MILITARIZING MARRIAGE

War and Militarism in African History

SERIES EDITORS: ALICIA C. DECKER AND GIACOMO MACOLA

Sarah J. Zimmerman
*Militarizing Marriage: West African Soldiers'
Conjugal Traditions in Modern French Empire*

Militarizing Marriage

*West African Soldiers' Conjugal Traditions
in Modern French Empire*

Sarah J. Zimmerman

OHIO UNIVERSITY PRESS ⁕ ATHENS, OHIO

Ohio University Press, Athens, Ohio 45701
ohioswallow.com
© 2020 by Ohio University Press
All rights reserved

To obtain permission to quote, reprint, or otherwise reproduce or distribute material from Ohio University Press publications, please contact our rights and permissions department at (740) 593-1154 or (740) 593-4536 (fax).

Cover image: "Le pont de la Salamandre," in Joseph-Simon Gallieni, *Deux campagnes au Soudan français, 1886–1888* (Paris: Hachette, 1891), 10–11.

Printed in the United States of America
Ohio University Press books are printed on acid-free paper ∞ ™

30 29 28 27 26 25 24 23 22 21 20   5 4 3 2 1

Library of Congress Cataloging-in-Publication Data
Names: Zimmerman, Sarah J., author.
Title: Militarizing marriage : West African soldiers' conjugal traditions in modern French empire / Sarah J. Zimmerman.
Other titles: War and militarism in African history.
Description: Athens, Ohio : Ohio University Press, 2020. | Series: War and militarism in African history | Includes bibliographical references and index.
Identifiers: LCCN 2019059725 | ISBN 9780821424223 (hardcover) | ISBN 9780821440674 (adobe pdf)
Subjects: LCSH: Soldiers--Family relationships--Africa, West. | Military spouses--Africa, French-speaking West--Social conditions--20th century. | Women--Africa, French-speaking West--Social conditions--20th century. | Africa, French-speaking West--History--1884-1960.
Classification: LCC DT532.5 .Z56 2020 | DDC 960.03--dc23
LC record available at https://lccn.loc.gov/2019059725

To Fatoumata Mbodj Faye, Samba Katy Faye, Ndeye Niawe Faye, and Mohamadou Lamine Faye

Contents

List of Illustrations — ix

Acknowledgments — xi

Abbreviations — xv

Introduction
French African Soldiers and Female Conjugal Partners in Colonial Militarism — 1

1 Marrying into the Military
   Colonization, Emancipation, and Martial Community in West Africa, 1880–1900 — 28

2 Colonial Conquest "en Famille"
   African Military Households in Congo and Madagascar, 1880–1905 — 58

3 *Mesdames Tirailleurs* and Black Villages
   Trans-Saharan Experiences in the Conquest of Morocco, 1908–18 — 88

4 Domestic Affairs in the Great War
   Legal Plurality, Citizenship, and Family Benefits, 1914–18 — 114

5 Challenging Colonial Order
   Long-Distance, Interracial, and Cross-Colonial Conjugal Relationships, 1918–46 — 139

Contents

6 Afro-Vietnamese Military Households in French Indochina
and West Africa, 1930–56   170

Epilogue
Decolonization, Algeria, and Legacies   195

Notes   215

Bibliography   263

Index   291

Illustrations

MAPS

0.1	Modern French Empire	3
1.1	French West Africa	30
2.1	French Congo / French Equatorial Africa	65
2.2	French Madagascar	69
3.1	French Protectorate in Morocco	89
4.1	Four Communes of Senegal	115
5.1	French Mandate Territories: Syria and Lebanon	141
6.1	French Indochina	172
7.1	French Algeria	197

FIGURES

3.1	"Casablanca.—Au Camp Sénégalais: Les futurs tirailleurs"	103
3.2	"Campagne au Maroc (1907–1909).—Ber Réchid—Camp et cuisines des Sénégalais"	105
6.1	"Sois actif et vigilant, LE VIET EST PARTOUT"	185
6.2	"Attention! Ta solde est pour qui?"	185

Acknowledgments

Research for this book spanned more than a decade and took place in six countries, twenty archival units, and the homes of over fifty West African veterans, widows, and their children. I benefitted from the resources and assistance of many actors, agencies, and institutions throughout the research and writing process. While I may not have the space or faculties of recollection to acknowledge all of them here, I am extremely grateful for their support.

At the University of California, Berkeley, I benefitted from Rocca Fellowships from the Center of African Studies, numerous grants and fellowships from the History Department, grants from the Townsend Center for Humanities, and Foreign Language Area Study Grants through UC Berkeley and Stanford University. The majority of early research was generously supported by a Fulbright-Hayes DDRA Grant.

At Berkeley, Tabitha Kanogo offered invaluable advice that allowed this project to radically evolve from its genesis to conclusion. Many thanks to Richard Roberts at Stanford University for his indispensable knowledge and guidance, as well as for providing me with an Africanist community. Tyler Stovall provided sound counsel and opened doors to a community of French colonial scholars who have drastically improved this book. Mariane Ferme, whose knowledge is unbounded, also read and provided critical insights. Rachel Giraudo, Noah Tamarkin, and Liz Thornberry provided formative feedback on the earliest versions of this book. The Bay Area provided a wonderful community of scholars, intellectuals, and friends throughout and beyond graduate school: Michael Allan, Jon Cole, Corrie Decker, Brandon Essex, Rozy Fredericks, Kemrexx George, Trevor Getz, Blake Johnson, Rico

Acknowledgments

Marcelli, Ivy Mills, Robin Mitchell, Laura Monnig, Erin Pettigrew, Jonathan Repinecz, Martha Saavedra, Maya Smith, Julia Elizabeth Swett, and Toby Warner.

Archivists, archival staff, librarians, and research center staff immensely facilitated the realization of this book. *Militarizing Marriage* outlasted the careers of several archivists and staff members at the National Archives in Dakar. Directors Papa Momar Diop, Babacar Ndiaye, and Fatoumata Cissé Diarra, as well as archival employees Mamadou Ndiaye, Mossane Diouf, Massamba Seck Sylla, Ibrahima Ndione Mbengue, and Albert Diatta, had great patience and immeasurably influenced this project. Papa Momar Diop provided introductions to Colonel M. L. Touré, Lieutenant Colonel Manga, and Mamdou Koné at the Senegal Museum of Armed Forces, as well as Abdoul Sow and Cheikh Faty Faye of the History Department at FASTEF. Professors Sow and Faye provided access to unpublished masters students' theses that were part of an oral history project concerning veterans of the *tirailleurs sénégalais*. At the West African Research Center (WARC) in Dakar, Ousmane Sène, a former teacher and now colleague, provided safe haven for research. WARC's staff is unparalleled in their hospitality and conviviality.

I am indebted to veterans, widows, and their grown children in Dakar, Saint-Louis, Thiès, Podor, Ziguinchor, Conakry, and Paris who spoke with candor regarding their experiences in French Empire. At the Veterans Bureau in Dakar, I specifically thank Director Alioune Kamara, Amadou Sall, Koly Kourouma, and Adjudant Ba for their assistance in this project. Among others, veterans Joseph à Lô, Allasane Wade, and Urbain Diagne spent many hours teaching me the history of French African soldiers. Sophie Diagne's friendship and interest in this project opened doors to the Afro-Vietnamese community in Dakar. In Saint-Louis, the concierge at the Veterans Bureau, Mr. Ndow, was a great help. Fatima Fall at the Centre National des Recherches Scientifiques and Ngor Sène at the Préfecture Archives facilitated research in Saint-Louis. Adjudant Sow served as my liaison to Thiès, where Veterans' Bureau Director Omar Diop and Ousmane Traoré's family provided support. The director of the Veterans' Bureau in Ziguinchor, Keba Touré, connected me with veterans. In Conakry, Captain El Hadj Thierno Conté and Marie Yvonne Curtis's family introduced me to a different set of military memories.

Acknowledgments

In Paris, I am indebted to the staff and archivists, particularly Mme. Découbert, at Service Historique de l'Armée de Terre and to Cyril Canet in the Service Iconographique in Vincennes. The staff at Établissement de Communication et de Production Audiovisuelle de la Défense in Mairie d'Ivry were also extremely helpful, as were those at the National Archives. Colonel Maurice Rives, former commander of *tirailleurs sénégalais* and military historian, provided new insights for this project. The staff at the National Overseas Archives in Aix-en-Provence and the Diplomatic Archives in Nantes were cordial and accommodating. Captain Eric Warnant at CHETOM in Fréjus went above and beyond the call of duty to assist in accommodations and to remedy a computer failure. In Rabat, Driss Idrissi, Driss Maghraoui, and the Institute des Études Africaines provided collegial support. The staff at the Bibliothèque Nationale du Maroc and Bibliothèque La Source assisted in research for this book.

During years of research, numerous people provided me with hospitality and collegiality along the way. Thanks to David Ansari, Arthur Asseraf, Amadou Ba, Ndiouga Benga, Jennifer Boittin, Emily Burrill, Audrey Celestine, Brandon County, Kelly Duke Bryant, Romain Deschateaux, Rick Fogarty, Ruth Ginio, Lindsay Gish, Cameron Gokee, Dave Glovsky, Walter Hawthorne, Larissa Kopytoff, Abdou Mbodj, Amadou Makhtar Mbow, Martin Mourre, Emily Musil Church, Minayo Nasiali, Derek Rhinehart, Marie Rodet, Lorelle Semley, and Makhroufi Ousmane Traoré. Several people have provided feedback on this book at critical moments: Corrie Decker, Rachel Jean-Baptiste, Trevor Getz, Martin Klein, Benjamin Lawrance, Liz MacMahon, Jonathan Miran, Michelle Moyd, Sue Peabody, and Elizabeth Schmidt. Thanks also to anonymous reviewers and the War and Militarism in African History series editors Alicia C. Decker and Giacomo Macola. At Ohio University Press, Ed Vesneske Jr., Nancy Basmajian, and others greatly improved this book. Thanks to Rachel Kantrowitz for the index.

At Western Washington University, I continued research and wrote in a collegial environment. The West African Research Association provided funding for summer research and the Camargo Foundation In-Residence Writing Fellowship provided a wonderful environment in Cassis, where I finished drafting this book. Through Western, I won several summer grants, as well as the Marjorie and Allen Hatter Research Grant and the Radke Family Faculty Awards Program for Innovations in the Humanities. My colleagues

Acknowledgments

and friends at Western have unwaveringly supported me as a young scholar and have immeasurably contributed to the completion of this work. Thanks to Charles Anderson, Kathryn Anderson, Kaveh Askari, AB Brown, Josh Cerretti, Andy Denning, Amanda Eurich, Michael Fraas, Steven Garfinkle, Jared Hardesty, Lenny Helfgott, Beth Joffrion, Damani Johnson, Tiana Kahakauwila, Kevin Leonard, A. Ricardo Lopez, Kristin Mahoney, Ed Matthieu, Polly Meyers, Johann Neem, Hunter Price, Diana Schenk, Jen Seltz, Silky Shah, and Sarah Zarrow.

My parents Suzanne and David Zimmerman have been steadfast in championing my ambitions. I am greatly indebted to their pragmatism, unwavering support, and enthusiasm for all things. In addition to creating the maps, Isaac Barry intellectually invested in this book. I am grateful for his love, wit, and companionship in the final stages of this project. For nearly two decades, my family in Senegal—Fatoumata Mbodj Faye, Samba Katy Faye, Ndeye Niawe Faye, and Mohamadou Lamine Faye—have ensured that Dakar will always be home. I dedicate this book to them.

Abbreviations

ADN	Archives Diplomatiques de Nantes, France
ANG	Archives Nationales de la Guinée, Conakry
ANOM	Archives Nationales d'Outre-Mer, France
ANS	Archives Nationales du Sénégal, Dakar
AOF	Afrique Occidentale Française
BAA	Bureau des Affaires Africaines
BMC	Bordels Militaires de Campagne
BTS	Bataillon de Tirailleurs Sénégalais
CFA	Colonies Françaises d'Afrique (1945–1958 / Communauté Française d'Afrique (1958–1960)
CHETOM	Centre d'Histoire et d'Études des Troupes d'Outre-Mer, Fréjus
EMPA	École Militaire de Préparation de l'Afrique, after independence becoming École Militaire de Préparation de l'Armée
FLN	Front de Libération Nationale
FWA	French West Africa
SHD-T	Service Historique de la Défense, Terre, Vincennes
V	Versement—in citations, refers to archival organization at ANS

Introduction

French African Soldiers and Female Conjugal Partners in Colonial Militarism

IN DECEMBER 1887, A CONTINGENT OF *TIRAILLEURS SÉNÉGALAIS* captured Mamadou Lamine Drame. The tirailleurs sénégalais were West Africans serving in the French colonial army. Mamadou Lamine Drame was a revolutionary West African jihadist leader whose campaigns to create a Muslim state based in Bundu occurred at a time in which the French colonial government, based in Saint-Louis, sought to bring the Senegal River valley under its formal rule. These incompatible visions of West African expansion led French military leaders to cast Drame as a religious zealot and enemy of the state. After his dramatic capture and murder, French military officials oversaw the distribution of Drame's conjugal partners—wives and concubines—to tirailleurs sénégalais.[1] These women became the "wives" of West African colonial soldiers because French officials believed that the transfer of women from the vanquished to the victors followed local martial and marital customs, as well as assuring these women's welfare in a politically unstable environment.[2] As soldiers' wives, these women became members of a large civilian contingent supporting African troops participating in France's conquest of inland West Africa. Some likely traveled with tirailleurs sénégalais to overseas deployments in French Congo and Madagascar in the following decade.

Seventy years later and 7,500 miles to the east in Hanoi, Abdou Karim Bâ, a French West African soldier, adopted Vuti Chat. Vuti Chat was a hospitalized eleven-year-old Vietnamese female war orphan of the French

Indochina War (1945–54). When the war concluded with Vietnam's independence, Abdou Karim Bâ was one of roughly twenty thousand West African soldiers deployed in the region. In 1956, Abdou Bâ moved Vuti Chat from Hanoi to Kaolack, Senegal. The French colonial military facilitated the relocation of members of tirailleurs sénégalais' Afro-Vietnamese households from Southeast Asia to their colonies of origin. Chat was one of hundreds, perhaps thousands, of Vietnamese women and children who relocated to West Africa in the 1950s. Bâ's mother and sisters raised Chat and, at age seventeen, she became Bâ's wife.[3] Chat and Bâ married in 1962, when the French Empire that had once connected West Africa and Southeast Asia no longer existed. Senegal became Chat's home and her foster family became her only kin. In 2008, Asstou Bâ, née Vuti Chat, was a childless widow, a socially marginal member of her husband's extended kin, and an infrequent participant in the diasporic Vietnamese community in Dakar. Due to Asstou Bâ's connection to the French military, she secured French citizenship during Senegal's decolonization and continued to collect a widow's pension.

These two examples of militarized conjugality bookend the imperial career of tirailleurs sénégalais. The first French governor of colonial Senegal, Louis Faidherbe, inaugurated the tirailleurs sénégalais in 1857. This locally recruited fighting force paralleled transformations in French colonialism's form and function in West Africa and French Empire over the subsequent century. West African soldiers served in the expansion, maintenance, and defense of France's empire in West Africa, Equatorial Africa, Madagascar, North Africa, the Levant, and French Indochina from the 1880s to 1962. Across the history and geography of modern French Empire, tirailleurs sénégalais advanced conjugal strategies and engaged in marital relationships with women at home and abroad. The coexistence of manifold marital practices and "customs" in French colonial militarized spaces influenced the processes through which civilian women and girls became the wives of West African soldiers. The French military managed African soldiers' sexuality, conjugality, and marital legitimacy in a range of consensual and nonconsensual war-front (and home-front) interactions with female civilians because soldiers' sexuality and their households were crucial to the operation of French colonialism. The French colonial military played a significant role in shaping masculinity, femininity, domesticity, patriarchy, and sexual behaviors among members of African military households in West Africa and across French Empire.

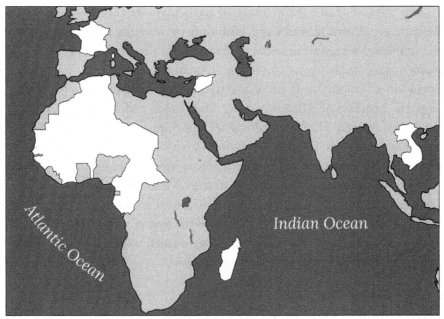

MAP 0.1. Modern French Empire. Map by Isaac Barry

Vuti Chat and the former conjugal partners of Mamadou Lamine Drame evidence an evolution in tirailleurs sénégalais' conjugal and marital practices. In the 1880s, French military officials witnessed the distribution of captured women to their local military employees—providing tacit sanction to a purported indigenous custom that shared characteristics with female domestic slavery. By the 1950s, military and civilian administrations coordinated their management of soldiers' marriages, soldiers' adoption of foreign children, and long-distance travel accommodations for members of their cross-colonial households. Over the decades, the French colonial military and state gradually took jurisdiction over the processes through which African soldiers' female conjugal partners and households acquired legitimacy. The French colonial military developed martial traditions emphasizing masculinity and celebrating family men. Gender, wives, and households were vital components of these ideals. Military officials progressively policed the boundaries of propriety related to tirailleurs sénégalais' sexual practices and partners.

Cynthia Enloe has noted that "women's myriad relationships to militaristic practices and to the military are far less the result of amorphous tradition or culture than they are the product of particular—traceable—decisions."[4] *Militarizing Marriage* traces the evolution of women's relationships with the tirailleurs sénégalais in order to demonstrate that sexuality, gender, and women were fundamental to violent colonial expansion and the everyday operation of colonial rule in West Africa and French Empire. To varying degrees, members of African military households and French colonial officials determined whether conjugal relationships were, or could become, legitimate marriages. Gender, heteronormativity, and racial order influenced processes of legitimation, and contestations over conjugal legitimacy shaped colonial welfare policies and military strategy. Tirailleurs sénégalais' conjugal practices and marital traditions evolved within nineteenth- and twentieth-century French colonialism. Vuti Chat and the former wives and concubines of Mamadou Lamine Drame illustrate that women were essential to the articulation of French militarism and colonialism.

MILITARISM, GENDER, AND TIRAILLEURS SÉNÉGALAIS

Mamadou Lamine Drame's former conjugal partners and Vietnamese migrant wives demonstrate the importance of studying gender and militarism in African and French colonial history. Amina Mama and Margo Okazawa-Rey write that colonial militaries "relied on military force, deployed along with a formidable array of political, economic and cultural technologies of violence, thus militarising the societies they conquered and governed in ways that extended far beyond the barracks, into the very fabric of peoples' lives."[5] West African soldiers' participation in the expansion and maintenance of the French colonial state had extensive gendered effects in their home-front communities and in foreign war-front societies. Simultaneously, soldiers' female conjugal partners (and their communities) influenced colonial military practice and policy. Tirailleurs sénégalais' households were at the center of diverse interests and stakeholders, which collectively illustrate the dynamic relationship between gender and militarism in the history of African colonial soldiers. According to Laura Sjoberg and Sandra Via, militarism "is the extension of war-related, war-preparatory, and war-based meanings and activities outside of 'war proper' and into social and political life."[6] Gender, or perceptions of sexualized and embodied difference, has a dynamic relationship with militarism. In multivalent and concerted ways, gender and militarism inform military and civilian norms and practices. Alicia Decker and Patricia McFadden have each pointed out that in postcolonial African examples, state militarism often involved, in Decker's words, a "reassertion of manhood undermined by colonial rule."[7] Colonial rule may have undermined the feminine and masculine authority of colonized civilians, but it certainly could bolster the masculine authority of African men enlisted in colonial militaries. *Militarizing Marriage* tracks soldiers' sexuality and conjugality to illustrate how African servicemen and the colonial military contributed to new iterations of gendered relations in West Africa and French Empire.

This book builds on an extensive historical literature dealing with African colonial soldiers that has gradually taken up the concerns of gender, sexuality, and militarism. Early publications concerning African colonial soldiers tended to glorify European officers, African enlistees, or important battles. In doing so, these older works reproduced narrow visions of what militaries were and what they did in colonial Africa.[8] "New" military histories, which deal with wide-ranging themes of war and society, portray the lived experiences of colonial soldiers. Many of these works include women, but they have a tendency to relegate them to the domestic realm or cast them as minor characters in soldiers' social worlds.[9] A number of studies have focused on soldiers' wives and households in order to understand how colonial statecraft and African housecraft operated in tandem.[10] Africanist military historians query how masculinity, patriarchy, and soldiering work together to produce discourses concerning African and colonial "martial races."[11] With an eye toward gender, Gregory Mann's *Native Sons* captures the complexity of active and retired tirailleurs sénégalais' navigation of shifting social, political, and economic forces in West Africa and French Empire.[12] Michelle Moyd's *Violent Intermediaries* illustrates that women and gender were integral to Askari ways of war and soldiers' participation in the everyday violence of German colonialism.[13] *Militarizing Marriage* joins a small field of works that address forced conjugal association, sexual violence, and female subjugation in colonial and postcolonial military histories of Africa.[14] In doing so, this book follows their lead and incorporates the concepts prevalent among studies of gendered violence in colonial and postcolonial conflicts.[15] West African soldiers' conjugal and marital traditions serve as the unit of analysis through which to understand how "war making . . . relies on gendered constructions and images of the state, state militaries, and their role in the international system" over the course of decades and across diverse geographies of French colonialism.[16]

Militarized women have long born the title "civilian." Civilian is a deceptive term which often reinforces false gendered distinctions between combatants and noncombatants, as well as trivializing the degree to which women are involved in war.[17] West African "civilian" women were auxiliary combatants, sutlers, and domestic laborers while accompanying their husbands to colonial conquest in West Africa, Congo, Madagascar, and Morocco through the First World War. The inclusion of African women in these colonial campaigns contradicts common narratives about the masculinization of nineteenth-century Western European armed forces. Historians have shown that women commonly provided essential services to land-based armies prior to the 1850s.[18] Afterward, the nationalization and professionalization of North Atlantic militaries led to the erasure of female civilians from state-funded armies.[19] These trends paralleled the modernization of the industrial-military complex and the emergence of the male citizen-soldier as an ideal model for civic membership in North Atlantic countries.[20] Dominant moral discourses concerning feminine propriety compelled state armies to progressively displace civilian women from military spaces. By the late nineteenth century, North American and western European armies were predominantly devoid of wives and female camp followers.[21] These symbiotic male soldier/female civilian relationships continued to exist in the European armed forces on the "fringes of empire."[22] Contrary to this narrative, *Militarizing Marriage* locates the colonial frontier at the center of late nineteenth-century European military practices. French military officials condoned tirailleurs sénégalais' conjugal traditions, which indicates the existence of paradoxes at the heart of military policy and colonial militarization in West Africa. Colonized African women and men lived these paradoxes as they became new members of an expanding French army.

Tirailleurs sénégalais' conjugal practices and marital traditions produced African military households. The contravention of premarital heterosexual practices and gender-based violence were among the constitutive processes that produced military households in West Africa and French Empire. The literature concerning forced conjugal association and gender-based violence in contemporary African conflicts offers historians theoretical and methodological tools to reexamine the intersection of warfare, gender-based violence, and conjugality in the African colonial past.[23] Contemporary feminist concerns with the globalization of militarism provide models for interrogating French imperial militarism and how the colonial army managed sexual violence and conjugality in war-front interactions.[24] Military officers seldom viewed tirailleurs sénégalais' sexual exploits as transgressing normative sexual behaviors affiliated with the colonial military. In rare, egregious cases, French officers took disciplinary action against West African soldiers for gender-based violence, but those measures did little to protect female colonial subjects from future transgressions. Militarization increased the vulnerability of women and their communities in French Empire. Combined with colonialism, militarization circumscribed female colonial subjects' and/or their guardians' ability to hold colonial soldiers accountable for violating local marital customs or normative sexual practices.

The presence of the French colonial army compromised the ability of traditional authorities—relatives and community leaders—to manage sexual relationships between tirailleurs sénégalais and civilian women. This had many consequences. Some communities and individuals encouraged women to enter into conjugal relationships with West African soldiers in order to mitigate the effects of conflict and conquest. Vulnerable and enterprising women could have seen military marriage as a strategy to leave previous marriages or domestic slavery, or to provide some stability in the upheavals accompanying colonial conquest and conflict.[25] Military officials became de facto authority figures in regulating the conjugal affairs of local women and tirailleurs sénégalais. Significantly, the military established and maintained state-funded brothels for their troops. In these spaces of transactional sex, they monitored troops' sexual behavior and discouraged conjugal or romantic inclinations.[26] In official correspondence related to soldiers' conjugality, military officials avoided terms like sexual enslavement or forced marriage to describe tirailleurs sénégalais' conjugal relationships. To do so would have opened the colonial army up to civilian, metropolitan, and international criticism.

Throughout much of the colonial period, the French military operated outside international, French, and colonial laws aiming to improve the conditions of women. Antislavery acts in 1848 and 1905, the 1926 Slavery Convention, as well as the French Family Code, the Mandel Decree of 1939, and the Jacquinot Decree of 1951 all aimed to shore up women's rights—the latter pieces of legislation setting minimum marriageable ages and requiring future brides' consent to marriage. French military officials often lacked the political will to enforce international and colonial statutes in relation to tirailleurs sénégalais' conjugal relationships with female colonial subjects. Instead, they operated through a corpus of marital tradition formed within the military, sourced from African soldiers' natal communities or from female conjugal partners' societal norms. The military's ad hoc application of pluralistic traditions and laws serves as historical prologue for contemporary debates in supranational bodies, like the United Nations and the International Criminal Court, that attempt to define, regulate, and adjudicate gender-based violence in recent African conflicts.[27]

The continuum of consent and coercion is useful for conceptualizing gender-based violence and war crimes in the colonial past. Consent assumes equality among individuals, as well as the ability of those individuals to give consent in contracts—like those pertaining to sexual intercourse or marriage.[28] French military officers wielded great authority in adjudicating conjugal disputes between tirailleurs sénégalais and colonized women—none of whom were fully endowed with rights vis-à-vis the colonial state. French military officials enforced the conjugal prerogatives of their military employees, following pervasive assumptions that colonized women were incapable of consent to marriage or of individual choice. Accordingly, female colonial subjects' "consent" was diffused across members of their lineage group and their community, who policed the boundaries of propriety and social reproduction. Military officials took for granted that fathers and communities maintained patriarchal authority over daughters and that husbands held ultimate authority over wives. Colonialism contributed to the extension of male and state authority over women's mobility via social institutions like marriage.[29] However, the French military frequently allowed tirailleurs sénégalais to violate these social prescriptions.

The use of marital terminology to describe tirailleurs sénégalais' conjugal relationships camouflaged the potentially illegitimate (and sometimes violent) means through which these relationships came into being. French military officials' use of "marriage" and "wife" shielded the ways in which the military allowed soldiers to contravene local traditions or international conventions regarding the rights of women and the institutions of marriage. In doing so, the French colonial military condoned conjugal relationships that soldiers, women, their respective communities, and French law would not sanction. There are few examples in which archival or oral evidence suggests that all individuals and collective bodies agreed that African military households were legal or legitimate marriages.

The use of the term "wife" to refer to tirailleurs sénégalais' female sexual partners is deceiving due to the manifold meanings embedded in the French word *femme*. *Femme* directly translates to both "wife" and "woman." Written sources and informants predominantly employed *femme* over épouse (female spouse) to refer to tirailleurs sénégalais' conjugal partners, which masked the degree to which state agents, women, or soldiers assigned legitimacy to the marital status of women. Depending on context, the word *femme* was an umbrella term for any number of the following meanings: official or unofficial wife, girlfriend, concubine, female slave, sex worker, or domestic partner. Military officials used *femme* to refer to women maintaining monogamous relationships with soldiers, as well as to cast aspersions on West African soldiers' extramarital, polyamorous, and polygynous romantic partners. As a result, throughout this book, the word "wife" remains imprecise, contested, and ambiguous—even when lacking scare quotes. I use "conjugal partner" throughout this book because the conditions of colonialism and militarism undermined the ability of tirailleurs sénégalais and female colonial subjects to consent to practices affiliated with matrimony. These conditions also prevented willing partners from legitimizing their conjugal unions with the state, or according to their own conventions.

The subjugation of women was essential to the manifestation and articulation of military power and colonial rule. Tirailleurs sénégalais' households, when considered as part of a longer tradition of martial matrimony, illustrate the ways in which gendered power operated through institutions of the colonial military, the civilian state, and individual actors in diverse geographic contexts. The conjugal relationships that tirailleurs sénégalais sought while serving in empire are comparable to Susan Zeiger's observation of twentieth-century American soldiers' overseas conjugal behaviors, which "existed in a matrix of warfront interaction between American soldiers and local women that encompassed courtship and dating, consensual and coerced sexual intercourse, informal and commercial prostitution, and sexual assault."[30] Tirailleurs sénégalais introduced new forms of marriage to French Empire because conquest and foreign rule altered local tradition around women's sexuality and conjugality. Tirailleurs sénégalais represented a particular kind of racialized, masculine power harnessed to French colonial order. West African soldiers' conjugal practices and marital traditions illustrate that ideologies of militarism and sexuality shaped social order from the nineteenth-century frontiers of French colonial conquest to wars of decolonization.[31]

MARRIAGE AT THE CONVERGENCE OF MILITARIZATION AND FRENCH COLONIALISM

The women distributed to tirailleurs sénégalais as wives in Bundu and Vuti Chat's journey from war orphan to expatriate to wife collectively demonstrate that establishing households and legitimizing conjugal relationships were significant life events during West African soldiers' military service. Households and marriage were integral components of political history in West Africa and French Empire, just as they were sites of intimate and emotional exchange.[32] Tirailleurs sénégalais households' domestic economy was bound up in France's imperial and military political economy. Instead of shoring up boundaries between the public and the private, African military households transcended these categories. They also eroded distinctions between military and civilian populations. Across eighty years, the French colonial military and state increased their direct involvement in soldiers' conjugal and marital relationships. Members of tirailleurs sénégalais households and the French colonial military modified prenuptial rites, altered pathways to marital legitimacy, and ultimately formed their own marital traditions. These traditions permit historians to take stock of continuity and change in multiple fields of inquiry because marriage is a multifaceted site of historical production.

Marriage became a key site of contestation where stakeholders—wives and husbands—disputed their obligations to their spouses and to the state. Individuals and states, via marriage, struggle over social reproduction and the articulation of state authority in the most intimate spheres of the human experience.[33] Marriage is a means to extend kinship networks, build new economic and social connections, and encourage social and biological reproduction. Religious rites, cultural practices, and legal obligations affiliated with marriage are geographically specific and historically contingent. In the case of tirailleurs sénégalais and female colonial subjects, marriage could secure legal status, provide access to military resources, and legitimize their children. Efforts to legitimate and/or invalidate these intimate encounters encompassed challenges to colonial power and complex contestations concerning marital traditions and rights. The military allocated resources to soldiers' wives and dependents when their relationships conformed to heteronormative, gendered, and racialized ideals of marriage. The colonial state approached West African soldiers' conjugal unions as important sites of moral order, which could normalize tirailleurs sénégalais' war-front sexual behavior. There were great risks and consequences for couples seeking to make their conjugal relationships legible to the French colonial army and/or state.

West African soldiers' conjugal practices and the gendered power relationships within African military households were part of colonial martial custom. Martin Chanock's seminal work notes that custom is a crucial index of identity.[34] Historians have used this point to debate the teleological traps and specious fixity affiliated with tribal identities.[35] The tirailleurs sénégalais was a military institution with a corporate identity historically tethered to French West Africa. The tirailleurs sénégalais was also a global institution, whose members reacted to and incorporated conjugal practices and marital customs from other regions of French Empire. Chanock's work also demonstrates that marriage was a key site to witness the codification of marital customs during the colonial period, a codification that shored up male authority and extended control over women.[36] Colonial courts and administrators took center stage in subsequent debates concerning the gendered power surrounding the transformation of marital traditions.[37] Few historians have interrogated colonial militaries' contribution to customary law. The tirailleurs sénégalais was an explicitly patriarchal institution and a violently coercive force that managed soldiers' customs related to sexuality, conjugality, and marriage. Colonial soldiers and their families were on the front line of what Emily Burrill has identified as the colonial state's marriage legibility project. African soldiers sought the military's sanction for marital legitimacy in order to acquire state-allocated benefits for their households. However, as the military narrowed and fixed definitions of military marriages through policy and decree, these marriages diverged from civilian West Africans' conjugal traditions.[38]

African military households sat at the convergence of West African, French, and military traditions of marriage within spaces of colonial conflict. African soldiers, their conjugal partners, and French officials had different ideas about prenuptial rites and what constituted legitimate marriage. In West Africa, marital rites differed according to community and were influenced by local and global religious beliefs—predominantly Islam. West African communities practiced polygyny and monogamy. Family organization occurred along matrilineal and patrilineal lines and extended beyond the nuclear family. Prenuptial customs for legitimate marriages could include the exchange of gifts, labor, or marriage payments. The socioeconomic rank, caste, or slave status/ancestry of prospective conjugal partners altered the ways in which individuals and communities observed premarital rites.[39]

The French colonial army made overtures toward codifying West African marital practices before the civilian colonial state made marital custom its prerogative. The military's goal was to recognize a limited set of practices that would make tirailleurs sénégalais' marriages more legible to military officials. The exchange of bridewealth was an early, favored standard for recognizing legitimate marriages in West Africa. As the colonial state and its military officials wedged diverse West African marital practices into French colonial and military traditions, they stripped them of value and complexity. Officials measured African marital traditions against definitions of marriage culled from French tradition and civil code. In late nineteenth- and twentieth-century France, marriage was often celebrated through Christian religious ceremonies and registered with a "secular" state. French marriage fell within the realm of civil affairs, which the state presided over in order to maintain its own authority and patriarchal power over women, primogeniture inheritance, and parents' authority over their children.[40] Marriages registered with the French state were monogamous, and, as a consequence, the French military rarely recognized or financially supported West African soldiers' second or subsequent wives. French military officials narrowed and rigidified "marital legitimacy" but stopped short of static definition. Their efforts steadily nudged tirailleurs sénégalais' marital practices away from West African and French civil customs toward marital traditions evolving within the French colonial military.

Military officials referred to an older French Atlantic marital tradition—*mariage à la mode du pays*—in order to describe tirailleurs sénégalais' conjugal behaviors when deployed in colonial frontiers of Africa and Madagascar. Mariage à la mode du pays was a conjugal tradition typified by African women forming temporary, though often protracted, sexual and domestic relationships with European merchants, administrators, and military officials.[41] Governor Louis Faidherbe infamously participated in a relationship of this nature with Dioucounda Sidibe, a fifteen-year-old Khassonké woman.[42] Sidibe lived with him in the governor's mansion in Saint-Louis and gave birth to their son, Louis Léon Faidherbe, the same year that Governor Faidherbe created the tirailleurs sénégalais in 1857. Temporary interracial conjugal unions continued into the late nineteenth century and early twentieth century, particularly with colonial officials serving in the interior of West Africa. However, the practice decreased in the more visible quarters of colonial society during the twentieth century.[43] French military officials used mariage à la mode du pays to describe tirailleurs sénégalais' conjugal unions, which condoned male soldiers' prerogatives in accessing conjugal labor and indicated the temporary nature of these unions. Further, these observers assumed that the sexual behavior of young soldiers, who lacked their elders' supervision, was representative of conjugal norms in West Africa.[44] Within military convention, the phrase *mariage à la mode du pays* became a rhetorical means through which to debase African soldiers' marital practices and their sexual moral economy in West Africa and in French Empire.

Paradoxically, military officials also believed that tirailleurs sénégalais were natural "family men."[45] African soldiers' ability to create families and shape colonial and local ideas about marriage were paramount to normalizing the manifestation of colonial power in intimate spheres. Embedded in this presumption were tirailleurs sénégalais' heteronormativity and preference for matrimony, which stand in contrast to French metropolitan concerns about the carnal desires of African soldiers in France during and after the world wars.[46] Despite counterexamples, colonial officials were convinced that tirailleurs sénégalais preferred conjugal relationships over transactional sexual experiences in military-maintained brothels or single-occurrence (often nonconsensual) sexual encounters. The "family man" ideology was powerful in its ability to transform nonconsensual, coercive sexual encounters into legitimate marriages and characterize tirailleurs sénégalais as male heads of household.

The French colonial military employed another patriarchal concept, the male-breadwinner model, to direct allocations and benefits to the members of tirailleurs sénégalais' nuclear households.[47] French military officials refused to recognize West Africans' households as nodes within extended networks of biological and fictive kin. During the Great War, the military began to require formal documentation of soldiers' marital status and members of their nuclear households—whether their marriages occurred prior to or during their service. Wartime legislation ushered in new forms of state welfare for active-duty soldiers, veterans, and their families. In the 1920s and 1930s, metropolitan France expanded its welfare state and initiated a veritable boom in benefits for heteronormative, racialized, and gendered citizens in metropolitan France.[48] This trend extended into empire and was most conspicuous in tax abatements and familial benefits promised to tirailleurs sénégalais' households. Colonial soldiers achieved basic benefits and tax relief decades before other colonial laborers and employees.[49] With the extension of formal state assistance to West African military households, the French army awarded legitimate status to soldiers' first wives, while divesting itself of responsibilities for subsequent wives—even though African soldiers' legal status allowed them to practice polygyny. In limited cases, tirailleurs sénégalais' children, irrespective of their mothers' wife order, could access state funds before reaching puberty. These measures created bureaucratic and fiscal relationships between soldiers' wives and children that flowed through African soldiers, which reinforced the male-breadwinner household model. This patriarchal construct cast military wives as nonearning household members and endowed soldiers with authority over their wives' interactions with the military or colonial state.

The extension of benefits to West African households occurred at a time when the French colonial military reduced the number of West African wives traveling within empire. As a result, the interwar period witnessed an uptick in tirailleurs sénégalais' cross-colonial relationships and requests to relocate foreign wives to West Africa. West African soldiers initiated these conjugal relationships without the approval of their families and/or often without the input of their future in-laws. In the absence of family oversight of these unions, the military was the primary entity capable of legitimating cross-colonial conjugal relationships. Even with the military's formal recognition of marital legitimacy and the funding of foreign wives' long-distance relocation to West Africa, cross-colonial couples faced the discerning scrutiny of West African communities. Foreign women experienced gendered and racialized discrimination in their new homes. Tirailleurs sénégalais' extended kin contested foreign war brides' legitimacy.

"War bride" was a commonly used term to describe the foreign wives accompanying repatriating American soldiers who served in twentieth-century conflicts—particularly from theaters of war affiliated with World War II and Vietnam.[50] War brides in the United States were defined by their relationship to powerful state institutions and their marital relationships with active soldiers.[51] The relationship between tirailleurs sénégalais' war brides and the colonial state was crucial to their households' survival since their long-distance relocations separated them from the kin and social communities that had sustained them prior to marriage. Cross-colonial military marriages bound foreign wives and tirailleurs sénégalais to state authority, even while conjugal partners contested that power. Even today, tirailleurs sénégalais' widows, like Vuti Chat, collect pensions from the French state. These regularly distributed allocations evince the reciprocal ties between a defunct French colonial state, its veterans, and their wives and/or widows.[52]

MOBILE SUBJECTS BUILDING EMPIRES

The tirailleurs sénégalais and their households were protagonists in an international colonial enterprise stretching from West Africa to Southeast Asia. African and other colonial soldiers have become a means through which to appraise and critique nineteenth- and twentieth-century colonialism. Histories of African soldiers are often geographically limited to a single colony, interrogate the history of a single ethnolinguistic group, or focus on the colonizer/colonized binary. The historiography of African soldiers widens out at the world wars.[53] African veterans of these global conflicts have featured in twenty-first century controversies concerning the legacies of colonialism, which has inspired historians to investigate tirailleurs sénégalais' place within transnational public history and collective memory. Images of soldiers on popular French breakfast cereals, the haunting iconography of war, and the Thiaroye Massacre are flash points that prompt questions about France's debt to its African veterans and African countries formally colonized by France.[54] This rapt attention to ten years of tirailleurs sénégalais' history blinkers us to the colonial institution's longevity and its importance in shaping French Empire for more than a century. *Militarizing Marriage* joins the work of other scholars who have recently begun to acknowledge the importance of West African soldiers' participation in building and defending empire.[55]

Tirailleurs sénégalais' lived experiences, their conjugal partners, and their families tell us much about the nature of colonialism. From the perspective of military households, we can query the theoretical constructions of colonial binaries, intermediaries, and the boundaries of subjecthood. Historians have identified indigenous African employees as social actors and colonial intermediaries in order to complicate interpretations of imperial power that rely on dichotomies like colonized/colonizer, subject/citizen, or African/European. Scholarship on intermediary concepts and actors has tended toward the historicization of men due to the gendered nature of colonial education and employment. The female conjugal partners of tirailleurs sénégalais provide an opportunity to examine women's contribution to the articulation of colonial governance, economies, and traditions. Military wives and households offer historians a means to address the ambiguous and inconsistent manifestations of gendered colonial power.[56] Colonial rule's daily operations would not have been possible without female and male colonial subjects who took advantage of the "new opportunities created by colonial conquest and colonial rule to pursue their own agendas even as they served their employers."[57] Tirailleurs sénégalais' motivations to become members of the French colonial army were innumerable and complicated by individuals' history and social context.[58] Tirailleurs sénégalais could have been seeking autonomy from their elders, resources to build households, or the ability to defy the constraints of communal authority. The means through which female colonial subjects became soldiers' wives were equally complex, with varying degrees of volition and consent. These women could have sought conjugal relationships with tirailleurs sénégalais in order to liberate themselves from the authority of their community, leave previous husbands, or for wanderlust.[59] The social and material interests of colonized women and men making up military households influenced the articulation of French colonialism for a century.

Tirailleurs sénégalais and their wives challenge the traditional chronologies affiliated with the onset, conclusion, and legacies of colonialism. For the former wives of Mamadou Lamine Drame, colonialism began with perfunctory nuptials and forced labor as military auxiliaries prior to the formalization of colonial rule in the upper reaches of the Senegal River. For women like Vuti Chat, colonialism ended not with Vietnam's independence in 1954, but in 1960 in Senegal—though she continued to collect a widow's pension from the postcolonial French state into the twenty-first century. Some tirailleurs sénégalais experienced decolonization three times—in Indochina, in Algeria, and in their home colonies. Their pensions served as a cause célèbre in postcolonial criticism in the 2000s. For many participating in these debates, French colonialism was an ongoing and palpable twenty-first-century experience.

The tirailleurs sénégalais and their marital traditions occurred within the Third, Fourth, and Fifth French Republics. The heralded universalism of French Republican law did not extend into tirailleurs sénégalais' households.[60] The majority of women and men in African military households were colonial subjects. The legacies of colonial exploitation were bound to the historical status of colonial subjecthood. Tirailleurs sénégalais and their conjugal partners lived in and traversed colonial contexts where they were beholden to ambiguous and shifting legal statuses and regimes. Cross-colonial households demonstrate that the ad hoc interpretation and application of colonial law—related to marriage—in West Africa could inform legal practices in other regions of French Empire. Legal practice or its exception was not tethered to a particular colony. For example, West African marital customs, which were in constant revision in order to accommodate local colonial rule, also informed soldiers' marital practices in Madagascar or Vietnam.

Via tirailleurs sénégalais' conjugal relationships, *Militarizing Marriage* expands the geographic horizons of West Africans' colonial history and places emphasis on the migration of female colonial subjects across empire. Women are often cast as "passive" migrants, which results from misrepresentations of women's (especially African women's) agency in initiating conjugal relationships or long-distance migrations.[61] Migrant female conjugal partners and tirailleurs sénégalais were part of elaborate systems of imperial labor migration involving the blunt manifestation of colonial power. Their imperial "presence and activities performed the crucial and complicated race-work and sex-work that contributed to racially hierarchizing and engendering 'free' labor" in late nineteenth- and twentieth-century French Empire.[62] West African colonial soldiers and their female conjugal partners sought to fulfill their own desires and sociocultural traditions while performing the work of colonialism. Concerns for the domestic realm were often central to the ways in which active soldiers labored for the colonial state and maintained conjugal relationships in and across empire.[63] Interests in maintaining shared household responsibilities and fulfilling domestic labor obligations motivated colonized women to do the same.

African military households participated in south-south migration. These trans-imperial movements challenge the core-periphery model of colonial history, where information and historical causality flow unidirectionally from the French metropole into its colonies. Studies of imperial migrant households tend to focus on the circulation of Europeans in empire.[64] The historical cross-colonial movements of West African soldiers and their female conjugal partners reveals connections and exchanges among radically different people brought together by war and colonialism. During the period covered by the first half of this study, migration "en famille" was a mechanism that provided official recognition of soldiers' conjugal relationships. After World War I, cross-colonial migration became a consequence of, not a precursor to, legitimate marriage. The long-distance migrations of soldiers' foreign wives demonstrated their independence, adventurousness, and willingness to transgress traditional expectations as much as it demonstrated their subjugation, victimization, and vulnerability in French colonial empire.

Trans-imperial relocation was a constitutive element of women's transformation from conjugal partner to legitimate wife. *Militarizing Marriage* follows female and male colonial subjects who traversed the terrains of imperial "bourgeois culture" and left their footprints in the drying concrete of colonial marital policy and imperial ideas related to racial order.[65] West African, inter-African, and interracial/cross-colonial military households relied on the colonial state for legitimacy because their marriages occurred within imperial labor schemes and outside the bounds of their own marital traditions. By financing the cross-colonial migration of African military households, colonial officials bound them to state power and authority.[66] Similarly, soldiers' households were crucial to state security and military strategy in the international/imperial sphere.[67] This colonial history of long-distance marital relationships and mobile conjugal partners antedates, but is informed by, literature on contemporary West African migrants and their transnational households.[68]

The diverse racial, ethnic, and geographic origins of tirailleurs sénégalais' wives challenged imperial racial order and influenced how the military determined West African soldiers' household legitimacy. Conjugal unions between European men and colonized women have received scholarly attention due to a growing interest in the confluence of race, sexuality, and power in colonial history.[69] The product of these unions, métis, "mixed" race, or interracial children are the focus of a number of recent publications historicizing colonial policy and the social integration of these minority colonial populations.[70] The interracial relationships between West African soldiers and colonized women from other parts of French Empire have received less attention, even though their conjugal relationships unfolded in arenas where dense and dangerous transfers of colonial power transpired.[71] This may have much to do with how contemporary historians have inherited the racial, "ethnic," and national constructs that the Europeans produced to organize their empire.[72] According to colonial logic, West African soldiers' cross-colonial conjugal relationships with Malagasy or Congolese women did not result in interracial children because French officials lumped all sub-Saharan Africans into the same race. *Militarizing Marriage* makes plain that tirailleurs sénégalais' inter-African, interracial, and cross-colonial relationships with women from the African continent and other parts of French Empire merit the same types of nuanced examination typical to studies of race and sexuality in colonial history.

SOURCES AND METHODS

Women and households were crucial to military and political expansion in French Empire, yet the women affiliated with tirailleurs sénégalais seemed to be "without history," or, at best, on the periphery of colonial and/or military history.[73] *Militarizing Marriage* draws upon a wide range of sources to foreground women, as well as recovering lived experiences and institutional traditions connected to tirailleurs sénégalais' conjugal households. Early chapters rely on archival documents and French officers' memoirs found in twenty archival institutions located in six countries. I read these texts across ministerial and geographical divides to better understand how tirailleurs sénégalais' conjugality broadly influenced the daily operation of colonial militarism. The prevailing ontologies of the colonial era marginalized women and households from the "high politics of governments and states," even though female actors and their conjugal unions are crucial to the colonial state's most "masculine" and violent institution—the French colonial army.[74] Tirailleurs sénégalais' conjugal unions, marital legitimacy, and sexuality, rare as they appear in the colonial archive, were important to imperial statecraft.

The voices of female and male colonial subjects at the center of this study rarely appear in military and colonial documents, and, when they do, are often distorted. Members of tirailleurs sénégalais households were the stakeholders most invested in, and vulnerable to, the decisions recorded in the archives. The discriminating and ambivalent power of the French colonial and postcolonial state is evident in archival materials. Once assembled in the archives, military documents conveyed "authority and set rules for credibility and interdependence; they help select the stories that matter."[75] African military households were minor concerns in military policy and fiscal expenditures, whereas military policies regulating marital legitimacy and family allocations had great import on the integrity and prosperity of these households. Inherent biases in the representation of women and colonial subjects typified the "grain" of the archive.[76] Gaps in information and the silences surrounding soldiers' conjugal practices and the quotidian domestic activities of their families were profound. Reading the archives "against the grain," or thinking comprehensively about contexts, individual and collective motivations, as well as risks taken to achieve optimal futures, allows for a more comprehensive representation of military families' lived experiences of war, separation, and migration.

Memoirs authored by French military officers, soldiers, adventurers, and entrepreneurs contain anecdotes concerning tirailleurs sénégalais households that offer sociocultural information that lies beyond the purview of officialdom. Imperial discourses on race and gender influenced how these colonial authors produced African military households in texts aimed at European audiences. African soldiers, veterans, military wives, and widows seldom published memoirs, though there are important exceptions.[77] Memoirs opened wider portals of observation into the intimate worlds of African military households. They collapsed public and private spheres, which affords opportunities to understand how households, the state, and the states' employees mutually influenced each other.[78]

Tirailleurs sénégalais' and their conjugal partners' life histories inestimably enriched this study. I accessed life histories via unpublished master's theses at the École Normale Supérieure (ENS) in Dakar, which were the result of a state-funded oral history project aimed at recovering the experiences of Senegalese veterans.[79] The majority of the master's theses were organized around formulaic questions and served the particular interests of the ENS History Department, the Senegalese archives, and governmental efforts to make veterans of the tirailleurs sénégalais more visible in a postcolonial world. Nevertheless, ENS master's theses contained valuable lines of inquiry that extended the scope of my research. Master's students interviewed veterans in languages other than Wolof or French in familial and rural contexts. I also collected life histories via sixty interviews with veterans, widows, and their adult children in Senegalese cities, Conakry, and Paris. Interview formats varied. I asked a wide range of questions about military service, interactions with civilians, and conjugal behaviors. Informants organized their historical experiences of war and marriage into personal narratives and global processes that continue to have bearing upon their lives. Their experiences of militarization and conjugality in French Empire were much more dynamic than the ways in which military records portrayed them.

The majority of my informants served in, or had conjugal partners who deployed to, French Indochina or French Algeria. I met veterans and widows through associational networks linked to regional veterans' bureaus. As a result, veteran or military widow status were integral components of their identities. When I conducted interviews between 2006 and 2011, the international scandals surrounding African veterans' frozen pensions reached a series of crescendos in France and its former empire.[80] Journalists, authors, and other historians preceded me into the courtyards and private homes of West African veterans. This media and academic attention predetermined aspects of the interviews that I later conducted with veterans and their families. Women and men were primed to speak about the injustices of paltry pensions, widows' allocations, and the negative legacies of colonial rule. Through conversation, I came to understand that their underlying concerns about pensions were less about historical injustices and more about maximizing resources for their families—past and present.

I interviewed veterans in public and domestic spaces. Other veterans, family members, and neighbors moved through or lingered in interview spaces, and their presence modified my interview questions and shaped the types of memories shared by veterans, widows, and their children. Irrespective of venue or community, veterans rarely framed their cross-colonial conjugal relationships as nonconsensual, initiated through violence, or transactional. Normative moral standards, and the erasure of historical excesses, prevented veterans from speaking candidly of military brothels and overseas sex workers. My gender, as well as my status as a foreigner and guest in veterans' homes, influenced how veterans recalled and reassembled the sexual relationships of their past. How they conveyed the past was directly influenced by the contemporary cultural prescriptions that maintain social decency between people of different ages, genders, and nationalities.[81] Contrary to sociocultural dictates regarding discretion about sharing others' private information, or *sutura* in Wolof, some interviewees divulged details about themselves and other veterans that were not part of public discourse in their communities.[82] Individuals circulated gossip and rumor to damage the reputation or diminish the credibility of other informants.

Oral sources did not prove to be a panacea for the biases of the colonial archives.[83] Historians have warned us about the ability of statist narratives to "suppress alternative narratives and challenges," as well as to shape the production of a counternarrative to the colonial state's archives.[84] Inadvertently, the "statist" narratives influenced how I identified informants, how I formulated my research questions, and how my informants organized and shared information.[85] Veterans' and widows' memories relied on the tangible reminders and external props generated by the state during their military service in order to recall and reconstruct their life histories.[86] Military decorations and official papers were the hooks upon which veterans hung their military careers. When describing courtship, conjugal relationships, and marriage that occurred during their military service, veterans built their affective histories upon the tours of duty listed in military passports—fished out of the deep pockets of their boubous or pulled from precariously balanced stacks of aging documents. Corporeal scars were also evidence built into chronologies of sacrifice, romance, and survival. Despite these personalized and intimate means of recalling the past, veterans often defaulted to tirailleurs sénégalais' marital traditions to refer to former female conjugal partners as wives—whether they achieved legitimate status or not.

Historians once believed that Africans' life histories could lead to the recovery of an "authentic" African past distinct from the colonial histories that subjugated them.[87] *Militarizing Marriage* demonstrates that African and colonial epistemologies are mutually constitutive.[88] These arguments echo historical concerns regarding the recuperation of African customs and traditions across the colonial divide. West African colonial soldiers' conjugal traditions portray that continuities accompanied the great ruptures once affiliated with the onset of colonialism. Scholars now understand that colonial rule could not destroy precolonial African traditions, nor alter them beyond recognition, due to the limits imposed on evolutions in African traditions.[89] Tirailleurs sénégalais' marital traditions extended beyond the precolonial/colonial/postcolonial divides. Contemporary interests in the legacies of French colonialism influence how veterans and their households fit in collective memory and public history. Adding the former wives of Mamadou Lamine Drame or Vuti Chat to this history accounts for the gendered legacies of colonial militarism and requires us to think more broadly about the history of the tirailleurs sénégalais and the legacies of Africans' military service in empire.

MILITARIZING MARRIAGE: AN ORIENTATION

Militarizing Marriage is chronologically and geographically organized to take account of tirailleurs sénégalais' conjugal practices across eighty years of military service in French Empire. Collectively, the following chapters track the evolution of African soldiers' conjugal traditions throughout the nineteenth and twentieth centuries. West African troops and their households heralded the onset of French colonialism and outlived its formal demise. As Myron Echenberg writes, "rather than being a caricature of colonialism, African soldiers were, perhaps more than any other groups, a mirror of colonialism and a reflection of its more basic contradictions."[90] By focusing on the French colonial military's treatment of African soldiers' conjugal partners and households, the gendered contradictions of colonialism come into fuller view. The women affiliated with tirailleurs sénégalais reveal how the universalism espoused by French Republican governments wavered at the intersection of gender, race, and colonial subject status. African military households result from legal exception and parallelism. The following chapters account for idiosyncratic themes salient to policy and practice specific to time and place in French Empire.

The governor of Senegal, Louis Faidherbe, inaugurated the tirailleurs sénégalais in 1857 at a time when Napoleon III's Second Empire dedicated more resources to spreading France's influence in Africa and Asia. The French Third Republic (1871–1940) used these troops to expand France's modern empire. This constitutional government inherited the universal principles of the French Revolution (liberty, equality, and fraternity), but did not extend these values to the new imperial populations of French Empire.[91] The contradictions inherent to Republican colonialism are at the foundation of the early expression of tirailleurs sénégalais' conjugal traditions in nineteenth-century West Africa. Chapter 1 highlights the French colonial military's reliance on domestic slavery and coerced labor in France's conquest of inland West Africa during the 1880s and 1890s. The recruitment of tirailleurs sénégalais and soldiers' acquisition of female conjugal partners contravened a major goal of colonialism in West Africa—slave emancipation. In para- and postconflict settings, French military officials maintained an ambivalent stance toward the means through which these soldiers obtained conjugal partners, formed households, and improvised marital legitimacy. In the swirl of colonial militarization, women's vulnerability heightened and consensuality became moot. Tirailleurs sénégalais' conjugal traditions formed at the confluence of these trends, which served as the shifting foundation for military policies and practices concerning the legitimacy of tirailleurs sénégalais' households for decades to come.

During the final decades of the nineteenth century, West African military employees extended France's rule in Congo and Madagascar. Chapter 2 interrogates how geographically distant settings affected tirailleurs sénégalais' ability to establish and maintain conjugal households. Long-distance migration and military officials' perceptions of sociocultural similarity and difference affected African military households' marital legitimacy. In an era when the French metropolitan army discouraged the presence of civilian women in official military spaces, the colonial military funded the relocation of West African women and households to new frontiers of empire. The military also encouraged tirailleurs sénégalais to engage in conjugal relationships with Congolese or Madagascan women. Outside of West Africa, concerns around soldiers' conjugal and marital legitimacy increased. Military officials perceived African military households composed uniquely of West Africans as legitimate. In foreign lands, these households became more dependent on the military for their survival, welfare, and repatriation. In Congo and Madagascar, tirailleurs sénégalais' inter-African or socioculturally heterogeneous conjugal households inspired multiple stakeholders to contest their legitimacy. Many of these inter-African military households followed prenuptial practices typical to West African conquest. As these practices moved into African empire, observers described tirailleurs sénégalais' sexual and conjugal practices with a vocabulary related to sexual assault and female enslavement.

French African Soldiers and Female Conjugal Partners in Colonial Militarism

The French military deployed West African soldiers and their West African wives—*mesdames tirailleurs*—in Morocco from 1908 to 1918. Morocco was one of the final territories integrated into France's overseas empire via military conquest. The debates surrounding the use of African military households in North Africa demonstrate that the French Third Republic believed in racial difference and hierarchy within empire. Chapter 3 examines how perceptions of racial difference influenced military officials to police boundaries between "North" African women and "sub-Saharan" African soldiers. They promoted mesdames tirailleurs as essential members of *villages nègres*. These "Black Villages" were racialized, segregated, and surveilled quarters within French military encampments in Morocco.[92] French military officials justified the deployment of West African military households in Morocco with references to the *abid al-Bukhari*—a historical Moroccan military institution made up of dark-skinned Moroccan military families. The comparisons drawn between the abid al-Bukhari and the tirailleurs sénégalais balanced upon perceptions of their shared sub-Saharan African origins, slave ancestry, and martiality. The Moroccan campaign, despite its contradictions, convinced the French Ministries of the Colonies and War to permanently invest in the tirailleurs sénégalais—on the eve of the Great War.

Chapter 4 examines critical transformations in French West African soldiers' marital traditions between 1914 and 1918. More than 170,000 West Africans mobilized in the war effort—conspicuously without their conjugal households. Instead, their wives remained in West Africa and dealt with new bureaucracies of wartime assistance. Citizenship status determined military wives' access to the state's resources. Senegal's first black deputy to the French National Assembly, Blaise Diagne, introduced wartime legislation that guaranteed French citizenship to a coastal Senegalese demographic minority—*originaires*. Originaires' wives and children were eligible to receive the same benefits as metropolitan French soldiers' families, while the majority of West Africans remained colonial subjects, served in the tirailleurs sénégalais, and received fewer benefits. Soldiers' citizenship/subject status and their polygynous practices challenged the French state's extension of social welfare into the colonial military. French military officials examined and debated the similarities and discrepancies among customary, Muslim, and French marital practices. Ambiguities in marital policy and family allocations extended into the interwar period.

Introduction

After the Great War, tirailleurs sénégalais served as occupying forces in North Africa, Madagascar, and France's newly acquired League of Nations mandate territories Syria and Lebanon. During the interwar period, tirailleurs sénégalais increasingly expected administrative assistance for their households at home and abroad. Chapter 5 examines evolutions in how military officials supported long-distance West African households and cross-colonial households. After 1918, the colonial military provided West African soldiers with a means to maintain households across long distances via separation indemnities, tax abatements, and other allocations. Cross-colonial households were interracial and made up of conjugal partners from different French territories who often possessed different politico-legal statuses. Imperial authorities debated jurisdiction and relevant marital customs for recognizing the legitimacy of these hyphenated military households. Evidence in this chapter demonstrates that the military found interracial military marriages irksome and that some cross-colonial households were more undesirable than others. In the aftermath of World War II, the military (in coordination with civilian government officials) used its control over oceanic travel, communication, and law to prevent mainland French women from joining their demobilizing conjugal partners in West Africa.

In stark contrast, hundreds, perhaps thousands, of Vietnamese women and Afro-Vietnamese children relocated to West Africa during and after the French Indochina War (1945–54). Chapter 6 examines Afro-Vietnamese conjugal households in Southeast Asia and West Africa. These households experienced World War II, the Vichy regime, Japanese occupation, the French Fourth Republic, and the beginning of anticolonial war in rapid succession. Afro-Vietnamese couples and children provide a means to understand the articulation of gendered and racialized colonial power during wars of decolonization. In this chapter, the "peripheries" of French Empire demand that we rethink the operation of race, sexuality, and family outside of the colonizer/colonized binary. In Vietnam, tirailleurs sénégalais' conjugal traditions adapted to the French military precedent, in which military personnel believed that Vietnamese women were sexually available to them via casual, transactional, romantic, and conjugal relationships. The French military attempted to regulate African soldiers' sexual relationships with local women by sanctioning transactional sex and discouraging "clandestine" romantic relationships. Their efforts failed. The French Indochina War came home with veterans, their Afro-Vietnamese children, and their Vietnamese brides. Once in West Africa, soldiers' extended families contested the incorporation of foreign war brides and interracial children into their communities—making their own arguments about conjugal legitimacy.

The epilogue appraises African military households' experiences in the final decades of the tirailleurs sénégalais and the legacies of this military institution in the twenty-first century. The French military introduced measures to professionalize the tirailleurs sénégalais in step with the restructuring of empire at the beginning of the French Fourth Republic in 1946 and the Fifth Republic in 1958. The French-Algerian War (1954–62) created the context for this constitutional transition, which altered the civil status of people residing in French Empire. In 1958, West African soldiers integrated into the French marine corps. In the same year, French Guinea became independent, which had great consequence for Guinean tirailleurs sénégalais serving France in Algeria. The life history of Guinean career soldier Koly Kourouma provides a harrowing tale of negotiating the decolonization of French West Africa. West African independence catalyzed discussions concerning the legal status of veterans and their benefits, which impacted West African widows and military households. After a half-century of political independence, the legacies of war and colonialism continue to affect veterans' households. West African veterans have become living symbols of the injustices and legacies of French colonialism, yet their families continue to look to postcolonial France for financial support.

1

Marrying into the Military

Colonization, Emancipation, and Martial Community in West Africa, 1880–1900

TIRAILLEURS SÉNÉGALAIS' CONJUGAL TRADITIONS COHERED AT A TIME in which France intensified and expanded its military presence in West Africa. During the final decades of the nineteenth century, locally recruited troops across the African continent played important roles in the escalation of everyday violence, social destabilization, and the operation of colonialism. Their presence in the ranks of the European-commanded armies influenced local expressions of militarization and colonial rule. In West Africa, soldiers participated in France's violent conquest of regions extending from the Senegal River basin to the shoreline of Lake Chad and along the coasts of what would become Guinea, Côte d'Ivoire, and Dahomey. French colonization coincided with, and exacerbated, regional conflicts led by politicized Muslim leaders in the West African savannah and Sahel. Tirailleurs sénégalais fought in pitched battles with the adherents of Mamadou Lamine Drame in Bundu, Samory Touré across his Wassulu Empire, and Ahmadu Seku Tall in Segu—the capital of the Tukulor Empire. The French military eliminated opposition to colonial rule with superior military technology and tirailleurs sénégalais. Via tirailleurs sénégalais, France incorporated West African territories into the nascent colonial state. Subsequently, these soldiers assisted in initiating processes and introducing institutions meant to foster postconflict stability.

Empowered by the colonial state, African soldiers influenced changes in important sociocultural traditions, including slavery and marriage. They simultaneously engaged in conjugal practices that would serve as the foundation for tirailleurs sénégalais' marital traditions.

The earliest manifestations of the French colonial state and military depended on West African women and the households they created with tirailleurs sénégalais.[1] The importance of women in these institutions has not been adequately addressed in the historical literature on colonial armies in Africa. Early publications focused on military technology, battles, and political power, as well as relying on the troublesome dichotomies of colonizer versus colonized and/or narratives of collaboration versus resistance.[2] Unintentionally, these works produced political histories of conquest that disregarded the subtle (and not so subtle) effects of militarization across African sociocultural landscapes. In the past decade, Africanist military historians have begun to locate women's experiences in Europe's conquest of the continent, as well as to map gendered results of colonial and postcolonial militarism.[3] This chapter examines how women and gender were consequential to the early iterations of the French colonial military and state. Women participated in military campaigns stretching from Atlantic coastlines into southern Saharan towns. West African communities experienced the tragedies of war and profound transformations in gerontocratic and gendered authority. Colonial militarization altered local institutions that gave social order to West African societies— armies, slavery, and marriage. With conquest, the colonial military and its African soldiers brought heteronormative marriage and slave emancipation under their jurisdiction, which had wide-ranging effects on conjugal behavior and marital legitimacy within the tirailleurs sénégalais. Military records concerning tirailleurs sénégalais' households during colonial conquest allow historians to track changes and continuities in West African marital traditions before civilian administrators set up indigenous court systems in the early twentieth century. West African women, soldiers, and the French colonial military contested marital customs within military spaces, where masculinity and paternalism weighed on decisions concerning legitimate marriage and divorce. Tirailleurs sénégalais' emergent conjugal traditions would later inform civilian administrators about West African marital rites.[4]

Warfare, slave emancipation, and marriage were processes that influenced how African women became tirailleurs sénégalais' conjugal partners and/or

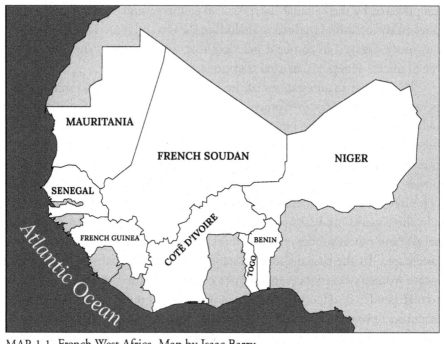

MAP 1.1. French West Africa. Map by Isaac Barry

auxiliary members of the French colonial army. Conjugal traditions cohered in military contexts, but were informed by precolonial West African and French marital and martial customs. In order to track their origins and transformations, this chapter pays careful attention to the relationship between slavery, emancipation, and military service. Precolonial states and the French colonial state relied heavily on enslaved and/or formerly enslaved men to fill the ranks of their armed forces. Relatedly, the dynamic relationship among female slavery, emancipation, and marriage informs our understanding of how West African women, across the colonial divide, came to be affiliated with military men. The trial of Ciraïa Aminata, detailed below, illustrates how colonial agents obscured the distinction between female slave and wife in colonial African military households. Militarization increased women's vulnerability and reduced their social ties and status within their natal communities. When colonial soldiers were involved, nineteenth-century West African communities lost their authority over the marital rites and traditions that provided legitimacy to conjugal relationships in West Africa.

French conquest introduced new mechanisms and institutions that provided displaced West African women and men with gendered pathways toward emancipation and marriage. Military officers created Liberty Villages, which tripled as safe havens, spaces of emancipation, and sites of labor recruitment for the colonial state. Men became soldiers and women became their wives. Similar to Mamadou Lamine Drame's conjugal partners (described in the introduction), West African women experienced "emancipation" from slavery and "marriage" to tirailleurs sénégalais as analogous or coterminous processes. Military marriages, when paired with emancipation, served to liberate men into the public sphere and women into the private sphere or household.[5] Efforts to eradicate slavery through military conquest gendered the emancipation process—masculinizing the colonial state and its employees.[6] The French military's support of these gendered processes made West African women crucial to recruitment efforts and labor stabilization within the tirailleurs sénégalais. Female West Africans—slave or not—transformed into colonial subjects and *mesdames tirailleurs*.[7]

The French colonial military expected mesdames tirailleurs to provide their husbands with domestic labor, as well as to provide other troops with essential services like food preparation and laundering services. Active soldiers campaigned with their families and/or established new households near war fronts while serving state interests. African military households conformed their traditions of familial reciprocity and patron-client relationships to the hierarchical structure of the colonial military.[8] Tirailleurs sénégalais households depended on each other and the colonial state. They reproduced precolonial sociocultural hierarchies and relationships of exchange while adapting to the colonial military's systems of redistribution and its allocation of resources to their military families. West African conjugal traditions evolved within French conquest. African military households on the frontiers of the colonial state result from dramatic transformations in gendered power in nineteenth-century West Africa.

SLAVES AND SOLDIERS:
INDIGENOUS AND COLONIAL MILITARY TRADITIONS

During the 1880s and 1890s, the French military benefited from recruitment practices that constrained African men's liberty and put them to work for the nascent colonial state. Slavery and coerced labor were key features of the

French colonial military and African military households in the late nineteenth century. Governor Louis Faidherbe created the tirailleurs sénégalais in 1857 in response to several contingent nineteenth-century processes—a renewed and growing presence of French concessionary companies along West African coastlines and waterways, colonial state expansion, and the protracted abolition of slavery. French colonization in late nineteenth-century West Africa occurred through military conquest. The French military recruited West African men for extensive inland campaigns. Many tirailleurs sénégalais were former slaves who had secured their freedom by enlisting in the colonial military. At the front lines of French colonization, these slaves-turned-soldiers assisted in liberating and protecting other recently emancipated slaves. The French colonial military's dependence on slaves and former slaves paralleled indigenous West African military practices. Nineteenth-century French colonial labor schemes—*laptots, engagé à temps, rachat*—employed enslaved laborers, who were also channeled into the tirailleurs sénégalais.[9] Additionally, Liberty Villages served as entry points into military service. French colonial officials and village chiefs compelled able-bodied men in these sites of refuge to enlist in the tirailleurs sénégalais.

The military conquest of inland West Africa followed France's universal declaration of slave abolition in 1848 and the Third Republic's (1871–1940) commitment to eradicating forms of slavery in empire. In the 1880s, the emancipation of domestic slaves was a formal objective of colonization, which would deeply entangle military officials in processes of emancipation, recruitment, and conjugal affiliation. Forms of domestic slavery were pervasive to the processes that produced African soldiers and military households.[10] Domestic slavery describes a continuum of forms of human bondage that were subtler, if no less brutal, than the chattel slavery affiliated with the plantation colonies of the Americas. Scholars have described domestic slavery as a transitional process, where outsiders were incorporated into new kinship groups/communities through an initial phase of enslavement.[11] French civilian and military administrators believed in this assimilationist model and argued it was standard to African and Muslim forms of slavery in West Africa.[12] Through transgenerational social integration, enslaved people would become full community members and gradually efface their slave origins or foreign status. Domestic slavery enabled powerful lineages to accumulate dependents and secure labor. Nineteenth-century French observers viewed domestic slavery as essential to the social fabric of West African societies.[13] They were hesitant to enforce wholesale emancipation in their West African territories because they feared it would create social upheaval and inhibit their ability to manage recently acquired territories. Instead, early colonial officials fostered institutions that moderated the enforcement of emancipation and accommodated local practices dependent upon slavery. The military used emancipatory mechanisms that assimilated marginalized West Africans into the nascent colonial state and provided them with limited opportunities to achieve social mobility. Membership in the tirailleurs sénégalais provided former slaves with circumstances in which they could accumulate resources and acquire conjugal partners and dependents. The gradual amelioration of their low social status during their military careers extended to their offspring. In this way, the tirailleurs sénégalais' measured integration into the colonial state was analogous to the ways in which the French believed noncasted domestic slavery functioned in West Africa.

The colonial state's incorporation of enslaved men and men with slave ancestry into the tirailleurs sénégalais resembled aspects of precolonial West African military recruitment practices.[14] Many West African societies valorized martial skills. Men (and in some cases women) in those societies were trained in military skills at various stages of maturation.[15] The Bamana kingdoms of Ségou and Kaarta exemplified warrior-based states in nineteenth-century West Africa.[16] Some societies designated specific lineages or castes to specialize in martial skills. Martial lineages or castes were affiliated with slave status, like the *ceddo* of the Wolof kingdoms. Although affiliated with slave status, soldier castes often held privileged positions among the slave classes.[17] Expansionist states absorbed prisoners of war and refugees into their military forces. Many of Samory's *sofa*s, or soldiers, were captives prior to their conscription into his army.[18] Sofas acquired, employed, and incorporated slaves into the expansionist Samorian state as groomsmen, attendants, and orderlies. Enslaved women, who provided domestic and auxiliary military services, were among sofas' wives and dependents.[19] Many new recruits in the tirailleurs sénégalais were refugees or former sofas looking for new patrons. They lacked the ability to return home and reclaim their homes or farms. Enlisting in the tirailleurs sénégalais provided these men with the opportunity to earn wages, as well as to secure access to other types of resources provided by the colonial military state. Sofas-turned-tirailleurs sénégalais also continued Samorian practices of acquiring wives on campaign.[20] The colonial military allocated rations to soldiers and allowed them to set up family homesteads adjacent to military posts. In some cases, the colonial military assisted tirailleurs sénégalais in locating and liberating their dispersed kin.[21]

The French colonial military's methods of recruitment and retention of soldiers expanded upon earlier nineteenth-century colonial labor schemes. Laptots provide a historical through line, which connects Atlantic African forms of slavery with French colonial labor systems that include the tirailleurs sénégalais. Laptots were men employed on limited-term contracts to crew and provide security on French merchant and military ships between trading posts in the Senegambia. Laptots first appeared in the colonial record during the early eighteenth century, when they worked for French royal charter companies participating in the transatlantic slave trade. In the nineteenth century, laptots hailed from a variety of ethnolinguistic groups and included free men, slaves, and former slaves. Emancipation could occur before, during, or after laptots' period of employment. In some cases, representatives of the French state freed the slaves that became laptots. In other examples, slave owners hired out their slaves to work in laptots corps. In this type of arrangement, masters received enslaved laptots' enlistment bonus and part of their wages. This practice existed contemporaneously with engagé à temps, a labor scheme in which French merchants or state employees rented slaves and/or contracted non-slave laborers from local populations.[22] Working in the laptot corps provided men with the ability to accumulate resources, manumit themselves, and become merchants and/or slave owners.[23] Financial independence provided enslaved and formerly enslaved laptots with the means to marry, support multiwife households, and become full members of their communities.[24]

The rachat, or repurchasing, system was another means through which enslaved men entered the laptots corps. French recruiters initiated this process of gradual emancipation by purchasing slaves from their masters. After ten to fourteen years of contracted labor, these former slaves were free of their obligations to their masters and the French colonial state.[25] The rachat labor system conflicted with the Second French Republic's abolition of slavery in its colonial territories.[26] The 1848 declaration of universal emancipation was intended for France's agricultural plantation and settler colonies in the

Caribbean, which may explain why the French military continued using rachat in West Africa into the late 1880s. In 1857, the same year that Faidherbe inaugurated the tirailleurs sénégalais, local French administrators circulated a confidential note outlining the 1848 legislation's relevance to West Africa. The decree of emancipation affected the regions that had already been incorporated into the colony of Senegal at the time of the declaration on 27 April 1848—nine years earlier. This meant that the decree applied to Gorée, Saint-Louis, and the military posts along the Senegal River. All of the West Africans living outside of those specified zones became subjects of France. As subjects, they retained the right to hold and trade in slaves.[27] French military leaders in West Africa accommodated slavery because local political leaders and slave owners supplied them with enslaved men for military service into the late 1880s.[28] After 1857, the rachat system and other emancipatory mechanisms steered male slaves and former male slaves away from the laptots corps and into the ranks of the tirailleurs sénégalais.[29]

Liberty Villages were another colonial institution involved in the production of emancipated slaves, tirailleurs sénégalais, and their conjugal households. Lieutenant Colonel Joseph-Simon Gallieni established the first Liberty Villages in Kayes and Siguiri in the 1880s. These villages sheltered West African refugees—displaced people, prisoners of war, and fugitive slaves—following regional conflicts triggered by French conquest as well as conflicts initiated by local religious and political leaders.[30] Samory Touré's sofas razed conquered villages in his expansionist wars south of the Niger River. Ahmadu Seku Tall and Mamadou Lamine Drame attempted to maintain and expand their influence in Segu and Bundu, respectively. Colonel Henri Frey's overzealous punitive actions against the Soninke villages allied with Mamadou Lamine Drame resulted in large numbers of Soninke (some of whom were former laptots and tirailleurs sénégalais) seeking sanctuary in the Liberty Villages.[31]

The French colonial military established Liberty Villages adjacent to military posts in the Senegal and Niger River watersheds. This proximity to the state provided residents with limited protections and provided a space in which French military officials could recruit soldiers and reward veterans for previous service. French military officials and their West African military and civilian employees regulated access and residency in these villages. Liberty Village inhabitants acquired certificates of liberty through a protracted process that began when they registered with the village's administrator on the day of their arrival. Within ninety days, villagers could obtain their liberty certificate, which protected them from enslavement or reenslavement.[32] Liberty certificates, and the record of their receipt, were admissible evidence in the ad hoc colonial tribunals formed in military posts, Liberty Villages, and recently conquered towns. Military officials, village chiefs, and other colonial personnel presided over these tribunals, which had jurisdiction over civil suits concerning individuals' slave status. During the three-month period of liminal emancipation, refugees worked for the local administration in order to pay for the rations and resources supplied to them by the colonial state. Men predominantly provided manual labor in construction and farming. Women gathered firewood, fetched water, cooked, and participated in other domestic services. During the ninety-day waiting period, masters could reclaim runaway slaves residing in the Liberty Villages. This clause upheld slave owners' rights to their slaves, as well as contravening the abolitionist imperatives of the French Third Republic. However, the French established themselves as the ultimate authority that adjudicated slave ownership in their conquered territories. Tribunal officials required masters to present witnesses and testimony in order to verify their ownership of Liberty Village residents. If a master successfully reclaimed a runaway slave at a Liberty Village, they were required to reimburse the local administrator for the resources consumed by their slave, at a rate of fifty centimes per day.[33]

Male residents in Liberty Villages had greater opportunity than female residents to shield themselves from former masters. If they joined the tirailleurs sénégalais, former masters could only reclaim them within thirty days of their enlistment. This option could have been attractive to fugitive slaves, but it came with some of the same conditions as rachat. Men enlisting in the tirailleurs sénégalais in Liberty Villages were expected to serve for ten to fourteen years in order to guarantee their freedom.[34] If they survived the length of their service, the French colonial state offered veterans employment opportunities that ameliorated their socioeconomic status. Some tirailleurs sénégalais veterans returned to their ancestral villages, some reenlisted, and others took administrative positions in the expanding colonial state.[35] Former tirailleurs sénégalais also secured chieftaincies in newly established Liberty Villages. In this way, former slaves-turned-soldiers gained authority and responsibilities that would have been inaccessible to them as slaves or low-status individuals.

Liberty Village chiefs assigned new arrivals usufruct rights to land for farming, allotted them materials to build homesteads, and presided over marriage ceremonies.[36] To potential recruits, these colonial soldiers-turned-chiefs were paragons of the social and political mobility that could result from colonial military service. Liberty Village headmen also acted as recruitment agents who encouraged newly incorporated male villagers to enlist in the tirailleurs sénégalais. Liberty Village chiefs performed many of the same tasks as other West African headmen, but their authority depended on their relationship with the colonial state—not on claims of traditional legitimacy or community sanction.

EMANCIPATING MESDAMES TIRAILLEURS: FORMER FEMALE SLAVES AND THE BONDS OF MARRIAGE

Colonial labor schemes and Liberty Villages provided refugee, enslaved, and formerly enslaved women with fewer postemancipation possibilities than men. The French did not protect former female slaves' liberty by offering them employment in the colonial state. Instead, military administrators encouraged women to marry West African colonial employees, predominantly tirailleurs sénégalais, in order to protect them from enslavement or reenslavement. Marriage was also thought to stabilize the colonial military's labor force and increase stability in postconflict areas.[37] Enslaved women were emancipated into the bonds of marriage and many became mesdames tirailleurs. From the perspective of the French military, African military households provided hierarchical and gendered organization to biological and social reproduction within the military and along the colonial frontier. Tirailleurs sénégalais could absorb and channel French colonial authority into their households. Marriage provided a platform through which the nascent colonial state could reinforce patriarchal authority and male prerogatives, as well as efface women's and men's slave origins.[38] An administrator in Siguiri argued that male slaves could not attain liberty until they had taken a wife and begun a family.[39] Tirailleurs sénégalais' conjugal relationships initiated new forms of female subjugation and dependency in the nascent French colonial era. In doing so, the colonial army maintained and altered gendered aspects of domestic slavery within African military households in a postemancipation landscape.[40] The emancipation of male slaves did not automatically extend their newfound liberty to wives and children. Female household members could not attain the same degree of liberty as their husbands.[41] Their "free" status was not protected outside of the domestic households and their limited liberties were further constrained by their husband's authority. The gendered effects of militarization and emancipation were bound up in tirailleurs sénégalais' nineteenth-century conjugal traditions.

African military households perpetuated female domestic slavery. The majority of domestic slaves in nineteenth-century West Africa were women.[42] For many French observers of that time, being female in West Africa connoted subservient status. If women were not slaves, they were the wards or dependents of their husbands or other male relatives.[43] Like many other former female slaves in early colonial Africa, mesdames tirailleurs often became "political minors in the postslavery landscape."[44] Military officials viewed mesdames tirailleurs as the responsibility of soldiers. The sanctity of marriage and the presumed patriarchal authority operating within African military households deterred most French administrators from intervening in their domestic affairs. French colonial officials perpetuated freed West African women's inferior status by "excluding marriage from . . . antislavery policies," which "reinforced the patriarchal family" within the colonial military.[45]

Some tirailleurs sénégalais and mesdames tirailleurs grew up in matrilineal societies. They confronted and conformed to new iterations of gendered familial authority in the army. Administrators upheld patriarchal and patrilineal claims to wives and daughters in the interest of maintaining regional political stability.[46] In the 1880s, tirailleurs sénégalais households accompanied troops on campaign. This mobility isolated mesdames tirailleurs from broader West African kin networks, which increased their responsibilities in the conjugal home and increased husbands' authority over them. These women lacked nearby kin who could compel husbands to comply with the expectations and obligations typical to legitimate marriages. Mesdames tirailleurs also lacked familial networks necessary for access to agricultural land, assistance in childrearing, and other necessities normally fulfilled by reciprocal kin-based relationships. Their ability to acquire resources hinged upon the rank and/or status of their husbands within the French colonial military.

French colonial administrators imagined tirailleurs sénégalais households as nuclear-family households that conformed to male-breadwinner models of economic distribution. Both had little precedent in nineteenth-century

West Africa.[47] The male-breadwinner economic model assumed that senior male family members were the unique wage earners within a household made up of their heteronormative partners and offspring. The wages and other resources that male heads of household acquired were subsequently redistributed to other household members.[48] Most West Africans, irrespective of gender, consumed what they produced and used local and long-distance trade networks for scarce or luxury goods.[49] French military officials believed that women's labor contributed to an economy circumscribed by the needs of their households and extended families. These private spheres of economic domesticity were ostensibly discrete from the public sphere, where the colonial economy existed. To the contrary, women across West Africa participated in the production of crops and artisanal goods as well as selling their wares in daily or weekly rotating markets. Extensive and overlapping modes of resource redistribution existed among extended matrilineal and patrilineal kin. Foodstuffs, goods, and gifts moved through and around conjugal households. Despite some familiarity with the complex web of familial relations and the ubiquity of market women, French colonial observers characterized their African soldiers as the conduits through which the colonial economy reached the members of their households.[50]

The French military sanctioned tirailleurs sénégalais' acquisition of wives through means that paralleled concubinage and enslavement. In order to avoid the language of slavery, French military observers deployed the language of matrimony and legitimacy in describing vulnerable women's incorporation into the tirailleurs sénégalais community. One of the most striking examples of this process, referenced in the introduction, occurred after the capture of seventeen of Mamadou Lamine Drame's conjugal partners. Lieutenant Colonel Gallieni oversaw the redistribution of these women to his most distinguished tirailleurs sénégalais. Gallieni made the exceptional violence involved in forced conjugal association mundane by depicting the transfer of women from one man to another as a West African "tradition." He blurred the distinctions between slavery and marriage by equating husbands, in this case tirailleurs sénégalais, with masters.[51] French colonial military historical documents are replete with examples of code switching between the language used to describe gendered roles in African military households and the language used to describe the gendered dynamics between enslaved women and male slave owners.

Mainland French abolitionists and journalists became aware of the gendered paradoxes of emancipation in West Africa in June 1887. They scandalized metropolitan France by accusing the French colonial military of trafficking female sex slaves among the tirailleurs sénégalais. Colonel Henri Frey defended the allocation of liberated women to tirailleurs sénégalais as a necessary step in protecting their freedom.[52] The different vocabularies used in the reporting and defense of these practices reveal the degree to which the French military believed in tirailleurs sénégalais' entitlement to family life, irrespective of whether or not their marriages perpetuated forms of domestic slavery. The processes through which vulnerable women wed tirailleurs sénégalais were less than ideal. Mesdames tirailleurs located on campaign often suffered brutality and humiliation during their incorporation into soldiers' households. When Gallieni distributed Drame's conjugal partners to his most distinguished tirailleurs sénégalais, he labeled the last woman to be chosen as the "ugliest" of the seventeen women. Gallieni later granted a divorce to the tirailleur sénégalais who had lived a brief, disagreeable marriage with her.[53]

French administrators believed that, despite the perfunctory nature of African military nuptials, former slave women would be better off once they "adjusted" to living with tirailleurs sénégalais.[54] Mesdames tirailleurs habituated themselves to the duties of military wives, while tirailleurs sénégalais obtained the status of married men, fathers, and patrons. The French colonial military protected soldiers' rights to wives acquired through forced conjugal association. Once married, the colonial state reinforced soldiers' authority over women made vulnerable by militarization across West Africa. As emancipated men and household heads, tirailleurs sénégalais engaged in strategies that improved their social status.[55] In the early years of the colonial era, male members of African military households had greater opportunity to reinvent themselves; some even took European names while in the military.[56] Marriage and making households were crucial to their reinvention.

FEMALE SLAVERY, PRENUPTIAL IDEALS, AND MARITAL TRADITIONS IN WEST AFRICA

Tirailleurs sénégalais' conjugal practices followed and diverged from legitimate marital customs in West Africa. Marital practices in West Africa encompassed rites and rituals that conferred legitimacy on conjugal unions and their offspring.

Legitimate marriage had great significance in organizing many spheres of the human experience. Marriage provided a mechanism through which to extend and monitor kinship networks, forge or maintain economic connections, and encourage social and physical reproduction. Marital traditions varied from community to community in West Africa. Social status, spiritual beliefs, family dynamics, and a host of other factors influenced processes of betrothal, marriage, and the community's ongoing support of a marriage throughout its duration. In ideal circumstances, West Africans aspired to marry with the consent and approval of their parents and guardians. Public celebrations of weddings aimed to acquire the support of the broader community, which brought honor to newlyweds' unions and legitimated their future children. West African communities expected postpubescent individuals to marry and procreate. Youth often could not meet all cultural expectations or obey socially imposed constraints on premarital intimate interactions. Community elders superintended the heterosexual relations of youth and exercised gerontocratic authority over prenuptial rites. Young women were subject to greater surveillance and moral sanction than male youth because of proscriptions against pregnancy out of wedlock. Elders' supervision protected the virtuousness of pubescent women, which further preserved the honor of families and future generations. Various household and lineage members participated in the marital unions of individuals and pressured youth to accept arranged marriages. Young men had greater flexibility regarding when and whom they married. They also had greater autonomy in choosing their second or third wives. Aside from the rare exception, women could not marry more than one spouse at a time, but often had greater authority over choosing new husbands after divorce or the death of their first spouses.[57]

Many West African communities practiced polygyny. Family constellations extended beyond nuclear families through matrilineal and patrilineal hereditary lines. Households could consist of a husband, several wives, and their immediate descendants, as well as extended relations. Senior women in multiwife households organized shared domestic work among wives. Women gained prestige among their peers and within their families with live births and children that survived infancy. Marriage was a conduit through which lineage members could access the labor of their descendants. Children provided predominantly agricultural and pastoral communities with labor.[58] Marriage enhanced economic stability because it was crucial in determining who could farm arable land or have access to grazing land. Kinship ties facilitated long-distance trade because merchants extended credit and the welcome mat to distant relations.

The accumulation of dependents and resources enabled extended families to acquire greater economic, social, and political status. In some regions of West Africa, the accumulation of resources led to the development of socioeconomic classes and lineage-based castes that specialized in specific trades and the production of artisanal goods. Marriage figured prominently in maintaining these social distinctions, as well as ensuring that elite lineages retained prestige and economic resources. Through marriage, already powerful elite families reinforced their social and political power and also shored up sociocultural status through the exclusion of other classes and castes. Economic elites and noble lineages developed symbiotic relationships with their lower-class counterparts through patron-client relationships. Marriage and concubinage served as vehicles to incorporate foreigners, slaves, or members of other castes and classes into prominent families. Powerful elite families maintained their status through intermarriage and the redistribution of their wealth through the customary exchange of gifts surrounding marital ceremonies.[59] The value and abundance of these gifts publicly displayed these families' wealth and prestige, as well as the degree to which they esteemed their future in-laws.

French colonial documents tend to portray bridewealth as the mobilization of valued goods or labor from the groom's kin to the family of the bride. Bridewealth symbolized the sociocultural value of a bride and the groom's family's respect for and admiration of their future in-laws. The absence of bridewealth exchange often indicated an individual's low social status or community disapproval of the union. Prolonged conjugal affiliation without marriage—concubinage—signaled the low social position of one or both unmarried romantic partners. Concubinage resided at the intersection of slavery and marriage and occurred between free men and slave women or among enslaved people.[60] Communities condoned these romantic relationships in order to incorporate low-status women and their children into kin groups. Concubines also bolstered the prestige of important men by increasing their responsibilities and dependents. The social status of individual marital partners influenced their obligations and responsibilities to each other and the conjugal home. Concubines performed the same duties as wives, but they lacked the rights and privileges that accompanied legitimate marriage.[61]

French colonial authorities regarded bridewealth as the most salient feature of legitimate marriage in West Africa. Simultaneously and contrarily, they also associated bridewealth with female slave trafficking. In either interpretation, French colonial observers stripped bridewealth of its profound sociocultural meaning and reduced it all too often to a transactional value. French officials' position toward bridewealth grew ever more paradoxical in their sanction of romantic unions between tirailleurs sénégalais and female slaves or prisoners of war. Military observers labeled these conjugal unions "marriages," despite their consummation without the exchange of bridewealth. Concubinage was an integral component of early tirailleurs sénégalais marital traditions. The French sanctioned these unions for many of the same reasons that West African communities accepted concubinage—greater social stability, bolstering the prestige of men, and the incorporation of vulnerable women into the protection of the community and/or state.[62]

Militarization and French colonization altered the ways in which West Africans achieved marital legitimacy. Tirailleurs sénégalais had elevated status and power because of their employment in the colonial military. The expansion of colonial authority across West Africa enabled these men to assert their conjugal prerogatives and simultaneously dodge local social prescriptions pertaining to marriage. Military officials—French and West African—acted as powerful lineage members who backed tirailleurs sénégalais' conjugal behaviors. Military authority also constrained the ability of female spouses' kin to consent to the union or ensure that tirailleurs sénégalais observed appropriate premarital rites. Without the participation of extended communities in prenuptial rites, bridewealth became increasingly transactional. Unlike extended relatives in West Africa, the military did little to ensure that tirailleurs sénégalais' marriages were enduring or successful. Nineteenth-century military officials viewed West African soldiers' marriages as temporary arrangements that benefited soldiers and the army. Commanding officers supported soldiers' polygynous and polyamorous conjugal behaviors because they paralleled other colonial conjugal arrangements in West Africa.

French Atlantic forms of conjugal cohabitation and concubinage evolved in the nineteenth century. As France's colonial presence expanded beyond the West African Atlantic littoral, the term *mariage à la mode du pays* traveled with the colonial military—retaining some of its former meaning as well as acquiring new significance as military officials applied the term broadly to encompass relationships between military personnel and civilian women.[63] Significant changes in the term's usage included an emphasis on the temporary nature of sexual relationships, which no longer included an investment in shared domestic living or recognizing paternity of children. Within the military's usage at the end of the nineteenth century, mariage à la mode du pays no longer uniquely referred to conjugal relationships between European men and African women. Officials came to refer to tirailleurs sénégalais' conjugal and sexual relationships with female prisoners of war and former female slaves as mariage à la mode du pays, which simultaneously and ambivalently portrayed these heteronormative relationships as marriage and not marriage. This questionable legitimacy remained a dominant feature of tirailleurs sénégalais' marital traditions into the interwar years.

THE AFFAIR OF CIRAÏA AMINATA

The affair of Ciraïa Aminata provides a snapshot of the dynamic confluence of militarization, colonization, emancipation, and marriage in nineteenth-century West Africa. Aminata's brief appearance in the historical record illustrates the ways in which French conquest destabilized West African communities and how early institutions of the colonial state opened and closed gendered pathways toward emancipation and prosperity. The military asserted its political and juridical authority over West Africans' sociocultural practices and traditional institutions in newly colonized spaces. There are many excellent historical studies that examine the operation of the colonial state's juridical power over slavery and marriage in West African colonial court records.[64] Ciraïa Aminata's day in the ad hoc military tribunal exemplifies how military officials' intervention into the conjugal affairs of tirailleurs sénégalais households inscribed paternalism and masculine authority into the institutions of the nascent colonial state. Militarization coincided with the articulation of juridical authority over African women's liberty and marital status.

Ciraïa Aminata appeared before a hastily assembled tribunal in Siguiri's Liberty Village in March 1888. Three different men brought forward competing claims of ownership and/or spousal authority over Ciraïa Aminata. Her day in court provides intimate details of one woman's survival in the volatile borderlands of Samory's Wassulu Empire and French Empire in contemporary northeastern Guinea-Conakry. In the years preceding the trial, Aminata's lived experiences demonstrate how militarization of the region caused the rise of masculine authority over women and increased women's vulnerability to male authority.[65] Emboldened men, particularly men affiliated with armed forces, took advantage of sociopolitical instability to advance their household strategies outside of normative conjugal traditions. Ciraïa Aminata became affiliated with three different men through processes that blurred the distinctions between enslavement, forced conjugal association, and marriage. In court, military officials wielded the colonial state's new juridical power and provided the ultimate authority over the marital status of Ciraïa Aminata. The colonial state shored up the power of tirailleurs sénégalais over vulnerable women, while condoning conjugal practices that contravened colonial imperatives to eradicate slavery. Military officials blurred the discrete categories of slave women and wives, which created an ambiguity about the status, rights, and obligations of female members of tirailleurs sénégalais' households.[66]

Gallieni recorded the trial concerning Ciraïa Aminata's matrimonial and slave status in 1888.[67] Aminata's story began with an abduction while she collected water from a stream near Baté in the Milo River valley. According to Gallieni, Ciraïa Aminata's captor subsequently married her by force. Gallieni referred to her captor as a "ravisher," which indicated that the conjugal relationship began with an act of nonconsensual sex. Gallieni acknowledged that Aminata's marriage to her captor circumvented the standard rites and procedures preceding local marital custom. Despite this, Gallieni used the language of matrimony, which indicates he believed that forced conjugal association could be a precursor to legitimate marriage. Alternatively, Gallieni may have believed that the mere act of sexual intercourse provided a degree of legitimacy to West Africans' conjugal unions. His observations evince widely held beliefs among colonial officials that West African women's consent to sex or marriage was unnecessary in legitimizing conjugal unions. By sanctioning the marriage while casting doubt upon the prenuptial process, Gallieni provided himself with the cover to later delegitimize this marriage when adjudicating Ciraïa Aminata's case at Siguiri's tribunal.

Ciraïa Aminata's captor, referred to by Gallieni as her first husband (*premier mari*), was captured by a sofa serving in Samory Touré's army. The sofa sold Ciraïa Aminata's first husband into slavery in Kaarta to a Tukulor from Kouniakry and then replaced the original captor as Ciraïa Aminata's second husband (*deuxième mari*). The sofa, who was an active member of Samory Touré's army, participated in battles against the French near Bamako. Ciraïa Aminata followed her new husband on these campaigns and likely provided domestic and auxiliary military support to her husband and his fellow soldiers. Afterward, the second husband left Samory's army in order to set the couple up in a small village in Wassulu. Fearing forced reenlistment in Samory's armies, the couple left Wassulu and relocated to Siguiri. In Siguiri's Liberty Village, the demilitarized sofa and Ciraïa Aminata could expect a degree of French protection from Samory's recruitment agents.

By seeking refuge in the Liberty Village, the couple surrendered some of their sovereignty to the legal and bureaucratic authority of the colonial state. Their temporary sanctuary provided the setting for the unraveling of their union. The disintegration of their marriage resulted from the intervening authority of the colonial state. Liberty Village chiefs and French administrators presided over the processes of marriage and divorce among inhabitants of Liberty Villages. In Siguiri, two different men used Gallieni's tribunal to challenge the retired sofa's matrimonial claims to Ciraïa Aminata. The first was her captor from Baté, who Gallieni labeled her first husband. After his enslavement in Kaarta, he had eventually manumitted himself and enlisted in the Seventh Company of the tirailleurs sénégalais. The Seventh Company was under the command of Gallieni and encamped in Siguiri in March 1888. He caught sight of Ciraïa Aminata in the adjacent Liberty Village when he returned to Siguiri from campaigning in Manding. The second plaintiff was Ciraïa Aminata's original master. This man, referred to by Gallieni as her *premier maître* (first master), claimed to have proprietary rights to Aminata that predated her abduction near Baté. This original master had come to Siguiri, fleeing Samory, in order to access arable land in the Liberty Village. By happenstance, he had crossed paths with Ciraïa Aminata in the village and attempted to seize her. Gallieni's interpreter brought Ciraïa Aminata and the three men with matrimonial and/or ownership claims to her before the tribunal.

In the late nineteenth century, French administrators and their local interlocutors possessed a great deal of latitude in adjudicating cases according to their interpretation of local custom, the applicability of French legal norms, and restorative justice. As demonstrated above, members of the colonial state had conflictual and deeply ambivalent ideas about marital legitimacy and female slavery in West Africa. Gallieni used *maître* (master) and *mari* (husband) synonymously to describe Ciraïa Aminata's ostensible husbands. His conflation of these two terms was symptomatic of an extensive belief held by French colonial officials regarding the interchangeability of these terms. Each of the men making claims on Ciraïa Aminata had experienced displacement and had become a client of the colonial state. Any one of these men could have successfully argued their entitlement to Ciraïa Aminata's conjugal labor. If Ciraïa Aminata had resided in the Liberty Village for less than ninety days, the original master would have had the right to reclaim his former slave. The retired sofa, or second husband, could have argued that his marriage to Ciraïa had occurred along the same principles and processes central to tirailleurs sénégalais' marital traditions. However, it was the first captor from Baté, turned tirailleur sénégalais, who walked out of the tribunal with Ciraïa Aminata on his arm.

Gallieni presided over the tribunal. In newly colonized spaces in West Africa, military authorities asserted their jurisdiction over civil affairs and tipped the scales toward their soldiers. The original master would have likely had the strongest claim over Ciraïa Aminata in terms of ownership. In his description of Ciraïa Aminata's history, Gallieni delegitimized the process through which the first husband/ravisher had acquired Ciraïa Aminata as a wife. This abductor-turned-tirailleur sénégalais may have also had the weakest case when viewed through local understandings of slave ownership and marital tradition. Yet the first husband's transformation from abductor to tirailleur sénégalais positively influenced his case in the eyes of the colonial state. The retired sofa, or second husband, may have had the most viable claim over Aminata as a wife because they had set up homesteads in Wassulu and in Siguiri's Liberty Village. The presence of children could have influenced the outcome of the tribunal, but there were no details concerning paternity in the account.

Ciraïa Aminata's ability to determine her possible future was circumscribed by the colonial state's narrow vision of emancipated women's destiny as wives. Gallieni claimed that Ciraïa Aminata's status as a resident of Siguiri's Liberty Village gave her the freedom to choose her husband from among the three successive masters/husbands. By framing her act as one of choice, Gallieni perpetuated the myth that West African women obtained liberties through the emancipatory processes on offer in Liberty Villages, when, in fact, Ciraïa Aminata's only "choice" was marriage. Ciraïa Aminata "chose" the tirailleur sénégalais who was her first abductor/ravisher and first husband. She elected to become a *madame tirailleur* as opposed to the wife of a civilian. Upon leaving the tribunal with Ciraïa Aminata, her tirailleur sénégalais husband purportedly commented, "women always prefer handsome tirailleurs sénégalais to civilians."[68] Captured for posterity in Gallieni's *Deux campagnes*, the words of a gloating braggart signal several assumptions made by colonial soldiers and their commanders: martiality, affiliation with the colonial state's authority, and access to its resources made African colonial soldiers ideal spouses. For Gallieni, the affair of Ciraïa Aminata was an allegory for the "benevolent" power of military colonization.

There are other reasons that may explain why Ciraïa Aminata chose the tirailleur sénégalais over the other men. The possibility of economic and social stability would have been appealing to her, having recently experienced a rapid succession of life-altering events and intimate affiliations. She may have recognized that the tirailleur sénégalais's gainful employment held more promise than the other men, who were refugees in an increasingly crowded Liberty Village. Marriage to a tirailleur sénégalais could safeguard against future reenslavement because the colonial military protected soldiers and their conjugal partners from former and potential future masters. Ciraïa Aminata may have also been aware of the fact that Gallieni donated domesticated animals and grains to new military households. Membership in an African military household made mesdames tirailleurs eligible for regular rations and gave them preferential access to land.[69] Ciraïa Aminata's choice of husband corresponds with the historical arguments regarding the "strategies of slaves and women" in politically tumultuous regions. Marriage to important men or colonial employees was an avenue through which women could reduce their vulnerability to reenslavement or forced conjugal association.[70] However, marriages between West African women and tirailleurs sénégalais were not simply the result of a cost-benefit analysis on the part of vulnerable women. Physical and emotional attraction certainly influenced how women maneuvered through the postslavery landscape of militarism and colonialism. Remarkably, Ciraïa Aminata chose a husband that Gallieni had labeled an abductor and a sexual assailant. Her "choice" may indicate that Gallieni misunderstood that day near the stream in Baté. If Ciraïa Aminata was a slave when she was collecting water near the Milo River, she could not marry without the authority of her master.[71] The task of gathering water would have given her brief reprieve from the mindful and authoritative eyes of her master and his household. In those precious unescorted moments, she may have absconded with her abductor—who could have been her liberator and lover. Abduction, or perhaps elopement in this case, would have been a means for two people of low social status to circumvent normative marital practices in nineteenth- and twentieth-century African societies.[72]

Gallieni portrayed Ciraïa Aminata as a woman capable of making choices within the constraints of war, colonization, and emancipation. He used her story to illustrate the success of the tirailleurs sénégalais and Liberty Villages as colonial institutions that facilitated processes of slave emancipation and postconflict social stability. Yet Ciraïa Aminata's experience at the Siguiri tribunal was exceptional when compared with other women who became mesdames tirailleurs in nineteenth-century West Africa. Historical evidence suggests that West African women partnering with tirailleurs sénégalais "had little choice" in the matter and that freed slave women needed the protection of colonial soldiers because they "would be enslaved again by the first man who came along."[73] However, Ciraïa Aminata broadens our understanding of the complex processes that preceded mesdames tirailleurs' partnerships with colonial soldiers. Love and emotional investment are difficult to historicize in the gendered silences of the nineteenth-century French colonial historical record. However, the absence of evidence portraying emotional attachment does not eliminate it as a motivating factor for women to join African military households.[74] These households became part of a tirailleurs sénégalais military community that cultivated its own marital traditions where West African and colonial societies overlapped.

MEMBERS ONLY: EXPLORING FAMILY LIFE IN TIRAILLEURS' MILITARY COMMUNITIES

> Someone sent them reinforcements: ten tirailleurs flanked by their families, wives, children, captives, monkeys, cats, chickens, parakeets, each dragging behind him Noah's Ark.
>
> —Paul Vigné d'Octon, *Journal d'un marin*[75]

A curious spectacle to some, tirailleurs sénégalais households became a common feature of the French West African military landscape at the end of the nineteenth century.[76] Mesdames tirailleurs lived as wives and military auxiliaries in the violent swirl of French colonial conquest. From the 1880s, household migration was an important feature of colonial soldiers' conjugal traditions. Once in the French military community, mesdames tirailleurs and tirailleurs sénégalais adjusted their domestic responsibilities to the daily rhythms of camp life and military campaign. The military promoted its own hierarchical organization, but it did not replace West African social organization—caste, slave ancestry, ethnicity—with meritocracy. West African military households conformed their traditions of familial reciprocity and patron-client relationships to the ranks and divisions of the colonial military. The French colonial military became an extended family, or kinship network, that provided newlyweds with basic resources and social security. African military households depended on each other and created fictive kin relationships within their regiments. The military allocated resources to them, which fueled these relationships and made these households reliant on the colonial state. Unlike French soldiers serving in the army, tirailleurs sénégalais brought wives and children with them on campaign and in their frequent garrison changes.[77] These practices untethered tirailleurs sénégalais households from specific geographies, communities, and familial kin, while strengthening their ties to the French colonial military.

Above, I highlighted how civilian women became soldiers' wives through conflict and emancipation. Civilian women living near tirailleurs sénégalais encampments were also incorporated into the military community without the violence affiliated with war. The French colonial military did not enforce boundaries between soldiers and civilians. Sometimes, with little formality, civilian women became soldiers' wives. West African campaigns depended on the continual incorporation of civilians into the military community. Campaigning regiments relied on local villages to provide spaces for bivouacking and basic foodstuffs. Villages supplied female laborers, often enslaved women, to perform domestic tasks for campaigning soldiers that ranged from pounding millet to sexual services.[78] Military encampments constructed near urban centers were busy sites of commerce and exchange. Local female and male merchants found ready consumers for basic and luxury goods among tirailleurs sénégalais households. Military encampments were also sites of civilian labor recruitment. French officers and West African infantrymen hired women and men to supply their regiments as they crossed

West Africa.[79] Market women and hired women's protracted presence in tirailleurs sénégalais' encampments could make them members of the African military community and/or specific households.

Mesdames tirailleurs acutely experienced the structural transformation of West African households in the colonial military. These women followed regiments with the disassembled components of their homesteads and their husbands' effects (excluding rifles and bullets) loaded on their heads, while bearing young children on their backs.[80] They made temporary homes among the piles of equipment and provisions on the decks of French military river barges.[81] On campaign, mesdames tirailleurs constructed temporary and semipermanent homes in open-air bivouacs. Where possible, mesdames tirailleurs constructed their households on the margins of military and administrative spaces in order to create a distance between their households and French officialdom.[82] From this distance, these women raised children, pounded millet, prepared rationed food, and laundered their husbands' uniforms.[83] Mesdames tirailleurs' innumerable responsibilities were central to the functioning of this mobile colonial military community. They participated in the refashioning of ancestral social, ethnic, and gendered hierarchies within the context of the French military community.

The rank of individual tirailleurs sénégalais could influence their households' social status among their peers, but ethnolinguistic tensions and caste hierarchies influenced intra- and inter-household relations.[84] The continuing salience of slave ancestry in the military community curbed former slaves' aspirations for social mobility in the ranks of the tirailleurs sénégalais. French officials avoided promoting former slaves because they believed these men had "an innate mentality for servitude," which made them ineligible for leadership roles in the military.[85] African soldiers of free status would not obey the command of petty officers who had slave ancestry. They also refused to serve under men who were slaves—for example, the men serving in the tirailleurs sénégalais through the engagé à temps system.[86] The colonial military did not foster meritocratic advancement in the tirailleurs sénégalais and former slaves rarely achieved the stripes of a corporal or a sergeant.

African military households' ethnolinguistic groups and lineage affiliations affected social relationships among members of the military community. France's conquest of Bundu occasioned the liberation of many Bamana and Malinké female slaves. These captives were subsequently integrated into the tirailleurs sénégalais serving in the region. According to military observers, these liberated women fortuitously found their countrymen among the tirailleurs sénégalais, some of whom had grown up in the same villages. These common geographical and ancestral ties facilitated a number of conjugal relationships within the tirailleurs sénégalais.[87] Ethnic diversity and tensions within the ranks of the tirailleurs sénégalais also hampered troops' discipline and confidence. The history of El Hajj Umar Tall's Tukulor conquest of the Bamana states of Kaarta and Segu embittered Bamanakan toward Tukulors serving side by side in ranks of the tirailleurs sénégalais. These feelings also incited quarrels between Bamana and Tukulor mesdames tirailleurs. In Bafoulabé (contemporary southwestern Mali), a French commander incarcerated two particularly bellicose women at the police station for a twenty-four-hour period in order to set an example for the "feminine world" in the military community.[88] This was a rare example of French officials directly disciplining mesdames tirailleurs.

As with many West African households, senior infantrymen and African officers displayed their status and wealth through their belongings and the comportment of their wives. Some tirailleurs sénégalais had multiwife households that included numerous other dependents—orderlies, slaves, and children. Larger households evidenced the greater prosperity of tirailleurs sénégalais and their wives. Military wives exhibited their household's wealth with their clothing, accessories, and comportment. On a steamer traveling up the Senegal River, Aïssata, the wife of sergeant N'gor Faye, posed for a photo displaying a remarkable quantity of jewelry and other ornaments.[89] Outside of Koulikoro (northeast of Bamako), mesdames tirailleurs accessorized themselves picturesquely, wearing beautiful wraparound skirts (*pagne*s) and long flowing dresses (boubous), with their hair tucked under light handkerchiefs. Jewelry covered their hands, arms, ears, noses, ankles, and toes. Many wives cosmetically altered their nails' color with henna and wore antimony (kohl) on their lips.[90] Through ornamentation, cleanliness, and propriety, mesdames tirailleurs distinguished themselves from civilian women on campaign and in town.[91]

Men's and women's gendered roles in the maintenance of the military community complied with military exigencies while cherry-picking from and conforming to gendered expectations affiliated with West African village life. In the bivouacs shaded by enormous baobabs or in the military camps adjacent to arid Agadez, gendered work and leisure organized the activities of African military households.[92] Mesdames tirailleurs were responsible for maintaining households, preparing meals, and raising children. They also provided sexual services to their soldiering husbands. Many tirailleurs sénégalais spoke of their wives while away on campaign and anticipating returning to them.[93] The pull of domestic life led many married tirailleurs sénégalais to spend their leisure time with their households, which provided a site to entertain guests and maintain families.[94] Married soldiers' leisure differed from that of unmarried tirailleurs sénégalais, who engaged in homosocial male activities like consuming *dolo* (a fermented beverage made from sorghum), smoking pipe tobacco, engaging in convivial conversations, and seeking romantic partners in nearby civilian populations.[95]

Tirailleurs sénégalais and mesdames tirailleurs wanted their conjugal unions to map onto local traditions so that their marriages gained a semblance of legitimacy. In the absence of the tirailleurs sénégalais' lineage elders, military officials provided the authority to welcome newlyweds into the extended family of the tirailleurs sénégalais community. By the end of the nineteenth century, the French military offered potential recruits enlistment bonuses in order to supply soldiers with the means to pay bridewealth for their future wives.[96] Ranking officers provided infantrymen with opportunities to locate new wives on campaign and in camp. French military officers acted as officiators in Christian marriage ceremonies.[97] Officers supplied domesticated animals for sacrifice and consumption in Muslim and pagan marital celebrations occurring near military camps.[98] Brides of indigenous officers and favored infantrymen could expect gifts of cloth or other household items that would assist newlyweds in establishing households. The French colonial military accommodated the increasing number of tirailleurs sénégalais families residing near posts by establishing separate married housing by the end of the 1890s.[99]

In some exceptional instances, French officials acted as intermediaries or extended kin in their soldiers' conjugal affairs in life and death. Their power to shape the contours and sanctity of marriage buoyed the prerogative of their soldiers over local tradition and against traditional authorities. In one case, Samba, a marabout and a military interpreter for the tirailleurs sénégalais, married a woman of noble lineage in Manding.[100] The interpreter had not completed bridewealth payments to his father-in-law. After the death of the couple's first child, the father-in-law threatened to dissolve the marriage. French officer Marie Étienne Péroz intervened on the behalf of his interpreter and sent an expedited message to the father-in-law saying that he would regulate the affair in person.[101] In addition to intervening in family affairs, military officials made limited efforts to support widowed mesdames tirailleurs. French officials liberated female slaves who were the wives of fallen tirailleurs sénégalais in acts of emancipation that followed local and Muslim practice.[102] Family allowances and widow's pay were not standardized in the nineteenth century, but the military awarded limited and inconsistent benefits to tirailleurs sénégalais' widows and orphans. Some widowed women remarried within the military community, which became an accepted practice that shared characteristics with "levirate" marriage. This marital tradition encouraged widows to marry male relatives of their deceased husbands in order to maintain lineage connections and familial wealth.

The relationship between the French colonial state and mesdames tirailleurs was ill-defined. Mesdames tirailleurs were not official employees of the French colonial army. As members of the tirailleurs sénégalais community, they were expected to withstand hardship without complaint and obey military discipline.[103] In an extreme example of the degree to which mesdames tirailleurs complied with military discipline and authority, the wife of soldier Moussa Traoré gave birth while marching on campaign. She went into labor while following a regiment from Sikasso to the Mossi region. The commanding French officer left two tirailleurs sénégalais with her while the rest of the regiment continued to their destination. The new mother arrived a couple of hours later. In order to maintain her affiliation with her husband and the military, she had walked the final stage of the march with her newborn in her arms.[104]

As accepted and recognized members of a growing military community, wives acquired food rations, housing, and a degree of social security. In the vein of the breadwinner model, the colonial military transmitted orders and disciplinary measures to mesdames tirailleurs via their husbands. They also channeled rations and resources into military households via soldiers. When husbands were away on lengthy assignments, these women lacked the resources normally allocated to them via their husbands. A group of mesdames tirailleurs protested before Colonel Combes because they lacked the basic means of survival. Colonel Combes threatened to whip them if they did not disperse. The mesdames tirailleurs fled, then regrouped and brought their grievances before Gallieni. Eventually, the gendarmerie broke up the protesters and military officers dispatched couriers to their campaigning husbands.[105]

French military officials rarely intervened in the domestic affairs of African military households. One official claimed that "conjugal correction" was the responsibility of tirailleurs sénégalais.[106] Patriarchal prerogatives could transgress the bounds of proper decorum, but the line between domestic discipline and abuse was hard to locate. French observers wrote about the extreme lengths that tirailleurs sénégalais took to ensure the fidelity of their conjugal partners. One group of tirailleurs sénégalais built a small earthen enclosure with chest-high walls, where they left their wives guarded while they were away on campaign. Suspicious of the guard, tirailleurs sénégalais supplied their wives with chastity belts. Another group of West African soldiers stationed in Zinder kept their conjugal partners hidden in a house, guarded by an old blind man, in an unfrequented part of the city. These efforts shielded conjugal partners from the sexual advances of French officers and other tirailleurs sénégalais. Read another way, soldiers' female conjugal partners were prisoners. By physically restricting their mobility, tirailleurs sénégalais prevented newly acquired conjugal partners from returning to their home communities. In his memoir, French sergeant Charles Guilleux recounted these activities and cited a Nigerien male civilian who believed that "Senegalese and Soudanese soldiers are liars and thieves, who take our women from us."[107] French observers witnessed these behaviors and in condoning them made them part of African colonial soldiers' conjugal practices.

Gender-based violence was an accepted component of tirailleurs sénégalais' marital traditions. French observers generally overlooked soldiers' mistreatment of civilian women because forced conjugal association did not contravene military order and corresponded with the paternalistic authority accompanying colonial rule. French commanding officers interfered in conjugal abuse when the women were known members of the military community. Abusive behaviors needed to reach egregious levels—like attempted murder—before commanding officers reprimanded and disciplined tirailleurs sénégalais. Indigenous corporal Hannah Ramata, stationed in Matam (present-day Senegal), stabbed his wife below her right breast in a fit of jealousy. Ramata's superiors sentenced him to fifteen days of imprisonment in irons. His commanders reduced his diet to biscuits and water.[108] French commanders took responsibility for the families of imprisoned soldiers and ensured that they continued to receive rations while the "head" of family served his sentence.[109]

French commanding officers were poor substitutes for familial, village, or community leaders. The French military's distribution of justice and social welfare was insufficient for maintaining a moral economy. They were not invested in curating the reproduction of their military community. Nevertheless, the community affiliated with the tirailleurs sénégalais had the potential to become an extended family united by uniform, common resources, and trials faced on campaign. Once in African military households, women and men could build communal ties, reduce their outsider status, and increase their socioeconomic worth despite slave origins. Women's membership in the colonial military community provided them with access to resources often unavailable to women unaffiliated with tirailleurs sénégalais. These possibilities came with the hardships affiliated with life on the road with the tirailleurs sénégalais. The patriarchal and misogynist culture of military conquest created gendered inequities and increased risk for mesdames tirailleurs.

After her marriage to a tirailleur sénégalais in March 1888, Ciraïa Aminata exited the written historical record. As a madame tirailleur, she may have participated in Samori Touré's capture, the fall of Dahomey, or conquest in Madagascar. She, and other West African military wives like her, experienced the onset of colonization in the most intimate realms of human experience—in their conjugal relationships and within their households. Many mesdames tirailleurs experienced emancipation and marriage simultaneously. The French colonial military encouraged, expedited, and sanctioned these unions without fully legitimating them. By most West African customs, mesdames tirailleurs' marriages shared characteristics with concubinage or lacked the prenuptial rites that would have made them legitimate. Within the military community, the conjugal practices of nineteenth-century West Africa served as the foundation for marital traditions that traveled with the tirailleurs sénégalais as they deployed to new frontiers of colonial conquest. Marriage, once a mechanism to protect vulnerable women from social instability, became

Colonization, Emancipation, and Martial Community in West Africa, 1880–1900

a vehicle through which West African women acquired resources, gained membership in an extended colonial family, and migrated long distances to the frontiers of French Empire in Africa. By the time West African military employees deployed to Congo and Madagascar, their households were a sacrosanct feature of the colonial military landscape. In 1911, one French observer commented, "Ce qu'il y a de précieux chez le tirailleur, c'est sa femme" (That which the tirailleur holds precious is his wife/woman).[110]

2

Colonial Conquest "en Famille"

African Military Households in Congo and Madagascar, 1880–1905

> For the last twenty years, the colony of Senegal has supplied the contingents of all the missions and expeditions formed for the conquest of Africa . . . private industry and foreign colonization alike have drawn their elements from Senegal.
>
> —Governor-general of French West Africa to the minister of the colonies, Saint-Louis, 26 July 1899[1]

FRANCE HAD HISTORICAL TIES TO CONGO AND MADAGASCAR through its participation in global oceanic African slave trades. During the final decades of the nineteenth century, France converted its nominal presence in these regions to formal colonial rule. Tirailleurs sénégalais and other West Africans participated in France's colonial expansion into the Congo and Ubangi-Shari River basins of Equatorial Africa and across the mountainous spine of Madagascar. Congo and Madagascar are understudied episodes in tirailleurs sénégalais' historiography and neglected regions of African and French colonial history.[2] This chapter examines these regions in parallel because they showcase how different, yet contemporaneous, nineteenth-century contexts shaped the formation of African military households. In Congo and Madagascar, tirailleurs sénégalais and their conjugal partners continued and modified conjugal practices imported from West African campaigns. These military households challenged local traditions of marital legitimacy.

West Africans maintained and expanded their households while carrying out the work of empire in radically different political and geographic settings. In the Congo River basin, West Africans participated in a series of exploratory missions led by Savorgnan de Brazza during the 1870s and 1880s. The earlier missions were funded by the Geographic Society of Paris and the International African Association. De Brazza encountered multiple chiefdoms and signed trading treaties with them. In 1880, at the Malebo Pool, Chief Makoko of the Bateke/Tio kingdom ceded land for a French trading post, which became the foundation for Brazzaville. French public and private organizations funded the formal establishment of trading and military posts throughout the Congo region. Ultimately, imperial and capitalistic interests would parcel the region into large privately owned concessions. Around the same time, West African laborers in Congo shifted from being primarily carpenters and porters to serving as soldiers. These soldiers defended French interests when challenged by local authorities and by the expansionist maneuvers of the nearby Belgian Congo Free State.

France's gradual conquest of Congo through trade ambitions and its limited use of martial forces starkly contrasts with the concerted and coordinated military campaigns of the 1890s in Madagascar. France's military conquest of the large island followed decades, if not centuries, of Europeans' participation in Indian Oceanic trade and regional affairs. In the early nineteenth century, the Merina Kingdom—under the monarchical power of Radama I and his successor Queen Ranavalona I—expanded and consolidated its authority over much of Madagascar. During their rule, increasing numbers of foreign diplomats, travelers, and missionaries relocated to the island. France launched several military incursions into Madagascar with varying goals and results. The campaign of 1883–85 ended with a treaty placing the Merina Kingdom/Madagascar under a French protectorate. From 1885, a French resident oversaw the terms of the peace deal and Madagascar's payment of postconflict indemnities to France. In subsequent years, the Merina Kingdom faltered in its ability to maintain political continuity and hegemony over the island. French expeditionary forces arrived in the 1890s to improve social stability and enforce France's formal domination of Madagascar.

Military campaigns included seasoned tirailleurs sénégalais as well as West African laborers serving in auxiliary capacities.

West Africans performed a variety of functions in France's colonization of Congo and Madagascar. The origins, identities, and titles of West African colonial employees and their conjugal partners multiplied as they circulated among imperial ports and military campaigns. Governor Louis Faidherbe recruited the original regiment of the tirailleurs sénégalais from the northern region of Senegambia. By the campaigns of the 1880s, recruitment expanded to incorporate more men from the Niger River basin—particularly Bamanakan—making tirailleurs *sénégalais* a misnomer within a generation of its inauguration. West Africans shipping out to Equatorial Africa and Madagascar served France as tirailleurs sénégalais, laptots, and *miliciens*—militiamen predominantly hired to accompany civilian exploration missions. In French African empire, Congolese and Madagascan communities transformed the terminology and monikers used to identify the foreign Africans accompanying conquest. The distinction between military and civilian colonial employees blurred as West Africans completed their labor contracts and remained in Congo or Madagascar to work in the industries accompanying colonialism. Irrespective of origin or employment status, once in Congo or Madagascar, local officials and populations often referred to these diverse West Africans as "sénégalais." West African men working abroad took up and modified tirailleurs sénégalais' conjugal practices and marital traditions.

West Africans' conjugality appeared in debates concerning the articulation and future of French colonialism. Their conjugal practices traveled to new destinations and evolved alongside colonial conquest. In late nineteenth-century West Africa, tirailleurs sénégalais' ability to establish and build households was an expected benefit affiliated with military service. In Congo and Madagascar, West African employees arrived with their West African wives and/or sought local conjugal partners. Tirailleurs sénégalais brought their conjugal practices to campaigns in foreign Africa. French officials condoned soldiers' conjugal behaviors in West Africa, but hesitated to do so in Congo and Madagascar. Geographic and sociocultural differences gave military officials pause in ascribing marital legitimacy to soldiers' inter-African households. In Congo and Madagascar, French officials recorded episodes of sexual violence, female abduction, and forced conjugal association perpetrated by West African colonial employees.

Race and other forms of sociocultural difference appeared in empire-wide debates concerning "sénégalais" conjugality and marital legitimacy. These discussions began among administrators in West Africa and Southeast Asia regarding the possibility of deploying tirailleurs sénégalais in Vietnam. These far-flung officials supported West African soldiers' access to women's domestic and sexual labor, but debated the ideal racial composition of their households—West African women and men or Vietnamese women and African men. These discussions also occurred in Congo and Madagascar, but relied on slightly different sociocultural taxonomies and fumbled through the broad racial categorizations that served to organize and distinguish populations in French Empire. Evidence from Congo and Madagascar suggests that local officials made more nuanced distinctions. They readily recognized the legitimacy of West African military households in Congo and Madagascar. Conversely, they struggled to legitimize conjugal relationships between "sénégalais" and *congolaise* (Congolese) or *malgache* (Madagascan) women. These households transgressed sociolinguistic and geographical boundaries in Africa, which prompted officials and local populations to question consensuality and legitimacy. The gendered violence affiliated with colonial militarism threw the distinctions among West Africans, Congolese, and Madagascans into stark relief. West African men's relationships with congolaises and malgaches catalyzed new debates in the colonial administration about female slavery, forced conjugal association, and the colonial military's tolerance of "sénégalais" exploitation of women in foreign colonial territories.

Historical actors and historians have struggled to locate the most accurate and appropriate terminology to identify sociocultural organization and its transgressions on the African continent. Race, tribe, ethnicity, clan, and lineage groups are popular and contested categories that fail to capture the dynamism of social organization and lived experiences in Africa and beyond. However, these differences have consequences—particularly in matters related to sex and social reproduction. Grand schemes of French colonial racial order lumped all sub-Saharan Africans into one category of blackness, or *noir*. Achille Mbembe has argued that "the racial unity of Africa has always been a myth."[3] Recent historical publications have qualified his assessment by examining interracial and multiracial communities that resulted from colonial encounters inside and outside of white settler colonies.[4] The conjugal relationships between West African men and congolaises or malgaches challenge persistent misconceptions of Africa's racial homogeny and demand that we employ concepts and terminology that accurately describe these heterogeneous African colonial military households. In the introduction, I argued for the application of "interraciality" beyond the colonizer/colonized divide. In this chapter, I use "inter-African" for mixed African military families to highlight the deep cultural divides between women and men from different regions of Africa who formed households on the frontiers of French Empire.

GOING THE DISTANCE: WEST AFRICANS IN FRENCH EMPIRE

West African soldiers' conjugality played a prominent role in determining where they deployed in nineteenth-century French Empire. Household composition and tirailleurs sénégalais' conjugal practices featured in administrative discussions about the effectiveness of West African troops in other regions of French Empire—French Indochina (contemporary Vietnam, Cambodia, and Laos), French Congo (contemporary Republic of Congo, Gabon, Central African Republic, and Chad), and Madagascar. Discussions about tirailleurs sénégalais' utility in empire began in Southeast Asia, but they did not deploy to Vietnam until 1948. *Mesdames tirailleurs* were consequential to these deferred actions. Military officials believed that tirailleurs sénégalais' West African households were sacrosanct to French colonial military campaigns and Indochinese officials did not. Officials disagreed about whether tirailleurs sénégalais should serve *en famille* (with their West African households) in Vietnam or should deploy as single men who could participate in prolonged conjugal unions or temporary marriages with Indochinese female colonial subjects. Household migration and local conditions in Vietnam, Congo, and Madagascar influenced the degree to which West African women and/or local women became legitimate members of "sénégalais" households.

A decade after the creation of the tirailleurs sénégalais, administrative officials in southern Vietnam broached the possibility of employing tirailleurs sénégalais as part of a permanent security force in French Indochina. Vietnamese officials specified that a small percentage of soldiers could bring their West African wives and recommended that most soldiers locate temporary local wives.[5] The initial request in 1867 went unmet. Conversations regarding the use of West African soldiers in Southeast Asia periodically resurfaced over the next forty years. French officials in Indochina explicitly connected West

African soldiers' martial utility with their sexuality and conjugal practices. Officials wrote of West African men's carnal desires and paternalism as if these were inveterate qualities. Indochinese officials queried tirailleurs sénégalais' preferences for West African women and their desire to maintain racially homogenous households. These officials regarded the presence of West African women in Vietnam as a potential threat to the conjugal conventions that French colonial occupation had created in Southeast Asia. Since colonization in 1862, French soldiers stationed in Vietnam developed traditions of temporary conjugal and/or transactional sexual relationships with local women.[6] If West African soldiers deployed to French Indochina, officials expected them to abandon aspects of their conjugal and marital practices to conform to local precedent.

Administrators in Indochina and West Africa agreed that West African soldiers required access to women's conjugal and domestic labor, but disagreed on the importance of shared racial origins and nuclear household models for tirailleurs sénégalais' conjugal practices. These debates continued into the 1890s, when it became clear that Indochinese officials no longer considered the presence of mesdames tirailleurs in their colony viable. By the turn of the twentieth century, an official requesting one hundred Senegalese or Soudanese tirailleurs for policing purposes in Laos unambiguously stated that these soldiers "must come to Laos without their families" and should "take one or several wives in-country."[7] In this proposed scheme, married tirailleurs sénégalais could leave their households in West Africa and engage in polygynous, extramarital, and polyamorous relationships with local women while deployed in Southeast Asia. Officials predicted that these soldiers would repatriate to West Africa after two or three years of service in Laos. There was no mention of their Laotian conjugal partners or potential children accompanying them home. This Indochinese official thought little of West African soldiers' fidelity to their conjugal households on the home front. French soldiers' widespread practice of temporary conjugality in Vietnam may have led administrators in Southeast Asia to assume that tirailleurs sénégalais could adapt to the same sexual practices. Following, there is a sense in the documents that these officials were unconvinced that mesdames tirailleurs were legitimate wives. Therefore, mesdames tirailleurs could be replaced with local Indochinese women who could perform similar conjugal labors without committing adultery. Indochinese military officials endorsed conjugal strategies in which tirailleurs sénégalais entered into temporary conjugal relationships at a time when West African military officials encouraged soldiers' domestic stability in the form of racially homogenous mobile African military households.

Administrators across empire differed in how they viewed soldiers' household integrity and the role of West African women in colonial conquest. They were unable to agree on how to define these conjugal unions—marriage, casual romantic liaison, temporary marriage, or concubinage—because of disagreements over where West African troops should locate romantic partners and how the military would support them. West African administrators lauded mesdames tirailleurs as essential to troop retention and stabilization on colonial campaigns. A West African administrator described tirailleurs sénégalais' households as monogamous strongholds held together by enduring bonds. Another argued that prolonged separation would adversely affect tirailleurs sénégalais' households.[8] There was overwhelming West African–based administrative support for mesdames tirailleurs' participation in the military expansion and maintenance of empire. These strong beliefs defeated a proposal to create a local committee in Senegal to maintain West African wives during their husbands' active service in Indochina. The rejection of this proposal buttressed an implicit nineteenth-century belief—the military was not obligated to support tirailleurs sénégalais' conjugal partners if they did not live within mobile military units. Despite these extensive imperial debates, tirailleurs sénégalais and their military households did not deploy to French Indochina until the mid-twentieth century. However, these debates illustrate how the French colonial military transformed a "tacit" understanding into a defensible privilege—tirailleurs sénégalais became entitled to wives while they served in French Empire.[9]

CONGO

Beginning in 1875, French military leaders, civil servants, and entrepreneurs collectively expanded France's heretofore modest presence on the right bank of the Congo River. By the turn of the twentieth century, French Congo encompassed a territory that includes the contemporary countries of Gabon, Republic of Congo, and Central African Republic, as well as regions of Cameroon and Chad. Beginning in 1875, Savorgnan de Brazza, a French-Italian aristocrat with an elite military school pedigree, led several West African

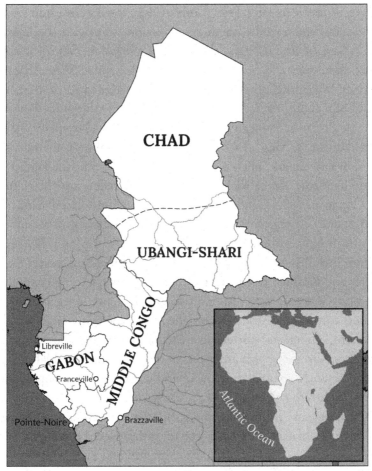

MAP 2.1. French Congo / French Equatorial Africa. Map by Isaac Barry

missions into Equatorial Africa. These missions explored the Ogowe, Congo, Sangha, and Ubangi River basins with the intention of acquiring trading rights and increasing French entrepreneurs' access to land and locally produced resources. Twelve laptots from coastal Senegal were members of the first mission, which explored the Ogowe River basin from 1875 to 1878. West Africans' presence in Congo increased with each subsequent mission led by de Brazza (1879–82 and 1883–85). At the height of European conquest of Africa, de Brazza became the general commissioner of Gabon and Congo in 1886. A dozen years later, France carved Equatorial Africa into enormous parcels of land and awarded them as concessions to private commercial investors.[10] West African military laborers were integral to these processes.

State-sponsored and privately hired agents recruited West African men for security forces and other skilled professions needed in de Brazza's missions and other commercial enterprises in Congo. By the third West African mission, de Brazza had recognized the incomparable and irreplaceable talents of West Africans serving in Congo. Sergeant Malamine Camara was celebrated above all others. The only indigenous sergeant in the laptots corps, he single-handedly defended France's territorial claims on the right bank of the Congo in 1881. Camara stared down Belgium's hired hand, Henry Morton Stanley.[11] Sergeant Camara was also instrumental in recruiting 169 West African laptots for de Brazza's third mission in March of 1883. This expedition included a panoply of West Africans, including former tirailleurs sénégalais and Krumen recruited from coastal areas spanning contemporary Liberia and Côte d'Ivoire.[12] In addition to tirailleurs sénégalais regiments and laptots corps, West African men signed up to serve in Congo as miliciens (militiamen), muleteers, porters, construction workers, and railway men. Despite these diverse origins and titles among these recruited laborers, once in Congo, French colonial employees and autochthonous populations referred to this heterogeneous group as "sénégalais."[13]

The "sénégalais" in nineteenth-century Congo were a diverse and mobile population managed by a variety of authorities. These West Africans blurred distinctions between military employee and civil contractor. They changed employment frequently, swapping state-funded contracts for private enterprise. West African laptots and tirailleurs sénégalais were institutionally distinct, yet in Congo these titles could refer broadly to armed West Africans affiliated with French and other European agents.[14] Some of these men were military employees, but many were civilians recruited specifically for exploration and infrastructure projects. At the conclusion of their contracts, laptots, tirailleurs sénégalais, and miliciens transitioned into noncombatant employment in Congo. They deployed myriad strategies to remain in Congo. These men integrated into local communities through marriage, hired themselves out as guides to foreign merchants, and became successful traders in their own right.[15] Due to budgetary shortfalls, a ministerial decree disbanded the garrison housing laptots and tirailleurs sénégalais in 1891.

Decommissioned soldiers became an integral part of local militias recruited by private enterprises in the Congo basin.[16] West African military and civilian employees in French Congo traversed colonial boundaries in search of better-compensated work. Men abandoned their contracts with the French and sought higher-paying work across the river in the Belgian Congo Free State.[17] The Congo Free State also recruited "sénégalais" directly from French territories in West Africa—with and without the approval of French colonial authorities.[18] Once they arrived in Belgian Congo, these laborers, hired for road building and rail laying, found themselves press-ganged into military service.[19] Deserters fled west across the Congo River in search of French administrative assistance and return passage to West Africa. Others sought work within the French colonial state or as security forces for concessionary companies.[20]

Soldiers, civilians, and colonial officials from West Africa had a heavy hand in the colonization of Congo. They brought tirailleurs sénégalais' conjugal traditions with them. At different moments in conquest, French officials encouraged their West African employees to travel en famille and/or to seek local conjugal partners. West African women were not listed in the inventories of employees in the first three West African missions.[21] Colonial records rarely included soldiers' female conjugal partners as official members of military campaigns and scientific missions. Their absence in the official record does not indicate that West African women were not present in these colonial endeavors. However, occasional references to West African men poorly executing domestic chores, which would have otherwise been allocated to their female domestic partners, suggest that mesdames tirailleurs did not have a large presence in Congo during the 1870s and 1880s. Biran Fall, a "sénégalais" serving in de Brazza's second West African mission, was removed from kitchen duty because he washed dishes with spit, then wiped them dry with soiled socks.[22] West African servicemen's families began traveling with them to Equatorial Africa in the mid-1890s.[23] In June 1894, the wives of a tirailleurs sénégalais battalion sent to Congo were erroneously left behind in Saint-Louis. In order to remedy the situation, a local official proposed that the military earmark a portion of their husbands' pay in order to support their abandoned families in Saint-Louis.[24] This proposal came at a time in which administrators across French Empire debated the conjugal and marital proclivities of tirailleurs sénégalais. Despite West African officials' overwhelming support for the mobility and integrity of African military households, the majority of West African female conjugal partners remained on the home front. Most of the "sénégalais" serving in Equatorial Africa at the end of the nineteenth century sought female conjugal partners among local populations. French officials encouraged and supported their West African employees' access to and unions with Congolese women.

West African and inter-African military families coexisted in Congo. There is evidence from the twentieth century that speaks to their durable presence. West Africans and congolaises set up their domestic households adjacent to military posts and colonial trading centers. Some West Africans chose to remain in Equatorial Africa after the conclusion of their contracts and established family compounds in growing colonial towns like Libreville, Franceville, and Brazzaville. By 1905, African military households had established their own village at the edge of Brazzaville.[25] At the beginning of the First World War, urban colonial officials channeled most West Africans into Poto-Poto, the "African" neighborhood of Brazzaville. Poto-Poto has an avenue named for Sergeant Malamine Camara and continues to serve as a locus for West African migrants today.[26] The West Africa populations residing in contemporary Poto-Poto are seldom the descendants of tirailleurs sénégalais and mesdames tirailleurs households. An official decree in 1905 withdrew government assistance for the relocation of mesdames tirailleurs to Congo. Even so, there was an inquiry from Kayes in 1906 regarding whether locally recruited miliciens could bring all, or some, members of their families to Congo.[27] By 1909, the prohibition on mesdames tirailleurs' travel to Equatorial Africa influenced some potential male labor recruits to remain in West Africa and seek work locally.[28] West African men continued to travel to Congo as independent entrepreneurs and contractors. If so inclined, they would have sought conjugal partnership among local populations.

MADAGASCAR

French colonization of Madagascar brought significant numbers of West Africans to the Indian Ocean island. Formal colonization in Madagascar occurred gradually in the early nineteenth century and came to challenge the dominion of the Merina and Sakalava kingdoms in the latter half of the century.[29] In the 1890s, France accelerated its conquest of Madagascar and brought military forces to the island, which included a variety of mainland

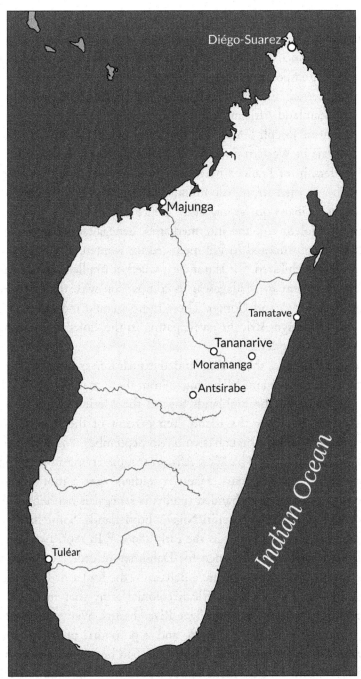

MAP 2.2. French Madagascar. Map by Isaac Barry

Africans whose origins extended from Saint-Louis to Brazzaville. Some of these tirailleurs arrived with their families. Troop and household composition reflected France's military conquest of West and Equatorial Africa in earlier and contemporaneous years. France's violent incorporation of Madagascar into French Empire shared casts and characteristics with previous episodes of mainland African conquest. Large-scale revolt in the mid-1890s brought General Joseph-Simon Gallieni, former commander of the tirailleurs sénégalais in Western Soudan, to Madagascar to assume military and civilian leadership of France's newest colony. Gallieni relied on West African women and men to impose military order and then encouraged them to remain as civilians on Madagascar. "Sénégalais" gained a reputation on the island as violent colonial intermediaries. Senegalese soldiers serving in Madagascar were rumored to kill men, reduce women to slavery, and pull the hearts out of children.[30] It is not clear whether tirailleurs sénégalais were exceptionally violent in Madagascar in comparison with their previous exploits in West Africa and Congo. These rumors could indicate widespread disapproval of foreign Africans participating in the violence accompanying French colonial conquest.

In December 1894, the French landed expeditionary forces at the strategic ports of Toamasina and Mahajanga. From these coastal enclaves, French troops marched into the highlands toward the Merina capital to enforce France's prerogative over the island. Ten percent of the fifteen thousand French troops entering Antananarivo on 30 September 1894 were West and North African soldiers.[31] The West African troops serving in this campaign were labeled *haoussa* tirailleurs. Haoussa soldiers were a motley crew that had been recruited from disbanded tirailleurs sénégalais battalions and new recruits from contemporary Benin/Nigeria borderlands. Some had served as tirailleurs sénégalais in Congo in the early 1890s.[32] In 1891, two companies of tirailleurs sénégalais left Congo for Dahomey in order to participate in France's conquest of the kingdom.[33] Behanzin, the leader of Dahomey, surrendered in 1894 to a French African colonial army that included troops recruited from the Senegal and Niger River basins, West and Central Africans previously residing in Congo, and a potpourri of troops recruited from Dahomey and its environs. The French had begun recruiting this final group in 1893 and labeled them haoussa soldiers. The traditional homeland of Hausa speakers is located north of the confluence of the Niger and

Benue Rivers. The French recruited haoussa soldiers from across the border in Yoruba-speaking areas under British colonial control in neighboring Nigeria. There were likely a minority of Hausa speakers among the haoussa troops and the French military's use of the term is misleading and misrepresents the ethnolinguistic origins of their soldiers. These mislabeled haoussa servicemen from the Dahomeyan campaign were among the first troops to serve France in Madagascar.[34] Evidence from the Madagascan campaign suggests that conjugal partners were with these haoussa soldiers, but it is unclear whether these women traveled with West African tirailleurs to Madagascar or were malgache women whom soldiers had incorporated into colonial regiments during their march from coastal ports to Antananarivo.[35] Hundreds of porters and muleteers from the Senegal and Niger River basins were also among these forces, but these militarized civilian employees rarely brought their households into French Empire.[36]

After the initial French troop buildup in Madagascar, leaders of the Merina Kingdom—Queen Ranavalona III and Prime Minister Rainilaiarivony—signed a treaty with France on 1 October 1895. This treaty unambiguously made Madagascar a French protectorate state. France faced a range of thorny social and political issues on the island. Merina state control over low-status men had faltered as their system of forced labor, the *fanompoana*, devolved in the 1890s. The fanompoana had channeled these men into state infrastructure projects and the Merina military. The destabilization of the monarchy prompted many imperial Merina subjects to flee conscription and engage in banditry on the margins of Merina's empire.[37] The capitulation of the royal family weakened the state military and strengthened marauding bands whose membership began to include defecting soldiers and former slaves. In a context of increasing instability, the Menalamba uprising began in earnest during November 1895. *Menalamba* refers to the red shawls that the participants wore. These women and men sought to violently remove foreigners and foreign influence from Madagascar.

The French inadvertently bolstered the number of Madagascans participating in the Menalamba uprising by abolishing slavery in August 1896. This decree occurred in tandem with the formal designation of Madagascar as a French colony. The estimated number of slaves in Madagascar at the moment of emancipation varies from five hundred thousand to one million slaves—on an island with a population of two and a half million.[38] The

French fueled social chaos in Madagascar by untethering at least 20 percent of the islands' residents from their former masters and the Merina state. Former slaves joined the ongoing uprising in order to survive without their former patrons.[39] As the numbers of Menalamba participants grew, the nascent French colony responded by consolidating military and civilian power in the hands of recently promoted General Joseph-Simon Gallieni.

Gallieni landed in Madagascar on 28 September 1896 with a contingent of tirailleurs sénégalais that included mesdames tirailleurs among its ranks.[40] The number of West Africans serving on the island mushroomed after Gallieni's arrival.[41] These new troops integrated themselves into previously established encampments and posts guarded by haoussa tirailleurs.[42] These semipermanent encampments included trappings of domestic life—temporary dwellings, communal cooking areas, kitchen gardens, and female conjugal partners. Early in France's conquest of Madagascar, West African soldiers maintained households with mesdames tirailleurs and malgache women in proximity to military camps and bivouacs. The female members of racially homogenous West African soldiers' households in Madagascar could have grown up in Senegambia, the Niger River basin, Dahomey, Congo, or Madagascar.[43] The wives of haoussa tirailleurs arrived in Madagascar in a cloud of rumors asserting that some among them were former "Amazons" of Dahomeyan leader Behanzin.[44] Erroneously labeled "Amazons" by European observers in the mid-nineteenth century, this female fighting force was a militarized arm of the female dependents/protectors (*ahosi*) of male Dahomeyan rulers.[45] They played an important role in defending Behanzin and Dahomey during Colonel Alfred-Amédée Dodds's conquest of the region in the early 1890s. The purported "Amazons" arriving in Madagascar with haoussa tirailleurs could have been female prisoners of war—former combatants and noncombatants—incorporated into African military households during and subsequent to Dahomey's fall. Irrespective of origin, colonial officials and local communities in Madagascar recognized these women as mesdames tirailleurs or *mesdames sénégalais*. Their importance in France's conquest of the island echoes into the present. In contemporary Antananarivo, there is a neighborhood called the "quartier des femmes de Sénégalais."[46]

Documents related to labor recruitment efforts in West Africa for Madagascan conquest illustrate the importance of soldiers acquiring wives before they deployed overseas. Newly recruited West African servicemen acquired wives and celebrated marriages while they marched from their point of enlistment to coastal ports for overseas departure. A contingent of railway workers destined for Madagascar gained four wives with marriages celebrated between Kayes and Saint-Louis in 1897.[47] These couples bedded down in Saint-Louis's military encampments while awaiting military steamers to the Indian Ocean. Tirailleurs sénégalais also acquired new conjugal partners after they arrived in colonial port towns to await departure for Madagascar. These military couples expected to ship out as a household, but there were instances in which mesdames tirailleurs missed the boat. The first contingent of 250 tirailleurs sénégalais sent to Madagascar on 14 October 1895 left without their wives. Military agents alerted abandoned mesdames tirailleurs that they could join their husbands by boarding the next steamer leaving for Mahajanga. Nearly seven months later, forty-eight wives and twenty-four children left for Madagascar on 6 July 1896.[48] Archival evidence does not provide information about the reunification of these households in Madagascar.

Scant and inconsistent sources illustrate that between 19 and 42 percent of tirailleurs sénégalais served in Madagascar with female conjugal partners. If their wives reunited with them, 19 percent of the tirailleurs sénégalais in the first contingent deployed to Madagascar had West African wives with them. Two companies of tirailleurs sénégalais (134 men) departing from Mahajanga for Antananarivo in 1896 included fifty-six wives and fifteen children, which meant that roughly 42 percent of the troops had spouses with them on campaign.[49] This source does not detail whether these wives were mesdames tirailleurs or Madagascan women. The terminology used to describe these unions employed the legitimating language of marriage, but the author of the source claimed that most of these unions were intentionally temporary due to the nature of war and the rules that organized camp life.[50]

AS conquest subsided in Madagascar and Congo at the turn of the twentieth century, colonial administrations replaced West African military employees with locally recruited security forces. The French began training Madagascan soldiers as early as 1884 and their numbers increased drastically during the late 1890s.[51] In Congo, administrators used West African soldiers to train Gabonese and Congolese miliciens and tirailleurs.[52] In the 1890s, West Africans volunteered less often for military service or labor contracts in distant overseas territories.[53] In 1899, Colonel Combes noted that soldiers returning to Kayes from Madagascar declined reenlistment and spread rumors about abusive commanding officers in overseas territories.[54] Haoussa volunteers dwindled as British agents in Nigeria increasingly monitored the border they shared with French colonial Dahomey.[55] In 1901, the French disbanded their haoussa tirailleurs and shifted remaining active soldiers into tirailleurs sénégalais regiments.

At the turn of the twentieth century, African military households became constitutive elements of grander schemes of commercial and colonial development. In 1898, Savorgnan de Brazza's departure from Congo coincided with parceling the region into concessionary claims. West African employees in Equatorial Africa—miliciens, tirailleurs, and laptots—transferred into private security forces or engaged in their own commercial enterprises. De Brazza believed that miliciens should find local wives, live near colonial outposts, and provide a lasting front line of effective occupation in Congo.[56] Gallieni's military administration released tirailleurs sénégalais from service obligations and encouraged them to locate civilian employment in public and private industries in Madagascar.[57] In West Africa, Gallieni had provided new military couples with land and resources. Similarly, Gallieni awarded plots of land to retiring tirailleurs sénégalais in Madagascar. Married or not, Gallieni encouraged West African soldiers to find local wives in an effort to strengthen France's presence in Madagascar.[58] De Brazza and Gallieni believed that African military households would play important roles in the future of French African Empire.

MARITAL LEGITIMACY, SOCIOCULTURAL DIFFERENCE, AND SOLDIERS' WIVES IN EMPIRE

West African military households brought a range of traditions associated with colonial conquest to Congo and Madagascar. Most significantly, West African colonial soldiers and their wives believed they could expand their households and community through the incorporation of new dependents—often female prisoners of war—while serving on French colonial frontiers. While those practices were accepted (even encouraged) in West Africa, tirailleurs sénégalais, mesdames tirailleurs, French military officials, and local populations contested the incorporation of Congolese and Madagascan women into colonial military encampments. Conflicting ideas concerning tirailleurs sénégalais' conjugality followed them into empire. First, they were family men invested in building heteronormative monogamous or polygynous military households. Second, they were polyamorous and incapable of long-term conjugal commitments. The colonial military invested more explicitly in the former idea and mobilized resources to ensure that West African military households remained intact in empire. The French colonial military accorded mesdames tirailleurs the privilege of traveling with their husbands to Congo and Madagascar. As West African military employees' families moved further from the Niger and Senegal River basins, military officials accepted their households as a standard feature of the colonial military landscape. French military officials referenced the second idea—that West African soldiers were consummate polyamorous bachelors—when referring to inter-African conjugal relationships.

The French military and civilian administrations never officially sanctioned mesdames tirailleurs' migration out of West Africa, but military officials came to view long-distance wifely accompaniment as an entitlement for West African soldiers serving in empire. Military commanders moved considerable resources and invested energy in the inclusion of West African wives on military campaigns in Congo and Madagascar. In Saint-Louis in October 1895, Brigadier General Boilève discovered that a regiment of tirailleurs sénégalais shipped out to Madagascar without their wives. He moved quickly to rectify this oversight and tasked battalion leader Ferras to find and assemble these women.[59] Ferras directed native officers in Saint-Louis to locate those abandoned wives so that they could join their husbands in Madagascar.[60] Eventually, a group of West African women and children departed on the long oceanic journey to join tirailleurs sénégalais in Madagascar. Boilève's and Ferras's actions demonstrate that by the 1890s, French officers believed that West African soldiers were entitled to family accompaniment, no matter the distance.

Administrative support for tirailleurs sénégalais' West African households incrementally increased and inconsistently extended across empire in the late nineteenth century. The informal promises of conjugal entitlements and allotments of land in and around military posts transformed into official acknowledgement of West African women in empire as spouses, who could access ad hoc social welfare from the military. If soldiers were incapacitated in some way—convalescence leave or imprisoned for indiscipline—the military could supply mesdames tirailleurs with an advance on their husbands' pay.[61]

Military officials acknowledged their increasing obligations to West African military families in empire because they lacked kin-based assistance. Mesdames tirailleurs had difficulty supporting their families without the resources and protections provided by the colonial state in Congo and Madagascar. A ministerial dispatch in 1900 introduced specific allocations to tirailleurs sénégalais' families traveling by steamer from Dakar to Mahajanga. On board, the French allocated two hundred francs to mesdames tirailleurs, which was the same amount allocated to their husbands. For each of their children older than three, couples received another one hundred francs' worth of food and supplies. At the turn of the century, a decree acknowledged France's financial obligations to the civilian members of their regiments.[62]

Military practice, colonial norms, and marital legitimacy shifted as soldiers deployed to overseas theaters of colonial conflict. The colonial military encouraged West African military households to modify their marital traditions and family structures to fit within a mobile nuclear, male-breadwinner family model.[63] Transoceanic voyages en famille strengthened bonds of mutual dependency among enlisted and civilian members of West African military communities. Long-distance migration reduced these African military households' genetic kin to their nuclear families and replaced their extended familial relations with other members of the tirailleurs sénégalais community. West African military couples were minorities on the frontiers of French Empire and depended on the authority and resources of the colonial military more than they had in West Africa. West African military employees serving en famille rarely deserted. Commanders allocated rations to tirailleurs sénégalais, who redistributed them among the members of their households. Mesdames tirailleurs accessed resources through their husbands and other troops. The gender imbalance in West African colonial regiments placed greater burden on women to provide domestic services, like meal preparation and laundering services, for soldiers who were not their conjugal partners.[64] In the absence of extended kin on distant frontiers of French Empire, child-rearing obligations fell heavily on mesdames tirailleurs.

Military officials financially supported West African military households and encouraged veterans to settle in Congo and Madagascar, while casting aspersions upon inter-African conjugal relationships. West African military couples' marital legitimacy increased in empire, whereas a variety of stakeholders contested the legitimacy of inter-African military households. West

African administrators condoned tirailleurs sénégalais' means of acquiring female conjugal partners in West Africa, then used the language of marital "entitlements" or "tradition" to justify the expense of sending female non-combatants—mesdames tirailleurs—to Congo and Madagascar. That language shifted when referring to inter-African conjugal military households.

In empire, the tirailleurs sénégalais military community expanded through the incorporation of women in Congo and Madagascar, which caused discord on campaign. In the spring of 1897, at a military bivouac in Maharidaza (200 km north of Antananarivo), Calixte Savaron, a retired French soldier traveling with a West African platoon, witnessed the intimate tensions surrounding African soldiers' conjugal practices in Madagascar. While he was lunching, a young Hova woman burst into Savaron's tent with a tirailleur sénégalais on her heels. Hova predominantly resided in the central Madagascan highlands. Many Hova had become the coerced porters and conjugal partners of West African soldiers as they destroyed Hova villages on the march from the coast toward Antananarivo. The Hova woman pleaded, "Save me, this Sénégalais wants to take me by force, save me, monsieur." When Savaron intervened, the tirailleur sénégalais declared, "Captive, my wife."[65] Here, the tirailleur sénégalais illustrated that military conjugal traditions blurred distinctions between marriage and enslavement, which permitted soldiers' incorporation of vulnerable women into their households. By recounting this incident, Savaron questioned the viability of these conjugal practices outside of West Africa.

This confrontation escalated quickly and came to involve military officials, feinted gun shots, and the imprisonment of the tirailleur sénégalais in question. Word of the event quickly spread to other members of the West African military battalion, inspiring further disorder. A day later, at a bivouac in Kinajy, military officers tried to enforce a command from General Gallieni—the liberation of Madagascan prisoners of war/captives living in the tirailleurs sénégalais battalion. Officers attempted to do so while most of the enlisted men were working on infrastructure projects away from camp. The mesdames sénégalais remaining in camp opposed this action. A Catholic *madame tirailleur* named Marie proclaimed, "The female captives will remain with us, the Senegalese have the right to have wives." A French officer rejoined, "That's understood, but not against their will." Marie's claim about having access to enslaved female labor was rooted in marital traditions cultivated during French conquest in West Africa. In the highlands of Madagascar, disagreements over access to Madagascan women's domestic labor demonstrate how military officials, colonial employees, and female civilians continued contested marital traditions, as well as the obligations and responsibilities that accompanied conjugal association. The incorporation of new Madagascan wives, via enslavement, into tirailleurs sénégalais households would have provided West African women and men with invaluable labor and resources. When Marie adamantly claimed that mesdames tirailleurs and tirailleurs sénégalais were entitled to Madagascan captives, her assertion adhered to West African colonial military and marital traditions. In Congo and Madagascar, French observers vilified the processes—concubinage and domestic slavery—that had created many military households in West Africa.

As West African couples migrated across empire to new sites of colonial conquest, tirailleurs sénégalais households evolved in their demography and function. Gendered responsibilities shifted and mesdames tirailleurs shouldered new obligations in the highlands of Madagascar. Several sources from the French conquest of Madagascar portrayed mesdames tirailleurs as recalcitrant and violent women.[66] Yet Mesdames tirailleurs seldom appear in the colonial military record, which suggests that their actions rarely approached the level of insubordination witnessed in Kinajy. We could interpret behavior like Marie's as evidence of how mesdames tirailleurs struggled to maintain and reproduce the same traditions of emancipation and matrimony that had incorporated West African women into tirailleurs sénégalais households in previous years. Marie's strong assertion regarding mesdames tirailleurs' rights to the labor of female Madagascan captives followed West African traditions of first-wife authority and the integration of low-status vulnerable women into their homesteads. Tirailleurs sénégalais' acquisition of wives from among prisoners of war was common practice in West Africa.[67] Marie's verbal confrontation with military personnel was one of the rare instances where colonial records portrayed West African wives' desired outcomes—unhindered access to more women who could share the burden of domestic and military labor.

This confrontation in Kinajy delayed the release of the captives several days until the captain of their platoon, Mazillier, threatened a handful of tirailleurs sénégalais in camp with insubordination charges and the retribution of General Gallieni. The majority of the mesdames tirailleurs were not fluent in French and Marie made as if to speak, but she was silenced. In order to avoid any unnecessary violence, the men were removed from the camp once more. Then, Captain Mazillier turned to the Madagascan captives—who were all women—and told them they were free to leave. According to Savaron, several among them stayed seated because they had made conjugal arrangements with "sénégalais" men.[68] Captain Mazillier's conception of "free will" was blind to how Hova women experienced France's colonization of the Madagascan highlands. Military conquest gendered the ways in which Madagascans experienced colonialism and emancipation. Marriage to an African military employee was a strategy that vulnerable women accepted in a world of shifting and shrinking possibilities.

In Congo, inter-African relationships unfolded in similar and different ways. Militarization accompanied French colonialism in the region, but it was not the fundamental driver of conquest. In 1894, Savorgnan de Brazza was the commissioner general of French Congo. He took a slightly different approach to supporting the conjugal practices of West African employees living in Equatorial Africa. He instructed the colonial official in charge of the Upper Sangha River basin to implement new standardized allocations that would encourage miliciens to marry and set up households adjacent to colonial outposts. Up to 1894, miliciens received their pay at the conclusion of their contracts. De Brazza stipulated that miliciens married to Congolese women according to local tradition should have advance access to a third of their pay in order to support their wives. If they had children, they should have access to three-quarters of their pay. By encouraging West African miliciens' attachment to their site of deployment through familial ties, de Brazza hoped that "sénégalais" would be part of an affective and effective colonial occupation. In order to convince miliciens to extend their contracts and remain in Congo, de Brazza announced that local wives could not travel with their husbands outside of French Congo—unless they had married according to the legal traditions of French civil marriage.[69] West African men would not be able to return home with their Congolese conjugal partners.

In the 1890s, administrators in French colonial empire did not create a uniform, empire-wide system of support for African military households. French assistance for West African colonial employees' wives differed from region to region. Civilian members of tirailleurs sénégalais households continued to seek assistance from the French imperial state through ad hoc means and informal channels that followed traditional relationships of patronage and clientage. In one compelling example, an orphan of empire made an appeal to Albert Veistroffer, a veteran member of de Brazza's West African missions. This young man approached Veistroffer on a vessel sailing from Libreville to Saint-Louis: "Good morning, commandant. You don't recognize me? I am Alfa, son of Sergeant Taouré. . . . He died and I left Gabon to return to my mother's homeland, where I was born in Porto Novo. I will perhaps locate my mother, but I don't know her."[70] Alfa's father's surname was a common Bamana patronym. Porto Novo had accepted French protection in 1863. Twenty years later, the French incorporated the city into their colony of Dahomey in 1883. Tirailleurs sénégalais' presence in Porto Novo began at roughly the same time. Alfa's parents' conjugal relationship lasted long enough for his father to recognize his paternity and claim guardianship of his son. Curiously, the meager details of Alfa's life seem to indicate that his mother did not join Sergeant Taouré's mobile household. Veistroffer decided to employ the orphaned fifteen-year-old Alfa Taouré as his personal steward.

In the service of Veistroffer, Alfa Taouré went on to live in Dakar, Paris, Marseille, and Fernand-Vaz in Gabon, where he parted ways with his employer after two years of service. Due to Taouré's international parentage—the son of a Dahomeyan woman and a West African tirailleur sénégalais—he came of age within the networks of French colonial military expansion in Dahomey and Congo. As part of a mobile military household, Taouré's extended family consisted of the colonial employees surrounding posts and garrisons. His ability to speak French enabled Alfa Taouré to tether himself to sympathetic European employers in empire. Taouré capitalized on his connection to the colonial military via his father to secure employment and access to resources, as well as to continue traveling within French Empire. The coexistence of patrimonial and bureaucratic connections between members of tirailleurs sénégalais' households and French African colonial administrations demonstrates that West African military communities could create durable ties. These ties transformed as tirailleurs sénégalais' households became entangled in multiple frontiers of conquest in Dahomey, Congo, and Madagascar.

"THE SENEGALESE DON'T RAPE, THEY MARRY": FORCED CONJUGAL ASSOCIATION, SLAVERY, AND MARITAL LEGITIMACY IN CONGO AND MADAGASCAR

The entanglement of marriage, domestic labor, and slavery in France's conquest of Congo and Madagascar illustrates how conjugality remained at the dynamic confluence of colonialism, abolition, and marital traditions. Colonial intermediaries—missionaries and African soldiers—complicated the colonial state's ability to uniformly enforce the moral and legal prerogatives of emancipation. The processes that facilitated the incorporation of vulnerable women into the colonial military community in 1880s and 1890s West Africa were discredited and acquired harsher labels in Congo and Madagascar—human trafficking and female slavery. French officials continued to support West African soldiers' conjugal prerogatives, but began using the language of consent and volition to question tirailleurs sénégalais' methods of incorporating Congolese and Madagascan women into their households. Local populations regarded West African soldiers' conjugal relationships with malgaches and congolaises as intimate, violent transgressions of their social order and autonomy. Local populations contested the consensuality and legitimacy of West African military employees' conjugal practices. These contestations heralded transformations in how colonial observers labeled these relationships.

Consent, or lack thereof, was an important factor in scandals surrounding tirailleurs sénégalais' inter-African sexuality and conjugality. Colonial soldiers' conjugal intentions were also important in determining the nature of these sexual liaisons. Their willingness or unwillingness to participate in prenuptial rites to win the approval of congolaises' or malgaches' communities influenced the tenor of local populations' protests against inter-African military households. From the perspective of colonial observers, a wide range of sometimes contradictory traditions were used to determine consent and the legitimacy of inter-African sexual encounters: the premarital and marital customs affiliated with wives' communities in Congo and Madagascar, French colonial observers' marital rites, and West African traditions. Soldiers' transgressive conjugal behaviors received the tacit approval of their commanding officers and high-level colonial administrators, but not that of local communities and French missionaries. The French colonial military's detractors insisted that tirailleurs sénégalais were enslaving and trafficking women in Congo and Madagascar. Historical sources fail to portray tirailleurs sénégalais' quotidian treatment of local women. Instead, only tirailleurs sénégalais' most egregious violations of local marital custom reached upper-level colonial administrators. Gross sexual misconduct inspired violent reprisals against employees of the colonial state. French missionaries in Congo and Madagascar intervened on the behalf of local populations and wrote direct appeals to regional military and civilian leadership. Despite these entreaties, French colonial officials rarely intervened in tirailleurs sénégalais' conjugal relationships with local women in African empire.

In Congo, Catholic missionaries denounced the transgressive conjugal behaviors of "sénégalais" and the French military officials who condoned them. When confronted with missionaries' disapproval of West Africans' sexual and conjugal activities, Albert Dolisie, the highest French official in Congo, claimed that West African Muslim soldiers, by virtue of their religious beliefs, were entitled to practice polygyny.[71] Bishop Alexandre Le Roy wrote a response to the minister of the colonies from Alinda, Gabon, in 1899. His letter condemned Dolisie's statement and denounced French administrators' complicity in tirailleurs sénégalais' transgressive sexual relationships with Congolese women.[72] Polygyny was a common marital practice in West and Equatorial Africa. However, French officials in Congo traded on Ottoman and Muslim stereotypes in order to condemn and/or justify tirailleurs sénégalais' multiwife inter-African households.[73] Bishop Le Roy brought some specificity and nuance to the debate. "Perhaps this right should be limited to awarding [them] the liberty to exercise polygyny in other peoples' households, especially those of our Christians."[74] Le Roy referenced incidents where "sénégalais" had incorporated female Congolese Christian converts into their military households despite the fact that these women had already married according to Catholic rites.[75] Congo administrators and military officials condoned tirailleurs sénégalais' marital traditions over Catholic traditions. These incidents illustrate how French military officials callously defended tirailleurs sénégalais' forced conjugal association and marital infidelity. French military and civilian officials paradoxically used the legitimating vocabulary of marriage to describe these transgressive conjugal unions. Étienne Grosclaude's 1896 assertion that Senegalese men in Madagascar "don't rape, they marry" conformed to this discursive practice.[76]

The colonial state wielded military force and used extrajudicial means to arbitrate conjugal affairs between West African men and Congolese women. In 1888, an inquiry into the murder of four laptots in Lastourville (in contemporary Gabon) found that the laptots' deaths were connected to an Aouangis woman's abandonment of her conjugal home. This unnamed woman had been the conjugal partner of a West African laptot. She deserted her husband's household and fled to her family's homestead in a nearby village. Wives' abandonment of the conjugal home often connoted unresolvable domestic problems. In many places on the African continent, wives deserted their husbands in order to make their grievances public. This was an opportunity for the community to intervene and assist in conflict resolution. The families of conjugal partners had the greatest stake in ensuring that the marriage endured and resulted in numerous offspring that would extend their kinship lines and provide new dependents. Conjugal partners' communities rarely participated in prenuptial rites for marital unions between West African men and women in Congo or Madagascar. When disputes among conjugal partners occurred, their kin could not provide mediation because tirailleurs sénégalais' kin were not present. Instead, congolaises' and malgaches' kin appealed to French colonial representatives to deal with couples' quarrels or West African men's illicit conjugal practices. If local community members approached French colonial agents regarding local women affiliated with West African men, they most often sought to extract the women from unsanctioned or abusive conjugal relationships. When given the opportunity, they sought the assistance of sympathetic religious authorities. Very few sought assistance from the colonial state in restoring and maintaining unions between local women and West African colonial employees—for good reason. "Sénégalais" received preferential treatment, which encouraged many West Africans serving in Congo to extend their original three-year contracts.[77] Latouche, the head French administrator in Lastourville, asserted the conjugal prerogative of the Aouangis woman's military husband and sent eight armed laptots and five Krumen to physically return her to the laptot. Unable to retrieve the wife, this band of West African military employees imprisoned two other village members. The villagers responded by killing half of the laptots with firearms.[78] The rapid escalation of violence suggests that the laptots' inter-African household had formed outside of Aouangis marital customs. It also hints at a history of tense relations between Aouangis and "sénégalais."

The desired outcomes of female members of inter-African military households are rarely accounted for in the historical record. In June of 1897, West African sergeant Bakari's conjugal behavior was the center of a dispute between Chief Onwango Amane and French commander Manas, who resided in Lambaréné (in contemporary Gabon). This incident illustrates how "sénégalais" brought the subversive violent authority of French colonialism into the most intimate affairs of family and community. It also may reveal how local actors took advantage of the presence of foreign colonial workers to reestablish matrilineal authority over marital contracts. Sergeant Bakari had incorporated a young woman, Yandjo, into his household inside the military garrison at Lambaréné. Chief Amane and local missionaries leveled accusations of sexual misconduct at Sergeant Bakari. Collectively, their accusations included adultery, rape, bigamy, abduction, concubinage, forced prostitution, and enslavement. In Lambaréné, prenuptial traditions included the consent and input of a young bride's extended kin. The exchange of bridewealth symbolized their approval of a marital union, but may not have granted male relatives or her husband control over the bride's sexuality.[79] When conjugal unions occurred outside of these processes, lineage members acted on behalf of the bride to remedy what the community considered illegitimate conjugal behavior. In the context of French colonial militarism, the bride's kin seldom succeeded in influencing civilian or military officials to intervene in conjugal unions between congolaises and "sénégalais."

Chief Amane wrote Commander Manas to notify him of Sergeant Bakari's illicit conjugal union with his niece Yandjo. In this letter, Chief Amane established his legal, political, and gerontocratic authority over Yandjo. Yandjo's mother was deceased. For the past two years, her father had been engaged in trading activities at Lake Avanga, several days journey down the Ogowe River. In the absence of direct parental authority, Chief Amane claimed that he, as Yandjo's maternal uncle, was the only member of the family who could superintend issues related to Yandjo's sexuality and conjugality. In addition to asserting familial right over his younger female kin, Chief Amane informed Manas that he had already given Yandjo in marriage to a man named Agninga, who had provided five hundred francs in bridewealth. Amane had already distributed portions of this bridewealth to Yandjo's father and maternal aunt.

Enter Yandjo's husband, Agninga, who attempted, unsuccessfully, to recuperate his young wife from the colonial garrison. Agninga suffered physical harm as a result of asserting his entitlement to Yandjo as his wife. A "sénégalais" functionary at the post placed Agninga in prison until he renounced his marriage and accepted a "reimbursement" of bridewealth from Sergeant Bakari that was a fraction of the original amount. The reduction of bridewealth to an economic transaction violated normal procedure, as did the circumvention of Yandjo's family in this decision. Chief Amane claimed that the dissolution of Yandjo and Agninga's marriage could only occur after local judges pronounced a divorce, at which point Chief Amane's family would reimburse Yandjo's bridewealth to Agninga's kin.

Chief Amane's letter spelled out in no uncertain terms that Sergeant Bakari's conjugal relationship with Yandjo was extraordinary in its violation of local marital practice. The letter also illustrated that Chief Amane believed that female in-laws had undermined his authority with this inter-African marriage. Yandjo's two maternal aunts, the sisters of her deceased mother, had facilitated Yandjo's union with Sergeant Bakari. They had received compensation from Sergeant Bakari for their efforts. Local missionaries ignored the importance of this detail in their assessment of the colonial state's violation of local communities' traditions. While these aunts could have arranged Yandjo's second marriage in order to line their own pockets, it is also possible that they assisted her in escaping an undesirable marriage brokered by her uncle. Chief Amane, the French missionary making a scandal of the affair, and the military's defense of Sergeant Bakari's actions all use patriarchal prerogative to explain whether Sergeant Bakari and Yandjo's conjugal union was legitimate or illegitimate.[80] These men were most interested in reestablishing patriarchal order, which they viewed as central to colonial and local traditions. Perhaps only her maternal aunts concerned themselves with what may have been Yandjo's desired future.

French military and civilian administrators in nineteenth-century Congo and Madagascar failed to standardize the basic components and procedures required for the colonial state to validate the inter-African conjugal unions of "sénégalais." French officials, clergy, and colonial employees lacked a clearly defined set of marital practices that would have enabled them to implement and protect local custom. French colonial officers encouraged laptots, tirailleurs sénégalais, and miliciens to locate conjugal partners while serving in French African Empire, but did not provide them with an accessible and straightforward means through which to register their marriages with the colonial state. There were a few half-hearted initiatives to encourage Congolese populations to do so. At the end of the nineteenth century, thirty-four civilian and military posts in Congo had marriage registers. In March 1900, administrators returned empty, unused registers to Libreville.[81] Congolese did not seek official recognition of their marriages. Offering Congolese the opportunity to record their marriages with the colonial state, without simultaneously providing a judicial system to enforce civil disputes related to marriage, was a futile exercise. Further, these registers were not intended for marriages between West African colonial employees and local women.

Civilian observers accused tirailleurs sénégalais and the colonial military of human trafficking and female enslavement, which contributed to a blossoming sex trade in French Congo. Albert Veistroffer, a French employee stationed in Congo, brokered marriages for several West African men in his employ with local Bandjo women in 1899. According to Veistroffer, the "sénégalais" under his command found Bandjo women extremely desirable as wives (*épouses*), but they were difficult to obtain (*se procurer*). Veistroffer bought (*acheter*) female Bandjo slaves (*esclaves*) for his West African employees with surplus merchandise. Veistroffer's "sénégalais" were married (*mariés*) with priority and ahead of his local Congolese employees.[82] Unlike many of his contemporaries, Veistroffer did not mask the outright purchase of local women with the language of bridewealth. Similar to his contemporaries, Veistroffer made female enslavement and marriage synonymous.

A shocking example of sex trafficking involved the barely pubescent daughter of a West African man and a local woman in Franceville (Gabon). The mother recuperated her daughter from a Catholic mission to enlist her in transactional sex work. Her clients were predominantly European and West African workers employed in French Congo.[83] Female members of inter-African military households were likened to sex slaves in an elaborate human trafficking scheme along the Bight of Benin. Administrators in French Congo grew suspicious of the number of women moving from Congo to join their foreign conjugal partners in German Cameroon. In order to curb "illegal immigration," they introduced bureaucratic procedures that would authenticate marriage and require passports for Congolese women desiring to relocate within the Gulf of Guinea.[84] The unused marriage registers, mentioned above, were absurdly cited as integral to this process. Additionally, the French placed a hundred-franc price tag on passports, which would encourage subterfuge and fraud instead of matrimony.

Étienne Grosclaude's assertion that tirailleurs sénégalais married, as opposed to raped, captured the paradoxes and ambiguities surrounding the conjugal unions shared between West African colonial employees and women in Congo and Madagascar. Most military officials strove to provide a degree of official sanction to inter-African households without legally obligating the colonial state to intervene in West Africans' military households in empire. By championing ambiguity, the state dodged grievances and abuses, conjugal or otherwise, articulated by women, local chiefs, and French missionaries. Local detractors accused "sénégalais" of concubinage, polygyny, female slavery, and forced prostitution in postemancipation Congo and Madagascar. Tirailleurs sénégalais had been integral to processes of female slave emancipation in West Africa. In Madagascar and French Congo, they earned a reputation for practices that today would be labeled female enslavement or forced conjugal association. Even though civilians and military officials were uncomfortable with the processes through which tirailleurs sénégalais set up inter-African military households, they condoned them. The colonial state encouraged West African employees to establish conjugal unions with Congolese and Madagascan women, but did not legalize them. As a result, officials like Grosclaude could use the word "marriage" to obscure forced conjugal association and sexual assault.

In the final decades of the nineteenth century, tirailleurs sénégalais and their households participated in colonial campaigns in West Africa, Congo, Dahomey, and Madagascar. Their family histories provide empirical evidence of the interconnectedness of France's imperial conquest of disparate regions of Africa. African military household members' origins diversified and the words used to describe them expanded, contracted, and became misnomers. Long-distance migration served to legitimize socially homogeneous conjugal relationships between West African women and men. In Congo and Madagascar, tirailleurs sénégalais' inter-African conjugal unions struggled to acquire legitimacy. These households were simultaneously labeled as both marriage and enslavement by different stakeholders. In the following chapter, racial similarity and common origins became the primary reason that military officials celebrated African military households in Morocco. They prohibited interracial conjugal relationships between tirailleurs sénégalais and Arab or Berber women.

3

Mesdames Tirailleurs and Black Villages

Trans-Saharan Experiences in the Conquest of Morocco, 1908–18

IN 1908, APPROXIMATELY SIXTEEN HUNDRED TIRAILLEURS sénégalais disembarked steamships in Casablanca to participate in France's military conquest of Morocco. An unreported number of West African wives, with infants tied to their backs and household items balanced on their heads, accompanied them down the gangplanks. Their arrival in the Maghreb followed the Treaty of Algeçiras in 1906, which divided the management of Morocco's foreign relations between France and Spain. In 1908, the French military capitalized on local uprisings aimed at foreign residents in Casablanca to launch direct military intervention in Morocco.[1] During subsequent years, tirailleurs sénégalais and their African military households participated in campaigns to secure the port towns of Casablanca and Kenitra, then the inland imperial cities of Meknes, Fez, and Marrakech. By 1912, the Sultan of Morocco had bankrupted his treasury and relied on French occupying forces to protect his dynastic seat from fraternal competition. African military households were vital members of the colonial forces that maintained France's protectorate rule in Morocco from 1912 to 1956.

In North Africa, mesdames tirailleurs' presence in the ranks of the tirailleurs sénégalais acquired new historical, racialized, and gendered significance. They featured in empire-wide discussions surrounding the use of West African soldiers in Morocco (the troupes noires debates) and whether the French state

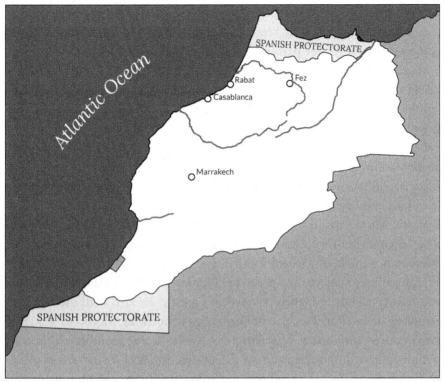

MAP 3.1. French Protectorate in Morocco. Map by Isaac Barry

should permanently invest in the tirailleurs sénégalais as a tool of twentieth-century empire. The troupes noires debates appeared in upwards of forty-three hundred publications and featured in numerous public meetings.[2] As indicated by the name of the debates, French officials invested in a broad racial categorization—black—to refer to tirailleurs sénégalais. They made sweeping generalizations about sociocultural differences that mapped onto populations living north and south of the Sahara. They imagined these differences in polemicized terms: "Arab" and "black."[3] Additionally, French officials transformed West African households' raison d'être on military campaign. In the nineteenth century, the French believed that tirailleurs sénégalais were better soldiers when they served en famille. In twentieth-century Morocco, mesdames tirailleurs and their households became a colonial tool to reify racial differences between West African colonial soldiers and North African civilians.

French officials went to great lengths to legitimize the existence of African military households in Morocco because they were apprehensive about transgressing what they perceived as fixed racial hierarchies in North Africa and across the Sahara. Their actions were informed by a diverse set of ideas about race, gender, and power relations among populations living north and south of the Sahara. French military officials believed that Arabo-Berber populations had attained greater civilizational development than sub-Saharan Africans. This imagined racial order originated, in part, from France's participation in the Atlantic slave trade and the use of enslaved Africans in French Caribbean plantation colonies.[4] French military officials also considered local history and the legacies of slavery and race inherited from Alawi dynastic Morocco and the trans-Saharan slave trade.[5] The *abid al-Bukhari*, a seventeenth-century Alawi military institution made up of dark-skinned Moroccan households, served as a template and a foil to twentieth-century French military strategy. The process of locating a "usable" indigenous Moroccan history to justify French colonial conquest coincided with the rapid assemblage of a colonial archive of knowledge concerning Morocco.[6] Roughly two hundred years apart, West African and dark-skinned southern Moroccan women played important roles in the production and reproduction of the abid al-Bukhari and the tirailleurs sénégalais—military institutions integral to ambitious, expansionist states in Morocco. The presence of mesdames tirailleurs in Morocco maintained and intensified local and colonial racial beliefs that affiliated blackness with martiality and slave origins. Centering mesdames tirailleurs in this history enables us to see how race and gender worked together in creating French colonial order in twentieth-century North Africa.

Tirailleurs sénégalais' households took a prominent position in the visual representation of France's conquest of Morocco. New technologies of image production and their wide circulation informed imperial audiences of racially homogenous African military households' livelihoods on campaign. Picture postcards from the Moroccan campaign depicted African military households engaged in domestic activities in their racially segregated living quarters. "Black Villages" were a colonial invention for North African conquest.[7] Racial segregation discouraged tirailleurs sénégalais from fraternizing with local civilian women and men.[8] This gendered military strategy heightened the racial distinctiveness of African military households in Morocco.

Officials championed Black Villages as spaces of refuge among the epidemiological and climatic challenges that West African troops encountered north of the tropics. According to the troupes noires debates, mesdames tirailleurs provided soldiers with medical care and domestic comfort, which inspired tirailleurs sénégalais to overcome the hardships affiliated with Moroccan conquest. Conversely, Black Villages signaled to other French troops and North African civilians that tirailleurs sénégalais could not conform to modern military practices—male-restricted military service. Racial segregation drastically altered the experiences of tirailleurs sénégalais and their conjugal partners in Morocco—mesdames tirailleurs' final theater of French imperial expansion.

CONSTRUCTING DIFFERENCE WITH HISTORY AND RACIAL SCIENCE

In North Africa, the French colonial military community reappraised tirailleurs sénégalais' and mesdames tirailleurs' roles as empire builders. The troupes noires debates created a vocabulary and a discourse that would convince a broader public of West African troops' ability to overcome any physical, social, and epidemiological hardships that could negatively impact their performance in North Africa. The troupes noires debates built their arguments on two sets of racial discourses. The first mined local histories concerning slavery and soldiering in Alawi Morocco. The second appropriated ideas from nineteenth-century European racial sciences in order to reaffirm and challenge biological determinism and the racial "fixity" of black Africans. Debates about West African troops' versatility linked up to discussions about the viability and/or professionalization of the tirailleurs sénégalais. These interministerial and empire-wide discussions coalesced around the publication of Lieutenant Colonel Charles Mangin's *La force noire* in 1910.[9] This significant text selectively culled images and ideas from Moroccan history and French scientific discourses to celebrate West African soldiers' ostensible innate martial prowess and their universal utility in French Empire. *La force noire* convinced the ministers of war and colonies to finance the introduction of quota-based conscription in French West Africa in 1912. *La force noire* created a vocabulary and a repertoire of ideas about the tirailleurs sénégalais that echoed across French Empire and survived its fall.

Lieutenant Colonel Mangin made sweeping racialist claims about black Africans and their diasporic descendants' martial talents. For Mangin, black slavery was a key factor in producing martial races. He cited military institutions made of up slaves and/or descendants of slaves that aided expansionist historical states across time and space. Mangin connected tirailleurs sénégalais with African American troops in the American Civil War and the abid al-Bukhari. Also known as the Black Guard, this historical Moroccan institution merits significant attention because of how Mangin twisted this army of enslaved men into a celebrated antecedent of the tirailleurs sénégalais. *La force noire* lacked citations, but Mangin likely cribbed French Orientalist Octave Houdas's translation of Ahmad az-Zayani's history of the Alawi dynasty for information on the abid al-Bukhari.[10] *Abid* in Arabic translates to slaves, servants, or devoted followers. In this case, *abid* denoted the soldiers' devotion to one of the foundational texts of Islamic jurisprudence—the *Sahih al-Bukhari*.[11] Moroccan sultan Mawlay Ismail (r. 1672–1727) created this military institution. Early in his reign, Mawlay Ismail assembled dark-skinned women and men in his imperial capital of Meknes to inaugurate a black army. After recruitment, Mawlay Ismail's agents provided members of the Black Guard with clothing and arms, then directed them to Mashra ar-Ramla camp, located in the outskirts of Meknes.[12] The members of this racially determined military encampment became the support system for, and the members of, the abid al-Bukhari. In describing the process of induction, Houdas's French translation conveyed that the conscripted Moroccan women and men were already slaves when they entered military service. Most were not. Military service and enslavement were conterminous processes for households in the Black Guard. Houdas collapsed the important distinctions between slave status, slave ancestry, and sub-Saharan African origins in seventeenth-century Morocco. Mangin carried forward Houdas's historical oversights.

In *La force noire*, Mangin backfilled the creation of the Black Guard with historical context, explaining why large numbers of people of West African descent lived in Alawi-ruled Morocco. Dodging the longer history of the trans-Saharan slave trade, Mangin focused on an episode in which a powerful Moroccan sultan invaded the Songhai Empire. In 1591, eighty years before Mawlay Ismail's reign, Sultan Al Mansur sent a large contingent of musketeers across the Sahara. According to historians, Al Mansur's motivations for the trans-Saharan assault included jihad, increasing Morocco's access to salt and gold, and regional military strategy.[13] According to Mangin, Al Mansur invaded West Africa for the explicit purpose of acquiring men from the southern Sahara to build an imperial army. Al Mansur's bid for trans-Saharan domination yielded thousands of prisoners of war and an annual tribute of enslaved women and men. Deemphasizing these processes of enslavement and forced migration, Mangin used this example to justify France's conscription of West African men. With an army made up of captives sourced from West Africa, Al Mansur strengthened his rule in the Maghreb and defended his realm from Iberian and Ottoman threats.[14] According to Mangin, with an army of West African conscripts, France could likewise assert its prerogative over Morocco.

During the three or four generations separating the reigns of Al Mansur and Mawlay Ismail, most of the prisoners and subsequent levies of enslaved women and men integrated into Moroccan communities. Many (particularly women) did so by entering into conjugal relationships with Moroccans, which gradually strengthened their local social ties. Others converted to Islam, or, for those already Muslim, made their religious convictions more evident. Religious conversion and marriage were well-trodden paths toward slave emancipation and improving social status. Social integration facilitated the gradual reduction of outsider and slave status in the trans-Saharan world.[15] In the late seventeenth century, Mawlay Ismail's agents used physical traits affiliated with West African ancestry to identify potential recruits for the abid al-Bukhari, without regard for their free status. Government officials conscripted over 150,000 dark-skinned people for the abid al-Bukhari—effectively creating a racialized military institution made up of people enslaved by the Alawi state. Men became soldiers and women became soldiers' conjugal partners, who provided the state with a range of military and domestic support services. Mawlay Ismail's agents enslaved these people despite the vehement protests of religious leaders. Muslim authorities contended that the sultan's actions contravened sharia law because many members of the Black Guard were Muslim. For Mawlay Ismail, West African ancestry outweighed their free status as Muslims. Historian Chouki El Hamel argues that the creation of the abid al-Bukhari ushered in social transformations in Alawi Morocco because West African origins, slavery, and martial qualities cohered in novel ways to produce new racial distinctions and hierarchies.[16] This influenced many free Arabo-Berber Moroccans to imagine themselves as distinct from and superior to the members of the abid al-Bukhari and the

Moroccans that looked like them. Moroccan communities and ruling aristocracies came to question dark-skinned peoples' religious convictions and to see them as innately predetermined for servitude in Morocco.[17] Roughly two centuries later, *La force noire* proved Mawlay Ismail's success in fusing West African origins with slave status and martial qualities. Mangin claimed that black Africans and members of their diaspora were incontrovertibly predetermined for military service.

The troupes noires debates muddled the theories of French naturalists, anthropologists, and other social scientists in order to argue that West African soldiers could serve the French in any environment or climate.[18] Mangin championed biological determinism in referring to West Africans' ability to adapt to "all privations and all dangers," yet acknowledged environmental factors' influence upon human conditioning.[19] Mangin and his supporters cherry-picked language from nineteenth-century French discourses on racial science in order to substantiate their claims that black Africans were innately suited for military service and could adapt to any environment.[20] Accordingly, West Africans could provide France with versatile troops for the arid Moroccan plains and the frigid passes of the Atlas Mountains. The fiction of black Africans' universal strength and adaptability had the unfortunate result of influencing a new type of military-supported science—a science of negligence, detailed below.

Mangin tapped popular nineteenth-century racial assumptions about sub-Saharan Africans and their diaspora to strengthen his claims. His text compared African American soldiers, Egyptian Mamelukes, and the Black Guard to argue that black Africans could acclimatize, transgenerationally, to a wide range of temperatures and topographies.[21] Mangin believed that the African diaspora's martial qualities—particularly obedience and resilience—were acquired genetically, environmentally nurtured by tropical Africa's harsh climates, and socioculturally instilled due to the historical experiences of slavery.[22] Mangin cavalierly celebrated black slavery as an antecedent to martial prowess. He envisioned military service as a means through which to orient slaves and former slaves toward the productive forces of empire building. This echoed those nineteenth-century abolitionist and colonial discourses that championed the state's role in emancipating both domestic African slaves and enslaved diasporic Africans, in order to prepare them for participation in French Republican colonialism.[23]

Mangin was not alone in capitalizing on facile comparisons between the abid al-Bukhari and the tirailleurs sénégalais. Louis-Hubert Lyautey, the top colonial official in France's Moroccan Protectorate (1912–25), maintained that military occupation should encompass processes normally overseen by civilian governments—social policy, nation building, and more.[24] He believed tirailleurs sénégalais could play an essential role in establishing and perpetuating the French protectorate in Morocco. Lyautey had commanded West African soldiers in Madagascar's southern military region during the late 1890s.[25] Once in Morocco, Lyautey amalgamated the familiar with the historical. If diasporic African soldiers represented the authority of seventeenth-century Alawi Sultans, tirailleurs sénégalais could serve to legitimize French rule in twentieth-century Morocco. To this end, Lyautey created his own Black Guard made up of tirailleurs sénégalais.[26] His was the ultimate appropriation of imperial Moroccan history—adopting precolonial symbols of power in order to give colonial rule a veneer of legitimacy.

Lyautey's and Mangin's glorification of historical military institutions dependent upon black slave labor conflicted with contemporaneous efforts in French West Africa to alter how civilian West Africans perceived the tirailleurs sénégalais as a military institution made up of slaves and former slaves.[27] High-level officials in French West Africa linked dwindling numbers of voluntary soldiers with the successful implementation of emancipation in West Africa, as well as increased opportunities for low-status men to access expanding economies in agricultural, industrial, and service sectors.[28] From 1909, Mangin and the governor-general of French West Africa, William Ponty, coordinated their efforts to encourage enlistment by altering the image of the tirailleurs sénégalais among potential recruits. They standardized and increased compensation, as well as systematizing recruitment practices across West Africa.[29] These efforts, in combination with the success of *La force noire*, resulted in the 1912 Recruitment Decree, which introduced quota-based conscription to French West Africa. With federation-wide conscription, Mangin and Ponty hoped that recruitment classes would better represent the demographic diversity of West Africa, efface the connection between soldiering and slavery, and ensure the longevity of the tirailleurs sénégalais as a colonial institution.

At the same time, in French colonial North Africa, slavery, West African origins, and soldiering cohered to produce another set of ideas. Known as *saligan* in Moroccan Arabic and *saligani* in Algerian Arabic, the tirailleurs sénégalais' participation in French conquest in the Maghreb disrupted the historical ways in which North Africans interacted with, and imagined their relationship with, people from West Africa.[30] Under the rubric of French colonialism, African military households introduced ideas that West Africans in Morocco were foreign, unassimilable outsiders who inevitably returned to their homelands south of the desert. African military households contradicted epistemological ideas about people of West African descent having origins in Morocco. French officials made gross errors when they superficially adapted the abid al-Bukhari to their twentieth-century military ambitions in the Maghreb. In the seventeenth century, the members of Mawlay Ismail's abid al-Bukhari may have been physically distinct, but they were Moroccans.[31] Tirailleurs sénégalais were West Africans employed and outfitted by the French colonial military, cast as interlopers in France's colonial bid for North Africa.[32] As a result, North Africans came to affiliate West African soldiers with foreign and illegitimate political intervention.[33]

French colonialism in West Africa and North Africa altered the centuries-old processes through which many sub-Saharan Africans had arrived in and integrated into Moroccan societies. French colonial officials impeded long-distance slave trading in the Sahara by attacking the institution of slavery in West Africa and the public sale of slaves in Morocco. Officials north and south of the Sahara approached this task differently. The civilian administration in French West Africa eliminated slavery as a legal category in all colonial courts in 1905. In 1912, French military officers prohibited slave markets in Moroccan cities under French control, but did little to alter the legal status of slaves or to enforce emancipation. French officials continued to affiliate their own soldiers in Morocco with present and historical enslavement. In September 1912, Captain Cornet instructed his Bamana-speaking orderly, Nama Diara, to seek his countrymen among the slaves for purchase in a Marrakech public market. Cornet assumed that a tirailleur sénégalais shared geographic origins and ethnolinguistic characteristics with the enslaved in Morocco.[34]

LIVING SEGREGATION AND RACIAL SCIENCE ON CAMPAIGN

Tirailleurs sénégalais and their families experienced unnecessary hardship on Moroccan campaign. Widely held fallacious beliefs that African soldiers were "innately" invincible led military officials to experiment with the line between subsistence and undernourishment.[35] In nineteenth-century West Africa, Equatorial Africa, and Madagascar, tirailleurs sénégalais depended on conjugal relationships with local women for supplemental resources and domestic labor. Mesdames tirailleurs and tirailleurs sénégalais plundered civilian fields and homesteads for essential foodstuffs. In Morocco, the French military limited contact between African military households and civilian populations. This new prohibition boxed in West African families' household economy. The military commissariat provided the majority of the resources consumed by West African households. Due to pervasive myths about the predisposition of black Africans to be able to perform arduous tasks with inadequate caloric consumption, the commissariat allocated smaller rations to tirailleurs sénégalais than to other troops serving on Moroccan campaign. French officials were slow to acknowledge and respond to these drastic changes in tirailleurs sénégalais' household economies, which had fatal consequences.

Shortly after West African households landed in Morocco, there was an outbreak of beriberi among soldiers stationed in Chaouia, a rural area east of Casablanca.[36] Beriberi is caused by deficiencies in thiamine (vitamin B1) and is characterized by degenerative changes in the immune, digestive, and cardiovascular systems. Thiamine is essential for the body's metabolic processes and is ample in plants and animals. Many grains, like rice, are deficient in B-complex vitamins. In Morocco, the most prevalent carbohydrate was couscous, made from wheat semolina. The central carbohydrate in most West Africans' diets was rice or millet. In order to satisfy their dietary preferences, the military imported rice from West Africa and Asia for tirailleurs sénégalais households in Morocco—and provided them with little else. West Africans were the only soldiers among the ranks of the colonial army affected by the outbreak of beriberi. After the 1908 beriberi outbreak, the military diversified West Africans' diets. Despite these implemented measures, individual cases of beriberi continued to hospitalize tirailleurs sénégalais in Morocco over the next five years and there was another outbreak in 1913.[37] Military records do not account for how beriberi affected West African women and children.

When soldiers felt the deleterious effects of malnourishment, they rebelled against French authority. In April 1913, Moussa Sambaké refused to don his military pack during a training exercise on the Merzaga plateau. The following day, two other members of his battalion, Mambé Keita and Digbo Missaté, refused to march double-time in formation. French commanding officers sent these recalcitrant soldiers to police headquarters. When they attempted to resume drills, Karifa Missaré shouted to his fellow tirailleurs sénégalais in Bamana, "Anyone who picks up their pack will be known as an incestuous cur," which incited general disorder. On his way to the police station, Missaré placed his hand on his standard-issue machete and said, "I will go to prison, but I will not carry my pack."[38] At first blush, these Bamana-speaking soldiers called into question the stereotypes concerning the martial proclivities that made them ideal, obedient soldiers.[39] At the conclusion of a lengthy report on this multiday affair, an administrator noted recent decreases in sugar, coffee, and cooking oil rations. Tirailleurs sénégalais' recalcitrance looked like collective protest against austerity measures. Commanding officers were lenient in disciplining Missaré, Keita, and Missaté and increased the battalion's daily rations. One can only imagine how reductions in these essential goods affected mesdames tirailleurs and their children.

West and North Africa are distinct epidemiological and environmental zones. The French belatedly implemented policies that could reduce West Africans' susceptibility to pathogens common in North Africa. Tirailleurs sénégalais serving in Morocco frequently contracted respiratory and pulmonary infections, as well as tapeworm and filariasis.[40] In 1913, a report disclosed that 910 out of 5,962 West African servicemen—roughly 15 percent—were hospitalized for pneumonia, dysentery, severe fever, tuberculosis, and typhoid.[41] There are no numbers available for their wives or children. French officials did not implement basic measures that could have improved the sanitation of encampments and the overall health of their troops. Military officials belatedly realized that West African soldiers required warmer uniforms, close-toed shoes, and extra bedding on North Africa's temperate coasts and in the mountainous interior. Six years after the first battalion of tirailleurs sénégalais deployed to Casablanca, high-level administrators acknowledged that West African soldiers required at least one or two years to acclimate to Morocco and that they should not deploy in the Atlas Mountains during the winter.[42] A report from January 1915 illustrated the dire situation of a column of tirailleurs sénégalais marching through sleet and whipping wind in the high elevations northeast of Fez. Several mounted West Africans fell off their mules because they were numb with cold and/or suffering from frostbite. Twenty tirailleurs sénégalais died as a result of this wintry high-elevation march.[43]

Language and cultural barriers between tirailleurs sénégalais and their commanding officers inhibited troops' ability to register their discontent over substandard uniforms and insufficient rations. Medical reports illustrate that West Africans sought to prematurely terminate their military service by making themselves ill through the ingestion of inedible or toxic items. Others attempted suicide and several were successful. Some soldiers tried to make themselves ineligible for service through acts of self-harm or self-mutilation. In one example, a tirailleur sénégalais picked a fight with another soldier to provoke disabling physical retribution that could prematurely terminate his tour of duty. Another African infantryman intentionally discharged his rifle into his leg. Tirailleurs sénégalais attempted desertion and aided or abetted their compatriots' efforts to go AWOL.[44] Documents from nineteenth-century campaigns in Madagascar and French Congo rarely mention comparably grave incidents resulting from soldiers' despair and general malaise. This could have something to do with the introduction of conscription in 1912 to French West Africa and/or the inability of tirailleurs sénégalais to create social and conjugal relationships with local Moroccan women.

The troupes noires debates cast mesdames tirailleurs as solutions to West African soldiers' medical issues and low morale in Morocco. Wives improved the quality of tirailleurs sénégalais' cuisine and the cleanliness of their living quarters. Mesdames tirailleurs provided health care to those debilitated by disease, as well as palliative care to injured soldiers. Soldiers' households could improve the psychological health of enlisted men because the responsibilities of family life offered soldiers immediate and meaningful purpose. The sociability inherent to intimate domestic relationships could provide distraction from the hardships of campaign. Officials praised West African women in Morocco as bulwarks against the spread of sexually transmitted infections among tirailleurs sénégalais, which affected metropolitan French troops and locally recruited North African forces in far larger percentages.[45] French officials touted mesdames tirailleurs as a panacea for a triad of unwanted behaviors and practices that they believed tirailleurs sénégalais were particularly susceptible to in Morocco—alcoholism, homesickness, and homosexuality.[46]

Homosexuality rarely appears in the historical record affiliated with the tirailleurs sénégalais. Reference to it in a laundry list of the advantages affiliated with mesdames tirailleurs in Morocco merits further examination and contextualization. Historian Marc Epprecht has identified a pernicious, ubiquitous myth that sub-Saharan Africans, particularly men, are incontrovertibly heterosexual.[47] I have found only one source, authored by a French surgeon who claimed to work among tirailleurs sénégalais stationed in Saint-Louis in the 1880s and 1890s, that explicitly identified homosexual practices among enlisted men. The surgeon's 1893 text, published under a pseudonym, identified two recent recruits who participated in a same-sex relationship with each other. The surgeon did not identify these men as homosexuals. He claimed that West African men only engaged in temporary homosexual behaviors when they could not locate female sexual partners. He explained that these men had become tirailleurs sénégalais after their emancipation from slavery. According to "Dr. Jacobus X," slave status and the homosocial existence associated with the barrack life provided the contexts for these purportedly anomalous homosexual practices.[48]

Writing at the time of Moroccan conquest, Maurice Delafosse believed that homosexuality was extremely rare among West African populations. He claimed that where the sexual practices affiliated with homosexuality existed, they had been introduced by Europeans or "Arab tribes."[49] This is important for understanding why French officials believed it was possible for mesdames tirailleurs to safeguard tirailleurs sénégalais from homosexuality in Morocco. In the twentieth-century French imagination, Arab-speaking North Africa was an exotic space in which European men could locate young male Arab lovers. These predominantly intergenerational affairs were sometimes well-known and openly written about by French authors like André Gide. French men employed in the colonial service or enlisted in the Bataillon d'Afrique were rumored to engage in sodomy while serving in North Africa.[50] Opposing arguments contended that French men were seduced by an atmosphere of homosexual permissiveness in North Africa or that French men with homosexual proclivities could convince Arabs to engage in these relationships.[51] It is unclear whether French officials feared that West African soldiers would engage in sexual relations with each other or with Moroccan men. French officials believed that their West African troops were paragons of masculinity and martial prowess, yet they feared their troops' susceptibility to what they believed were North African sexual practices. Mesdames tirailleurs became an important tool for maintaining sociocultural boundaries that allowed French officials to respect what they perceived as racial, gendered, and sexual order in Arabo-Berber North Africa.

MESDAMES TIRAILLEURS, BLACK VILLAGES, AND GENDERED RACIAL ORDER IN MOROCCO

Mesdames tirailleurs' presence in the conquest of North Africa attracted great attention because of the troupes noires debates and advances in image production technology. Picture postcards featuring African military households in Black Villages on Moroccan campaign circulated within empire. Tirailleurs sénégalais seldom formed interracial households with Moroccan women and the presence of their West African families in the Maghreb racialized colonial military service in new ways. French military discourse added new elements to tirailleurs sénégalais' conjugal practices and marital traditions that emphasized racial homogeneity and colonial order. Black military wives sit uncomfortably at the confluence of Moroccan military traditions and colonial military practices. Mesdames tirailleurs were civilian members of military households serving the French colonial state in Morocco. Their presence emphasized the racial distinctiveness of tirailleurs sénégalais. They performed domestic and auxiliary military roles that were disarmingly similar to the work performed by diasporic African women affiliated with the abid al-Bukhari. In Morocco, mesdames tirailleurs became twentieth-century solutions for medical and social ills experienced by West African colonial troops serving outside of the tropics. French observers conveniently cast West African women as gendered scapegoats for sudden outbursts of racialized violence in Morocco. In the troupes noires debates, African military households were crucial to military discourses promoting tirailleurs sénégalais' universal utility in French Empire. Incongruously, Morocco was mesdames tirailleurs' final stop in empire.

On Moroccan campaign, African military households were the exclusive members of Black Villages. The French military physically segregated West African troops from other people serving France's armed forces in Morocco. These racialized military villages shared characteristics with historical Moroccan military traditions, as well as challenging local customs in order to serve twentieth-century French military ambitions and colonial racial order. In the seventeenth century, Sultan Mawlay Ismail racially engineered his Black Guard to amplify the racial distinctiveness of the African diasporic troops serving in the Alawi military. His representatives across Morocco produced free and slave women for arranged marriages with members of the abid al-Bukhari. Alawi state agents considered women eligible for these forced conjugal relationships based on the visible signs of their sub-Saharan African ancestry, which purportedly connoted their slave past and/or pagan ancestors. Once incorporated into the abid al-Bukhari, women received training in obedience and the domestic arts in the Sultan's harems.[52] The children of military couples entered into domestic service in the Sultan's palace or other governmental offices. When they came of age, boys became soldiers and girls became wives.

These practices effectively racialized military service in the expanding Alawi state, segregated Moroccans by physical appearance, and simultaneously marginalized yet increased the visibility of diasporic Africans in Morocco. The *makhzen*, or imperial government, isolated families of the abid al-Bukhari from the general population and Moroccan civil society began to view them as agents of the imperial state.[53] Soldiers in the abid al-Bukhari deployed to conflict zones with their families. Their family members provided domestic and auxiliary services that enhanced troops' performance and encouraged troops' fidelity to their units. Families accompanied soldiers during the campaigning season in the southern Sous region and into the Atlas Mountains. According to Chouki El Hamel, the abid al-Bukhari's temporary garrisons provided a "buffer zone to control tensions between Arabs and Berbers" in the outreaches of the expanding Alawi state.[54] The Alawi state considered diasporic Africans serving in the abid al-Bukhari ideal military intermediaries.

Little more than two hundred years later, Mangin highlighted points of confluence between the abid al-Bukhari and the tirailleurs sénégalais. French observers believed the Black Villages provided tirailleurs sénégalais with the appropriate space and demographic makeup to reenact the social and cultural life affiliated with their ancestral villages. Racial segregation was meant to improve troops' morale and enhance their performance on campaign.[55] Like Mawlay Ismail's government, the French introduced educational services and employment pathways for soldiers' offspring. The Écoles des Enfants de Troupes offered literacy classes, vocational training, and drilling exercises for

FIGURE 3.1. "Casablanca.—Au Camp Sénégalais: Les futurs tirailleurs," 2K 148 Michat Album Algésiras/Chaouia/Casablanca 32, © Service historique de la Défense.

young male children on campaign.[56] The conical tents of the Black Villages provided the backdrop for postcards from the Moroccan campaign, bearing captions reading "The Future Black Army" or "The Future Tirailleurs," which portrayed groups of West African children flanked by French officers (see fig. 3.1).[57] In neighboring Algeria, a general argued that tirailleurs sénégalais would provide a cordon sanitaire between French settlers and indigenous Algerians.[58]

There were important distinctions between the Black Villages and the abid al-Bukhari encampments. The abid al-Bukhari's camps were racially distinct, but their amenities and lifestyles varied little from other troops in the seventeenth-century Alawi military. In the twentieth century, Black Villages were antithetical to French military efforts to professionalize the tirailleurs sénégalais and to modernize the French state's colonial military. The presence of civilian wives in Black Villages countered trends in metropolitan France where camp followers, sutlers, and soldiers' wives were phased out of official military spaces during the early Third Republic.[59] Postcard images of West African soldiers en famille on Moroccan campaign were incompatible with French ideals of male Republican citizens providing military labor for a nationally defined state.[60] West African troops could not embody ideals of individualism and continue to live in households on campaign. The racialized physical segregation of African military households from other troops participating in France's conquest of Morocco heuristically educated local civilians and other men serving France that tirailleurs sénégalais were incapable of conforming to the demands of modern military service. The presence of mesdames tirailleurs on campaign reinforced racialized ethnic, physical, and "civilizational" differences between West Africans and North Africans. Black Villages communicated that the French military supported the continuation of these differences through the prohibition of sexual contact and conjugal relationships between West African troops and Maghrebi female civilians.

Contrary to French officials claims, Black Villages failed to reproduce West African village life because of the demographic controls that the French military imposed on them. Unlike the abid al-Bukhari's camps, Black Villages were not designed for transgenerational social reproduction. Age and gender imbalances were extreme. West African couples had children while on campaign, but could not rely on extended kin and older generations to participate in child rearing. French commissariats at West African Atlantic ports regulated freight and weight on military steamers bound for Morocco. They determined that roughly 25 percent of tirailleurs sénégalais could deploy to North Africa with their wives.[61] This percentage resulted from weighing women's contributions to soldiers' morale and military efficacy against the added logistical burden of campaigning with households. Black Villages deviated from West African village life as well as nineteenth-century military conjugal practices. Evidence from previous campaigns in West Africa, Equatorial Africa, and Madagascar demonstrated that tirailleurs sénégalais participated in polyamorous and polygynous conjugal relationships involving local women and mesdames tirailleurs. In Morocco, the French portrayed tirailleurs sénégalais as heteronormative, monogamous husbands and fathers who did not seek local conjugal partners.

In Black Villages, the French reshaped West Africans' traditional social relationships as well as retooling the gendered divisions of space and labor common to tirailleurs sénégalais' ancestral communities.[62] Villages consisted of conical canvas tents organized along latitudinal and longitudinal corridors (see fig. 3.2). Social and domestic activities like dining and fraternizing took place in common, open-air spaces adjacent to tents. Laundering, bathing,

FIGURE 3.2. "Campagne au Maroc (1907–1909).—Ber Réchid—Camp et cuisines des Sénégalais," 2K 148 Michat Album Algésiras/Chaouia/Casablanca 32, © Service historique de la Défense.

and other domestic chores occurred at natural water sources located near encampments. Tents' canvas fabric likely served as a visible barrier between intimate and public spaces. Sources do not indicate how the French military allocated tents or whether families and unwed soldiers shared sleeping quarters. Married and unmarried West African troops congregated in small groups around women who made their preferred cuisine, spoke their language, and shared ancestral and/or linguistic ties.[63] Mesdames tirailleurs adapted Moroccan food staples to West African culinary fare. They laundered the uniforms and personal effects of their husbands and other tirailleurs sénégalais.[64] Mesdames tirailleurs' presence on campaign allowed for a gendered division of labor that benefited their husbands, other soldiers, and the colonial state. In his memoir, soldier Bakary Diallo wrote that the West African women on Moroccan campaign provided their husbands with affection and obedience, which granted low-ranking tirailleurs sénégalais a bit of authority in a hierarchical and racialized landscape. He also commented on the women's sacrifices for their families, which included going hungry, thirsty, and suffering other privations.[65] Mesdames tirailleurs participated in camp work and fatigue duty. These women protected and vigorously defended West Africans' encampments while soldiers were away on campaign.[66]

Mesdames tirailleurs' unpaid labor contributed to tirailleurs sénégalais' cost-effectiveness, which the troupes noires debates highlighted. Tirailleurs sénégalais received lower wages than French metropolitan or North African troops serving in Morocco. In 1909, an article estimated that a West African soldier cost the French army 550 francs per year, while Algerian soldiers cost 810 francs.[67] Two years later, the French military paid tirailleurs sénégalais 676 francs annually, while Algerian soldiers earned 872 francs.[68] French infantrymen's wives could not accompany them to Morocco and they were paid roughly three times more than tirailleurs sénégalais. The French military allocated metropolitan officers' families travel and maintenance allowances, but their family members remained at coastal ports or military bases. The tirailleurs sénégalais who brought mesdames tirailleurs to Morocco experienced double economic hardship because of their paltry pay and the added financial burden of supporting families while on campaign.

In Morocco, mesdames tirailleurs could not independently supplement their husbands' allocated pay and rations with foodstuffs or labor appropriated from nearby civilian populations. In West Africa, Congo, and Madagascar, wives of tirailleurs sénégalais had grown spice gardens and other agricultural products to supplement the provisions distributed by the French military. Mobility, climate, and ecological differences in North Africa impeded mesdames tirailleurs from cultivating small gardens, which made them much more reliant on the French military for their own survival. These limitations compelled Black Village residents to participate in a military male-breadwinner economy. Soldiers became the link through which wives and children could access financial resources, food rations, and household materials. Married West African soldiers received a monthly premium of ten francs and their wives received the equivalent of half an active soldier's food ration. The flawed logic behind the tiered distribution of basic goods failed to recognize the productive and reproductive labor mesdames tirailleurs invested in maintaining Black Villages, their children, and troops.[69] This inadequate distribution system could have disastrous effects. In 1911, a French doctor reported that tirailleurs sénégalais' pitiful wages and insufficient rations could not nourish soldiers, let alone their dependents.[70]

Mesdames tirailleurs deployed strategies for survival within the conditions of Moroccan campaign. They engaged in entrepreneurial activities within the military community. They took on the laundering and cooking duties of unmarried soldiers, who compensated them for their work. The French military occasionally provided mesdames tirailleurs with store credit in nearby Moroccan markets.[71] With this limited contact with civilian populations, West African wives ran illicit enterprises like bootlegging and trafficking luxury goods. Military commanders prohibited tirailleurs sénégalais from consuming alcoholic beverages while on campaign in Morocco. Contrary to this embargo, mesdames tirailleurs purchased locally fermented beverages and resold them to tirailleurs sénégalais.[72] These activities allowed mesdames tirailleurs to persevere, but threatened military order. Intoxicated soldiers had greater inclination for insubordination. Local alcoholic beverages were often blended with adulterated liquor, which increased incidents of sickness for infantrymen.

Five years into the "pacification" of Morocco, the French military broached the topic of raising troops' rations of grains and salt in order to avoid any "regrettable incidents."[73] The colonial military courted charitable private donors in order to provide basic necessities for mesdames tirailleurs and their children. In French-language Moroccan newspapers, the French army solicited the benevolence of local, French-owned businesses in Morocco to contribute monetary donations to improve the conditions of West African wives.[74] Their advertisement stated that mesdames tirailleurs only accessed five francs per month for maintaining their families. Banks and other businesses responded by donating funds and by early May 1913 they had raised 22,140 francs for African military households in Morocco.[75] The distribution of these funds was not detailed in newspaper or military sources.

Insurmountable linguistic difference and cultural ignorance could explain French officials' and troops' general disregard for the basic welfare and health of mesdames tirailleurs and their children. When three tirailleurs sénégalais battalions deployed to the Chaouia region, their households remained in camp near Casablanca. With the chain of allocation and communication disrupted, roughly six hundred West African women and three hundred children soon lacked the basic necessities ordinarily passed on to them by their husbands.[76] Women and children lacked sufficient blankets and warm clothing. The military was slow to distribute necessary basic supplies to mesdames tirailleurs separated from their soldiering husbands.[77] Mesdames tirailleurs had difficulty accessing medical care. A medical report commented that it was "difficult, especially in the absence of their husbands, to appraise the health and hygiene of the Black Villages. Wives do not make timely requests for medical care." The report went on to blame mesdames tirailleurs for increased infant mortality rates.[78] The French military's standardization of mesdames tirailleurs' malnourishment likely reduced their fecundity and negatively affected their ability to carry pregnancies to term. Health consultations between male medical army staff and mesdames tirailleurs would have been replete with miscommunication, miscomprehension, and mistranslation.

Images and rhetoric from Moroccan conquest portrayed tirailleurs sénégalais' wives as the font of a new generation of colonial soldiers. Raising infants and toddlers in a politically hostile foreign warscape was no insignificant task.[79] Pediatric, obstetric, and gynecological specialists were not standard in the French colonial military's medical staff in early twentieth-century Morocco. French health professionals' lack of fluency in West African languages, healing, and reproductive practices created an exasperating chasm between mesdames tirailleurs and army medical officers. In the majority of French West Africa, obstetrics and midwifery were components of a constellation of esoteric knowledge largely entrusted to postmenopausal women. Midwives often gained their skills through apprenticeships with senior female relatives.[80] Pointedly, the French military did not bring West African female elders to Morocco in order to assist mesdames tirailleurs in childbirth. The military restricted mesdames tirailleurs' access to local Moroccan midwives. In their communities of origin, West African mothers would have relied on mutually dependent relationships with extended family members, other wives, and neighbors to aid them in raising their children. Childrearing included initiating children in the community through cultural rites and social education. This social instruction was absent, or nearly so, in North Africa.

Even though mesdames tirailleurs experienced great hardships in Morocco, the pool of women desiring to accompany enlisted men to North Africa surpassed the number awarded passage.[81] The French colonial army limited the number of women eligible to accompany soldiers to North Africa by establishing criteria, albeit flexible and inconsistently enforced, for marital legitimacy. This was an important innovation in tirailleurs sénégalais' marital traditions—military evaluation of African households' legitimacy prior to their departure for French imperial frontiers. French military officials attempted to decipher and culturally translate local marital customs to legitimize soldiers' conjugal unions. This would be quite a feat, considering the brevity of France's presence in inland West Africa and the number of marital traditions practiced by its disparate communities. A survey conducted in Guinea during the first decade of the twentieth century revealed great regional variation in communities' traditions related to marriage and divorce.[82] Despite this diversity and nuance, French colonial officials and military administrators made bridewealth the most salient determining factor for marital legitimacy.[83] The French focused on the monetary value of goods and services exchanged between marrying parties. They sidelined the complex negotiations and prenuptial rituals preceding a marriage. The military identified "enduring cohabitation" as another marker of legitimate marriage, but declined to attach a specific, requisite length of time necessary to determine durability.[84] These oversimplified and vague qualifications of marital legitimacy permitted mesdames tirailleurs and tirailleurs sénégalais to continue their conjugal relationships overseas irrespective of whether they conformed to West African communities' standards for marital legitimacy. Several French officials acknowledged that they could not know whether mesdames tirailleurs in Morocco were legitimate wives.[85] The North African campaigns of the early twentieth century were the final frontier for this kind of ambiguity regarding African military households' legitimacy.

In Morocco, there were significant changes to tirailleurs sénégalais' conjugal practices related to the incorporation of local women. The military discouraged contact between Moroccan civilian women and tirailleurs sénégalais. This proscription radically altered West African martial tradition—the military ceased to support African soldiers' acquisition of local conjugal partners from newly conquered populations. This policy quickly and effectively racialized African military households, as well as orienting them toward imperial racial order. West African women were the only female conjugal partners in Black Villages. In order to ensure that "racially appropriate" women completed tirailleurs sénégalais' households, the military used wifely accompaniment as recruitment and retention tools.[86] The French military also worked to unite families separated by military service. In 1911, Aissata Koné submitted a formal request to join her husband, Mamadou Coulibaly, who was serving in North Africa. Once Coulibaly confirmed his desire to have Koné and their two children with him on campaign, the

French military approved the request and made arrangements to expedite their reunification.[87]

Military officials north and south of the Sahara coordinated their energies and budgets in order to maintain soldiers' West African families in Morocco. Their efforts communicate a conviction that West African men were better soldiers when offered the opportunity to continue their family life on campaign. French officials continued to question the legitimacy of marital unions by shifting their scrutiny and criticisms onto mesdames tirailleurs' conjugal behavior in Morocco. French observers variously portrayed mesdames tirailleurs as steadfast committed wives and as promiscuous adulterers who could take advantage of their gender minority in the close quarters of the Black Villages and practice polyamory or polyandry. Casting aspersions on West African women's sexual and conjugal habits in Morocco occurred concurrently with conversations going on in French West Africa.[88] When a French officer in Morocco found it "difficult to distinguish the difference between married and single tirailleurs sénégalais because their type of marriage is informal and divorce is frequent," he tapped into the "mariage à la mode du pays" discourses as well as traditional assumptions about camp followers' and *vivandières*' flexible morals and marital ties.[89]

French colonial observers demeaned the moral character of mesdames tirailleurs when they highlighted incidents emphasizing mesdames tirailleurs' passionate and inherently uncontrollable nature. They did so in order to feminize and racialize unacceptable, disorderly conduct occurring within a militarized landscape. Significantly, West African women on Moroccan campaign were in a unique position because they belonged to tirailleurs sénégalais regiments but were not contractually bound to their discipline. Military expectations of obedience were not explained to wives through formal training or enforced through chain of command. The French military expected wives to act in accordance with military order because they provided mesdames tirailleurs' transportation, sustenance, and living quarters. These women had greater contact with Moroccan civilians because they acquired provisions for cooking, cleaning, and childrearing from local populations. They did not wear uniforms into Moroccan markets, which would have visibly communicated their official status as members of the tirailleurs sénégalais regiments. Yet they bore the physical characteristics of West African origins, which were inextricably tied with slave ancestry and newly linked to foreign occupation.

The dynamics of colonial conquest and the legacies of the slave trade weighed heavily upon mesdames tirailleurs' interactions with Moroccan civilians. French officials labeled the gendered and racial tensions between Moroccan and West African women as "primordial," which illustrated mesdames tirailleurs' hysterical, unbridled "nature." A dispute at a well in Zahiliga (a rural military post east of Casablanca) is a germane example of how French officials represented mesdames tirailleurs as unruly operatives who surrendered to their "primal" instincts when confronted by adversity. Pierre Khorat published the following account of an altercation in his *Scènes de la pacification marocaine*:

> Justly made impatient by the size of the queue, a Senegalese woman attempted to fill her water receptacle before her turn. The wife of a Moroccan colonial soldier vehemently protested. With calm insolence, the Senegalese woman wedged an enormous bowl under the water stream. "It's truly spiteful to monopolize the fountain," sniggered the Moroccan woman, "all that water won't make your skin white!" "What did you say?" gulped *madame sénégalais*. "It's true, I'm black, but my body and my clothes are clean. You can rub them and they won't change color. One couldn't say the same for you." The women chortled at one another.
>
> The Moroccan woman ostentatiously displayed the relative paleness of her face and her arms. Rendered furious by the mockery, the Senegalese woman dampened her scarf and with a firm hand rubbed her face and chest, and proudly displayed that the fabric had not altered in color. Then, leaping upon the Moroccan woman, she gripped her vigorously and roughly rubbed her down with the moist scarf. The face of her victim lightened under the rubbings, and suddenly the scarf's fabric grayed from the dirt that came off the Moroccan's face. Triumph on her side, the Senegalese woman had achieved her victory by routing her adversary, and with clenched fists and her neck swollen by the effort, she yelled: "Moroccans are savages!! Moroccans have dirty faces, dirty clothes, and are all dirty. If we were dirty like you, our husbands would beat us."[90]

Khorat heard about this incident secondhand and likely embellished the women's behavior in order to satirize them. This altercation could not have occurred in a language simultaneously comprehensible to French military agents, mesdames tirailleurs, and Moroccan women. The wholesale invention of this exchange for the purposes of substantiating French assumptions about racialized animosities between North and West Africans is a possibility. This is a staggering indictment of mesdames tirailleurs' behavior and illustrates French colonial anxieties about the operation and intersection of gender and race on Moroccan campaign.

In the verbal exchange, the two women traded insults that referenced and questioned sociocultural hierarchies drawn from the legacies of the trans-Saharan slave trade. Skin color and West African origins took pride of place in this dispute. The Moroccan woman wielded racial superiority by insinuating the West African woman needed to possess lighter skin in order to improve her social position. The madame tirailleur's response shifted the argument from physical characteristics to cleanliness. The madame tirailleur successfully shamed the Moroccan by publicly exposing her unwashed face, which had important connotations in Muslim societies regarding honor, virtuousness, respectability, and morality. The quarrel devolved into public shaming and physical abuse. According to the source, the conflict concluded with the intervention of French officers and tirailleurs sénégalais.

French military racial anxieties intersected with gendered conjugal concerns when West Africans affiliated with the French colonial army came into contact with Moroccans on and off the battlefield. Khorat's potentially allegorical tale emphasized that soldiers' wives from north and south of the Sahara could not suppress their innate mutual revulsion. Colonial officials presumed that the smallest pretext could easily lead to an "explosion" that required the intervention of their husbands.[91] Purportedly, African soldiers could keep the expression of these types of racial animosity in check. French observers believed that this restraint resulted from military training and the greater ability of men to control their emotional responses. These conclusions ignored the social controls that the French military had put in place prohibiting interracial sexual contact in Morocco. Khorat's observations about the "nature" of mesdames tirailleurs in Morocco failed to recognize that these West African women and their children suffered from social isolation, malnourishment, and overwork in a foreign war zone. The French military blamed the character of women for racialized violent encounters and conveniently absolved itself and tirailleurs sénégalais of any role in catalyzing or exacerbating these purportedly civilian adversarial conflicts.

The production of images and anecdotes about tirailleurs sénégalais' households on twentieth-century Moroccan campaign illustrate how French military officials participated in broader imperial discourses about the place of African military households in Moroccan history and French colonial order. They drew upon Alawi dynastic history, the legacies of the trans-Saharan slave trade, and twentieth-century Moroccan assumptions concerning race and social status in order to champion mesdames tirailleurs' and Black Villages' presence in the conquest of North Africa. The gendered and racial dynamics of the abid al-Bukhari and the tirailleurs sénégalais hinged upon the inclusion of West African women and diasporic African Moroccan women in state militaries. Tirailleurs sénégalais' marital traditions adapted to the racialized and gendered exigencies of Moroccan conquest. Mesdames tirailleurs acquired new symbolic significance as remedies to, and causes of, a range of racial, health, and environmental problems that African soldiers faced in Morocco. West African women and men played integral roles in completing the image of racially distinct, loyal, and obedient military forces in colonial modernity.

Charles Mangin's *La force noire* and the accompanying troupes noires debates convinced French administrators to invest in a permanent West African colonial fighting force. Even as officials lauded mesdames tirailleurs' presence in Morocco, the recruitment law of 1912 would reduce their numbers in Morocco. Quota-based conscription drastically altered the average age of new recruits in the tirailleurs sénégalais. Twenty-year-old unmarried men filled the ranks. Over the next few years, transoceanic steamships between West Africa and North Africa carried fewer and fewer mesdames tirailleurs. The Great War grounded mesdames tirailleurs in West Africa because they could not accompany troops deploying to mainland France. Their conjugal legitimacy came to depend on regimes of paper produced by increasingly complex colonial and military bureaucracies. After 1914, mesdames tirailleurs' work for the French colonial military as auxiliary combatants or domestics decreased. With the introduction of benefits and allocations to the wives of active soldiers, mesdames tirailleurs became the colonial military's indirect clients.

4

Domestic Affairs in the Great War

Legal Plurality, Citizenship, and Family Benefits, 1914–18

> The Sergeant-Major read a report. It was a bit long and we only understood two things: "Germany had declared war on France . . . and France has made a call to all of its children."
>
> —Bakary Diallo[1]

GERMANY'S DECLARATION OF WAR WITH FRANCE FOUND BAKARY Diallo in Casablanca, on leave and preparing to return to French West Africa after completing a tour in Morocco. In 1914, there were approximately seven battalions of West African troops serving in Morocco, two battalions of tirailleurs sénégalais in Algeria, and one battalion in Madagascar.[2] Germany's declaration of war prompted the French military to relocate tirailleurs sénégalais from African Empire to mainland France. Compared to West Africans' previous participation in colonial conflicts, their mobilization for World War I differed in size and scope. Over the next four years, France mobilized 170,000 sub-Saharan Africans toward the war effort. Conspicuously, mesdames tirailleurs remained in West Africa. Soldiers' households fragmented across French Empire and their conjugal traditions evolved to accommodate long-term and long-distance spousal separation. During the Great War, soldiers' marital legitimacy increasingly became a matter for the

Legal Plurality, Citizenship, and Family Benefits, 1914–18

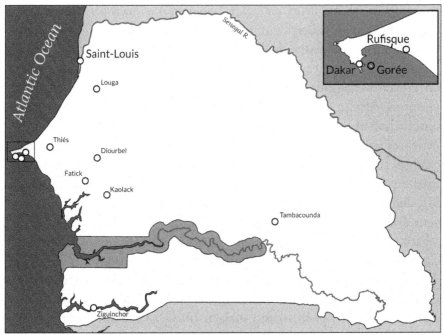

MAP 4.1. Four Communes of Senegal. Map by Isaac Barry

colonial state. The French military formalized its relationship with tirailleurs sénégalais' households through regimes of paper and the regular distribution of allocations to wives in West Africa—making soldier/husbands legally necessary, but no longer requiring their immediate proximity.

The men serving in the tirailleurs sénégalais came from all over French West Africa, which was a colonial federation administered by France. Career soldiers and veterans of the conquest and occupation of French Africa made up the early levies of troops for the war effort. As the conflict deepened into 1915, younger, conscripted recruits shipped out to mainland France. Introduced in 1912, quota-based conscription had provided France with a stable military population in French West Africa. During the war, the institutions and mechanisms of military conscription provided the means to raise 170,000 soldiers—and demonstrate the power of the colonial state over West African women and men.[3] The demographic makeup of the tirailleurs sénégalais expanded and Bamanakan and Malinké from Upper Senegal, Upper Volta, French Guinea, and Côte d'Ivoire came to dominate the ranks of the tirailleurs sénégalais.[4] Soldiers' conjugal partners mirrored these demographic shifts.

There is an extensive body of academic work that examines the actions and consequences of tirailleurs sénégalais' wartime activities, on and off French battlefields.[5] The Great War was a time of reversals and juxtapositions. African colonial subjects interacted with and captured the racial imagination of people in mainland France.[6] African military households' experiences of the war occurred predominantly in West Africa, where policy changes concerning military service, citizenship, and marriage altered the lived experiences of soldiers' family members on the home front. The laws of 1915 and 1916 pushed through the French National Assembly by Blaise Diagne disambiguated French West African citizens and subjects. They created separate sets of military service obligations and compensations for soldiers.[7] These laws further entrenched the legal pluralisms introduced to French West Africa in 1903 with the reorganization of the justice system and the creation of separate sets of laws to organize the civil affairs of French West African citizens (*originaires*) and subjects (*indigènes*). Adding to the confusion, the French military had some jurisdiction over the marital affairs of their active soldiers because of their fiscal obligations—in the form of allocations and tax abatements/exemptions—to soldiers' legitimate households. The military and civilian administrations relied on each other to confirm the legitimacy of active soldiers' wives, which led their agents to think creatively about how to support multiwife military households—whether citizens or subjects.

The Great War heralded the French state's intensified interest in, and regulation of, soldiers' wives' marital legitimacy. Many couples were unable to formalize their unions with the military/state prior to new recruits' departure for France. Military service truncated or delayed young men's marital ambitions. For those who had completed some premarital rites—like bridewealth payments or labor obligations—the war interrupted the formalization of their households. As new enlistees relocated from their villages to regional military camps and/or port cities, their conjugal households often followed them. Cities like Saint-Louis and Dakar were wives' last stop because tirailleurs sénégalais became an all-male fighting force when they deployed to Western Europe. Female conjugal partners created encampments adjacent to military spaces. For the first time in the historical record related to African military households, military and civilian authorities portrayed mesdames tirailleurs as expendable liabilities. The formalization of marital and citizenship status opened up new means for the state to discriminate against the conjugal partners of tirailleurs sénégalais. Coincidentally, these processes also opened up the colonial state to new claims of affiliation, obligation, and clientage from members of African military households.

LEGISLATING FRENCH AFRICAN CITIZENS AND SUBJECTS

Legislation introduced to West Africa at the turn of the twentieth century greatly impacted the military's management of tirailleurs sénégalais' households during the Great War. In the mid-1890s, the Ministry of Colonies formally established French West Africa as a governable unit and began a decade-long effort to wrest control of the region from the French military. Many military officials remained in high governmental positions across French West Africa after civilian rule began in 1904–5. Governors-General Ernest Roume (1902–7) and William Ponty (1908–15) presided over the establishment and entrenchment of plural legal regimes that bifurcated along the citizenship status of people residing in French West Africa.[8] In 1903, Roume reorganized the administration of justice in order to assure that colonial subjects could maintain their local customs without contradicting French principles of humanity and civilization.[9] Most issues related to marriage—legitimacy, spousal abuse/neglect, child custody, divorce—fell within customary law and under the jurisdiction of native tribunals, which were subject to the oversight of French agents and their local intermediaries. For enlisted men, questions related to marital legitimacy also came under the purview of the colonial military, which retained authority over the mobility of soldiers' wives and the allocation of benefits to soldiers' households.

Two key pieces of legislation in 1912 affected the ways in which military service, citizenship, and martial custom dynamically coalesced during the Great War. Referenced briefly in the previous chapter, Lieutenant Colonel Charles Mangin's 1912 Recruitment Law introduced quota-based conscription to French West Africa in order to establish a "black reservoir" of soldiers for French military needs.[10] This law increased West Africans' obligations to the French imperial state, while redefining and standardizing the state's compensation to soldiers and their dependents. Physically sound men between the ages of twenty and forty could expect to serve in the French colonial military for three years, with a requisite deployment outside of French West Africa. The law created enlistment bonuses and other fiscal incentives for soldiers to volunteer for service. Volunteer tirailleurs sénégalais served longer initial tours of duty than conscripted soldiers. This legislation profoundly affected French colonial subjects, or indigènes, who made up the majority of French West Africa and the tirailleurs sénégalais. At the time of its introduction, it was unclear how this recruitment law affected a minority population in French West Africa—the originaires or French West African citizens of coastal Senegal.[11]

Another important legal change came in August of 1912, when Governor-General William Ponty revamped the legal system in French West Africa to subject all West Africans to the jurisdiction of native courts and defined French African citizens as those who had completed the formal process of naturalization. This second legal change affected originaires' citizenship status and West African soldiers' households. A brief history on the originaires explains why. In 1848, the Second French Republic abolished slavery and extended voting rights to male inhabitants of Saint-Louis and Gorée—French coastal enclaves on the Senegambian coast. These islands were once key entrepôts in French Atlantic commerce and their inhabitants had participated in French political and legal institutions to varying degrees since the French Revolution.[12] In 1872, these West African island communities accessed the same rights as mainland French communities, which was taken by many to mean French citizenship. By 1887, those residing in Dakar and Rufisque acquired the same status. These four coastal enclaves became known as the "quatre communes de plein exercise," or four communes endowed with fully exercisable rights. Their inhabitants became known as the "originaires" of the Four Communes.

There were some notable differences among the responsibilities and obligations that originaires and mainland French citizens owed the state. Unlike mainland French citizens, adult male originaires were not required to serve in the French military. They also possessed anomalous civic rights that allowed them to practice polygyny, subscribe to sharia, and use Muslim courts.[13] Male originaires' singular set of civic privileges was protected by their *statut personnel*, or personal status. This exclusive status had come into existence during Louis Faidherbe's tenure as governor of Senegal. The statut personnel entitled Muslim originaires to live in accordance with the legal and familial customs of Islam. Originaires' statut personnel directly conflicted with the French Civil Code of the Third Republic, which defined the French state as secular and required French citizens to practice monogamy. Although nineteenth-century colonial rhetoric extolled the virtues of assimilation, the French imperial state sanctioned its West African originaires to engage in plural legal and cultural practices that contravened the principle of universal, secular French citizenship.[14] Remarkably, Muslim originaires secured rights that were not extended to Muslim Algerians.[15] Originaires' civic rights contravened French civil law and were exceptional within French metropolitan and imperial juridical practice.

Ponty's revision of the legal system in 1912 undermined originaires' citizenship status, which many had assumed was their birthright. He also "challenged the privileged status of originaires as 'citizens'" because originaires could henceforth be tried in native courts if residing or traveling outside of the territorial limits of the Four Communes.[16] Originaires reacted strongly. By late 1913, originaires began to politically mobilize against legislative challenges to their citizenship status and unique civic privileges. During the previous half century, Bordeaux businessmen and *métis*, or mixed-race, politicians in Saint-Louis had dominated electoral campaigns in the Four Communes. Rumors circulated in Senegal that an African candidate would run for the Four Communes' seat in the upcoming French National Assembly elections. Blaise Diagne, born on Gorée and a veteran of imperial colonial service, campaigned on a political platform centered on protecting originaires' exceptional legal status and expanding rights for all West Africans. Originaires hoped that Diagne would convince the National Assembly to link originaires' citizenship with mandatory military service in the French metropolitan army, while simultaneously protecting their unique civic rights.[17] With this platform, Diagne beat the incumbent with a record turnout of new voters.

Fortuitously, Diagne took his seat at the French National Assembly four months prior to the outbreak of war in 1914. Diagne manipulated France's need for greater manpower and the high absenteeism in the National Assembly during the war to ratify bills that protected originaires' rights, citizenship, and statut personnel. He argued in the National Assembly that if the French government granted originaires inalienable citizenship in unambiguous language, then male originaires would become obligated to serve in the French military upon reaching twenty years of age. The Diagne-proposed laws of October 19, 1915, and September 29, 1916, tethered male originaires' citizenship to obligatory military service, guaranteeing them enfranchisement, educational opportunities, and civil rights. The 1916 law unambiguously stated, "The natives of the Four Communes of Senegal and their descendants are, and will remain, French citizens obligated to the military duties previously defined in the law of October 15, 1915."[18] The 1915 law had awarded French citizenship to originaires according to birthplace (*jus solis*). The 1916 law extended this legal status to their descendants (*jus sanguinis*) regardless of their place of birth.

Both the legislation itself and the historiography related to the Diagne laws neglect women. It is unclear how female originaires exercised the rights of French citizenship in the Four Communes.[19] They did not serve in the French military. They did not vote in elections, as women in mainland France were not universally enfranchised until 1946. Originaire women became the conveyors of male citizenship and military service, passing these rights and obligations from their husbands to their sons. Active soldiers wrote constantly of potential future wives, familial relations, and gossip related to romantic liaisons.[20] Female originaires felt the onus of military service as their husbands, brothers, and sons deployed to mainland France. Citizenship status combined with the statut personnel to shape the ways in which the French military managed originaires soldiers' households during the Great War. As I will demonstrate below, originaires' conjugal partners experienced the discriminating attentions of the military and civilian administrations in new ways during the war.

The Blaise Diagne legislation sharpened differences between West African citizens and subjects, as well as making originaires' privileges more pronounced in and outside of the military.[21] The first law, ratified in 1915, removed active originaire soldiers (who had been serving as volunteers) from the tirailleurs sénégalais and transferred them to the mainland branch of the French armed forces. West African colonial subjects continued serving in the colonial army under the communal title of tirailleurs sénégalais. Diagne failed to win comparable fiscal and political concessions for tirailleurs sénégalais during the Great War. French administrators commented on this failure and cast the Diagne legislation as discriminatory against West African colonial subjects. Critics of the Blaise Diagne laws claimed they negated

French Republican values of egalitarianism. Ironically, the use of egalitarianism in this case meant that critics believed all West Africans should share the same status—making them equal in their inequality to mainland French citizens. The legislation discriminately awarded political and civil rights to a minority population coincidently born in the Four Communes or descended from their residents. In 1915, Governor-General François Joseph Clozel of French West Africa claimed it paradoxical to enfranchise men born in the Four Communes, while the aristocratic sons of indigenous African elites remained indigènes and colonial subjects. Further, Clozel warned against crafty or criminal colonial subjects who would take advantage of the exceptional legal regimes governing citizenship in the Four Communes. For instance, a pregnant indigène woman from French Guinea or Côte d'Ivoire, brought to Dakar or Saint-Louis for the prosecution of a crime, could give birth during trial and her offspring would, ipso facto, have French citizenship.[22]

After the 1915 and 1916 Blaise Diagne laws, protests arose in the colonial administration as the onus of locating and enlisting eligible originaire soldiers fell on military and administrative employees in French West Africa. Not all originaires were aware of their new duty and many did not come forward voluntarily to serve in the trenches of World War I. Determining who was and who was not an eligible soldier required an examination of erroneous and incomplete colonial administrative records. The Diagne laws necessitated a heavier reliance on birth and marriage certificates, which exposed systemic fraud, malfeasance, and clerical errors in the Four Communes civil records.[23] French officials wading into this bureaucratic disarray blamed West African civil servants for allowing inaccurate recordkeeping to become custom.[24] West Africans in French employment understood the limits of French authority over their individual actions as functionaries of the imperial state.[25] Civil servants were susceptible to giving and receiving favors, which fell in line with practices of accumulating social capital and resources in patron-client relationships. These types of relationships were widespread across West Africa, but this was not a universal practice among West African civil servants. These agents had a great deal of power in collecting and corroborating information within the French West African colonial administration—and many of them were originaires. In order to curb malfeasance and corruption on the part of West African employees, a military official proposed rescinding the plenipotentiary powers that France had allotted to West African intermediaries, particularly the judges serving in the Muslim tribunals in Saint-Louis. Lieutenant-Governor Gabriel Angoulvant took a hard-line stance against the Muslim tribunals due to the findings of an official inquiry in 1916. A French military officer found that the judges had accepted bribes to falsify important civil documents and that many were unqualified to serve as judges.[26]

Irregular, incomplete, or missing documentation impeded military officials' ability to locate newly obligated originaires recruits. On Gorée in 1915 and 1916, there were at least thirty-six complex military cases involving the enlistment of originaires.[27] Many "errors," like inaccurate names or birth places/dates, in civil records represented spaces in which originaire men could maneuver and manipulate new protocols pertaining to military service. Shortly after the ratification of the 1915 law, the French military publicly posted the names of male originaires in the Four Communes who were required to report for duty. The Lieutenant-governor of Senegal, Raphaël Antonetti, predicted that of the nine thousand names listed on the recruitment rolls, perhaps fifteen hundred would be found.[28] He estimated that three-quarters of the residents in Saint-Louis, the most populous of the Four Communes, practiced name-switching. Some officials regarded name-switching as an evasive tactic on the part of originaires to avoid their new military obligations. West Africans often went by names that were not on their civil documents or chose new names when they entered the colonial state's official record—like at the moment of enlistment.[29] West African name-switching was another point of slippage between French bureaucratic practice and African social norms. This disjuncture created problems in recruitment drives and the allocation of resources to African military households on the West African home front.

Unauthorized recruit substitution hindered the military's levying and training of originaire troops. Illicit recruit substitution demonstrates how families and local authorities managed the burden of conscription with their own familial priorities. In the post-1915 enlistment process, the example of Malick N'Diaye exposed layers of fraud and forgery, as well as the lengths to which originaire families went to protect their sons from service in the Great War. In the egregious abuse of a minor, the family of Malick N'Diaye presented a fourteen-year-old youth, by the name of Amadou Mery, to a recruitment board in the place of Malick N'Diaye. N'Diaye, according to the presented birth certificate, was twenty-eight years old at the time of his enlistment in January 1916. The military medical staff examining Amadou Mery (posing as Malick N'Diaye) found physical evidence of the recruit's adolescence. When questioned, members of the N'Diaye family asserted that the male youth was twenty-eight years old. The N'Diaye family convinced medical practitioners, via means outside of the historical record, that a fourteen-year-old boy was a man twice his age. This case of recruitment substitution came to light because Amadou Mery found training too physically challenging and divulged his true age to his drill sergeant. He was discharged from the military.

Mery was too young for military service. There were other factors that could have disqualified him from military service as a French citizen in early 1916. His father was an originaire, but Mery was born to his father's second wife outside of the Four Communes.[30] In early 1916, it was unclear if French citizenship, and by extension obligatory military service, extended across originaires' multiwife households because they did not conform to French norms. Further, Mery's birth outside of the Four Communes made him eligible for service in the tirailleurs sénégalais. This example demonstrates that the universal conscription of male originaires (between the ages of twenty and forty) conflicted with N'Diaye familial prerogatives. From the viewpoint of most African communities, household heads and community leaders made collective decisions regarding which member of a family was most appropriate for military service. Mery had likely been coerced by his extended family members to take Malick N'Diaye's place in the military. Importantly, the Malick N'Diaye/Amadou Mery case occurred in the gap between the 1915 and 1916 Blaise Diagne laws. The second law extended originaire status to the descendants of originaires, irrespective of birthplace. After September 1916, Mery would have been obliged to French military service when he came of age.

The military acted as though originaires' status was inheritable patrilineally and matrilineally. After 1916, the state also traced it patrilineally through multiwife households. The 1915 and 1916 laws were retroactive, which meant that there were many new originaires and the men among them were required to provide the French with military service.[31] The French colonial government and military administration waded deeper into inchoate civil records to locate these men. The governor-general of French

West Africa estimated that there were at least five hundred originaires living outside of the Four Communes in Senegal, a thousand in Upper-Senegal-Niger, sixty in French Guinea, twenty-five in Côte d'Ivoire, ten in Dahomey, six in Niger, and ten in Mauritania.[32] Military and civilian officials relied on traditional leaders to produce these missing recruits. Recruitment agents depended on local communities' knowledge of originaires' whereabouts, due to the dearth of civil records outside of the Four Communes. This opened a wider space for maneuvering on the part of originaires living outside of the Four Communes. The multiple layers of interlocutors and intermediaries controlled knowledge regarding birth, residence, age, physical appearance, and names. Protective webs of contradictory or concealed information enabled originaires to escape military service. Originaires also resided in neighboring, non-French colonial territories. The French were forced to rely on their imperial competitors—Britain and Portugal—to assist them in locating originaires living in Guinea-Bissau, Gambia, Sierra Leone, Gold Coast, and Nigeria.

The Blaise Diagne laws strengthened originaires' statut personnel in the realm of marriage, which elicited French military criticism of the legitimacy of originaire soldiers' households. The lieutenant-governor of Senegal estimated that only 2 to 3 percent of originaires' marriages met the stipulations of the French Civil Code.[33] The military had little alternative but to condone originaires' polygynous marital practices. Ultimately, it was to the French Army's advantage to support originaires' polygynous practices because multiwife households meant more future soldiers. If originaire soldiers were married, most of them had celebrated their union through Muslim or customary practices. Local decrees and the French Civil Code often contradicted one another over polygynous families' rights. The coexistence of three legal systems in West Africa—French law, sharia, and customary law—provided originaire soldiers and French officials with latitude in managing marital legitimacy and distributing funds to soldiers' polygynous households. No standardized procedures existed for recognizing multiwife households or for regulating the distribution of the military's family allocations to more than one wife.

Originaire soldiers and their wives were newly emboldened clients of the French military. The women of these households ensured that the French state made good on its obligations to the wives of these citizen-soldiers.

French African citizens' wives were entitled to the same allocations and advantages as mainland French soldiers' wives. Originaire soldiers and members of their households prevailed upon officials to sanction and safeguard their polygynous practices. Surprisingly, some civilian and military administrators would go to great lengths to acknowledge and accommodate originaires' polygynous households. French military officials became entangled in the intimate affairs of French African citizens due to irreconcilable household disputes related to family allocations. While unwelcome by most, originaires' polygynous households took advantage of this new, pronounced military presence in their lives. State acknowledgement of legitimate marriage—monogamous or polygynous—increased their access to family benefits. Armed with vague standards for marital legitimacy—bridewealth and enduring cohabitation—French military agents plodded into the arena of originaire soldiers' households' domestic issues.

Military agents negotiated between parallel legal systems in order to approximate equitable distribution of resources to multiwife households of active originaire soldiers. The fixed allocation for originaires' wives was thirty-seven francs and fifty centimes per month—more than double the amount dispensed to wives of tirailleurs sénégalais. The resources distributed to African women were worth proportionately more than the allocations accorded to the wives of mainland French soldiers. Due to price differentials in basic goods and living standards, originaires' wives had greater purchasing power in West Africa than mainland wives had in wartime France.[34] Military and civilian officials could not reduce benefits dispensed to originaires' wives, but they attempted to regulate, standardize, and redesign the system through which these funds were disbursed. This impulse also entangled them in domestic conflicts far beyond the purview and comprehension of the state. In response to these incursions into their private lives, originaires framed their marital problems through the misappropriation and irregular distribution of family allocations. In doing so, originaire soldiers induced agents of the colonial state to settle their domestic affairs in their absence. Once involved, these representatives found themselves parsing Muslim and customary laws related to marital legitimacy and social ranking among wives in polygynous households.

West African officials offered a collection of proposals regarding how to allocate funds to originaires' wives. Governor-General Clozel weighed in to assert that only one wife of polygynous French African citizens should receive the family allocation and he suggested that originaire soldiers should choose which wife could collect the allowance from the military.[35] Significantly, his suggestion contravened Islamic prescriptions regarding equal treatment of each wife in a polygynous household. Clozel further suggested that originaires' children, irrespective of their mother's rank, should receive the fifty-centime supplements guaranteed to them.[36] In this scenario, the military would protect children fathered by originaire soldiers and deny funds to the mothers of these children. Ironically, this suggestion would monetize and make more visible the imperial state's connection with French African citizens' children—children that the French Civil Code would have deemed illegitimate. This proposal contravened previous military practice, in which breadwinner models emphasized the legitimacy of first wives and their integral role in household maintenance. Clozel's suggestion did not become law. The fiscal values and proportions of resources allocated to originaires' multiwife households remained contested and irregular into the interwar period.[37]

During World War I, French legislators could modify the amount and means of allocations for originaires' multiwife households. The example of Ali N'Diaye's household demonstrates how members of polygynous originaire soldiers' families could take advantage of the French military's irregular policies for managing family allocations.[38] Ali N'Diaye was born in Saint-Louis. His first wife was Bineta Gueye. His second, Makhoni N'Diaye, gave birth to their daughter in early 1917. According to the French military's understanding of local custom, the senior wife in a multiwife household retained the lion's share of authority and responsibility in that household, particularly in the absence of the husband. The French military awarded Bineta Gueye all of Ali N'Diaye's family allocation. According to the common social prescription of wives' rank, Gueye should have distributed some of the allocation to Makhoni N'Diaye and her infant daughter. In an ideal situation, Ali N'Diaye would have been present or relied on extended kin to address this inequity. Since he was overseas and the French military distributed the allocation meant to sustain his family in his absence, N'Diaye relied on colonial agents to intervene. N'Diaye framed his senior wife's transgressive behavior as a resource distribution error that could be resolved by modifying the military's means of dispensing family allocations. After an official inquest, a French military commission decided that Ali N'Diaye's allocation would be split equally between the two wives, who would each collect eighteen francs and seventy-five centimes per month.[39] This verdict revealed the degree to which the French military seriously considered originaire soldiers' requests for assistance in supporting their polygynous households.

The result differed when the wives of originaire soldier Seïdou Saar appealed to the French administration in Senegal to resolve a quarrel concerning the apportionment of Saar's family allocation. Both of his wives, Binta Saar and Fatou Diouf, felt entitled to receive resources from the state while their husband was stationed in France. Archival evidence suggests that Fatou Diouf recognized her subordinate position as second wife, but argued that it did not preclude her from collecting part of the family allocation. In order to adjudicate this case, the attorney general of French West Africa sifted through legal precedent in local West African decrees, the French Civil Code, and military legislation. Curiously, he did not consult traditional law or sharia, which would have shed some light on polygynous originaires' social and marital practices. In accordance with French colonial West African legal precedent, the attorney general concluded that if the French state sanctioned Seïdou Saar's marriages, then the French military should evenly split Saar's family allocation between Binta Saar and Fatou Diouf.[40] Ultimately, his decision was not implemented because further inquiries found that neither woman had been married to Seïdou Saar according to French, Muslim, or customary practice. Since Binta Saar was residing in Seïdou Saar's home at the time of the inquiry, she became the sole recipient of Saar's family allocation due to evidence of cohabitation.[41]

The Ali N'Diaye and Seïdou Saar households illustrate the high stakes and unpredictable outcomes resulting from the direct involvement of French officials in polygynous originaires' household allocations. The Blaise Diagne laws protected originaires' citizenship status and statut personnel, while compelling French African male citizens to serve in the French military. The French military adjusted their marital traditions to accommodate originaires' legitimate multiwife families. Military and civilian officials collaborated to interpret plural legal traditions in order to guarantee family benefits to originaire soldiers' wives. Citizenship was a key factor in bifurcating military conjugal traditions in French West Africa during the Great War. The exceptions won by originaires were not extended to indigènes. During the war, tirailleurs sénégalais' households bore the discriminatory burden of the difference between citizen and subject.

INDIGÈNES, DISCRIMINATION, AND MARITAL RESOLUTIONS

The Blaise Diagne legislation created new, distinct pathways for West African men serving in the French armed forces. Originaires served alongside mainland French troops and indigènes continued to populate the ranks of the tirailleurs sénégalais. Despite his initial aims, Blaise Diagne was ultimately unable to extend greater benefits to men serving in the tirailleurs sénégalais. After 1916, the designation "indigène" replaced "militaire" in tirailleurs sénégalais' military passbooks, which clearly indicated their subject status and their exclusion from the benefits of French citizenship.[42] Veterans of the tirailleurs sénégalais, from the Great War to contemporary times, expressed bitter and bemused opposition to the tangible inequities ushered in with this division.[43] These inequalities directly affected their households' welfare. The French military rarely recognized the existence of tirailleurs sénégalais' wives beyond the first wife.[44] First wives were the unique recipients of military benefits, which differed in scope and scale when compared to originaires' wives' benefits. Most young indigène recruits were not informed of their rights to familial allocations or of the processes required to register their marriages and children with the colonial state and/or military. This was an issue of French language literacy, as well as of the arbitrary and discriminatory way that the colonial government and military treated colonial subjects. The state's reliance on rural intermediaries (*commandants de cercles* and *chefs de cantons*) in the recruitment of soldiers and the distribution of family allocations added a partisan layer of bureaucracy between soldiers' wives and the military's treasury. Colonial subjects were the overwhelming majority of West Africans who served in the French armed forces during the Great War. Their households' adverse experiences of the military's welfare were more ubiquitous, yet less evident in the historical record.

This legal distinction between mobilized originaires and indigènes affected how their conjugal partners interacted with and benefited from the French military and civilian colonial state. Tirailleurs sénégalais did not have the legal and civic protections guaranteed to originaires. Across the citizenship divide, African military households obtained different fiscal rewards through separate administrative channels. During the war, originaires' families received 1.25 francs per day and an additional fifty centimes for each child under the age of sixteen. The amounts allocated to tirailleurs sénégalais' families were much less, which circumscribed their wives' spending power, political leverage, and social status. The colonial state allocated fifteen francs per month to indigènes' wives—and only if their husbands deployed outside of French West Africa.[45] Colonial subjects' families could access tax abatements and other benefits, like emergency assistance for needy families. Wartime recruits often selected older male relatives or their mothers as beneficiaries of military/state welfare. They designated members of their families to be responsible for the consumption and redistribution of their allocations, which followed patriarchal, matriarchal, and gerontocratic traditions of power and responsibility in West Africa.

Tens of thousands of tirailleurs sénégalais served in the Great War, which corresponded to a large number of indigène wives in need of allocations. Their disproportionate appearance in the archival record could indicate that the colonial state often failed to distribute benefits to households living in rural villages. Allocations were withheld from tirailleurs sénégalais' wives and children if the state lacked the formal evidence to recognize their legitimate standing. Agents of the colonial state advocated for systems of resource distribution that discriminated against the wives of tirailleurs sénégalais. The governor-general called for flexibility in designating recipients of allocations in order to accommodate local custom, which allowed new recruits or commandants de cercle to identify beneficiaries among soldiers' extended relations.[46] This system may have accommodated local management of tirailleurs sénégalais' benefits, but it also facilitated discriminatory practices against soldiers' wives and children. In the examples of the N'Diaye and Saar originaire households above, female conjugal partners directly accessed funds allocated by the state. Outside of the Four Communes, the state viewed soldiers' wives as gendered minors. Local gerontocratic and patriarchal authorities acted as tirailleurs sénégalais' wives' custodians. Acting as intermediaries, they collected and withheld family benefits from their targeted population. By allowing this process to occur, the colonial state disempowered tirailleurs sénégalais' wives and accommodated what civilian administrators perceived as patriarchal and communal authority over West African women.

During the Great War, tirailleurs sénégalais' wives appeared in the colonial archives as troubled and troublesome figures. Long-term and long-distance separation were difficult to endure because the military failed to convey timely news concerning the whereabouts, health, or death of tirailleurs sénégalais serving in France. The absence of husbands and the inconsistent allocation of family benefits to military households influenced wives to locate other sources of affection and income. Some wives of tirailleurs sénégalais sought new conjugal partners. The French colonial military tolerated tirailleurs sénégalais' polygyny by bureaucratically ignoring its existence and choosing not to support wives subsequent to the first wife. However, the military would not accept the polyamory or polyandry practiced by soldiers' wives. The French colonial military policed tirailleurs sénégalais' wives' sexuality and invalidated wives' new conjugal relationships, which appear in the historical record as "illegal" remarriages and "illegal" divorces.

"Illegal" remarriages described conjugal arrangements in which tirailleurs sénégalais' wives sought new conjugal partners during their husband's period of deployment in Europe. Many West African indigène military wives received no information regarding the whereabouts or status of their husbands for years during the war. Many assumed that their husbands were unlikely to return to West Africa. Their "illegal" remarriages were strategies to secure affection as well as to improve their social and financial security. Historical documents construed these women as bigamous, unpatriotic, and capricious. The lieutenant-governor from Zinder stridently called for the expansion of military authority in Niger in order to prevent the wives of tirailleurs sénégalais from living with other men, specifically other unmarried tirailleurs sénégalais stationed in West Africa.[47] Due to the number of "illegal" remarriages, Governor-General Joost van Hollenhoven made a general declaration on 27 April 1918 that made remarriage illegal for the wives of tirailleurs sénégalais unless they possessed an official death notice for their husbands.[48] His declaration fortified the power of absentee husbands over their home-front conjugal partners. This is evident in the case of Sergeant Mamadou Bâ. At the war's end, Bâ was convalescing in Menton, France. He had had little contact with his wife since he had left Dakar several years earlier. His wife, Aissatou N'Diaye, wrote to him from Dakar in August of 1918 to inform him that she had married another man.[49] Sergeant Bâ's response was not addressed to his wife. Instead, he wrote to a French military official in French West Africa. He claimed that his wife had committed an act of injustice and implored the colonial army to intervene on his behalf. They were willing.

The documents surrounding Bâ's case illuminate the military's patriarchal authority in policing wives' conjugal fidelity and monogamy, as well as the dangers affiliated with opening up their intimate affairs to military scrutiny. The military agents were not benevolent actors and their investigations could lead to undesired or unanticipated outcomes. Ultimately, the French military discovered that Sergeant Bâ and Aissatou N'Diaye had never legitimated their conjugal union. She had moved into his domicile roughly six months prior to his departure for France in 1916, which meant that she could be recognized as Bâ's wife through the stipulation of cohabitation. Since Bâ's deployment, N'Diaye had collected fifteen francs per month from the French military. Between 1916 and 1917, Aissatou N'Diaye moved in with a day laborer, Bilaly Diallo, who had given her sixty francs in bridewealth. Although she received allocations from the French military for her marriage to Bâ, Aissatou N'Diaye was more likely to be viewed by the French colonial state as married to Diallo since their union met marital traditions of cohabitation and exchanged bridewealth.[50] As of 27 January 1919, N'Diaye no longer lived with Diallo and had returned his bridewealth.[51] Bâ's request made its way up the chain of the colonial administration at a time in which the minister of the colonies reinforced van Hollenhoven's April declaration.[52] His decision took husbands' prerogatives a step further and robbed wives of the ability to petition for divorce.

During the Great War, the French colonial military forbid "illegal" divorces. In this case, illegal meant undesirable. The sanctity of matrimony became a matter of troop morale and served as justification for the military, in coordination with the civilian administration, to impede soldiers' wives' ability to divorce their husbands. The military's direct intervention in these conjugal matters contravened French West African legislation that had ceded jurisdiction over marriage and divorce to customary courts in 1903. The military was not unique in deploying its extrajudicial authority to preside over its employees' divorces, but French military officials were exceptional in how they eschewed military conjugal traditions, sharia, French Civil Code, and West African custom.[53] The military aimed to preserve African military households, but coincidentally undermined the colonial state's efforts to protect the prerogatives of gerontocratic power in West Africa. Officials strengthened the husbandly authority of young, male soldiers and reduced the power of religious and elders' authority within their communities.[54]

Prior to World War I, tirailleurs sénégalais' divorces rarely showed up in the military historical record. During the first two decades of the twentieth century, women initiated a large number of divorce cases in colonial West Africa. West African women, especially the enslaved and formerly enslaved, used colonial courts to leave their masters, former masters, or bad marriages.[55] Divorce was common in West Africa, particularly for urban Muslims.[56] Women seeking divorce in sharia courts were granted divorce fairly regularly if they presented proof of impotence, abuse, neglect, or their husbands' absence for more than four years.[57] The duration of tirailleurs sénégalais' tours of duty in wartime France and the limitations of communication in the 1910s could substantiate claims to neglect and prolonged absence. Divorce was a tool to leave marriages with active-duty tirailleurs sénégalais, as well as a tool to leave civilian husbands to marry tirailleurs sénégalais.[58] When the military became involved in soldiers' wives' attempts to divorce, military exigency superseded the needs of female conjugal partners. Military efforts to maintain African military households dovetailed with the civilian administration's prohibition of female desertion of the conjugal home.[59]

Military and civilian officials moved the goalposts around divorce throughout the Great War. In 1915, the attorney general of French West Africa announced that in the absence of both members of a marital union, local representatives vested with colonial authority—like village chiefs and Muslim tribunals—could grant divorces between tirailleurs sénégalais and their wives.[60] The response from lieutenant-governors across French West Africa was fast and furious. They predicted that divorce in absentia could create complex bureaucratic problems, which prompted several among them to call for legislation to outlaw divorce for wives of tirailleurs sénégalais.[61] These administrators construed the home-front wives of West African servicemen as self-serving and unfaithful.[62] Financial and social security may have been a motivation for some women to seek divorce from their deployed soldier/ husbands. In the absence of news, many wives probably guessed that their husbands were among the large number of unreported deceased or missing West African soldiers. These women took it upon themselves to initiate divorce or new conjugal relationships.

During the war, the French military took on the role of arbitrating cases of divorce among African military households. Officials referenced a range of marital traditions to assess whether divorces should occur, but they were nearly unanimous in recognizing bridewealth reimbursement as a condition of legal divorce.[63] In one case, the military used bridewealth reimbursement to reprimand a tirailleur sénégalais petty officer's household negligence. Sergeant Biram Sakho and his wife Anttia Cissé were divorcing in early October of 1918. Representatives of the French military stepped in to regulate Cissé's return of 1,110 francs of bridewealth to Sergeant Sakho. Cissé claimed that she should have received family allowances from the military during Sakho's tours of duty. She maintained that Sakho had withheld the majority of these funds from her, which detrimentally affected their child. Cissé received only 90 of the 870 francs allocated to her by the French military, which meant that her husband had retained or directed these funds elsewhere. The French administration took Cissé's claim into consideration and required her to return only 320 francs of her bridewealth, which allowed her to retain 780 francs in compensation for her husband's fraudulent behavior.[64] This case illuminates that by the Great War, the military recognized conjugal military partners as nuclear households. They were the only stakeholders that the military dealt with in marital and child custody disputes. The direct reimbursement of bridewealth to a wife, as opposed to her kin, is either oversight or indifference on the part of the colonial military in observing West African marital customs.

Military officials selectively took on some of the social responsibilities of West African communities in regard to the maintenance and prosperity of African military households. The military prioritized soldiers' patriarchal and paternalistic power in the soldiers' households. Wives' advocates were few in the historical record. The military enforced the intended use of family allocations for members of tirailleurs sénégalais' households. Military officials categorically rejected military wives' appeals for divorce or granted them with the stipulation of bridewealth reimbursement. Unlike African military households' kith and kin, military officials would not encourage couples to reconcile their differences or modify their marital behaviors. The French military was invested in the sanctity of tirailleurs sénégalais' marriages in order to improve troop morale. It was not as invested in African military households to ensure the trans-generational longevity of West African lineages or societies.

West African women and communities understood that there were social and financial benefits that accompanied an affiliation, directly or by proxy, with tirailleurs sénégalais. The Great War provided the context for the military to become an intermediary and regulatory body between deployed soldiers and their home-front conjugal partners. Wives were likely aware that the military managed African military households' affairs in arbitrary ways, so they circumvented, challenged, and compromised the authority of the French Army in French West Africa by seeking new male companions and conjugal resolutions within and without the colonial state. Other women sought to strengthen their traditional claims of marital legitimacy by maintaining a close proximity to their husbands. The nineteenth-century military traditions of wifely accompaniment ended with the Great War.

MIGRATING WIVES AND ISSUES OF MOBILITY

The Great War demilitarized and demobilized the female conjugal partners of French African soldiers. This conflict fragmented French African soldiers' households across empire. Wives of newly enlisted tirailleurs sénégalais remained on the West African home front. New recruits' wives and children followed them to military encampments near large ports, which was common practice up to 1914. Conjugal households found themselves grounded by the military when their husbands deployed to mainland France. These abandoned women and children continued to reside in, or adjacent to, military camps. They were joined by mesdames tirailleurs of the Moroccan campaign who repatriated to French West Africa when their husbands deployed to France from Casablanca. As they alighted from military steamships docked at West African ports, the moniker "mesdames tirailleurs" faded in the historical record. In the absence of their husbands, abandoned wives dealt with new types of military interventions into their marital decisions, as well as military efforts to control wives' mobility and place of residence throughout the war. Very few African military households possessed documents providing evidence of their marriage with tirailleurs sénégalais at the outbreak of hostilities. The new emphasis on documented marital legitimacy endangered family members squatting on the periphery of military bases. Officials cast them as protagonists in insurmountable sanitary, social, and economic problems that affected military order. Once valued and celebrated military auxiliaries, African soldiers' female conjugal partners became troublesome and unmanageable figures.

West African women followed their enlisted husbands to military camps and port cities—like Dakar and Saint-Louis—on foot, carrying infants and their possessions. This was military conjugal tradition. The long-distance migration of women in the early twentieth century was also a consequence of slave emancipation and the draw of the expanding wartime economy in colonial cities. Women untethered from the bonds of servitude used migration and marriage as means to leave their slave pasts behind and create new family connections.[65] Recently freed female slaves entered conjugal relationships with tirailleurs sénégalais and became attached to military posts in the West African interior.[66] Wives of tirailleurs sénégalais collected fifteen francs a month from the French Army. For those women who relocated to coastal urban centers, fifteen francs did not cover their monthly expenses. Along Dakar's western coastal road, soldiers' female conjugal partners formed communities on the peripheries of the Madeleines military base and engaged in activities to supplement their allocations. French military officials alleged that the majority of these women falsely claimed to be the wives of tirailleurs sénégalais in order to maintain close proximity to the large population of ready consumers. These women provided their husbands and other tirailleurs sénégalais with goods and services. Many remained near military bases after their husbands deployed to France. Without tirailleurs sénégalais present to vouch for their legitimacy, the French military delegitimized, dehumanized, and criminalized them to justify West African women's physical removal from the fringes of camps.

The majority of these wives had traveled great distances overland in West Africa and overseas in French Empire. Once in Dakar, many of these women lacked nearby kith and kin. They established temporary residences and created new communities near military bases. In Senegal, an estimated one thousand women lived near Dakar, Thiaroye, Ouakam, Rufisque, and Thiès by mid-1916. Near the Madeleines base on the western corniche of the Cap Vert Peninsula, wives had settled in Abattoir Village, lined the road between Ouakam and Dakar, and resided in the Hok neighborhood. The majority of the migrant wives in Dakar lived in Abattoir Village. Created in 1913 and named for the Wolof and Tukulor butchers who plied their trade adjacent to the base, Abattoir Village experienced a large influx of people during World War I.[67] Most buildings in Abattoir Village were constructed out of scrap wood and topped with salvaged sheet metal. According to military sources, there were approximately ten shopkeepers in Abattoir Village who sold libations—predominantly wine and adulterated gin—to tirailleurs sénégalais and women lodging in the village. The French military believed that up to fifty landlords operating in the village exploited migrant wives with high rents. A room with a bed leased for twelve to thirteen francs a month and a room without a bed ranged between seven and a half and ten francs per month. Lodging alone nearly exhausted wives' fifteen-franc monthly allowances. The majority of tirailleurs sénégalais' conjugal partners lacked documented proof of their marriages and the military denied them access to allocations or rations disbursed during the war. High rents and the inflated prices of basic goods compelled women in Abattoir Village to participate in the growing urban cash economy. Some sold roasted groundnuts and fried millet pastries, but these activities rarely accrued enough revenue to afford basic amenities. According to the French officers stationed in Dakar, many women in Abattoir Village engaged in sex work.[68]

The conjugal partners of tirailleurs sénégalais entered Dakar's labor economy by selling domestic services that included cooking, entertaining, and sex work.[69] The wartime and colonial economies attracted young populations to urban spaces. West African women joined the growing cash economy by entering into casual yet sustained relationships with soldiers. In exchange for resources, these women took on temporary domestic and conjugal roles for their clients. These women fashioned precarious webs of economic and social security among a population in constant renewal. The French colonial military has a long history of state-funded brothels, employing indigenous women, for French soldiers serving in empire.[70] Outside of these state-regulated sites of transactional sex, the military seldom tolerated "clandestine" prostitution. Military officials blamed women residing in shanties adjacent to the Madeleines base for growing cases of sexually transmitted infections among soldiers in Dakar. According to the military, women who engaged in sex work often had between ten and fifteen steady partners with whom they exchanged favors and meals.[71] These women threatened the colonial military and state because they were autonomous agents lacking male parental or spousal authority.[72]

The colonial military cast Abattoir Village's female residents' entrepreneurial and survival strategies as adultery, polyamory, and prostitution. By asserting that tirailleurs sénégalais' conjugal partners were engaging in behaviors antithetical to moral propriety and matrimonial sanctity, military officials in Dakar created moral and/or ethical justification for removing them from the margins of colonial military spaces. The French colonial military debated how to carry out comprehensive removal. One official suggested denying these women their family allocations in Dakar, which would require wives to collect these funds in the village where the military had recruited their husbands.[73] This plan did not take into consideration the distance to those villages and the fact that abandoned wives might not have kin and community in their husbands' natal villages. Nor did officials consider the recent emancipation status of some of these women, who could risk reenslavement if they returned to their natal communities. One proposal suggested forcibly removing women to their villages of origin. Another proposed razing Abattoir Village.[74] At one point during the war, agents of the colonial military and Dakar's municipal police entered Abattoir Village with the intent of expelling any woman lacking identification papers that linked her to a tirailleur sénégalais serving abroad.

Ultimately, the French military acted tactfully with the wives of the tirailleurs sénégalais because not all of the women squatting near the Madeleines military base had most recently come from the West African hinterland. Mesdames tirailleurs who had repatriated from North Africa after the death or redeployment of their husbands survived in the peripheries of colonial military spaces in Dakar and Saint-Louis. Unlike other female conjugal partners, mesdames tirailleurs were difficult to delegitimize, being unquestionably members of the French colonial military and wives of West African colonial soldiers who had served in North Africa. In the absence of their husbands, they became wards of the French colonial state. The colonial administration worked swiftly to relocate repatriating mesdames tirailleurs to their villages of origin. In 1916, the military depot in Dakar claimed that of 2,596 women (repatriating mesdames tirailleurs and other soldiers' wives), 572 had been passed on to the civil authority. The military reunited 17 with their husbands and repatriated 1,997 to their villages of origin.[75] Once the military had reassigned these women to the care of the colonial state, their communities of origin, or their husbands, it measured its obligation to these women in monthly fifteen-franc allocations.

The outbreak of the Great War catalyzed a shift in military conjugal traditions, as well as marking the beginning of the end of mesdames tirailleurs' direct participation in the conquest and maintenance of French Empire. Soldiers' conjugal partners demilitarized and became members of home-front households. With the onset of World War I, West African women matrimonially tied to tirailleurs sénégalais were no longer required to migrate long distances or provide auxiliary military labor in conflict zones. West African women's connection to the colonial army became contingent upon the documented legitimacy of their marriage to French African soldiers. The military recognized that legitimacy through regularly distributed state welfare. Benefits bifurcated across citizenship status. The Blaise Diagne legislation obligated originaires to military service, awarded greater benefits to their households, and guaranteed support for their polygynous households. Colonial subjects, or indigènes, served in the tirailleurs sénégalais, received fewer benefits, and only their first wives could access military allocations. The increasing complexity of bureaucracy surrounding African military households led to the military's greater scrutiny of female conjugal partners' legal marital status and wives' attempts to terminate marriages with active soldiers. Military and civilian officials collaborated to control the movements of these women in the name of troop morale and military order.

Blaise Diagne's personal involvement in the final 1918 recruitment effort for the Great War yielded roughly 63,000 indigène soldiers. While they were not the equivalent of originaires' benefits, Diagne won new entitlements, privileges, and possibilities for indigènes who enlisted in 1918. This round of recruits received larger signing bonuses and family allocations than those who enlisted before them. New recruits' families were exempt from paying taxes.[76] At the Great War's end, these young men enlisted for at least three years. The colonial military diverted these fresh recruits into the occupied Rhineland and into empire—particularly to France's new League of Nations mandate territories in the Levant. In these new spaces of colonial occupation, tirailleurs sénégalais' conjugality and sexuality remained an important aspect of their military service. During the interwar years, tirailleurs sénégalais managed long-distance relationships with female conjugal partners at home and/or in Morocco, Madagascar, Syria, and Lebanon.

5

Challenging Colonial Order

*Long-Distance, Interracial,
and Cross-Colonial Conjugal Relationships, 1918–46*

IN THE AFTERMATH OF THE GREAT WAR, THE FRENCH MILITARY orchestrated a large-scale demobilization of African soldiers from mainland France. This occurred in tandem with the relocation of battalions of tirailleurs sénégalais to the German Rhineland, North Africa, the Levant, and Madagascar. West Africans' role in French Empire shifted from that of conquerors to guardians. By 1921, there were 3,200 West African servicemen in France, 3,000 in Morocco, 2,500 in the Levant, 500 in Algeria, 300 in Tunisia, and 3,500 designated for occupation of the Rhineland.[1] In the mid-1920s, tirailleurs sénégalais fought in the Rif War in Morocco and the Great Syrian Revolt (also known as the Djebel Druze Uprising).[2] With the outbreak of the Second World War, West African soldiers deployed to mainland France once more. After the fall of France in September 1940, many tirailleurs sénégalais relied on French civilians to survive German occupation and the Vichy regime until the conclusion of the war. From 1918 to 1946, in these disparate locations, West African soldiers and female conjugal partners sought to register and legitimize their relationships—at home and abroad—with superior officers in the French army. The colonial state's recognition of marital legitimacy was paramount in mobilizing military resources for soldiers' spouses across French Empire.

The French government committed long-term funding to tirailleurs sénégalais as guardians of empire. A decree on 19 July 1919 augmented conscription in French West Africa to twelve to fourteen thousand recruits per year. The demographic composition of the tirailleurs sénégalais shifted because men from French Guinea, Côte d'Ivoire, and Upper Volta voluntarily enlisted as career soldiers in growing numbers.[3] The military divided West African conscripts into reservists and active soldiers. As the interwar period wore on, men realized that reservist was a euphemism for forced labor (*corvée*), which made membership in the reserves (the infamous *deuxième portion*) undesirable for many.[4] For active soldiers, minimum lengths of service remained at three years of active duty and tirailleurs sénégalais served at least one of those years abroad. As a result, a large number of troops experienced spousal separation as part of their military service during the interwar years. In October 1919, the military restricted allocations to legitimate wives and legitimate children younger than fifteen.[5] On 28 July 1921, the French colonial state introduced the *indemnité de séparation* (separation indemnity), capped at fifteen francs per month, for the legitimate wives and children of tirailleurs sénégalais serving abroad.[6]

From 1918 to 1946, tirailleurs sénégalais' conjugal traditions evolved in radically different geographies. Soldiers deployed overseas without West African conjugal partners. The majority of newly conscripted soldiers were too young to have completed the prenuptial rites required for legitimate marriage in their communities. Married troops left wives and households behind at the home front. Single and married tirailleurs sénégalais continued to seek new female conjugal partners while serving colonial state interests outside of French West Africa. Tirailleurs sénégalais strove to fulfill obligations to their families at home and/or the conjugal partners they acquired during foreign active service. After 1918, the colonial military provided West African soldiers with a means to maintain households across long distances via separation indemnities, tax abatements, and other allocations. The means through which the French military delivered these allocations illustrated how the colonial state prioritized patriarchal authority and supported African men's prerogatives in courts, politics, and the colonial economy.[7] As mentioned in the introduction, the military incorporated the male-breadwinner model into its systems of social welfare for soldiers' households. The bureaucratic and fiscal ties between the state and households required documented proof

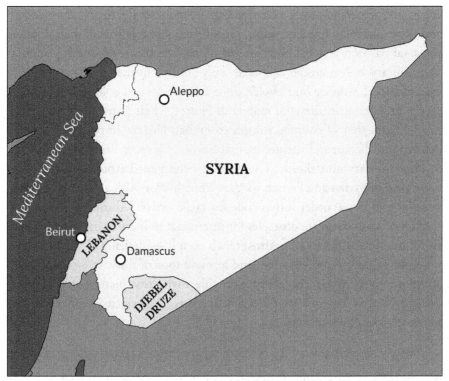

MAP 5.1. French Mandate Territories: Syria and Lebanon. Map by Isaac Barry

of marital and child legitimacy for the distribution of entitlements. After the Great War, military and civilian officials struggled with how to evaluate customary marital arrangements practiced by tirailleurs sénégalais—like child marriage and "levirate" marriage—because these officials increasingly relied on the statutes of the French Civil Code to determine marital legitimacy and the allocation of benefits.[8] The survival of long-distance African military households balanced on their decisions.

After the Great War, West African soldiers' foreign conjugal partners showed up in the archives in new ways. During the nineteenth century in Congo and Madagascar, accusations of sexual misconduct and forced conjugal association swirled around local women living in tirailleurs sénégalais' camps. In the interwar period, archival silences engulf the majority of incidents related to casual, transactional, and forced conjugal relationships among inter-African and cross-colonial couples. Instead, soldiers' foreign conjugal partners appear predominantly in requests for financial assistance and long-distance transportation. Tirailleurs sénégalais and their foreign conjugal partners adapted their conjugal practices to the expanding colonial and military bureaucracies affiliated with family entitlements. Members of cross-colonial military households came from federated colonies, protectorates, mandate territories, and mainland France. Their individual legal status ranged from that of colonial subject to French citizen. Imperial authorities debated jurisdiction and relevant marital customs for recognizing the legitimacy of these military households. These debates sharpened around the intended relocation of Syrian and French wives to French West Africa. Concerns about budgets and moral order (often code for racial order) led some military and civilian officials to create obstacles for interracial military couples—often insurmountable in the case of Afro-French couples—desiring to maintain the integrity of their households beyond a single tour of duty. In aggregate, the anecdotes presented in this chapter provide a wholistic picture of how tirailleurs sénégalais' conjugal traditions adapted to the exigencies of travel and bureaucracy in French Empire.

EVALUATING WIVES AND EXTENDED SEPARATION AFTER 1918

After the Great War, officials in the colonial state and in the French military became active participants in determining the legitimacy of West African soldiers' households at home and abroad. The state took on the formal role of assigning legitimacy to tirailleurs sénégalais' conjugal unions because the military expanded the benefits available to soldiers' households. Marital legitimacy continued to be a moving target. Examples from across French Empire demonstrate that no particular set of prenuptial rites dictated the ways in which tirailleurs sénégalais and their potential spouses acquired marital legitimacy for the purposes of allocations. Ultimately, enlisted men held the responsibility of registering their spouses with military commanders or civilian officials. Negotiating formal colonial bureaucracies across empire was an essential step in legitimizing conjugal relationships and receiving state assistance. For African military households, marital legitimacy and its attendant benefits became an evolving state affair between 1918 and 1946.

With the introduction of the separation indemnity in 1921, government funds flowed through West African soldiers in new ways. This legislation decided who the appropriate recipients were for monthly allocations and inheritable funds. The military used a male-breadwinner household model in the distribution of its welfare, which had the potential to wrest economic power from elders and place it in the hands of legitimate wives. Soldiers' extended kin were no longer eligible to receive military resources. These policies ignored West African family models and modes of economic redistribution. Benefits paid directly to soldiers' wives could marginalize soldiers' extended families from the process of redistributing soldiers' wealth—at least in the first transaction between the state and the recruit's wives and children.[9] These policies also ignored tirailleurs sénégalais' polygynous conjugal practices—which their *statut personnel* allowed them. The language of the separation indemnity outlined the colonial state's financial commitments to tirailleurs sénégalais' first wives. For the most part, second wives could not access compensation from the state and were beyond the jurisdiction of the French colonial military.

Regimes of benefits that were extended to West African soldiers' wives echoed the postwar social welfare programs aimed at heteronormative, nuclear families in mainland France.[10] Civilian social welfare in France encouraged population growth. In interwar West Africa, military welfare tended toward reducing the number of people eligible to receive benefits. The military used gender, age, and marital legitimacy to drastically reduce the number of civilians eligible for regularly distributed benefits. Officials complicated the process for registering legitimate marriages, wives, and children with the state. Deadlines and documented evidence expanded the opportunities for the state to scrutinize marital legitimacy and discriminate among soldiers' wives. Many soldiers were unaware of these benefits when they enlisted and scrambled to acquire the necessary documentation to register their wives with the state prior to deploying overseas. In 1935, the military administration received two hundred requests from tirailleurs sénégalais serving in empire to belatedly register marriages or deal with errors in the distribution of soldiers' remittances and military allocations.[11] Military and colonial administrators assumed that a large number of civilian women and West African soldiers claimed marital legitimacy in order to fraudulently obtain the meager fifteen-franc monthly separation compensation for wives.[12] In 1926, the military created a statute of limitations so that soldiers' beneficiaries could no longer access back pay or widows' pensions more than five years after the death of a soldier.[13]

West African soldiers and their conjugal partners became versed in the formal and informal processes of registering their legitimate marriages with the state. African military households exploited the overlapping and divergent conventions used to legitimate marriages in order to take advantage of the benefits available to them. Many processes or acts could meet the minimum requirements for legitimate marriage—filing required paperwork, the completion of customary rites, bridewealth, the allocation of benefits, a deep emotional tie, cohabitation, conjugal relations, or shared offspring. Couples gambled on inefficiencies and inconsistencies in colonial bureaucratic knowledge of local and imperial prenuptial practices and marital tradition. Colonial officials often lacked the evidence and capacity to confirm soldiers' and conjugal partners' marital status. The archives contain several examples of soldiers and wives misrepresenting their marital status in order to acquire military resources. The small number of cases indicates that most military households were legitimate or passed as legitimate. In 1933, a Dahomeyan soldier named Koto filed separation indemnity paperwork for his wife after he had already deployed overseas. After an inquiry, the military discovered that he had never been married and that his "wife" was the spouse of another individual.[14] Military officials used this case to argue for tightening restrictions upon when and where enlisted men could declare their marital status.

Despite the interwar colonial military's stronger stance on monogamous, heteronormative marriage, tirailleurs sénégalais continued to engage in multipartner conjugal relationships. They did not modify their conjugal practices, but strove to access allocations for the parts of their families that could pass as monogamous. Their conjugal partners used false names and/or took advantage of bureaucratic inefficiencies to collect allocations meant for first wives. Military inquiries into the misallocation of state funds opened up portals to career soldiers' household arrangements. Warrant Officer Demba Kone claimed that malfeasant state functionaries had swindled his wife, Koufiembaye Kone, out of her separation indemnity from 1930 to 1931. Upon investigation, higher-level administrators discovered the complexities of Demba Kone's conjugal life. Koufiembaye Kone had collected a few monthly allocations, then left Bobo Dioulasso (a colonial military center in contemporary Burkina Faso) for an unknown destination in southern Côte d'Ivoire. According to the inquest, Warrant Officer Demba Kone married another woman, Igoulelé Sori, who lived in his natal village, Tiefoura. He had not registered this wife with the colonial military. In order to shortcut the system, Sori tried unsuccessfully to collect a separation indemnity in Tiefoura under the name Koufiembaye Kone. Local functionaries in Tiefoura denied Sori the benefits but did not report the matter until Kone accused them of malfeasance. The officials may have refused to distribute the funds because of Sori's false identity, or perhaps they hoped to extort a percentage of the fifteen francs in order to overlook it. To complicate matters, a woman named Banafia, who lived in the military sector in Bobo Dioulasso, also tried to collect benefits from the military based on marital ties to Demba Kone. His conjugal relationships unfolded across the landscapes of his natal village and military posts. Kone's conjugal practices were not uncommon for career soldiers in the tirailleurs sénégalais. However, the ways in which he and his conjugal partners endeavored to access allocations was unusual, and eventually opened up this polygynous/polyamorous household to military scrutiny. Ultimately, the French designated all of Kone's conjugal partners as illegitimate wives. In effect, the military impeded Kone's ability to fulfill his conjugal obligations.[15]

The French military amended the qualifications for marital legitimacy and the separation indemnity throughout the interwar period in response to tirailleurs sénégalais' conjugal practices and their partners' attempts to access state allocations. The documentation necessary to register African military households multiplied. In the interwar period, most civilian births, marriages, and divorces remained within the jurisdiction of customary law and the colonial state did not register these life events. When civilians became soldiers, the military needed this information. Military officials relied on new enlistees and local actors to provide confirmation of basic civil status information and diverse traditions to render tirailleurs sénégalais' marriages legible to the state. The circulation of inquiries and information between regional capitals and rural districts slowed down the process of verifying the legitimacy of soldiers' conjugal unions. Protracted inquests, when combined with a clause stipulating that marriages needed to exist for at least two months prior to soldiers' foreign deployments, incalculably reduced the number of spouses and children eligible to receive separation indemnities. Modifications to separation indemnity policies elaborated that wives lost their rights to benefits in cases of divorce, remarriage, or being convicted of a serious crime. Wives could only access their benefits in the administrative districts corresponding to their husbands' registered domicile. They could not collect benefits if they abandoned their conjugal home or refused to relocate to their husband's family's homestead.[16] This particular clause contravened matrilocal traditions among some communities in West Africa. West African military wives' freedom of movement hit a new nadir in the interwar period. New decrees specifically stated that married women could not emigrate without the consent of their husbands and unmarried women needed the consent of the head of their family.[17]

The progression of changes to the separation indemnity during the interwar period accommodated or prohibited local marital customs that could qualify tirailleurs sénégalais' conjugal partners for military welfare. The French military struggled with local marital traditions that contravened French civil code. One such practice was child marriage.[18] In these types of conjugal relationships, families betrothed young girls to future spouses. These girls could transfer to the home of the designated groom (or the groom's family) at a young age, while he made bridewealth payments to his future in-laws. According to the tradition, the marriage was not celebrated or consummated before the girl and her husband reached pubescence. Active tirailleurs sénégalais participated in child marriage and could be responsible for the welfare of young girls who were their future wives. Regional colonial administrators in West Africa accused soldiers of using military benefits to pay the bridewealth of their future spouses.[19] Prepubescent fiancées were not eligible to receive separation indemnities. Military officials refused to recognize betrothed girls as wives prior to consummation of the marriage. Historical records do not detail how the military ascertained when tirailleurs sénégalais' child brides reached puberty or when these marriages were consummated. Marriage by proxy was another marital tradition prohibited by the colonial military.[20] West African traditions of wife inheritance challenged this policy. In 1933, a local administrator in Man, Côte d'Ivoire, found that a tirailleur sénégalais had inherited a wife, Dazahon, upon his father's death. Recognizing levirate marriage as viable local custom, the administrator recommended that the French military award Dazahon compensation while her new husband/son-in-law served outside of French West Africa.[21] The French colonial military accommodated these local marital traditions prior to the Mandel Decree of 1939. On the eve of World War II, the colonial administration prohibited proxy marriages, raised the legal age for marriage, and required the consent of brides in French West and Equatorial Africa.

The outbreak of World War II reintroduced wartime benefits to the families of tirailleurs sénégalais. Roughly a hundred thousand French African troops mobilized toward the war effort between September 1939 and the fall of France in May 1940.[22] From 1940, Marshal Philippe Pétain headed the French Vichy regime, which administered southern France, empire, and African colonial soldiers. France's former undersecretary of national defense, Charles de Gaulle, declared the armistice and Pétain's collaborationist government invalid. On 18 June 1940, de Gaulle called on members of France's armed forces to join him in London, where the Free French government-in-exile launched its activities against German and Vichy forces. West African soldiers fought for both Vichy and Free France across empire during World War II. The bifurcation of France interrupted and altered how West African military households accessed their benefits throughout the war.

In West Africa, the Vichy period began in late June 1940 and ended in July 1943, when Free French Forces reclaimed the federated colony. During that three-year period, Vichy's National Revolution promoted family values and patriarchal order in France and French Empire.[23] The regime's brief tenure prevented Vichy from implementing major changes to recognizing household legitimacy and disbursing benefits to soldiers' households. West African servicemen's conjugal partners continued to meet obstacles in collecting the benefits they were eligible for. War hindered the long-distance communication of basic information—births, deaths, marital status—between mainland France and West Africa. In May 1940, the French government introduced wartime urgent assistance (*secours d'urgence*) for families of tirailleurs sénégalais who had died, disappeared, or become prisoners of war.[24] Urgent assistance was available for the lateral and ascendant kin of active West African soldiers. Military and civilian administrations believed that wives should not collect both urgent assistance and the separation indemnity—the value of which had increased to twenty-five francs by the Second World War. Urgent assistance, in the form of daily rations and basic goods, could hold more value than the separation indemnity. Local administrators ironically acknowledged that "illegitimate" spouses, which was a catchall term for second wives and unregistered domestic partners, could access urgent assistance. Legitimate wives could not.[25] When long distances separated soldiers from their families, the military had greater authority in legitimating tirailleurs sénégalais' conjugal behavior and awarding benefits to their legal spouses.

DIFFERENCE, RACE, AND PLACE IN CROSS-COLONIAL CONJUGAL UNIONS

Roughly a quarter-million tirailleurs sénégalais served in the French colonial army during the 1920s and 1930s as reservists and active soldiers.[26] All active soldiers served outside of French West Africa. Whether married or single, tirailleurs sénégalais sought conjugal partners in new regions of empire. Civilian and military administrators had a strong hand in the success and longevity of cross-colonial African military households. Women and men from different regions of French Empire constituted cross-colonial relationships, which included inter-African and interracial partnerships. Racial difference and distinct marital customs in disparate geographies influenced how military officials determined the legitimacy of these relationships. Conjugal partners from different regions of French Empire depended on the state to subsidize the long-distance relocation of civilian family members. Tirailleurs sénégalais' cross-colonial conjugal relationships challenged French imperial order because West African men married Arab women in Morocco, Syria, and Lebanon, as well as French women. In the military historical record, administrators referred to all of these women as "white." Civilian government officials in West Africa and France strongly opposed the relocation of foreign wives to West Africa between 1918 and 1947. They invoked interwar austerity to deny soldiers' spouses and interracial children international travel assistance. The military took an ambivalent stance to cross-colonial relationships. However, military officials used their command of international waterways and state finances to control the movement of individuals, families, and their personal goods.

Civilian and military officials managed tirailleurs sénégalais' cross-colonial relationships within the racial, gendered, and legal hierarchies of twentieth-century French Empire.[27] Individual members of cross-colonial African military households could have different legal statuses managed by different political regimes within French Empire. Military officials handled requests for assistance in relocating female colonial subjects in Madagascar, female residents of the Moroccan Protectorate, women from the mandate territories, and female citizens in France. In order to access state funds for cross-colonial relocation and repatriation, female conjugal partners were subject to investigations that challenged the legitimacy of their marriages and their children, as well as calling their moral character into question. Inquests into tirailleurs sénégalais' cross-colonial marriages centered on wives—not soldiers. Racial difference and legal status dynamically influenced how military and civilian employees appraised wives' legitimacy and predicted foreign wives' ability to integrate into West African societies. Officials gave greater regard to French women and Arab women because they were not colonial subjects. Further, officials collectively categorized these women as members of the "white race," which grouped Syrian, Moroccan, and French women in racial opposition to sub-Saharan African and Malagasy "black" women. These latter women were predominantly French colonial subjects and often considered the legal wards of their parents, husbands, or the state. Their requests for international transport stalled because they required the permission of their husbands or male heads of household before they could emigrate.[28] Cross-colonial African military households' struggles to maintain their integrity create a wholistic picture of the evolution of tirailleurs sénégalais' conjugal traditions during the interwar period. Examples from Madagascar, Morocco, Syria, and France highlight the growing importance of imperial racial order between 1920 and 1946 and illuminate how racial discrimination affected the legitimacy and integrity of tirailleurs sénégalais' cross-colonial conjugal unions.

MADAGASCAR: LEGACIES OF CONQUEST, DISTANT HOMELANDS, AND CUSTODY BATTLES

After formal military conquest in Madagascar ended in 1905, tirailleurs sénégalais repatriated to West Africa and demobilized in Madagascar. Governor-General Joseph-Simon Gallieni awarded plots of land to demobilizing West African servicemen and encouraged them to seek local wives in an effort to strengthen France's presence in Madagascar.[29] Veterans obtained private- and public-sector jobs connected to the growing French colonial state presence as police, private security agents, and railway workers.[30] Tirailleurs sénégalais of the conquest era made Madagascar home with West African women who had accompanied them on campaign. They also made households with local female conjugal partners. In the 1920s, new West African recruits arrived in Madagascar. These young men also sought local conjugal partners, but, unlike their nineteenth-century predecessors, could not demobilize in Madagascar to support the households they created. Madagascan and French West African administrators fielded requests for travel assistance for members of African military households created during the era of conquest and the interwar period. They confronted the legacies of nineteenth-century conquest in repatriation requests from aging *mesdames tirailleurs*, as well as younger recruits' Madagascan conjugal partners and their interracial children.

In September 1926, sexagenarian widow Fatamata Bambara sent a handwritten appeal to the governor-general of Madagascar. With an *X* representing her signature at the bottom of the letter, Bambara requested state assistance to repatriate to her birthplace in French Soudan and rejoin her children after living for a quarter of a century in Madagascar. According to the letter, she had accompanied her husband, a tirailleur sénégalais named Bakari Sidibé, to Madagascar in the late 1890s. Like many other demobilizing tirailleurs sénégalais, Sidibé extended his stay in Madagascar as a civilian railway worker. Sidibé died in a work-related accident in 1902. After her husband's untimely death, Bambara remained in Madagascar under the charge of a relation, Samba Konaté. Konaté was a veteran of the tirailleurs sénégalais who had found employment in private enterprise in Madagascar. There were no details in the letter to suggest that Bambara had remarried or had any living children in Madagascar. In order to support herself, she had set up a roadside stand where she sold coffee, tea, and other refreshments to European and Senegalese workers at the mouth of the Gallieni Tunnel—where her husband had died. Twenty-five years later, Fatamata Bambara wanted to go home to family.

Bambara's relocation to Madagascar and her request for repatriation occurred at radically different political and economic moments in French Empire. When Fatamata Bambara accompanied Bakari Sidibé to the French conquest of Madagascar in the 1890s, the French military made promises to fund the return of tirailleurs sénégalais' wives and widows to West Africa. A generation later, high-level civilian administrators in Madagascar and French West Africa debated whether relocating Fatamata Bambara to her home in West Africa was worth the expense of international civilian transit. The handful of documents related to Fatamata Bambara's appeal provide a snapshot into the life history of a madame tirailleur who survived the French conquest of Madagascar. In 1926, Fatamata Bambara represented anachronistic military and conjugal practices once central to the expansion of French Empire in Africa. A brief synopsis of Fatamata Bambara's life starkly portrays the tragedy in interwar civilian officials' refusal to aid a sexagenarian widow of a tirailleur sénégalais to return to West Africa.[31]

Fatamata Bambara was born in the early-to-mid 1860s. Her surname was a term used by the French to designate Bamana speakers (*bamanakan*), who historically lived in the region between the Senegal and Niger River watersheds. Family names in West Africa provide roadmaps to ancestry, determine social order, and suggest guidelines for social belonging.[32] Bambara probably acquired her surname when the French military bureaucracy required her to have one. If she lacked a family name prior to her membership in the French colonial military, she may have had low social origins or slave ancestry. Bambara grew up in time and place where religious and political tensions threatened the social order of Bamana societies. Women were particularly vulnerable to kidnapping, capture, and enslavement due to expansionist wars launched by Umar Tall, Samory Touré, and the French in the Bamana-speaking areas in the 1880s. As demonstrated in chapter 2, military officers encouraged West African soldiers to incorporate vulnerable women into their households as wives and military auxiliaries.

Bakari Sidibé could have taken Fatamata Bambara as a conjugal partner in the aftermath of a battle. Or, she may have met him as a refugee in one of the Liberty Villages dotting the French West African post-conflict landscape. By the 1890s, West African women and their children were typical features of French military campaigns and encampments. Within this military community, Fatamata Bambara became a mother, a wife, and a world traveler. According to her request, Bambara had come to Madagascar with her "chéri," or darling, Bakari Sidibé. The couple likely arrived between 1896 and 1899, because Sidibé demobilized from the tirailleurs sénégalais in 1901. Their marital status was unclear at the time of their relocation to Madagascar. It is equally unclear whether Bakari Sidibé was the father of Bambara's children—Fatro, born in 1886, and Aisatra, born in 1891—whom she left behind in what became French Soudan. Bakari Sidibé found work in railroad construction and died as a result of an accident in the Gallieni Tunnel in 1902. In her midthirties at her husband's death, Bambara became the ward of Samba Konaté. According to her request, Konaté was Bambara's brother who had deployed to Madagascar as a tirailleur sénégalais around the same time as her husband. As a ward and a widow, Fatamata Bambara had maintained a close physical proximity to the colonial state at her refreshment stand, where railway workers completed the Gallieni Tunnel.

Samba Konaté, another tirailleur sénégalais and purported relation of Fatamata Bambara, became her guardian. Fatamata Bambara would have been roughly thirty-five when she became affiliated with Konaté. The word "brother," used by Bambara to describe her relationship with Konaté, could have referenced a range of social, economic, biological, and affective ties between them. Fictive familial ties, made tangible by conflict and long-distance travel, offered some security to the West African wives of tirailleurs sénégalais. Through her affiliation with Konaté, Bambara maintained a relationship with the French colonial military, which was one of the few common denominators in her adult life. Given her desire to return to French Soudan in 1926, it is unlikely that Bambara had children in Madagascar or a community that would provide her with assistance in the last decades of her life. Without in-laws or descendants in Madagascar to support Bambara in her postmenopausal years, she appealed to the governor-general of Madagascar for assistance.

Bambara's letter to the governor-general challenged the institutional memory of the colonial state. Her request probed the limits of the welfare offered to wives and widows of tirailleurs sénégalais. Bambara may or may not have been aware that the regimes of benefits for soldiers' spouses and households had evolved since her arrival in Madagascar. In the 1890s, the military allocated resources to mesdames tirailleurs based on their physical proximity to a soldier and their protracted presence on campaign. Regular monetized allocations had replaced this irregular distribution system. Fatamata Bambara's husband had died after demobilization. Neither her letter nor the accompanying administrative missives raised the possibility of her entitlement to a widow's pension. Her protracted residence in Madagascar timed her out of automatic access to funds from the military for repatriation. A decree from 3 July 1897, later modified in 1904, would have made Bambara eligible for fully funded repatriation from Madagascar to French Soudan within a year after her husband's demobilization. Past that deadline, the cost of repatriation fell on the civilian colonial government where the African military household resided.[33] After a series of telegrams, the governors of French West Africa and Madagascar rejected Fatamata Bambara's appeal for financial assistance.[34] In the 1920s, Fatamata Bambara was an anachronism, and civilian officials no longer felt responsible for her welfare.

Civilian administrations in Madagascar and West Africa willfully dismantled Afro-Malagasy households created during the interwar period. In the mid-1920s, the government received requests from repatriating tirailleurs sénégalais for assistance in relocating their Afro-Malagasy children to West Africa—conspicuously, without their mothers. These requests inspired debates about conjugal rights and guardianship that extended across empire. Even though most French civilian and military administrators lacked cultural proficiency in West African and Madagascan familial customs, they made pseudoscientific claims about traditional rights of guardianship and motherhood, which they supported with anecdotal evidence.[35] One official asserted that tirailleurs sénégalais' paternal prerogative was paramount, but nursing infants should not be separated from their mothers. Administrators waxed ethnographic regarding whether children conceived by Malagasy mothers could assimilate to West African societies. Tirailleurs sénégalais' paternal right to these children was never questioned. Officials feared that West African stepfamilies would reject Afro-Malagasy children.[36] The lieutenant-governors of Côte d'Ivoire and French Guinea strongly opposed transporting Afro-Malagasy children to French West Africa. They claimed West African polygyny and xenophobia would inhibit the children's integration into soldiers' extended families. In the end, the governor-general of French West Africa opposed the relocation of tirailleurs sénégalais' children from Madagascar to West Africa.[37]

The imperial circulation of Malagasy wives and mothers between Madagascar and West Africa seldom figured in these debates. A few Madagascan women relocated to West Africa. In 1926, Azana Dravalo and Ravao, wives of demobilized tirailleurs sénégalais in West Africa, requested state assistance to return to Madagascar. Their requests bore witness to domestic struggles and cultural differences among foreign wives and tirailleurs sénégalais' extended kin. Ravao was in constant battle with her disgruntled in-laws. Their inability to overcome their differences and live in proximity with each other led Ravao and her husband to declare their separation in front of local administrators.[38] Her request for repatriation stalled when civilian and military administrators in West Africa and Madagascar disagreed over what ministry should foot the bill.

MOROCCAN WOMEN IN SOUTHERN GEOGRAPHIES

After the First World War, tirailleurs sénégalais' mission in Morocco shifted from conquest to occupation. Resident-General Lyautey's enthusiasm for West African soldiers assured their tenure in the Moroccan Protectorate even as he expanded local recruitment and training of Moroccan soldiers. As support troops, tirailleurs sénégalais participated in violent campaigns to integrate rural Atlas Mountain communities into the protectorate throughout the 1930s. West African troops played an integral role in the Rif conflict, which occurred in the mountainous region spanning the borderland between French and Spanish protectorates in northern Morocco from 1924 to 1927.[39] During the 1920s and 1930s, only career soldiers and noncommissioned officers could take their West African wives to Morocco.[40] These women remained on base while their husbands patrolled towns or campaigned in the countryside. Wives were no longer members of racially segregated villages living on the margins of camp. Younger recruits, denied the privilege of wifely accompaniment, sought sexual and conjugal partners among female Moroccan civilians. It is unclear how and where African soldiers met and married these women in Morocco, but it seems as though the military rescinded its earlier prohibition on tirailleurs sénégalais' fraternization with civilian Moroccan women. Additionally, West African soldiers began to participate in the transactional sex industry affiliated with the French military. During the interwar period, tirailleurs sénégalais returned to West Africa with Moroccan wives in unreported numbers.

There were successful Afro-Moroccan military marriages, but the historical record tends to preserve those that ended in divorce or abandonment. Archival records related to cases of divorce and abandonment in West African households illustrate West African communities' and colonial governments' varying attitudes toward the integrity and legitimacy of Afro-Moroccan military households. In these cases, erstwhile Moroccan wives residing in French West Africa requested state assistance to repatriate to North Africa. These appeals were a consequence of failed marriages and Moroccan women's inability to subsist in West Africa without strong community or family ties. Colonial officials handled Moroccan wives' requests for repatriation differently than those of Madagascan women. According to administrators, Moroccan women's presence in West Africa disrupted racial and civilizational order. Colonial administrators in French West Africa referred to Arab women as "blanche" and assumed that Arab women were racially and culturally incompatible with sub-Saharan Africans. Concerns regarding the preservation of racial difference influenced officials' swift responses to Moroccan women's appeals for state funds to repatriate to Morocco. Administrators used the legal mechanism of indigence, which opened bureaucratic pathways and fiscal opportunities for repatriating Moroccan women to their natal communities. The Moroccan Protectorate often provided budgetary resources to expedite divorced Moroccan women's repatriation. The regular movement of military vessels between Dakar and Casablanca during the interwar period provided more opportunities for indigent divorcées to return to Morocco.

Fatou Diallo and Fatoum Haidara, both Moroccan women from Fez, relocated to Senegal in 1920 with tirailleurs sénégalais. Six years later, both women were divorced and living on charity in the streets of Dakar. The federal colonial government petitioned the resident-general of Morocco to fund their return.[41] Both women hoped to reunite with their families, whose names and addresses were provided within governmental correspondence. Protectorate staff contacted their families and gauged their receptiveness to Diallo and Haidara's repatriation from Senegal. Colonial agents took on the intermediary roles of extended family in ameliorating the experiences of abandoned or divorced "Arab" wives. In these examples, administrators acted as though the state had some responsibility in assuring the prosperity of foreign female colonial subjects residing in West Africa. The removal of these women from the streets of Dakar would prove beneficial to a colonial administration wary of how "white" destitute women living in public view compromised white supremacy and imperial racial hierarchy.

Another example illustrates how Afro-Moroccan marriages connected to legacies of the trans-Saharan slave trade. Saida Mint Saloum and N'Gor N'Diaye married in Marrakech in 1917. Fifty years earlier, Saloum's mother, Messaouda, had come to Morocco as an enslaved person. Messaouda was originally from Bandiagara near Mopti in French Soudan. Wife and mother-in-law accompanied N'Diaye to West Africa after a military authority in Marrakech witnessed and notarized the marriage. On November 5, 1919, the couple agreed by common accord to divorce in Fatick. Saloum's failing health in sub-Saharan Africa's climate was the cited reason. According to military reports, she was weak and anemic. Once divorced from her husband, she could be declared indigent and return to Morocco with state assistance. There was no word regarding Messaouda in documents related to Saloum's repatriation.[42] If Messaouda remained in West Africa while her daughter divorced and repatriated to Marrakech, the marriage between N'Diaye and Saloum acquires special significance—a vehicle for a formerly enslaved woman to return to her kin. There are no other reported cases where mothers accompanied brides from Morocco to Senegal. Despite an absence of fifty years, perhaps Messaouda located distant kin and remained in French Soudan.

Throughout the interwar period, colony-level administrators appealed to the governor-general to prohibit the relocation of foreign female colonial subjects to French West Africa. They cited examples like Zaira Bint Sidi Mohammed, who relocated from Morocco to Mauretania with her husband Amady Diara, as evidence. Once in Guidimaka, Mohammed suffered from her husband's brutality and neglect. Community members removed Mohammed from her conjugal home and provided her with temporary shelter. The foreign origin of Mohammed made her abuse and destitution more legible to the colonial state and induced officials to intervene in her case. The lieutenant-governor of Mauretania prepared to send her home on his colony's budget.[43] He also called for a law mandating that tirailleurs sénégalais obtain permission from a military administrative council before marrying in foreign colonies. This suggestion contradicted a 1923 decree in which the minister of war and pensions stated that indigenous troops desiring to marry outside of their colonies of origin could do so without the endorsement of military authorities. However, military officials were responsible for advising West African soldiers that their marriage entitled them to no special privileges in terms of lodging, medical attention, or transport. Officers could address family planning and inform foreign future brides of "the risk of leading an unhappy, or even miserable, existence in her husband's natal village."[44] Whether or not military officials dispensed this advice to potential brides, Moroccan women continued to relocate to West Africa with tirailleurs sénégalais.

Afro-Moroccan military households could not remain in Morocco because military protocol did not allow tirailleurs sénégalais to demobilize there. There is also evidence to suggest that Afro-Moroccan households would have faced adversity in Morocco. Tirailleurs sénégalais were members of a foreign occupying force and their sexual liaisons with local women transgressed racialized assumptions about soldiers' religious difference and slave ancestry.[45] Moroccan civilians' quotidian reactions to Afro-Moroccan sexual and conjugal relationships rarely appear in the historical record. Large-scale events do. In the aftermath of the Second World War, one racialized incident sparked violent reprisals from Moroccan civilians. During the night of 6 April 1947, a public quarrel between a Moroccan woman and a West African soldier in Casablanca's red-light district escalated into a large-scale brawl. The sixth of April was Easter Sunday and the majority of West African soldiers serving in Casablanca were on holiday leave. When civilian Moroccan men responded to the quarrel by attacking a handful of off-duty tirailleurs sénégalais, dozens of West African soldiers reciprocated and escalated the violence. Several opened fire on the Moroccan crowd gathered around the altercation, which resulted in 63 deaths and 118 seriously wounded.[46] On 8 April 1947, the military authority confined tirailleurs sénégalais to their barracks in Fez and Meknes for fear of civilian reprisals for events in Casablanca.[47] This was not a singular incident. French officers reported and trivialized low-level clashes that occurred between North African civilians and tirailleurs sénégalais in and near militarized sites of sex work throughout the twentieth century.[48] In a last-ditch effort to stem the flow of Moroccan wives to West Africa and ease racial tension in the post–World War II era, civilian authorities in France and West Africa proposed a reintroduction of pre–World War I practices, in which tirailleurs sénégalais stationed in Morocco could bring their West African households.[49] It was not approved.

MANDATE TERRITORIES: INTERRACIAL MILITARY HOUSEHOLDS IN NEW FRONTIERS

France's political negotiations for territories in the Levant began during the Great War. In May 1916, French and British wartime governments signed the Sykes-Picot Agreement, which detailed their plans to claim lands in the eastern Mediterranean in the event of an Allied victory and the fall of the Ottoman Empire. After the war, the League of Nations sanctioned this agreement by entrusting Syria and Lebanon to France as mandate territories. The French took on their role of administrating this region by increasing their military and political presence in Syria and Lebanon. After a series of political crises in Syria, the French military invaded Damascus in July 1920.[50] Tirailleurs sénégalais were numerous among these forces and many remained in Syria as occupation forces. Many of them transferred from occupied Rhineland directly to Syria. The number of West African soldiers in the Armée du

Levant plateaued at roughly four battalions or twenty-five hundred troops in the early 1920s.[51] The French managed Syria and Lebanon with an administration heavily reliant on military coercion and the assistance of indigenous political leaders. French mandate personnel discredited traditional leaders that opposed France's presence. Due to the reconfiguration of administrative districts and the displacement of defiant traditional leaders, dissidence grew in the southern region of Djebel Druze. This sentiment grew into opposition and then open revolt, headed by Sultan Pasha al-Atrash in August 1925.[52] In response, the French military sent sub-Saharan African troops south to participate in a hastily composed counterinsurgency against what became the Great Syrian Revolt. Amid the violence, West African soldiers located conjugal partners and repatriated with them.

In Syria, there was a strong reaction to the presence of the tirailleurs sénégalais in the Levant. Historian Elizabeth Thompson portrays the tirailleurs sénégalais' presence in Syria as part of a broader nonconsensual relationship, where Syrians rejected any vestige of their illicit presence. Tirailleurs sénégalais became affiliated with the most savage, masculine, and violent power of the French colonial state. West African troops became an important symbol that Syrians used to delegitimize France's colonial governance in the Levant. The tirailleurs sénégalais were blamed for the egregious violence committed by French soldiers during the Great Syrian Revolt. West African soldiers became a "target of nationalist propaganda in sexualized and racialized imagery that fused men's gender anxieties with outrage at French domination."[53]

Consensual and/or transactional sexual relationships between tirailleurs sénégalais and Syrian women also impacted Syrians' gendered sexual anxieties. Despite strong social proscriptions and military efforts to curb conjugal relationships between West African soldiers and civilian Syrian women, Afro-Syrian interracial couples appeared in the Levant and later relocated to West Africa. In Syria, these relationships led to violence. During World War II, in 1942, an incident erupted outside of a military brothel involving thirty intoxicated tirailleurs sénégalais and two Lebanese chauffeurs employed by the French colonial army. In the ensuing confusion, the tirailleurs sénégalais attacked Captain Massa, a West African warrant officer, who had attempted to intervene in the conflict. Massa was forced to defend himself with his belt until other French officers arrived on the scene.[54] The presence of the British in Syria after the defeat of Vichy French troops eroded the ultimate authority of France in its mandate territories. The war context exacerbated famine and drought. Wartime elections inspired protests and violent demonstrations in most major cities in the Levant throughout 1942 and 1943.[55] The French employed the tirailleurs sénégalais to carry out acts of violence and brutal reprisals against civilians.[56] French West African soldiers were not remembered fondly in Syria.

In West Africa, the French military's treatment of Syrian women shared similarities with their management of soldiers' Moroccan wives. Officials in French West Africa categorized Syrian women as "white" and treated them sympathetically. They claimed that these women faced great inconveniences, deceptions, and discomfort in tirailleurs sénégalais' villages. Military dossiers describing Syrian women did not raise questions about their morality and fidelity. Unlike West African wives, administrators did not insinuate that Syrian women entered into conjugal relationships with tirailleurs sénégalais in order to access state-allocated funds to military households. In the case of Syrian wives, officials cast tirailleurs sénégalais as duplicitous actors who misled their brides about the conditions and customs of their natal communities. West African administrators blamed their colleagues in Syria for allowing these war brides to leave the Levant. Here again, there were calls for military agents to counsel—read dissuade—Syrian fiancées about their marriages and future relocation to West Africa.[57] The military did not prohibit the migration of Syrian women to West Africa because, as residents of mandate territories, the French government's legal power over these women was circumscribed by local authority.

Raphaël Antonetti, lieutenant-governor of Côte d'Ivoire, was a vehement opponent of what he described as an "exodus" of Syrian women relocating to French West Africa with tirailleurs sénégalais. Antonetti insisted that the military stem the flow of Arab women to West Africa. He cited the example of Fadona Selim El Thomi as justification for mandating premarital counseling for Syrian women. El Thomi relocated to Côte d'Ivoire in 1923 with her thirteen-month-old child and her husband. Sekou Maiga was a career soldier retiring after fifteen years of service. In the coastal capital of Abidjan, El Thomi worked as a housekeeper at the tirailleurs sénégalais' military base. When her husband's service ended, she traveled up-country with him to his family's homestead. According to Antonetti, El Thomi disrupted normative social and cultural order in Maiga's natal community. Another Syrian woman, Kadidie, met insurmountable difficulties in Bouaké (also in Côte d'Ivoire). Both women ended up impoverished without the support of their husbands or in-laws. Antonetti argued that "it is not politically wise to lower the image of white women in West Africa to a condition of quasi-servitude, which would be humiliating for 'us.'"[58] Antonetti demanded funds for the repatriation of these women and their interracial children because he was committed to maintaining imperial racial order.

Female members of Afro-Syrian military households also remained in Syria. One example illustrates how a Syrian widow received preferential treatment by regional administrators. The documents related to Soulayman Diallo's inheritance portray the colonial state's greater regard for Levantine women when compared with sub-Saharan, Madagascan, or Moroccan wives of tirailleurs sénégalais. Soulayman Diallo died in Syria in April 1922. Diallo had served in the tirailleurs sénégalais since 1908 and had accrued a large pension—3,338.80 francs to be allocated in cash and another 1,600 francs in national defense bonds. Two women claimed entitlement to his pension. Aminé ben Mohamed el Abel requested that the government assist her in accessing her husband's pension. In Syria, el Abel and Diallo had married, lived together, and had a child. As a legitimate wife with a child, el Abel had legal entitlement to her husband's pension. Before el Abel contacted colonial ministries, Diallo's pension had been liquidated in November 1922 by Diallo's first and ex-wife, Della Mangassa. Mangassa had a son with Diallo, which normally would have entitled her to a portion of the pension. She had married another tirailleur sénégalais, Alpha Kamara, and lived with him in Saint-Louis. Having already liquidated Diallo's pension to Mangassa, there were few resources left for el Abel.

French officials in French West Africa and Syria delegitimized Mangassa's claim to Diallo's inheritance and portrayed her as avaricious and undeserving. They championed el Abel's claim, which they viewed as more critical due to el Abel's destitution and her interracial child. In the end, Mangassa would retain Diallo's pension and el Abel would inherit Diallo's movable objects and effects. The available documents reference an inventory of Diallo's possessions that was not preserved in the archives. The dossier relevant to this case contained no discussion about which agency or ministry would liquidate or ship Diallo's possessions. Five years after Diallo's death, el Abel had not received these resources.[59] The extent to which policymakers and military officials in Syria and French West Africa pursued el Abel's inheritance case demonstrates preferential treatment for tirailleurs sénégalais' widows from mandate territories. The attention and efforts evident in this inheritance case were extraordinary in comparison with other interracial households made up of tirailleurs sénégalais and foreign female colonial subjects.

MAINLAND FRANCE:
FRENCH WOMEN'S RACE, GENDER, AND CITIZENSHIP STATUS

During and immediately after both world wars, French military and civilian officials handled requests for repatriation, reunification, and financial assistance from members of Afro-French military households. Hundreds of thousands of tirailleurs sénégalais mobilized to mainland France during these conflicts. They met civilian French women while on leave, recuperating in hospitals, and during the interval between the cessation of hostilities and boarding military vessels bound for West Africa. The circumstances in which tirailleurs sénégalais and French civilian women entered into sexual and conjugal relationships were comparable to other cross-colonial relationships described above. Military and civilian governments treated Afro-French military households similarly to Afro-Moroccan and Afro-Syrian households—as undesirable challenges to French imperial racial and gendered order. Afro-French couples tested tirailleurs sénégalais' conjugal traditions because of the different legal statuses of West African soldiers and French women. Tirailleurs sénégalais were colonial subjects and customary law dictated their marital rites. French women were citizens and their marital legitimacy was beholden to practices defined in family law within the French Civil Code. Female partners of Afro-French military couples were literate in French, enlisted the assistance of municipal-level government officials, and leveraged their Frenchness—more often than their marital status—to make entitled claims to state assistance. These women also claimed that the state had a role in maintaining the integrity and virtuousness of their interracial households.

The presence of West Africans in mainland France during the Great War has received the greatest attention within the historiography of the tirailleurs sénégalais. Historians claim that the Great War was a watershed moment in dissolving myths of French social and cultural superiority that were fundamental to Republican colonial rhetoric.[60] Colonial troops in the metropole bore witness to the falsehoods of French superiority in the trenches and in their contact with French civilians.[61] The French feared West Africans' sexuality in the metropole because "miscegenation" threatened racial hierarchy and the very core of French society.[62] French women played numerous roles in tirailleurs sénégalais' experiences of France—*marraines de guerre*, military and medical staff, friends, companions, lovers.[63] Despite this academic attention, there were few Afro-French military households that entered the military or colonial record during the Great War.

At the conclusion of World War I, West African troops lingered near military bases in Saint-Raphael and Fréjus awaiting official word from Marseille regarding their formal demobilization and repatriation to West Africa. A champion of tirailleurs sénégalais, Lucie Cousturier wrote about her relationships with them in southern France. Cousturier was an artist and a writer who lived in Fréjus. West African troops sought out her residence for conviviality and French language education. In *Des inconnus chez moi*, Cousturier described young African men barely ready to take on the responsibilities of adulthood. Their conversation included concerns for mothers, wives, and families left behind in Senegal.[64] Other discussions addressed intimate experiences that tirailleurs sénégalais shared with French women, which ranged from friendship and courtship to conjugal relationships and transactional sex. Cousturier portrayed tirailleurs sénégalais in a way that revealed her sympathy for these men as they navigated cultural difference in seeking female companionship in France. In one extreme example, Cousturier questioned the veracity of a nearby townswoman's claim that a West African soldier had sexually assaulted her. Cousturier provided details that transformed the story into one in which a postmenopausal woman exploited the naiveté of a young tirailleur sénégalais and attempted to charge him for an undelivered sexual service.[65]

Interracial transactional sex was a military concern in the aftermath of the Great War. The military used rumors of transactional sex to delegitimize all interracial encounters. The French military administrators admonished tirailleurs sénégalais who "wasted" their pay on women, frivolous goods, and services. According to one colonial official, some soldiers returned to West Africa destitute, with nothing but their memories of the "women with loose morals that they met at the exits of military barracks."[66] Administrators in French West Africa feared the consequences of rumors spread in West Africa by repatriating soldiers who said that French women paid them for sexual encounters.⁶⁷ There were concerns that tirailleurs sénégalais, who had spent an extended period of time in metropolitan France, had become pretentious and no longer obeyed the racial hierarchy that French officials believed maintained order within empire. Administrators accused these soldiers of contracting "European" habits and living as foreigners in their own communities.⁶⁸ In the aftermath of the Great War, interracial sexual relationships contradicted efforts on the part of the French state and populace to reestablish France's cultural hegemony in its empire. The promotion of heteronormative and racially normative French families was integral to this process.⁶⁹

The number of active-duty tirailleurs sénégalais stationed in France decreased during the interwar period. France's declaration of war against Germany in September 1939 led to the rapid relocation of tirailleurs sénégalais serving in empire to mainland France. An additional hundred thousand West Africans mobilized toward the war effort between September 1939 and the fall of France in June 1940.⁷⁰ After France's capitulation, many sub-Saharan African soldiers were taken as German prisoners of war or repatriated to French West Africa.⁷¹ Some joined the resistance or took refuge with French civilians. Over the course of the war, West African troops interacted with sympathetic French people in a variety of contexts. Many ended up in military and civilian hospitals where they received the attention of French medical professionals and volunteers. Others demobilized and lingered in French cities near ports and military camps while awaiting repatriation to French West Africa. Hundreds of African prisoners of war joined these idle men when Germany released waves of prisoners throughout 1944. These men interacted with female French civilians and formed intimate bonds with them.

Throughout World War II and its aftermath, French civilians experienced waves of foreign occupation. German and Allied US and UK troops stationed in mainland France had engaged in nonconsensual sexual relationships with civilian French women.⁷² Tirailleurs sénégalais' sexuality remained a concern for government officials, but there is little evidence to suggest that French West African soldiers predominantly engaged in nonconsensual sexual relationships with French women.⁷³ Instead, civilian and military officials fielded requests from French female civilians soliciting assistance to maintain the integrity of their Afro-French households. This included French women relocating to West Africa and demobilized tirailleurs sénégalais relocating to mainland France. Various ministries moved to restrict French women's relocation to the colonies.[74] They had to be prudent in their methods. The new constitution of the French Fourth Republic enfranchised French women and the Lamine Guèye law of 1946 made tirailleurs sénégalais citizens—with conditions.[75] The minister of overseas France made sure to clarify to the high commissioner of French West Africa that indigenous soldiers and their households were required to renounce their statut personnel in order to enjoy the full rights of French citizens.[76] These new statuses altered the state's obligations to and regard for Afro-French military families. Military and civilian officials could not wield jurisdiction over these households' marital legitimacy, so they used their authority over international and oceanic travel to impede the long-distance relocation of French women to West Africa or West African men to France.

The military tasked indigenous African officers with surveilling demobilized tirailleurs sénégalais in France awaiting repatriation. These officers, particularly Lieutenants Philippe Aho and Sekou Koné, reported on troop morale and how unauthorized interracial conjugal relationships posed challenges to military order. Lieutenant Koné informed his commanders that the postwar shuttering of the Bordels Militaires de Campagne (campaign military bordellos, BMCs) led tirailleurs sénégalais to seek other forms of entertainment—particularly companionship among local civilian populations near their encampments. Koné expressed concern that tirailleurs sénégalais would engage in sexual relationships with French women, who, unlike women in BMCs, were not subjected to regular medical visits or supplied with prophylactics.[77] The impaired health of tirailleurs sénégalais would lower troop morale. Interracial children conceived out of wedlock created other significant problems.

Reports authored by Lieutenants Koné and Aho identified several causes for why Afro-French conjugal relationships seemed to multiply at the conclusion of World War II. Lieutenant Aho blamed municipal mayors—particularly those in northern and eastern France—for marrying sub-Saharan African men and French women without contacting military authorities beforehand. In the Mediterranean towns of Saint-Raphael and Fréjus, the military had a history of interposing itself between civilian authorities and tirailleurs sénégalais. The military obstructed civilian French women from marrying tirailleurs sénégalais in southern France. Civilian authorities in other parts of France were not accustomed to ceding their authority to military officials. There were no legal proscriptions on marriages between West African soldiers and French women and these mayors were "unaware of the principles which govern our tirailleurs or the unspoken rules that the military and local municipal leaders agree to enforce." Lieutenant Aho criticized civilian authorities that rewarded interracial couples with marriage certificates without "sufficient" inquiry into the various conditions that affected their eligibility for marriage—particularly soldiers' previous marital status or the timing of their repatriation.[78] Outside of southern France, civilian authorities unintentionally created long-distance marital relationships because they did not know that marrying French women would not prevent soldiers' imminent repatriation to West Africa. In some cases, these municipal authorities unknowingly made bigamists of West African soldiers and made French women second wives in polygynous households.[79]

According to legislation passed in March 1944, Afro-French military marriages were legal. However, mainland and colonial administrative officials undermined this legislation by questioning the degree to which it applied to Afro-French couples residing in empire.[80] Afro-French conjugal partners experienced parallel regulatory systems within civilian and military domains, as well as coexisting legal systems in mainland and imperial France. According to their personal status, tirailleurs sénégalais could practice polygyny. Monogamy was the only legal form of marriage for female French citizens. The 1946 constitution permitted them to maintain their own citizenship if they married foreigners—unlike previous decades when French women took on the citizenship status of their spouses upon marriage.[81] When it came to military benefits—in the form of spousal assistance, child support, and widow's pensions—the French military formally recognized the first wives of its indigenous soldiers. Technically, second wives (French or not) were ineligible to receive benefits. Yet tirailleurs sénégalais' French wives challenged the military's tiered and conditional system of allocations. The families of mainland French soldiers were entitled to far greater benefits than the families of tirailleurs sénégalais. In the case of Afro-French military households, French wives could access the entitlements normally awarded to mainland French soldiers' households. French women married to West African officers could access prenatal health care and state bonuses for live births.[82] Judging from documents generated around these interracial couples, individuals were not often aware of these legal and regulatory quandaries. In 1947, the government of French West Africa clarified that, irrespective of rank, West African soldiers married to French women had the same rights to family benefits as mainland French soldiers.[83]

Military officials portrayed polyamorous and polygynous West African soldiers in France as artful philanderers who dodged laws regulating monogamous marriage. During World War II and its aftermath, it is unlikely that African soldiers intentionally violated the law and acted duplicitously in their conjugal affairs. Creating multiwife households in different regions of French Empire was an inherited and accepted practice in tirailleurs sénégalais' conjugal traditions. Many West African soldiers had experienced isolation and trauma during the war. Creating intimate partnerships was a survival strategy in a conflict with unknown rules and uncertain ends. Tirailleurs sénégalais attempted to marry French women in accordance with French traditions and legal prescriptions. In a request initiated by the mayor of Toulon in 1946, Tiemoko Cissé attempted to divorce his wife in West Africa, Fanta Traoré, by proxy so that he could legally marry Gabrielle Maryse Josette Piegard. Cissé had married Traoré with the permission of his military commander in Segu in September 1943 before he deployed to France. Military authorities denied his request for divorce. While the military had the final word in the available documents, they did not technically have the legal jurisdiction to weigh in on affairs related to marriage. Between 1943 and 1946, soldiers' marriages and divorces became regulated by the civilian state.[84]

Metropolitan, colonial, and military authorities launched official inquiries seeking information related to soldiers' marital status. Inquests brought Afro-French couples' extended relations into conversations about the desirability and appropriateness of these interracial marital unions.[85] French military wives' mothers (often widows) were sometimes active agents assisting them in legalizing their conjugal unions—especially when interracial children were expected or already born.[86] When given the opportunity, West African families asserted their gerontocratic and patriarchal authority over the marital rights of junior members of their lineages. Tirailleurs sénégalais' extended kin refused to sanction these unions for a variety of reasons. These conjugal relationships had occurred outside of normative West African prenuptial marital traditions. Afro-French couples had taken shape in foreign territories, which denied West African parents and community elders their role in curating social reproduction. In 1946, Alioune Dieye, father of

Corporal Assane Dieye, formally opposed his son's marriage to Marie Louise Baliquet based on their religious differences.[87] Via military communication channels, Sacoura Ba's parents convinced him that his conjugal partner, Andrée Bertin, would be a bad marital match. Based on the chronology of the documents in this inquiry, it is possible that Ba and his parents were unaware that Bertin was pregnant with Ba's child.[88]

Military and colonial authorities used immigration legislation, transit costs, and other fiscal barriers to prevent Afro-French conjugal partners from living together—more so in West Africa.[89] Postwar interracial military households prompted Governor-General René Barthes of French West Africa to update the language concerning the admission of French people and other foreigners to West Africa. A decree on 14 September 1946 expanded mandatory documented information on French nationals' passports when traveling to French West Africa. Sojourners were also required to deposit a sum of 20,000 CFA with the company of transport before embarkation. These funds would be forwarded to the treasury of French West Africa. The deposit would pay for these French nationals' return trip in case of indigence or emergency.[90] Most French wives and tirailleurs sénégalais could not amass 20,000 CFA. The high cost of civilian transit between West Africa and France also created insurmountable obstacles for demobilized tirailleurs sénégalais—residing in West Africa—who desired to return to France and live with their French conjugal partners. In no uncertain terms, the minister of overseas France informed Hugette Pernot that she had the legal prerogative to marry Baye Seck, who had repatriated to Kébémer, Senegal, in 1946. In the same letter, the minister denied Pernot's request for fiscal assistance to bring Baye Seck back to France.[91] Some tirailleurs sénégalais tried another tactic, appealing to government officials for assistance in locating employment in France. Once demobilized, former soldiers needed proof of employment or apprenticeship to return to or live in France with their conjugal households.[92]

In appeals aimed at civilian and military officials, Afro-French couples cited their interracial children as justification for state assistance in maintaining the integrity of their households. Albert Yenou and Paulette Bastien began petitioning military and civilian authorities prior to Yenou's demobilization and repatriation to Dahomey in 1945. Their daughter, Micheline, was born while their requests aged on administrators' desks. Civilian authorities eventually granted Yenou permission to relocate to Vittel and wed Paulette Bastien. However, Yenou could not amass the 21,000 metropolitan francs necessary to return to France. This family remained on separate continents as of April 1948.[93] Historical documents convey a general disregard for the wellbeing of Afro-French military children. It is unclear whether the military allocated specific funds for the interracial children of the Afro-French military households they forced apart in the aftermath of World War II. Most of the children resulting from wartime conjugal relationships were infants and their biological needs necessitated an intimate proximity with their mothers. There was a pervasive bureaucratic assumption that interracial children would remain with their French mothers. This contrasted with historical and future military custody practices for interracial children in African military households. Military officials protected the paternal authority of tirailleurs sénégalais over their interracial children, irrespective of biological need, in Madagascar in the 1920s (see above) and in Vietnam in the 1950s (see next chapter). Remarkably, the military assumed that French women's custody over Afro-French children was sacrosanct.

During the aftermath of the Great War in West Africa, state authorities systematized the ways in which West African military household members accessed resources from the military and colonial government. In doing so, members of the colonial state and military became stakeholders in maintaining soldiers' familial relationships, as well as authorities in acknowledging and superintending their marital legitimacy. The French state increased its authority over African military household organization via the welfare it offered them. Families receiving military assistance, on paper if not in practice, conformed to male-breadwinner, heteronormative, and monogamous household models. The interwar period witnessed a widening divergence between colonial military conjugal traditions and West African marital and conjugal practices.

From one World War to the next, tirailleurs sénégalais came into greater contact with other populations across French Empire. Despite long distances, cultural differences, and manifold bureaucratic obstacles, tirailleurs sénégalais and their foreign conjugal partners endeavored to legitimize their conjugal relationships. Members of cross-colonial households faced official discrimination that most partners had little legal or political power to challenge. Race and racial order influenced how administrators obstructed or facilitated the long-distance movements of cross-colonial family members. In the next chapter, we will see how different citizenship statuses—among West African originaires and indigènes soldiers—further complicated how West Africans acquired legitimacy for cross-colonial households. West African originaires serving in French Indochina experienced conjugal and marital life differently than tirailleurs sénégalais. Originaires soldiers' Afro-Vietnamese households had greater prosperity and longevity.

6

Afro-Vietnamese Military Households in French Indochina and West Africa, 1930–56

IN OCTOBER 1950, THE GOVERNOR-GENERAL OF FRENCH WEST Africa received a telegram regarding Pierre Aguibou, an Afro-Vietnamese sixteen-month-old infant brought to Ziguinchor, Senegal, by Auguste Diba. Diba was a tirailleur sénégalais returning from a two-year tour in the French Indochina War (1945–54). Pierre Aguibou had been born to a French West African soldier and a female Vietnamese civilian. The child's surname was common to a large region of forested West Africa. Aguibou's name suggested his West African parentage but did not indicate filial ties with Auguste Diba. For reasons unstated in the telegram, Auguste Diba became Pierre Aguibou's guardian and transported the infant from Vietnam to Ziguinchor. Once in Senegal, Auguste Diba entrusted the care of the child to his sister, Moundo Diba.[1] Pierre Aguibou was part of the largest transimperial migration of foreign military wives and children to French West Africa. In colonial Vietnam, West African soldiers engaged in conjugal relationships with local women on a scale unparalleled in the history of tirailleurs sénégalais' marital traditions. Decades-old traditions of Franco-Vietnamese military conjugality preceded West Africans' deployment to Southeast Asia. Many of these relationships resulted in Afro-Vietnamese children. The military facilitated the relocation of Afro-Vietnamese military households to West Africa between 1946 and 1957. The fall of Dien Bien Phu in 1954 signaled the end of French Empire in Southeast Asia, which accelerated the migration of

Afro-Vietnamese families to West Africa and caused their fragmentation across empire.

Pierre Aguibou's arrival in West Africa offers an opportunity to rethink the operation of race, sexuality, and family in French imperial conflicts. Afro-Vietnamese children call attention to the limitations in historical studies of métis children in French Empire that follow the colonizer/colonized binary.[2] In Vietnam, "Africasian" was a subcategory of métis, or mixed-race people, used to describe these children.[3] When compared with French Mediterranean colonial territories and mainland France, West African soldiers confronted fewer socially and militarily imposed proscriptions when engaging in conjugal relationships with Vietnamese women.[4] Stories from the French Indochina War emphasize African soldiers' profound affection for wives and filial obligation to children.[5] The relocation of Afro-Vietnamese children to West Africa—in the absence of one or both parents—was a new trend in French African soldiers' conjugal traditions. French African soldiers viewed each other as fictive kin who shared the responsibilities of raising the children of fallen members of their battalions. They inherited or adopted other African soldiers' Vietnamese children. The French military invested in the paternity of their African soldiers and funded the long-distance removal of interracial children from Vietnam.[6] Soldiers' African wives, sisters, and mothers, often with no advance notice, became the caretakers of foreign war orphans and/or their male relatives' motherless infants. There are traditions of child fostering in West Africa, in which children circulate among extended family members, but these practices rarely involved foreign infants of nursing age.[7] The historical record does not comment on what Moundo Diba thought of her new maternal responsibilities.

In this chapter, "French African soldiers" broadly describes soldiers recruited south of the Sahara. More often, I will flag soldiers' origin and citizenship status because the differences between originaires and tirailleurs sénégalais drastically impacted soldiers' conjugal outcomes in Southeast Asia. West African citizens from the Four Communes of Senegal served in Southeast Asia from the interwar period until the fall of Dien Bien Phu in 1954. Perhaps a few hundred originaire soldiers served in French Indochina at any one time between 1930 and 1955. These West African servicemen and their Afro-Vietnamese families experienced World War II, the Vichy regime, and Japanese occupation in Southeast Asia. The French Fourth Republic

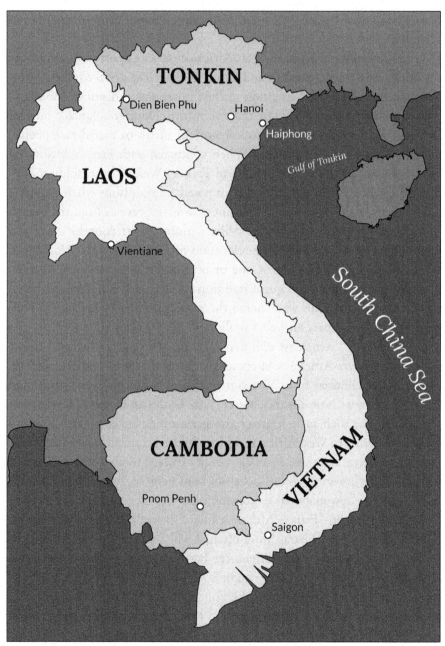

MAP 6.1. French Indochina. Map by Isaac Barry

reasserted its colonial authority in Vietnam after Japanese demobilization. On 2 September 1945, Nguyen That Thanh (Ho Chi Minh) declared the Democratic Republic of Vietnam's political independence. The French responded with war and predicted raising their occupying forces in Indochina to fifty thousand French troops. Colonial troops and the Foreign Legion would provide additional support.[8] Two years later, the first battalions of tirailleurs sénégalais began the long transoceanic voyage from Dakar to Saigon. During the French Indochina War, Guinean, Upper Voltan, and Equatorial African volunteers filled the ranks of the tirailleurs sénégalais.[9] This demographic shift resulted from new trends in recruitment. In response to criticisms regarding the use of conscripted soldiers in active theaters of war, the French National Assembly passed the Indochina Amendment on 11 November 1951. This decree affected all soldiers serving in the French armed forces and ensured that only voluntary soldiers would serve in the French Indochina War. In order to comply with the amendment and maintain a steady flow of African recruits, the French colonial military offered new economic incentives to entice young men to enlist as volunteers.[10] Tirailleurs sénégalais' numbers on the ground in French Indochina grew from 2,260 in 1948 to 19,731 in 1954.[11]

Over the course of the French Indochina War, tens of thousands of French African soldiers deployed to Southeast Asia.[12] Their numbers were far fewer than those who had mobilized to France in either of the world wars. Even so, Afro-Vietnamese conjugal households outnumbered interracial and/or cross-colonial military families in previous episodes of the tirailleurs sénégalais' conjugal history. French African soldiers served longer tours of duty in French Indochina, where decades of colonial occupation had normalized heteronormative interracial sexual and conjugal relationships. French military occupation and imperial masculinity facilitated the wide articulation of gendered and racialized colonial power over the bodies of Vietnamese women.[13] Encounters between Vietnamese women and foreign men affiliated with France ranged from extreme sexual violence to deeply affectionate care, but always occurred within the power dynamics of colonial militarism.[14] Industrialized prostitution was a prominent feature of the urban colonial military landscape. Military brothels were also prevalent in rural northern Vietnam (Tonkin).[15] The pervasive belief that Vietnamese women, sex workers or not, were sexually available to foreign men influenced the ways in which French

African soldiers formed casual, transactional, romantic, and conjugal bonds with them. These relationships signal that colonial constructions of racial and gendered order operated differently in Vietnam.

Interviews with veterans of the French Indochina War and Vietnamese widows provide intimate anecdotes of how citizenship status determined African soldiers' experiences in Vietnam and the aftermath of the war. This distinction impacted soldiers' ability to maintain conjugal relationships in Vietnam, as well as affecting whether their Afro-Vietnamese households would accompany them to West Africa. This chapter begins with the unique conjugal experiences of originaire soldiers in interwar Vietnam. These men survived World War II in Vietnam because of the intimate bonds they formed with local women. After they deployed to Southeast Asia in 1947, tirailleurs sénégalais' sexual and conjugal practices adapted to the context of wartime colonial Vietnam. Many engaged in interracial conjugal relationships and attempted to acquire official sanction of them. Once the colonial state recognized the legitimacy of these interracial military households, Afro-Vietnamese family members entered bureaucracies of social welfare that would endure the collapse of colonialism in French Indochina—and eventually of French Empire.

FRENCH WEST AFRICAN CITIZENS IN SOUTHEAST ASIA

Originaire soldiers' experiences in French Indochina were exceptional to those of other African servicemen deployed to Southeast Asia. The French military supported the prosperity of their interracial families in Vietnam. Originaire soldiers' conjugal practices recall the nineteenth-century, during which officials had debated the ideal racial composition and longevity of tirailleurs sénégalais' household arrangements in Vietnam. Beginning in the interwar period, originaire soldiers engaged in short-term, long-term, transactional, polyamorous, polygynous, and monogamous conjugal relationships with Vietnamese women. French citizenship endowed originaire soldiers with greater latitude in making choices about their military careers and their personal lives. Originaires could initiate, maintain, and legitimize their interracial households over the course of years because they had the ability to extend their tours of duty in Vietnam. Children in Afro-Vietnamese originaire households inherited French citizenship from their fathers via the Blaise Diagne law of 1916. They accessed resources offered by the French military and state—married housing, public education, health services, and eventually international relocation to West Africa. The outbreak of the Second World War II disrupted originaire households' access to government and military resources and they relied on their Vietnamese partners and in-laws to survive the war. The outbreak of the French Indochina War in 1945 made their advantages more obvious. Even though the French Union's 1946 constitution offered aspects of citizenship to French colonial subjects, originaires and erstwhile *indigènes* continued to serve in different branches of the French military, with different pay scales and benefits. Wifely accompaniment was an exceptional benefit. At least two originaire soldiers brought their West African originaire wives to Vietnam—a conjugal practice that nineteenth-century French officials in Vietnam had rejected and one that tirailleurs sénégalais had been denied since Morocco.[16]

The interwar period provided the context for two divergent, competing ideas about African men's sexuality and conjugality. On the one hand, the military endorsed an image of monogamous, heteronormative African family men. The other was one of hypersexuality, which emphasized black men's physical prowess and carnal desires. This second image may have resulted from the hysteria generated in France during the Great War and in Germany during African soldiers' occupation of the Rhineland. Propaganda had circulated in these countries that emphasized the ungovernable and libidinous nature of African colonial soldiers, with emphasis on the specter of miscegenation.[17] The sexuality and conjugality of black soldiers were a constant concern of French civilians and military personnel in colonial Vietnam. During the interwar period, West African originaires and diasporic African soldiers—predominantly from the French Caribbean islands of Martinique and Guadeloupe—served in Southeast Asia. They were a highly visible demographic minority populating the ranks of the regular French Army. Evidence suggests that these African and diasporic African soldiers engaged in a range of sexual and conjugal practices that were similar to those of their fellow French servicemen.

In interwar French Indochina, the colonial military's prurient concerns regarding black soldiers' sexuality were apparent in satirical anecdotes featured in colonial newspapers. A lampoon article, "À la recherché de Barnavaux: Le divorce de Thémélius Saint-Afrique," published in 1924, illustrated a range of French concerns and stereotypes pertaining to black masculinity and sexuality.

According to the article, a Vietnamese madam logged a complaint with a French military officer regarding black Martiniquan soldiers frequenting her brothel. The madam claimed that the physiological and anatomical disparities in the size of black soldiers' sexual organs and those of Vietnamese sex workers created physical discomfort for women in the brothel. The madam proposed regulations against black men's use of her brothel.[18] This article pulled from the colonial playbook of racial and gendered difference in empire and rearticulated stereotypes about African and Asian sexuality. Further, it communicated that Vietnamese women in distress seek the assistance of white French saviors to protect them from black Frenchmen. A former commanding officer of tirailleurs sénégalais in Vietnam, Colonel Maurice Rives, believed that the mythmaking around Africans' sexuality delayed the military's use of tirailleurs sénégalais in Southeast Asia.[19] At the outbreak of the French Indochina War, General Charles de Gaulle argued against using tirailleurs sénégalais in Southeast Asia in order to respect Vietnamese sociocultural hierarchies of race and gender. His detractors would eventually win the argument.[20]

Originaire soldiers formed conjugal relationships with Vietnamese women that would prove more steadfast than the French military's ability to support these troops during World War II. In June 1940, France surrendered to Germany. According to the conditions of the armistice agreement, empire came under the purview of Vichy France. Japan took advantage of these political changes and compelled the French in Indochina to cede economic control and border security to the Japanese military. Vichy France representatives struggled to maintain political and administrative authority in the region. The presence of Japanese troops in Indochina increased throughout World War II. In early 1945, the Imperial Japanese Army Air Force bombarded major cities, interned French military forces (including West African originaires) and eventually installed Bao Dai (Nguyen Phuc Vinh Thuy) at the head of an "Empire of Vietnam."[21] On 9 March 1945, the French Indochina colonial administration ceded its power to the Japanese military. These acts effectively severed contact between the West African soldiers living in Indochina and the rest of the world. It was not until after the Japanese surrender in August 1945 that Allied forces could reestablish French colonial authority in the region.

Ninh Beye (née Nguyen), the widow of originaire soldier Ibrahima Beye, vividly recalled the heightened presence of Japanese soldiers in Haiphong during World War II. Ninh Nguyen met Beye at a dancehall in Haiphong in 1939. Major Vietnamese urban areas—Saigon, Hanoi, and Haiphong—were sites where convivial nightlife enabled social intermingling between French soldiers on leave and the Vietnamese civilian population. Nguyen had not intended to date a black French soldier, but Ibrahima Beye energetically pursued her. She claimed that his persistence won her over. Beye was from Saint-Louis and had deployed to French Indochina before the news of World War II reached Southeast Asia. Indochina's severance from the rest of French Empire transformed Beye's two-year tour into an indefinite stay. Ibrahima and Ninh married and made a family. By 1945, Ibrahima Beye frequently spent nights off-base with his wife and their first child. Ninh Beye distinctly remembered the Japanese bombardments in March of that year because she ran for shelter through the streets of Haiphong with her young daughter tucked under her arm. Afterward, Japanese patrols increased in Ninh Beye's neighborhood. A few days after the bombardments, Japanese troops came to Ninh Beye's door looking for her husband—explicitly asking for the black French soldier. He was out at the time. With her fourteen-month-old interracial daughter hidden somewhere in the house, Ninh Beye claimed that she was unmarried and that no black man lived with her.

Had he been present, Ibrahima Beye would likely have been rounded up and interned in a Japanese imprisonment camp like other originaires and French troops serving in Indochina. After that terrifying night, the Beyes developed a plan to smuggle Ibrahima out of Haiphong. Ninh Beye dressed her husband in traditional Vietnamese women's clothing—flowing trousers covered with a shin-length tunic—in order to secret him out of the Japanese-occupied city. Ninh Beye claimed that her husband could pass as a woman in the cover of darkness because he had lost a significant amount of weight over the course of the war. Strict rationing measures had existed in Indochina since 1940. Dressed as a woman, Ibrahima Beye escaped from the city by swimming across the Haiphong River in the cover of night. He found safe haven among his Nguyen in-laws outside of town. Ninh and Ibrahima reunited after Japan surrendered to Allied forces in late 1945. When it was once again possible to travel between Southeast Asia and West Africa, they were one of the first Afro-Vietnamese households to relocate to Senegal in 1947.[22]

Jean Gomis experienced Vichy Indochina as a child in an Afro-Vietnamese military family. Gomis was born to Nguyen Thi Sau and originaire Emile

Gomis in Vietnam in 1933. Gomis's father had intended to return to West Africa for a visit when Jean was old enough to manage the six-to-eight-week boat ride to Senegal. The Second World War interrupted these plans and Gomis's family remained in Vietnam until 1946.[23] Jean Gomis grew up in a world dominated by French military culture and his mother's extended Vietnamese family. During his infancy and early adolescence, he attended French-language public schools with French expatriate, Franco-Vietnamese, and Vietnamese children. Jean Gomis experienced Vichy ideology in his early schooling and in 2011 remembered all of the words and melody of "Maréchal, nous voilà!"[24] Schoolchildren daily sang this anthem of Philippe Pétain's National Revolution in France and empire. State-funded spectacles promoted Vichy France's motto of "Patrimony, Work, and Family" in French Indochina.[25] Jean Gomis experienced this propaganda more intensely as an expatriate son of a French African servicemen in Indochina than he would have growing up in Dakar during the Vichy era.[26] Jean Gomis's memories of growing up in Vietnam hang next to memories of soldiering in Vietnam. He inherited his father's French citizenship and returned to Vietnam as a trained soldier a few days after the fall of Dien Bien Phu in 1954.

During the French Indochina War, originaires maintained their privileged status in relation to tirailleurs sénégalais. Despite valiant efforts on the part of West African politicians like Lamine Guèye to erase the divide between citizen and subject, the 1946 constitution of the Fourth French Republic maintained civic distinctions between residents of France and overseas inhabitants of the French Union. Originaires continued to have the same civic status as mainland French residents. Formerly referred to as French imperial subjects, French Union populations acquired the "quality of citizens," but not citizenship.[27] This ambiguity existed throughout the French-Indochinese conflict and maintained palpable distinctions between tirailleurs sénégalais and originaire soldiers. In a clear example of this privilege, a small number of originaires brought their West African wives to Vietnam. Urbain Diagne served in Vietnam between 1947 and 1957. While on leave in 1952, he married Marie-Désirée Simone, who was also an originaire. Simone worked as a stenographer for the secretary of commerce in Thiès, which facilitated administrative clearance for her relocation to Hanoi shortly after their wedding. They had three children (Sophie, Charles, and Paul) over the next five years in Hanoi and Saigon. Members of their African military household socialized with Afro-Vietnamese and Franco-Vietnamese families throughout the war. Marie-Désirée Diagne befriended Vietnamese military wives and raised her children with the assistance of Vietnamese nannies. The Diagnes attended elaborate church weddings in which French African soldiers married Vietnamese women with French officers and Vietnamese in-laws in attendance.[28] The French military supported this small French-African-Vietnamese community, which achieved a degree of prosperity described with nostalgia by its members over fifty years later.[29]

MOBILIZING THE HOME FRONT

At a time when the atrocities of World War II and the infamous 1944 massacre at Thiaroye were fresh in West African memory, young West African men volunteered in large numbers for military service in French Indochina.[30] Recruits in the 1940s and 1950s viewed military service as a means to acquire regular access to resources, which could help them in achieving a range of interconnected personal and familial goals. The powerful image of the uniformed tirailleurs sénégalais symbolized a shortcut to adulthood. Amady Moutar Gaye enlisted in the tirailleurs sénégalais in 1949 in order to gain autonomy from his father. His father was a veteran of World War II and tried to prevent his son's enlistment by hiding his birth certificate—a document required for voluntary enlistment. Amady Moutar Gaye sidestepped this bureaucratic formality by orally providing his birth details to a recruitment board eager to enlist volunteer soldiers bound for Southeast Asia.[31] Acquiring wives and building families continued to motivate young West African men to enlist in the tirailleurs sénégalais. Marriage was an important factor in veteran sergeant Omar Diop's decision to volunteer for the tirailleurs sénégalais. As a teenager, Diop apprenticed with his uncle, who was an electrician. They worked on installing the electric line between Bambey and Fatick in Senegal. After accumulating a year's pay, Diop returned to his hometown of Thiès in 1954 to initiate prenuptial arrangements with the family of his childhood romantic interest. The day Diop returned to Thiès was also the day of her marriage to a veteran of the French Indochina War. Shortly afterward, Diop enlisted in the tirailleurs sénégalais in order to emulate the man who had married his adolescent crush.[32]

Some soldiers used their enlistment bonuses to expedite their nuptials directly before their first deployment to Southeast Asia. Others married during home stays in between tours of duty.³³ Some married while serving in Southeast Asia. Evidence suggests that contingents of West African soldiers at the beginning of the French Indochina War were single more often than troops serving nearer to the conclusion of the conflict. Young, unmarried men nominated ascendant and lateral kin to receive remittances and to inherit soldiers' pay if they died in Vietnam. Of the fifty-two tirailleurs sénégalais boarding the *Pasteur* for Southeast Asia in September 1949, twenty soldiers chose their fathers as their emergency contact/beneficiary. Ten nominated a male sibling, seven each opted for their uncle or mother, and only one soldier chose his wife as the recipient of news, money orders, and military benefits.³⁴ In another example from 1950, three of fifty-five West African soldiers chose their wives as their beneficiaries, whereas more than half nominated their fathers.³⁵ These choices indicate that the majority of these recruits were likely single. At the conclusion of the war, a broad survey found that 35 to 40 percent of returning tirailleurs sénégalais were married.³⁶

For West African military households, long-distance married military life during the French Indochina War could be onerous for home-front wives. In the absence of soldiering husbands, patriarchal and gerontocratic familial authorities intervened to regulate the relationship between military representatives and soldiers' West African wives and children. While husbands served abroad, their West African wives acquired new obligations to their in-laws, as well as relying on them for assistance. Some communities in West Africa practiced patrilocality, a marital tradition in which wives physically relocated to the village/compound of their husband's kin. In these circumstances, soldiers' wives became new, minority members of their husband's lineage group. They could reduce their marginality and gain prestige by producing offspring. In the absence of their soldiering husbands, legitimate children were difficult to conceive. Wives yielded to the authority of soldiers' relatives, who took authoritative roles in superintending wives' activities and managed their contact with the French colonial military. Those wives who relocated to live with their husbands' kin groups had greater opportunity to benefit from the combined attention of their in-laws and the colonial military. Conversely, submitting to the authority of tirailleurs sénégalais' kin could be difficult—especially without husbands present to mediate disputes between wives and kin.³⁷

Familial and military interlocutors destabilized African military households and increased the challenges of maintaining long-distance relationships.

Young wives of tirailleurs sénégalais could find living with their in-laws untenable. For many, there was little alternative. Archival documents rarely provide details concerning the relationships between soldiers' wives and their kin. Wives expressed their dissatisfaction with these arrangements with their feet. Wives went missing.[38] Wives remarried and relocated without alerting their in-laws or the colonial government. These strategies signaled wives' discontentment with long-distance marital relationships. The colonial military viewed absent military wives, irrespective of their activities or intentions, as detrimental to soldiers' morale.[39] The colonial state encouraged wives' fidelity with the provision of family allocations and by endorsing soldiers' kin's guardianship of their nascent conjugal households. The colonial state became aware of tirailleurs sénégalais' broken conjugal households when money orders, remittances, news, and indemnities failed to reach their wives.[40] A curt telegram informed Sergeant Dieme in 1949 that a 2,600-franc money order had not reached its intended destination because his wife had remarried.[41] Military officials acknowledged some responsibility for lags and failures in communicating important information between tirailleurs sénégalais and West African military wives.

Home-front wives living in urban areas had greater opportunity to access remittances and information from the colonial military. Rural households rarely received news of soldiers' specific locations while serving in the Far East. Without this information, they could not send telegrams or letters to their loved ones, even when they were coaxed to do so by the colonial state.[42] In French West Africa, there were only eight sites where soldiers' home-front relatives could file new paperwork—Dakar, Saint-Louis, Bamako, Conakry, Abidjan, Cotonou, and two locations in eastern and western Niger.[43] Regional military headquarters were great distances from wives and families hoping to inform military officials of missing money orders or changes in soldiers' marital and/or parental status. Military officials had poor command of local African languages, which complicated bureaucratic processes. Misplaced or missing required documents—identification papers, marriage certificates, birth certificates, soldiers' enlistment documents—could void the sacrifices that African wives and family members made in traveling to military headquarters. Some tirailleurs sénégalais preferred to keep their pay until they returned home.[44] This was a risky decision, since remittances increasingly came to symbolize the strength of the link between soldiers and their West African conjugal households.

DATING ON THE WAR FRONT

West African soldiers had greater opportunity to form cross-colonial conjugal relationships in Vietnam than in previous twentieth-century imperial deployments. Many French African soldiers initiated intimate relationships with Vietnamese women, which often developed into monogamous conjugal households. The French military tolerated these relationships, though strongly advised against them. In the decades preceding the French Indochina War, French expatriates and French servicemen had contributed to the industrialization of transactional sex in Vietnam. Tirailleurs sénégalais were encouraged to visit military brothels but to refrain from establishing long-term relationships with female sex workers. Military brothels were controlled spaces of "appropriate" sexuality, where soldiers could engage in licit forms of masculinity.[45] Originaire soldiers and tirailleurs sénégalais dated Vietnamese women that they met in urban dancehalls or in villages neighboring their military posts. Occurring outside of the sanctioned brothels, the military labeled these romances with a variety of derogatory and degrading terms. French West African soldiers' conjugal traditions incorporated the language used in Vietnam to describe French soldiers' relationships with local women. *Concubinage* and *encongayement* were used interchangeably in official documents and interviews with veterans to describe heteronormative romantic relationships between men serving in French military forces and Vietnamese women. Both of these words connote the impermanence and illegitimacy of these interracial households in colonial Indochina. According to Frank Proschan, the Vietnamese term *con gai*, the root of encongayement, once meant "'young woman, girl, female child,' but its semantics in the French discourse shifted over time from 'woman' to 'wife' to 'mistress' to 'whore,' ultimately accomplishing linguistically the degradation of all womanhood to whoredom."[46] The military deployed *congaïe*, concubine, and "clandestine" wife in order to indicate that soldiers and Vietnamese women were participating in sexual relationships that lacked marital legitimacy. Veterans' recollections suggest that multiple meanings of *congaïe* coexisted during the French Indochina War. They deployed *congaïe* with romanticized nostalgia. Veterans used the term to describe women who worked in brothels, as well as women who formed long-term monogamous relationships and legitimate marriages with West African soldiers.

Vietnamese women and West African soldiers met and engaged in romantic relationships in a variety of settings in Vietnam. Several veterans spoke of dancehalls in Saigon, bearing names like Golden Lion and Blue Bird, where they went for amusement while on leave.[47] Known as "bar-dancings," these venues offered leisure, heteronormative conviviality, and live entertainment. These dancehalls differed in nature from the brothels that offered erotic entertainment and transactional sex. Large Saigon brothels, with fanciful names like Buffalos Park and Ice Cream Palace, were only open at night, when they filled with soldiers from all over French Empire. Estimates for the number of sex workers inside Buffalos Park varied from three to four hundred women. According to Jean Gomis, urban brothels were privately owned, yet the uniquely military clientele led soldier Marc Guèye to assume that the military owned and operated Buffalos Park.[48] Guèye's assumption had merit if one considers that soldiers patrolled them and military medical staff examined women working in them. Many tirailleurs sénégalais were unsatisfied with or repulsed by the transactional sex on offer at Bordels Militaires de Campagne (BMCs). According to French officers, African soldiers preferred conjugal relationships initiated outside of brothels.

In rural military outposts, French military agents coercively recruited local women for military-run brothels.[49] Here, the military controlled prices, required prophylactics, and subjected (involuntary) sex workers to routine gynecological exams.[50] Rural BMCs were tense sites of contestation because local communities objected to the employment of Vietnamese women as sex workers. The military mitigated this issue by recruiting out-of-town Vietnamese women for rural BMCs so that their connections with the local community were negligible.[51] Soldiers from different regions of French Empire expressed racial prejudices and discord within BMCs. In one example, a group of Vietnamese French colonial soldiers savagely assaulted a Nigerien soldier because he had been frequenting one Vietnamese soldier's preferred sex workers. This quarrel spun out of control and resulted in injuries ranging from light to severe for twelve Vietnamese soldiers and five tirailleurs sénégalais.[52] While they maintained a close eye on the functioning of local BMCs, French officials could not prevent soldiers' emotional attachment to women working in military brothels. According to a French military report from 1952 in Phu-Lang-Thuong, a tirailleur sénégalais murdered his African lieutenant because he discovered that they both were romantically involved with the same woman in a brothel.[53]

Despite these violent outbursts in and around state-sanctioned brothels, French officials were more apprehensive of intimate relationships between tirailleurs sénégalais and "clandestine" women. According to French propaganda, West African soldiers were inexperienced newcomers to Vietnamese guerilla warfare and had difficulty distinguishing between female Vietnamese civilians and female Viet Minh operatives.[54] Women were auxiliaries and combatants in the anticolonial struggle. The Viet Minh engaged in covert tactics that manipulated French colonial soldiers' assumptions about women and warfare. In one example cited in military archives, a group of male operatives dressed as women attacked a unit of tirailleurs sénégalais with grenades.[55] One veteran recalled a harrowing incident when Vietnamese village women tending their rice paddies fired upon his marching unit. The tirailleurs sénégalais had turned their backs on these laboring women, at which point the women retrieved rifles that they had previously submerged in the paddy water. They opened fire on the unsuspecting tirailleurs sénégalais and injured several.[56]

The French printed and circulated propaganda posters (see fig. 6.1) and booklets (see fig. 6.2) providing simple visual messaging about the duplicitous and dangerous nature of Vietnamese women.[57] According to these materials, Vietnamese women who sought the romantic attentions and patronage of African soldiers were entrepreneurial thieves or Viet Minh double agents. The French military blamed protracted liaisons between "congaïes" and African troops for military indiscipline—irregular absences, alcohol abuse, and desertion for love.[58] Military commanders held their troops responsible for contravening proscriptions on romantic relationships with clandestine women. Military officials handed out disciplinary actions, transfers, and demotions to men engaged in "dangerous" conjugal relationships. Erstwhile first-class soldier Konté's Vietnamese conjugal partner was implicated in a Viet Minh–led surprise attack on his rural military post. The post's commander demoted Konté and transferred him to another military sector.[59]

Whether initiated inside or outside the walls of military-operated brothels, Afro-Vietnamese conjugal relationships occurred in an uneven playing field of French colonial war. Colonial occupation and guerilla war made long-term relationships nearly impossible for tirailleurs sénégalais. Vietnamese conjugal partners were not allowed to follow tirailleurs sénégalais as they transferred from one military sector to another. Interracial couples made up

FIGURE 6.1. "Sois actif et vigilant, LE VIET EST PARTOUT," 10H 424, © Service historique de la Défense.

FIGURE 6.2. "Attention! Ta solde est pour qui?" in *Soldat africain, quelques conseils pour toi*, 10H 424, © Service historique de la Défense.

of colonial subjects lacked full rights and full integration into the political and legal regimes of France.[60] They had little recourse to challenge the French colonial authority's negligence of their conjugal relationships. Many African soldiers struggled with the strictures of military command, which compromised their ability to realize personal goals related to their Afro-Vietnamese households. The abandonment of their conjugal partners often resulted from soldiers' transfers within Vietnam and their repatriations to West Africa. The military did little to facilitate communication or correspondence between Afro-Vietnamese conjugal partners in Southeast Asia unless they were registered as legal spouses.

Despite familial and communal proscriptions on Vietnamese women's participation in relationships with French soldiers—black, white, Arab, or otherwise—Vietnamese widows, interviewed in Senegal, framed their participation in budding romantic relationships with West African soldiers as voluntary.[61] War and colonialism constrained their romantic choices. Vietnamese women entered into relationships with West African soldiers with social, political, and legal disadvantages. West African soldiers had the backing of the colonial government and the military. The colonial military turned a blind eye to acts of gender-based sexual violence in rice paddies and brothels, in order to shelter their colonial soldiers from sanction.[62] Vietnamese women's vulnerability to the whims of soldiers and the negligence of the colonial state were symptomatic of systemic gendered discrimination in colonial Vietnam generally and the French Indochina conflict in particular. Vietnamese women could face family alienation for dating *taî denh*, or black Frenchmen.[63] Marital legitimacy could reduce the moral and social derision they experienced in their communities as girlfriends of foreign soldiers serving in the French military corps.[64] Official sanction of their conjugal unions with West African soldiers translated into family benefits for wives and their interracial children.

Afro-Vietnamese conjugal relationships in French Indochina faced their greatest challenge at the conclusion of the war. The Viet Minh's capture of France's military installation at Dien Bien Phu signaled the end of nine years of civil and anticolonial conflict. For Afro-Vietnamese households, Dien Bien Phu marked the beginning of familial fragmentation, which encompassed the breakup of conjugal partners, separating parents from children, and/or the severance of Vietnamese wives from their social worlds. With the Geneva Accords of 1954, the international community recognized the political sovereignty of Vietnam, Laos, and Cambodia. These accords divided Vietnam at the 17th parallel, which served as the boundary between Ho Chi Minh's Democratic Republic of Vietnam and Emperor Bao Dai's Republic of Vietnam in the south. Ho Chi Minh's government insisted French Forces withdraw from northern Vietnam within three hundred days of independence.[65] The majority of French African soldiers had served in Tonkin (northern Vietnam) during the war and many had established Afro-Vietnamese households in Hanoi and Haiphong. As the French military began their demobilization from North Vietnam, one French officer estimated that more than a third of the four hundred thousand civilians residing in Hanoi would request assistance in evacuating south to the Republic of Vietnam.[66] The majority of Afro-Vietnamese households did not survive the division of Vietnam. Fewer successfully relocated to West Africa. The minority of interracial families that survived evacuation and repatriation intact would face new challenges in West Africa.

BRINGING THE WAR HOME

A fraction of Afro-Vietnamese households survived the French Indochina conflict, evacuation, and international relocation. Originaires' Afro-Vietnamese households were better positioned to survive these processes because originaires had registered their marriages with the French state. Originaires began to return to West Africa with their interracial households after Japan's withdrawal from colonial Vietnam in 1945.[67] Of the ten Afro-Vietnamese originaire families that relocated to Rufisque before 1951, three Vietnamese wives had remained in French Indochina.[68] Vietnamese conjugal partners accompanied tirailleurs sénégalais to West Africa in smaller percentages than with originaire soldiers. As seen with Pierre Aguibou at the beginning of this chapter, the children of tirailleurs sénégalais' Afro-Vietnamese households began appearing in West Africa in 1950. Interracial children arrived in West Africa in greater numbers than Vietnamese women. Military, colonial, and metropolitan legislation supported the paternal prerogatives of their West African soldiers. Due to the nature of the historical documents, it is difficult to assess the degree to which Vietnamese mothers could participate in deciding long-term custody of interracial children. Ultimately, the French colonial military subsidized the relocation of Afro-Vietnamese infants, often without their mothers.

"Africasian" was a distinct label for Afro-Vietnamese children. This term distinguished the children of West African soldiers from those of French soldiers in Vietnam. Historically, the interracial children of French men and Vietnamese women in the colonies were labeled métis, or mixed-race. Like other métis children, Afro-Vietnamese children were affiliated with bastardy, hybridity, and the transgression of racial order. The creation of a specialized term for Afro-Vietnamese children indicates that their numbers were not insignificant. The military and colonial state addressed the specific needs of Afro-Vietnamese children, especially orphans. From 1949, Vietnamese children of African descent began showing up in notable numbers at orphanages and other youth institutions in Vietnam. Afro-Vietnamese children were not accepted at some social-assistance agencies specifically dedicated to métis because of their obvious African parentage.

In 1950, Senegal's deputy to the French National Assembly, Léopold Sédar Senghor, called the attention of the colonial and military administrations to the plight of these Afro-Vietnamese children. Senghor had been taken as a prisoner of war while serving in the tirailleurs sénégalais in France during the Second World War and would become independent Senegal's first president. In 1950, he made an official inquiry into the military's bureaucratic policies for locating and assisting Afro-Vietnamese children and their families.[69] His request came at a moment when the Afro-Vietnamese population in West Africa was small and predominantly resided in the Four Communes of Senegal. Senghor likely anticipated the exponential growth of the Afro-Vietnamese population in West Africa, because the first tirailleurs sénégalais battalions were returning from Southeast Asia to West Africa in 1950. Senghor urged military and colonial representatives to devise a system through which West African soldiers could recuperate their children and other Afro-Vietnamese infants from orphanages and state institutions in order to repatriate with them to West Africa. At the time of Senghor's inquiry, two vessels, the *Cap Tourane* and the *Champollion*, left Saigon in August and November 1950, respectively. These military vessels carried a combined total of fifty-one Afro-Vietnamese children—twenty-three girls and twenty-eight boys between the ages of six and thirty months. West African fathers accompanied them to points of disembarkation in Dakar, Conakry, and Port Bouët.[70] These infants and toddlers were at an age that required the biological attentions of their mothers. The colonial state increased its assistance for Afro-Vietnamese children, but did markedly less to support the maternal prerogatives of Vietnamese mothers.[71]

Despite Senghor's call for a systemized approach to repatriating Afro-Vietnamese children with their fathers, ad hoc arrangements became standard during and following the French Indochina War. The widespread irregular practices affiliated with Afro-Vietnamese child location, adoption, and relocation floundered after the Geneva Accords in 1954, when the number of soldier and civilian requests for evacuation and relocation exponentially multiplied. Many West African troops had not registered their conjugal relationships with military administrators or the colonial state. The number of Afro-Vietnamese households in Vietnam in 1954 is incalculable. The whirlwind, multistage process of evacuation from Tonkin to Saigon, then Saigon to France and West Africa, severed tirailleurs sénégalais' contact and communication with their Vietnamese partners and children. The context of postwar decolonization placed new obstacles in front of soldiers who wanted to legalize their conjugal unions or register their interracial children prior to repatriation. Veterans claimed that military expediency and bureaucratic inefficiencies crippled their ability to locate and recuperate their Afro-Vietnamese conjugal households.[72] In French Indochina, marriages were processed by the civil administration, but tirailleurs sénégalais were expected to make formal requests for international passage through military channels. Several tirailleurs sénégalais extended their tours of duty in Indochina in order to file for and receive the marriage certificates that would allow them to repatriate their Vietnamese wives.[73]

In French Indochina, the French military employed West African noncommissioned officers—originaires and tirailleurs sénégalais—as agents in the Bureau des Affaires Africaines (BAA). These men shouldered the task of locating, registering, and channeling Afro-Vietnamese families out of Tonkin to southern Vietnam, as well as to their final destinations in West Africa and France. The BAA's resources and staff were insubstantial. Their bureau could not assist the majority of tirailleurs sénégalais hoping to leave Vietnam with their households. Even with the assistance of BAA agents, many West Africans could not locate their partners and children in the chaos that ensued after Dien Bien Phu. Many of these men lost contact with their conjugal partners during the war due to transfers, capture by the Viet Minh, or repatriation at the conclusion of their tours.[74] The limitations of telecommunications, reliable postal services, and proficiency in shared languages contributed to these issues. Jean-Bédel Bokassa, the leader of the Central African Republic from 1966 to 1979, left a wife (Nguyen Thi Hué) and daughter (Martine) in Vietnam during the French Indochina War. It is unclear why they were unable to accompany him to Equatorial Africa in the aftermath of the conflict. He eventually found them and with great pomp and circumstance brought them to Bangui in 1971.[75] Most veterans of the tirailleurs sénégalais did not have Bokassa's political power and economic resources. At the end of the war, some West African soldiers deserted in order to maintain their relationships.[76] Others deserted through a combination of love and political belief. A veteran recalled that one soldier, who became a proponent of anticolonialism during the war, deserted at its conclusion to remain with his Vietnamese wife and five children. He is rumored to have never returned from Vietnam.[77]

Urbain Diagne, an officer attached to the BAA at the end of the war, claimed that the French military pledged to finance the international transport of Afro-Vietnamese children but did not extend that promise to their mothers.[78] Throughout the war, women gave birth to interracial children out of wedlock. Some kept them and raised them, with or without conjugal partners. Others entrusted their interracial children to state- or church-run institutions. In the purview of the colonial military and the African soldiers that adopted Afro-Vietnamese children, these infants had achieved a degree of filiation because of the physical characteristics they shared with French African soldiers. BAA agents, tirailleurs sénégalais, and originaire soldiers adopted abandoned Afro-Vietnamese children and raised them in West Africa.[79] These children definitively lost contact with their mothers and their matrilineal relatives.[80] BAA agents registered Afro-Vietnamese children and assigned each to a transoceanic vessel and departure time. For children with known mothers, BAA agents requested that the mothers present Afro-Vietnamese children at the port for embarkation to Senegal. After registration, some mothers refused to deliver children to the docks on their assigned mornings. A rumor circulated among veterans that operatives in the independent Ho Chi Minh government were endeavoring to retain children fathered by West African soldiers as part of a program to eugenically engineer a taller race of Vietnamese people.[81] Perhaps more likely, emotional ties prevented mothers from parting with their children. The Vietnamese mothers who reported to ports to surrender their Afro-Vietnamese children to representatives of the French military did so in hysterics. Veteran Bakary Bieye believed that these women would have thrown themselves into the sea if there had not been a tall barrier at the quay.[82] A muted atmosphere on military vessels bound for West Africa resulted from the heart-wrenching public breakup of Afro-Vietnamese households just before embarkation. One Vietnamese widow recalled consoling bereft African soldiers aboard the *Claude-Bernard* as it repatriated numerous soldiers to West Africa without their wives and/or children.[83]

The Afro-Vietnamese families that survived the French Indochina War and the journey across empire faced new challenges when they arrived at major ports in West Africa. Their households had begun and expanded in Vietnam, far from soldiers' West African families. In West Africa, extended relations of brides and grooms normally participated in prenuptial rituals, which assured the legitimacy of well-maintained kinship lines. Lacking these participatory processes, which curried community approval and favor, soldiers' lateral and ascendant kin often questioned the legitimacy of Afro-Vietnamese households—particularly Vietnamese wives. In-laws often perceived Vietnamese wives as illegitimate outsiders.[84] Cultural differences were difficult to surmount. Soldiers' wives and children spoke Vietnamese or French and had learned social mores alien to West Africa. West African familial traditions that regulated honor, status, and femininity differed from those in Vietnam. Vietnamese women were unaccustomed to the social courtesies that Senegalese wives owed their in-laws. Many found the social and financial demands of their sisters-in-law incongruent with social practice in Vietnam.[85]

In order to adapt to Senegalese society and build social ties, Vietnamese women learned African languages and some converted to Islam. At the other extreme, Vietnamese wives refused social accommodation wholesale and retreated into their conjugal households. Those living in urban areas, like Saint-Louis or Dakar, could socialize exclusively within small Afro-Vietnamese military communities.[86] The strategies that Vietnamese women employed while adapting to living in West Africa often reflected the strength of their bonds with their husbands and the couples' unified commitment to raising their children. As noted above, Ninh and Ibrahima Beye survived the Japanese occupation of Haiphong. Ninh Beye converted to Islam sometime after she arrived in Senegal in 1947 with two biological and two adopted Afro-Vietnamese children. All of her children attended French-language schools in Senegal, where most excelled in their studies. She and her husband eventually raised eight children in a monogamous household that withstood social and familial pressures that encouraged Ibrahima to begin a second family. Many Senegalese families encouraged their returned sons either to divorce Vietnamese women, or to take advantage of their polygynous rights and begin second households deemed legitimate through local tradition and communal oversight.[87] Vietnamese women remained in less-than-ideal familial situations in Senegal because divorce meant severing ties with the limited legal, financial, and political protections that they accessed through their husbands.[88] In comparison with their Moroccan or Syrian interwar predecessors, divorced Vietnamese would have faced greater difficulty in returning to Vietnam because, after 1954, it was no longer part of French Empire.

Nearly thirty years after leaving Southeast Asia, a Vietnamese widow observed, "Senegal, the country of my husband, once represented the inaccessible, the mysterious. . . . Upon my arrival in Dakar, I nourished the hope of one day returning to Vietnam. I have since abandoned this idea. Senegal's soil is now somewhat my own, since it shelters the roots of my descendants."[89] Madame N'Diaye met and married her originaire husband, Karim N'Diaye, in Vietnam in the mid-1930s. Their Vietnamese family prospered over the next two decades until Vietnam's independence led to the relocation of their ten-person household to Senegal. Mme N'Diaye arrived in Senegal with her husband Karim, their eight children, and her elderly mother after the fall of Dien Bien Phu. Prior to relocation, the N'Diayes had lived as a monogamous household for upwards of twenty years. The parents had married in a Vietnamese Christian church and all of the children had Christian names. Mme N'Diaye faced social adversity in Senegal. Not long after their arrival in Senegal, Karim began practicing Islam after a twenty-year hiatus. Without informing his Vietnamese wife, he married a Senegalese woman from an important Saint-Louis family. Mme N'Diaye became the first wife of a polygynous household without consultation, which broke from local conjugal norms and Islamic legal practice. Without legal recourse to challenge the right of her husband to practice polygyny, Mme N'Diaye found herself in an inconsolable and disadvantaged position. Mme N'Diaye would have had difficulty securing guardianship of her children outside of wedlock in Senegal. Successive waves of decolonization in Vietnam (1954) and Senegal (1960) foreclosed any possibility of returning to a divided Vietnam caught up in the Cold War. Mme N'Diaye retreated into her nuclear family and rejected Senegalese culture and society.[90]

Mme N'Diaye did not enjoy the social benefits of her status as first wife in a multiwife Senegalese household. However, according to the postcolonial French military she was Karim N'Diaye's sole legal wife. She had married Karim N'Diaye while he was an active soldier, and she collected military benefits as a soldier's wife and later as a widow. Any concessions that the French military/colonial state made to originaires' polygynous families ended with Senegal's independence. Vietnamese wives and their Afro-Vietnamese children were the beneficiaries of any welfare allocated to French African soldiers who had married while serving in Vietnam. The amount of assistance they could access after Senegal's independence in 1960 depended on their husbands' citizenship choices. Most originaires lost their French citizenship with Senegal's independence, but many applied to "reintegrate" into the legal and political regimes of the independent French state.[91] Reintegrated originaire veterans extended their French citizenship to their spouses and children. French citizenship allowed these West African veterans and their widows to access considerably larger pensions than former tirailleurs sénégalais, who predominantly took the nationality of their independent countries. The Vietnamese wives of African soldiers maintained relationships with the French state that survived the decolonization of Vietnam and the political independence of West African countries. These women continue to collect pensions from the French government in the twenty-first century.[92]

The French Indochina War was the first war of decolonization that West African soldiers served in. It was not the last. However, this war had a more pronounced legacy than any other in the history of African military households due to the numerous Vietnamese women and Afro-Vietnamese children that relocated to West Africa. Their significance is more evident today than that of other interracial African military households that eventually settled in West Africa. The *nem*s (Vietnamese spring rolls) sold on the streets and the multiple locations of the restaurant chain Saveurs d'Asie in contemporary Dakar provide distant reference points to the French Indochina War coming home.[93] The small population of retirement-aged, copper-toned *dakarois* remind us that over sixty years ago Vietnamese women and interracial children like Pierre Aguibou made the transoceanic voyage from Vietnam to West Africa.

As Afro-Vietnamese households adapted to the demands of their in-laws, the ground shifted under their feet. After World War II, African military households experienced decolonization in a series of interlinked political and personal crises. The epilogue to this book follows military households' conjugal practices during the French-Algerian War (1954–62). While serving in this conflict, West African soldiers experienced the decolonization of their home territories—Guinea in 1958 and the remainder of French West Africa in 1960. Only six years after the fall of Dien Bien Phu, many Afro-Vietnamese families found themselves in independent West African countries. For some, the French military was the only consistent institution that supported their families through these politically turbulent times and in the postcolonial world.

Epilogue

Decolonization, Algeria, and Legacies

THE FRENCH INDOCHINA WAR DID NOT OCCUR IN A VACUUM and challenges to French Empire multiplied after the Second World War. Tirailleurs sénégalais participated in the suppression of anticolonial insurrection in Morocco, Madagascar, and Algeria in the 1940s through 1960s. In several of these uprisings, protesters and militants specifically targeted West African soldiers with violence and propaganda. African troops' sexuality and conjugal behaviors figured into these articulations of anticolonial sentiment. In French Empire, tirailleurs sénégalais had become symbols affiliated with the injustices of French colonialism. During the 1950s in French West Africa, young men enlisted in the tirailleurs sénégalais because military service became a viable career path. Many volunteered for the French colonial military in order to accumulate the resources necessary to attain autonomy from their parents and begin their own families. Many West African men sought careers in the tirailleurs sénégalais at a time in which French Empire was shrinking and West African independence was lingering on the other side of the horizon.

The French military introduced measures to professionalize the tirailleurs sénégalais in step with the restructuring of empire at the onsets of the French Fourth Republic in 1946 and the Fifth Republic in 1958. The French-Algerian War (1954–62) created the context for this constitutional transition, which altered the civil status of people residing in French Empire. The Loi Cadre (Framework Law) of 1956 dismantled divisions within the French armed forces and tirailleurs sénégalais ceased to officially exist. In October 1958, the French army dissolved the tirailleurs sénégalais and transferred West African soldiers into the French marine corps. In the same year, French Guinea became independent, which had great consequence for Guinean soldiers serving France in Algeria. The majority of Guinean soldiers experienced rapid demobilization, repatriation, and decolonization as seamless processes in early 1959. A minority continued their military careers and negotiated waves of decolonization with multinational families. Koly Kourouma's life history provides an exceptional example of a Guinean career soldier maintaining a relationship with the French military in order to survive the ends of French Empire.

Within two years of Guinea's independence, the decolonization of the remainder of French West Africa made veterans of tirailleurs sénégalais and originaire soldiers. West African independence catalyzed discussions concerning the legal status of veterans and their benefits, which impacted West African widows and military households. International debates concerning pension disparities between mainland French veterans and West African veterans reached a series of crescendos in the early twenty-first century. West African veterans became living symbols of the injustices and legacies of French colonialism. Their widows, wives, and families were seldom mobilized as part of this discourse, yet they remain important stakeholders in the afterlives of African military households. They continue to collect pensions from the postcolonial French state in the twenty-first century.

VIOLENT UPRISINGS AND WAR IN POST-1945 FRENCH EMPIRE

In the years immediately following armistice in 1945, Algerians, Madagascans, and Moroccans led regional uprisings against the French colonial state and its military employees.[1] On 8 May 1945, Allied forces acknowledged the unconditional surrender of Germany. On the same day, the French state staged a victory parade in Sétif, Algeria. Sétif is located in a mountainous region southeast of Algiers and the city was known for its popular opposition to French colonial rule. At the victory parade, the people of Sétif formed a second line. They protested colonial exploitation and called for the release of Messali Hadj—an Algerian labor organizer and anticolonialist imprisoned in France.[2] The parade ended in violent clashes among police and civilians. The brutal repression of this event led to thousands of deaths and there

Decolonization, Algeria, and Legacies

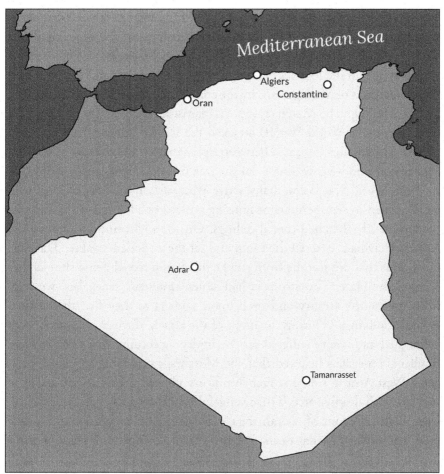

MAP 7.1. French Algeria. Map by Isaac Barry

were reports of Algerians shot in the back while fleeing the ensuing chaos.[3] Tirailleurs sénégalais had deployed to Algeria in small numbers since 1909. During the Sétif uprising they participated in the violent repression of protesters and the massacre of upwards of six thousand Algerians.[4] Historians and other scholars would later cast the events in Sétif as an antecedent of the French-Algerian War.[5] Tirailleurs sénégalais would deploy to Algeria in much greater numbers in the 1950s.

During March and April 1947, Madagascan and Moroccan civilians targeted tirailleurs sénégalais in violent demonstrations against colonial rule.

Epilogue

The deadly events of Easter weekend 1947 in Casablanca are detailed above in chapter 5. Here, I focus on incidents in Madagascar. By 1947, tirailleurs sénégalais had a long history in French colonial Madagascar. Their images were woven into the legacies of conquest and the lived experiences of at least two generations of Madagascans by the conclusion of the Second World War. During the night of March 29–30, Madagascan civilians (some of whom were veterans of World War II) attacked the French military base at Moramanga. Moramanga is located between Antananarivo and the eastern coast of Madagascar and was the long-term site of a tirailleurs sénégalais garrison. In the post–World War II era, many active West African servicemen lived with local women in semipermanent housing structures adjacent to the camp—predominantly thatched-roof dwellings. On the night under examination, Malagasy civilians entered the camp and set these residences afire. The African troops that did not die from smoke inhalation risked being shot as they escaped the blaze. The arsonists had stolen tirailleurs sénégalais' weapons from the camp's armory and fired upon soldiers as they fled their flame-engulfed lodgings.[6] During the night of the attack, thirteen tirailleurs sénégalais died and twelve suffered serious injury. According to French reports, tirailleurs sénégalais believed that the Moramanga uprising specifically targeted West African soldiers. French officers allowed tirailleurs sénégalais to retaliate with deadly force. These vengeful tirailleurs sénégalais attacked villages in the environs of Moramanga, razed domestic structures, and massacred a number of Madagascan civilians.[7] Their revenge took place within a broader French military response that had wide-ranging estimated casualties: 20,000 to 100,000.[8] This event has negatively shaped the Madagascan imagination pertaining to West Africans, in particular Senegalese nationals.[9] Many of the tirailleurs sénégalais who used deadly force against Madagascans would later serve in French Indochina and Algeria.[10]

The events at Moramanga were concurrent with the mobilization of West African soldiers to the French Indochina War. In the post–World War II period, tirailleurs sénégalais deployed into empire as counterinsurgent forces that defended French colonialism. Six months after the fall of Dien Bien Phu, the French-Algerian War began with a bang. Coordinated explosions erupted across Algeria on the morning of 1 November 1954. Bomb attacks targeted police stations, army barracks, and other sites of state infrastructure. The National Liberation Front (Front de Libération Nationale,

FLN) claimed responsibility for the bombings while simultaneously sending a rallying call for all Algerians to mobilize against French colonialism. This lengthy war encompassed anticolonial guerilla warfare, counterinsurgency forces, fratricidal attacks among militarized Algerians, and targeted assassinations of Algerians perceived to be French sympathizers or collaborators.[11] This war profoundly impacted the relationship between mainland France and its overseas territories. The French-Algerian War caused the dissolution of the French Union of the Fourth French Republic. French West Africa and French Equatorial Africa became independent in 1960, which precipitated the demobilization of French African servicemen two years before the Algerian War ended.

Many of the West African veterans interviewed for this book served in Indochina and/or Algeria. Those who served in Southeast Asia and Algeria emphasized the disparities between the two anticolonial wars. In Indochina, the majority of fighting occurred in rural areas and veterans remembered the major cities of Saigon, Hanoi, and Haiphong as spaces of relaxation and leisure.[12] In Algeria, FLN operatives and French paratroopers fought pitched battles in urban environments. In January 1957, General Jacques Massu and eight thousand paratroopers invaded Algiers and held the city hostage while the French military tracked down Algerian militants.[13] From 1958, Algerian armed resistance to French colonialism moved into rural areas. Fighting continued in the mountainous regions east and west of Algiers (Oranais and Kabylia, respectively), as well as in the southern margins of the Sahara. Throughout this conflict, the Algerian *moudjahidine*s relied heavily on civilians for supplies, shelter, and financing in the cities and the mountains. Moudjahidines (the term is derived from the same Arabic root as *jihad*) broadly considered themselves the resistance to France's illegitimate rule in Algeria. They used guerilla-style warfare against French forces in agricultural lands, urban streets, and private residences. Tirailleurs sénégalais serving in Algeria found themselves facing weapons that ranged from rifles to kitchen utensils.[14]

The guerilla violence of the French-Algerian War and its transgression of private civilian spaces adversely affected the tirailleurs sénégalais deployed in Algeria. The French colonial military monitored West African troops' morale in order to prevent psychological problems. Early reports authored by French officers on sub-Saharan African troops in Algeria found that veterans of the French Indochina War suffered PTSD when they later deployed to Algeria.

Epilogue

West Africans soldiers who transferred directly to Algeria from Indochina, without taking leave in West Africa, were hospitalized more often for mental illness and mood disorders.[15] One originaire veteran described bouts of amnesia that occurred at the onset of a psychological episode in Algeria. As a result, he spent time in a racially segregated military hospital in Constantine.[16] After the medical facility discharged him, the military deemed him unfit to serve and he repatriated to Saint-Louis. In 1955, the military's Psychological Bureau proposed a special division for sub-Saharan Africans, which had a more ambitious charge than the Bureau des Affaires Africaines had had in French Indochina. The West African officers in the Psychological Bureau became responsible for the production of all media—journals, periodicals, and photos—for military spaces of leisure where tirailleurs sénégalais congregated in Algeria. They organized motivational film screenings and radio programs targeting West African troops on Radio Algeria. They coordinated the importation and distribution of kola nuts and West African musical recordings among tirailleurs sénégalais. The French military also wanted West African officers to directly monitor the rank-and-file.[17] Archived reports from African officers Tiemoko, Tiecoura, Triande, Conde, and Fofana begin in 1959.

The prolific use of physical violence and torture in the French-Algerian War negatively impacted veterans of Indochina and newly recruited tirailleurs sénégalais. Frantz Fanon starkly portrayed the complex and violent roles that France assigned West Africans serving in Algeria. Fanon was a Martiniquan psychiatrist posted to Algiers during the early years of the war. Among the case studies presented in the final chapter of his seminal critique of colonialism, *The Wretched of the Earth*, Fanon described a French police inspector who sought psychiatric care in order to deal with trauma from the war, which led him to physically abuse his wife and children. The inspector recounted the methods of torture that he employed to extract information from Algerian prisoners. Physical torture wore prisoners down and exhausted those wielding it. "In the end your fists are ruined. So you call in the Senegalese. But either they hit too hard and destroy the creature or else they don't hit hard enough and it's no good."[18] This quote sparked a curiosity that resulted in this book. France's use of tirailleurs sénégalais in the torture chambers of Algeria was bewildering when I first encountered them there.

West Africans stationed in Algeria were assigned some of the dirtiest work of that war. They were subject to propaganda and counter-propaganda from the French military and the FLN. The militarized wing of the FLN, the National Liberation Army (ALN), welcomed tirailleurs sénégalais deserters. *El moudjahid*, the official publication of the FLN, enticed West African servicemen with anticolonial and pan-African propaganda. Fanon anonymously authored many articles published in *El moudjahid*. He used the pages of the newspaper to celebrate anticolonial cooperation and denounce the use of West African soldiers against other colonized people in Algeria.[19] The 1 November 1957 issue contained an article accompanied by a photograph of tirailleurs sénégalais posing with a rural unit of the ALN. The photograph's caption read "African fraternity forged in the Algerian maquis."[20] The fraternity celebrated by Fanon in *El moudjahid* was not widespread in the French-Algerian War. Despite Fanon's enthusiasm, French African soldiers rarely fraternized with local civilians.[21]

The conjugal practices prevalent in Southeast Asia did not transfer with African soldiers to North Africa. According to military reports, most of the contact between West African soldiers and Algerian women occurred in military brothels.[22] The French military believed that military brothels with healthy sex workers provided West African servicemen with needed diversion and improved their morale. Agents of the Psychological Bureau updated headquarters on West African soldiers' sexuality because they linked it to troops' well-being. Reports included details on mobile Bordels Militaires de Campagne, which traveled with tirailleurs sénégalais units.[23] These sexual policies and practices faintly echoed those championed in the *troupes noires* debates regarding the presence of *mesdames tirailleurs* in Black Villages in Morocco. However, they differed. because the military promoted transactional sex with local women in 1950s Algeria. Pointedly, West African soldiers and Algerian women did not cohabitate as households on campaign. There were few opportunities for West African soldiers to engage in non-transactional conjugal relationships with Algerian women. A small number of soldiers married and returned to West Africa with Algerian wives.[24]

A comprehensive accounting of Afro-Algerian conjugal relationships may be possible once the military records of the French-Algerian War are unsealed in 2062. I have relied on oral history and other types of sources to understand the drastic differences between West African soldiers' conjugal practices in French Indochina and in French Algeria. Interviewed veterans spoke of Algerian women as covert militants. One claimed that the FLN dispatched young Algerian women to socialize with tirailleurs sénégalais, coax them into states of intoxication, and then extract strategic information from them.[25] In popular media and publications, Algerian women appeared as perpetrators and victims of extreme violence. Historian Djamila Amrane found that roughly eleven thousand Algerian women mobilized during the French-Algerian War. They represented 3.1 percent of the Algerians who fought to end French colonialism.[26] Despite their minority, French security forces came to view all Algerian women as potential FLN operatives, terrorists, and/or enemies of the state. These widely held beliefs created a context in which the French government tolerated state agents' abuse and sexual assault of Algerian women. Sexualized violence—from body searches to penetrative rape—became routine during military sweeps of rural villages and in the treatment of imprisoned women. Rape and the threat of rape became strategies of France's counterinsurgency.[27] Two young Algerian women, Djamila Boupacha and Djamila Bouhired, experienced torture and sexual assault when French agents interrogated them about their participation in terrorist attacks in Algiers. French intellectuals drew public attention to their plight.[28] As noted in Fanon's *The Wretched of the Earth*, tirailleurs sénégalais were present in torture chambers, but the degree to which they participated in gender-based violence in Algeria is currently unknown.

LEGISLATION AND CHANGING STATUSES DURING DECOLONIZATION

Concurrent with the wars of decolonization in Indochina and Algeria, the French government passed important legislation that altered the future of French Empire, the tirailleurs sénégalais, and their families. After the conclusion of World War II, the Lamine Guèye law heralded the dismantling of the Indigénat—a legal "regime of exception" in French West Africa.[29] African politicians won other reforms that eliminated forced labor and redefined West Africans' rights and obligations within the Fourth Republic's constitution for the French Union (1946–58). For tirailleurs sénégalais, this legislation eliminated the loathed term *indigène* and replaced it with *africain*.[30] The Lamine Guèye law also signaled the eradication of the *deuxième portion*, which was a regime of coerced labor connected to military conscription since 1926.[31] The French constitution in 1946 awarded most West Africans the quality of citizen, while maintaining distinctions between the personal statuses of members of the French Republic and those of the French Union.[32]

This distinction preserved separate pay scales and service obligations between mainland French soldiers and soldiers recruited in the overseas territories making up the French Union. These ongoing forms of discrimination did not deter new West African recruits from joining the French military. Postwar legislation effectively transformed the tirailleurs sénégalais from a conscripted army into a voluntary corps of young West African soldiers.

A decade later, new legislation aimed to eliminate some of the inequities in civil status and military advancement across French Empire. Passed in 1956, the Loi Cadre (Framework Law) was designed to expand the imperial electorate and increase local authority within the French Union. The Loi Cadre continued the process of reducing distinctions between subject and citizen, which, in turn, gradually effaced regional and racial divisions within the French military. This legislation removed racial barriers and initiated the "Africanization" of the lower- and middle-ranking officers within the French Army. The military improved the professional development of West African soldiers and officers. The French Army reorganized the West African military preparatory schools (Écoles Militaires de Préparation de l'Afrique, or EMPAs), as well as inaugurating the École de Formation des Officiers Ressortissants des Territoires d'Outre-Mer (EFORTOM), an officer's training school in Fréjus for soldiers from France's overseas territories, in October 1956.[33] The limited number of seats in these institutions impeded the dramatic improvement and expansion of African officers' education.[34] West African men volunteered for military service during the 1950s due to increased wages and benefits as well as opportunities for career advancement. Voluntary recruits sought resources that could expedite their entrance into adulthood or improve conditions for their extended families. With their signing bonuses and wages, they could seek wives and support households without relying on extended family for financial support.[35]

The military aimed to dissolve the tirailleurs sénégalais and transfer African colonial soldiers into the French marines by 1 October 1958. From that point forward, West African servicemen would serve shoulder to shoulder with North African and mainland French troops. Despite this momentous institutional transformation, October 1st is not a major milestone in the collective memory of West African veterans. The Algerian War and September 28th are much more present. In the second half of 1958, most French African soldiers were serving in Algeria. There, they experienced seismic shifts in empire and the French Army. High-ranking French military and civilian agents seized the Algerian government in May 1958, which led to the fall of the mainland French government. As the Fourth Republic fell, Charles de Gaulle stepped forward to lead France toward a new constitution. He oversaw pacifying dissident French administrators and soldiers in Algeria, as well as restructuring the relationships between France and its empire.[36] De Gaulle's proposed Fifth Republic and French Community would retool French Empire so that colonial populations would have greater authority over their domestic affairs. Empire would vote on a constitutional referendum on 28 September 1958—three days before tirailleurs sénégalais were scheduled to become marines.

Populations across French Africa had the opportunity to vote for a constitution that offered them greater representative power within the French Community. However, the constitution maintained the ultimate authority of the French president and National Assembly over the Community. Alternatively, voters could opt for their territory's immediate independence from French Empire. The 1958 constitutional referendum proposed a single citizenship for all members of the newly conceived French Community envisioned for the French Fifth Republic. However, incongruities between nationality and citizenship persisted because individuals would hold the nationality of specific states in the French Community, while simultaneously possessing citizenship of the Community.[37] Tirailleurs sénégalais voted in the elections wherever they were stationed in empire. They also participated in monitoring the polling process and providing security for ballots across Algeria.[38] Most of the tirailleurs sénégalais serving in Algeria voted to remain in the French Community. The majority of colonies in French West Africa also voted for membership in the French Community. Ninety-five percent of Guinean voters opted for immediate independence.[39] Guinea's rejection of the constitutional referendum opened a fast track toward its political independence. Within the army, independence inspired discussions about Guinean troops' discharge from the French colonial army and France's postcolonial obligations to them.

KOLY KOUROUMA IN A DECOLONIZING WORLD

Career military serviceman Koly Kourouma's life history provides an exceptional opportunity to understand the experiences of Guinean tirailleurs sénégalais in the post–World War II period and in the aftermath of the September referendum.[40] Kourouma was born in 1933 in the village of Karo, near the headwaters of the Bafing, Senegal, and Niger Rivers in contemporary Guinea. He grew up in Macenta, then Conakry. He attended French-language elementary schools and inherited rich military traditions from male family members who had served in the world wars and North Africa. Other family members were public servants who worked in Conakry's municipal public sector.[41] This heritage of public service and militarism influenced Kourouma's decision to become an officer in the tirailleurs sénégalais. In the post–World War II period, military service was a pathway to male adulthood that growing numbers of Guineans chose.[42] Enterprising at sixteen, Kourouma lied about his age on his 1949 application to the EMPA in Kati, French Soudan. He passed as a nineteen-year-old and gained a seat at the exclusive school. Successful candidates acquired room, board, and an education. Graduating cadets were required to serve a minimum of five years in the tirailleurs sénégalais.[43] Upon completing his studies, Kourouma entered the tirailleurs sénégalais as a sergeant and shipped out to French Indochina in 1950. After a two-year tour in Cambodia, Kourouma returned to Kati and taught at his alma mater. At the conclusion of his five-year obligation in 1955, Kourouma opted to continue his military career.[44]

In 1956, Kourouma was in Morocco working on an officer's credential. He experienced Morocco's decolonization first hand. Kourouma then transferred from independent Morocco to wartime Algeria, where he commanded a unit in the region south of Oran. In September 1958, Kourouma and other Guinean tirailleurs sénégalais serving in Algeria were shocked by the results of the referendum. Most of them had cast their ballots to remain in the French Community.[45] Guinean soldiers in Algeria regarded a "no" vote as contrary to military duty and their future aspirations.[46] Soldiering was an integral component of their identities, which coexisted with their religious affiliations, ethnicities, and ancestral heritages.[47] A "no" vote also meant Guinean independence and the truncation of their military careers. In the weeks leading up to the referendum, Kourouma's government-employed relatives in Guinea witnessed the political rise of trade unionist Sékou Touré, European nationals' preemptive exodus, and a slowdown of economic activity in Conakry. Through correspondence, Kourouma's family members advised him to vote against independence and to continue pursuing his military career.[48] In the polling booth, Kourouma opted for French Community.

Epilogue

Four days after the constitutional referendum, Guinea became independent, with Sékou Touré as its first president. Touré called for the immediate demobilization and repatriation of Guinean tirailleurs sénégalais serving in Algeria. He also insisted that the French Army vacate Guinea by 1 November 1958—a mere month after the referendum.[49] There were approximately twelve thousand Guineans serving in the tirailleurs sénégalais in autumn of 1958. A third of these soldiers were in Guinea, of which two thousand were on leave. Three thousand Guinean troops were stationed across French West Africa and approximately forty-five hundred were deployed in Algeria.[50] In early October 1958, the French military countered Touré's demand and offered Guinean tirailleurs sénégalais an opportunity to remain in the French Army. Soldiers could choose to continue their military careers in order to receive full benefits after fifteen years of service. Alternatively, they could rupture their military contracts, demobilize, and repatriate to Guinea. If they chose the latter, they would be free of their military obligations after 1 January 1959 and stripped of their pensions and benefits.[51] Military officials estimated that approximately 10 percent of Guinean soldiers would remain in the French Army.[52]

During the early weeks of October 1958, the second voting process unfolded in an ad hoc manner across empire. One veteran, who was stationed in Algeria in October 1958, claimed that he repatriated to Guinea in early 1959 without a vote or any discussion of the matter.[53] Thierno Conté voted twice regarding his demobilization. Conté's commanding officer in Algeria was unsure as to whether a majority vote decided the fate of the entire unit, or if each Guinean soldier decided his own destiny.[54] When confronted with the choice of continuing their military career or demobilizing, many single-tour and early-career soldiers truncated their military service. Veterans interviewed in Conakry cited military duty and job security as major motivations for their "yes" vote in the referendum. Subsequently, they opted to quit the military out of solidarity with the Guinean people.[55] There is evidence to suggest that career soldiers with at least eight years of military service opted for delayed demobilization because they had completed more than half of the fifteen years needed to retire with a full pension.[56]

Koly Kourouma chose his military career, as did a minority of other Guineans. A Guinean serving in Madagascar during the referendum remained in the French Army due to his local family and his distrust of Sékou

Touré.[57] Guineans hitching their future to the French Army secured future resources from France, but they no longer had definable rights or political statuses. By retaining non-nationals in its regular military, France contravened its military traditions, which organized citizens, subjects, and foreigners into separate branches of the armed forces. Since the nineteenth century, French West African subjects had served in the colonial army, French citizens in the metropolitan army, and foreigners in the French Foreign Legion.[58] Transferring Guinean soldiers to the French Foreign Legion would have more clearly defined them as foreigners and provided them with a clearer path to French citizenship.[59] Instead, the French minister of overseas territories proposed exceptional processing for Guineans living outside of Guinea. These Guineans lost their claims to French nationality, but the French state continued to issue them passports for a limited time.[60] Guinean soldiers maintained a political affiliation with the French Community, but the "affiliation" lacked correlating citizenship in a member-state of the Community. This ill-defined political status carried a pending, unknown expiration date. Guineans serving in Algeria expressed interest in formal naturalization in order to eliminate that ambiguity, but their citizenship remained unresolved for years afterward.[61] Nearby West African member-states of the French Community could not absorb Guineans because their common constitution imposed constraints on processes of naturalization.[62] Guineans, made stateless by decolonization, relied on relationships forged in the military in order to survive Guinean independence.[63] French military officers were sympathetic to their plight and found ways to extend the careers of Guinean soldiers beyond French colonialism, as well as after the dissolution of the tirailleurs sénégalais.

After the referendum, Koly Kourouma put his personal affairs in order. During a brief period of leave in 1959, he returned to Kati to marry his first wife, Sira Komé, who had already given birth to their first child at the age of seventeen. The couple had courted while Kourouma was an instructor at the EMPA in Kati and Komé was a student attending a nearby school. After this marriage, Kourouma traveled with his young bride by air to Guinea, where he married his second wife, also in 1959.[64] By entering Guinea the year after the referendum, Kourouma put himself and his young family at risk. Another Guinean officer was arrested when he returned to Guinea in 1959 to collect his family.[65] Koly Kourouma relocated his wives to military housing in Dakar before deploying to French Soudan. With marriage, Kourouma attempted to legalize his conjugal partners and children, but in what state? Kourouma lacked citizenship or subject status in an existing political regime. His wives could claim French Community or Guinean nationality, respectively, but there was no centralized state that would recognize both marital unions. Local religious and familial authorities in Mali and Guinea could have recognized the legitimacy of these marriages, but their jurisdiction weakened when the household relocated to live in French military housing in Dakar. Perhaps Kourouma believed the French military would better support his multinational family in an era of independence—even though the French military only recognized the first wife in multiwife African military households.

Guinea's independence greatly affected active tirailleurs sénégalais' and veterans' abilities to access resources for themselves and their families. The French military promised severance pay to the soldiers who truncated their careers and demobilized in October 1958. The military also promised to pay their salaries up to a month after they boarded vessels in Algeria bound for Conakry.[66] Guinean veterans who had served between fifteen and twenty-five years in the French military could liquidate their pensions upon leaving territories in the French Community.[67] French officials vowed to protect repatriating Guineans' right to their pensions.[68] These were unkept promises. Guinean veterans watched their ability to collect retirement disappear as diplomatic relations between France and Guinea disintegrated. Tirailleurs sénégalais veterans and widows living in independent Guinea did not receive their pensions between 1965 and 1977—when Sékou Touré and Valéry Giscard d'Estaing reestablished diplomatic relations between Guinea and France.[69]

Kourouma left his nascent family in Dakar in 1959. West African political boundaries and allegiances continued to transform. In the aftermath of the referendum, political representatives from Senegal, French Soudan, Dahomey, and Upper Volta convened to engineer the Mali Federation within the French Community. Disagreements over the nature of political organization and authority within the Mali Federation reduced its members to Senegal and French Soudan by April 1959. Kourouma deployed to French Soudan a few months later. Between 18 January and 4 April 1960, the leaders of the Mali Federation negotiated independence from France. During these meetings, the French military promised five thousand military servicemen, predominantly of Soudanese and Senegalese origin, to assist the Mali Federation in training its independent army.[70] Koly Kourouma was among them.

Kourouma experienced the collapse of the Mali Federation in late August 1960. The acrimonious breakup of the Mali Federation catalyzed the repatriation of West African civil servants who were working outside of their home states.[71] Somewhere in the shuffle of repatriating state employees, Koly Kourouma headed to Dakar with the intention of recuperating his wives and catching a boat to Conakry. In Tambacounda, Senegal, a French officer took note of his dossier and suggested Kourouma continue serving France in independent Africa.[72] Kourouma became part of a corps of African officers who facilitated joint training operations and material assistance between France and its former colonies. In 1961, Koly Kourouma became a resident alien in Senegal and continued to work for the French military in former French colonial Africa.

On 13 January 1963, Koly Kourouma was aboard a French military vessel traveling from Dakar to Pointe Noire. The ship docked at Conakry to refuel and resupply. While anchored in Conakry, a military-led coup d'état in Togo culminated in the assassination of president Sylvanus Olympio.[73] The coup leaders, Étienne Gnassingbe Eyadéma, Emmanuel Bodjollé, and Kléber Dadjo were all recent veterans of the French Army. Sékou Touré's government reacted swiftly to the coup and increased security at Guinea's border crossings and international ports.[74] Port officials demanded the documents of all Guineans working on foreign watercraft and insisted these Guineans disembark for questioning. Koly Kourouma's captain protected his crew, fled port, and continued on to Congo-Brazzaville. By the time Kourouma returned to Dakar, Sékou Touré had placed his name on a watch list and formally requested his extradition to Guinea.[75] Senegalese president Léopold Sédar Senghor denied Touré's request.

After fifteen years of active service, Koly Kourouma retired from the French military in Dakar on 31 March 1965. According to his military documents, he was thirty-five years old. According to Kourouma, he was thirty-two. Many former tirailleurs sénégalais had enlisted in the independent armies of their new countries. Kourouma's ambiguous citizenship status made him ineligible for military service in Senegal or his native Guinea. He eventually found employment in a state-operated industrial agricultural developmental agency (SODAICA) in Senegal's southern region, the Casamance. Koly Kourouma naturalized as a Senegalese citizen in 1972.[76] In the same year, he married his third wife, whom he met while working in the Casamance. She remains the sole wife in the household with Senegalese citizenship. Kourouma's first and second wives, born in French Soudan and French Guinea, respectively, have not naturalized as Senegalese citizens. They are eligible for citizenship because their husband is a Senegalese citizen and they have lived in Senegal since 1959. The naturalization paperwork had yet to be filed in 2009.[77] Many Guinean tirailleurs sénégalais veterans' households remained in similar unregulated and ambiguous situations fifty years after Guinea's independence.

INDEPENDENCE, PENSIONS, AND THE AFTERLIVES OF TIRAILLEURS SÉNÉGALAIS

Between 1961 and 1962, ten thousand sub-Saharan African French troops demobilized from North Africa and repatriated to their independent countries. As mentioned above, originaires could "reintegrate" into French citizenship and continue to serve in the French Army. Debates regarding the "legitimacy" of originaires' wives and children reemerged as the decolonizing French government saw an opportunity to withdraw its support from polygynous households. By forcing these men to naturalize through official channels, the French state could legally limit originaire veterans to monogamy. There were a few cases where lax French administrators were accused of awarding French citizenship to polygynous veterans without negotiating a single legal formality.[78] High-ranking African officers could also petition to remain in the French Army and serve as commanding officers within the French military units stationed in their West African country of origin. Colonel Amadou Fall, former chief of staff of the Mali Federation's military, exploited this opportunity.[79] Aside from these rare examples, the majority of former tirailleurs sénégalais became citizens of West African countries. Their military households' postcolonial relationship with France continued in the form of pensions and widow's stipends. They have also become central to a political discourse of debt, reciprocity, and the negative legacies of French colonialism in the twenty-first century.

West African politicians participated in the diplomatic negotiations that froze tirailleurs sénégalais veterans' pensions with independence in 1960. West African leaders in the Mali Federation agreed to stipulations that led to the French Finance Law of 1960, under which African soldiers from the former

French Community would have their pensions' base rates fixed at 1960 levels in perpetuity.[80] According to one veteran, Senegalese and Malian leaders agreed to this decision so that former French colonial servicemen would not receive pensions greater than the pay of West African civil servants in independent West African states.[81] The decision to freeze, or "crystalize," veterans' pensions would create profound inequalities between mainland French veterans and veterans from former French West Africa. In recent decades, West African veterans have become part of a political discourse that repositions retired servicemen as "sites" and "sights" in a public history concerned with French colonialism and its negative legacies in Africa.[82] Photographs of aged veterans cradling faded, creased service records or wearing military decorations on pristine white boubous became commonly circulated images reminding broad audiences of veterans' sacrifices to France.[83]

Veterans were incorporated into a public discourse that criticized French colonialism and the production of its history.[84] The massacre of repatriating prisoners of war at Thiaroye in 1944 and the frozen pensions of living veterans were salient elements in an increasingly audible outcry against the abuse and mistreatment of former West African colonial soldiers. Even though the majority of living veterans served in French Indochina and Algeria, they found themselves wedged into an increasingly narrow set of contemporary academic, media, and political interests—the legacies of the world wars and French colonialism. Former Senegalese president Abdoulaye Wade captured the public's imagination by investing state funds in scholastic initiatives and veterans' events to increase their visibility locally and internationally.[85] Numerous publications responded to this discourse, which strove to expose France's amnesia toward its historical exploitation of West African soldiers.[86] Public and scholarly debates focused on tirailleurs sénégalais' service in France during the world wars, which sidelines tirailleurs sénégalais' participation in creating and defending French Empire.[87] They have also ignored the ways in which tirailleurs sénégalais' conjugal strategies on the home front and the war front impacted the articulation of French colonialism. Women played a formative role in this institution, which becomes readily apparent in tirailleurs sénégalais' imperial history. The sacrifices that colonial women made for their husbands and for the institution of the tirailleurs sénégalais were muted in the mainstream discourses on veterans' sacrifices for the French.

Since West African independence, veterans of the tirailleurs sénégalais have endeavored to secure more resources for their families and dependents. A few naturalized as French citizens. Others took advantage of a legal loophole which stipulated that if West African veterans resided in France most of the year, they could receive pensions equivalent to those of mainland French veterans. Some West African veterans moved permanently to France and continued to support their families in France or in West Africa. Other West Africans migrated between Paris and Dakar with the seasons. Octogenarians summered in France and wintered in Senegal. Elderly veterans shared apartments in Bondy, a suburb of Paris where many French people of sub-Saharan and North African descent live. They split rents or squatted with other veterans and/or their descendants in order to access larger pensions.[88] Veterans' pension migrations demonstrate that France has failed its West African veterans. Their annual circuits between West African towns and Parisian suburbs also illustrate that independent West African countries and the global economy have failed veterans' descendants. Postcolonial West African economies resulting from structural adjustment and neoliberalism are characterized by underemployment. Elderly veterans continue to support immediate and extended family members with the paltry pensions they collect from postcolonial France. These quarterly distributed benefits have served as a means for veterans' children and grandchildren to survive in the contemporary world.

On the eve of Bastille Day in 2010, French president Nicholas Sarkozy announced the full "de-crystallization" of West African veterans' pensions for early 2011. It was estimated that this decree would increase fiscal advantages for upwards of thirty thousand people: ten thousand veterans and twenty thousand widows and heirs.[89] With the equalization of pensions, the discourse around tirailleurs sénégalais and *anciens combattants* has evolved. While the tirailleurs sénégalais may remain a salient representation of the explicit exploitation of West Africans and West African resources in the past, they are no longer a governmental agenda item. The excesses of Abdoulaye Wade's administration and its emphasis on the memorialization and commemoration of the tirailleurs sénégalais ended with the elections of Senegalese president Macky Sall in Senegal and French president François Hollande in 2012. The symbolism remained, but its tenor changed.

In 2017, after decades of trying to legally "reintegrate" into France, twenty-eight veterans of the tirailleurs sénégalais were awarded French citizenship.

Aïssata Seck, deputy mayor of Bondy, had taken up their legal battle the previous year. Seck was the granddaughter of a tirailleur sénégalais and she celebrated with the veterans at a public event that included the French president.[90] Among the octogenarian and nonagenarian veterans, there were twenty-three Senegalese, one Ivoirian, two Congolese, and two men from the Central African Republic.[91] In a speech delivered at the event, President Hollande recycled the rhetorical points that had become common within West African veterans' debates since the 1990s. He referenced blood debts and sacrifice. In a separate statement, Aïssata Seck came a little closer to what was at stake in extending French citizenship to West African veterans. She emphasized how French citizenship, access to France's welfare state, and securer pensions would improve the well-being of veterans and their households.

Tirailleurs sénégalais' conjugal traditions continue to evolve in the twenty-first century. International attention to postcolonial France's unequal treatment of West African veterans created a repertoire of images and discourses concerning world war veterans. Vuti Chat and the conjugal partners of Lamine Drame are difficult to locate in that discourse. The gendered violence affiliated with African military households forged in wars of conquest and decolonization is notably missing. The militarization of colonized women is absent. Female enslavement, forced marriage, and forced conjugal association are not associated with the wives and widows of contemporary veterans. The pension debates mask the dangerous ways in which West Africans engaged in conjugal relationships while serving in French Empire. Further, there has not been a public discussion regarding how France could compensate former tirailleurs sénégalais' wives and households for providing unpaid long-term medical and psychological care for veterans with PTSD and physical impairments.[92] Negligible investment in health services in West Africa demonstrates that the French military continues to rely on the labor of veterans' female conjugal partners in the postcolonial period.

Twenty-first-century pension debates evince the success of interwar military policies concerning marital legitimacy and welfare for African soldiers' monogamous heteronormative nuclear families. The contemporary French state distributes resources to veterans' first wives and the legitimate children resulting from that marriage. Widows of French African soldiers lose rights to these benefits if they remarry. The postcolonial French military continues to disregard the realities of African military households. Veterans support

Epilogue

lateral kin and generations of direct descendants. Pensions and benefits continue to be allocated according to the male-breadwinner model introduced in the interwar period. This model preserves gendered assumptions about women's economic contributions to African military households. The post–World War I vision of militarized men and civilian women continues to reign. The mesdames tirailleurs of the nineteenth- and early twentieth-century campaigns of conquest are forgotten. The neglect of these women is a consequence of academic and public focus on African soldiers' participation in the world wars.

The French military and tirailleurs sénégalais relied on colonized women in the expansion, maintenance, and defense of French Empire. French African soldiers' conjugal traditions unfolded in empire. African military households problematize categories, geographies, and chronologies affiliated with French colonialism. Veterans, their conjugal partners, and their interracial descendants live in France, Vietnam, North Africa, West Africa, Madagascar, and Equatorial Africa. French African soldiers' households illustrate the importance of sexuality, conjugality, and women in the study of colonialism and militarism. Cross-colonial families demonstrate the limitations of focusing on the colonial-metropole axis in imperial histories. African military households antedated and outlasted formal French Empire. Each time Ninh Beye (née Nguyen) collects her widow's pension in Dakar, tirailleurs sénégalais' marital traditions demonstrate their durability.

Notes

INTRODUCTION: FRENCH AFRICAN SOLDIERS AND
FEMALE CONJUGAL PARTNERS IN COLONIAL MILITARISM

1. Joseph-Simon Gallieni, *Deux campagnes au Soudan français, 1886–1888* (Paris: Hachette, 1891), 121–22; Michael A. Gomez, *Pragmatism in the Age of Jihad: The Precolonial State of Bundu* (Cambridge: Cambridge University Press, 1992).

2. Martin A. Klein, *Slavery and Colonial Rule in French West Africa* (Cambridge: Cambridge University Press, 1998), 94–96.

3. A. Bâ, interview, Dakar, 2 February 2008.

4. Cynthia Enloe, *Maneuvers: The International Politics of Militarizing Women's Lives* (Berkeley: University of California Press, 2000), 34.

5. Amina Mama and Margo Okazawa-Rey, "Militarism, Conflict and Women's Activism in the Global Era: Challenges and Prospects for Women in Three West African Contexts," *Feminist Review*, no. 101 (2012): 98.

6. Laura Sjoberg and Sandra Via, eds., *Gender, War, and Militarism: Feminist Perspectives* (Santa Barbara, CA: Praeger, 2010), 7.

7. Alicia C. Decker, "What Does a Feminist Curiosity Bring to African Military History? An Analysis and an Intervention," *Journal of African Military History* 1, no. 1 (2017): 102; Patricia McFadden, "Plunder as Statecraft: Militarism and Resistance in Neocolonial Africa," in *Security Disarmed: Critical Perspectives on Gender, Race, and Militarization*, ed. Barbara Sutton, Sandra Morgen, and Julie Novkov (New Brunswick, NJ: Rutgers University Press, 2008), 149.

8. Shelby Cullom Davis, *Reservoirs of Men: A History of the Black Troops of French West Africa* (Chambéry, France: Imprimèries Réunies, 1934); Alexander S. Kanya-Forstner, *The Conquest of Western Sudan: A Study in French Military Imperialism* (London: Cambridge University Press, 1969); Charles John Balesi, *From Adversaries to Comrades-in-Arms: West Africans in the French Military, 1885–1918* (Waltham, MA: Crossroads, 1979).

9. Ronald Lamothe, *Slaves of Fortune: Sudanese Soldiers and the River War, 1896–1898* (Rochester, NY: James Currey, 2011); Timothy Stapleton, *African Police and Soldiers in Colonial Zimbabwe, 1923–80* (Rochester, NY: University of Rochester Press, 2011);

Timothy H. Parsons, *The African Rank-and-File: Social Implications of Colonial Military Service in the King's African Rifles, 1902–1964* (Portsmouth, NH: Heinemann, 1999); Myron Echenberg, *Colonial Conscripts: The Tirailleurs Sénégalais in French West Africa, 1857–1960* (Portsmouth, NH: Heinemann, 1991); Echenberg, "Slaves into Soldiers: Social Origins of the Tirailleurs Senegalais," in *Africans in Bondage: Studies in Slavery and the Slave Trade*, ed. Paul E. Lovejoy (Madison: African Studies Program, University of Wisconsin–Madison, 1986).

10. Amadou Ba, *Les "Sénégalais" à Madagascar: Militaires ouest-africains dans la conquête et la colonisation de la Grande-Île (1895–1960)* (Paris: Harmattan, 2012); Michelle Moyd, "Making the Household, Making the State: Colonial Military Communities and Labor in German East Africa," *International Labor and Working-Class History*, no. 80 (Fall 2011): 53–76; Camille Duparc, "Les Femmes des Tirailleurs Sénégalais de 1857 à nos jours" (master's thesis, Université du Havre, 2009); David Killingray, "Gender Issues and African Colonial Armies," in *Guardians of Empire: The Armed Forces of the Colonial Powers c. 1700–1964*, ed. David Killingray and David Omissi (Manchester: Manchester University Press, 1999); Timothy Parsons, "All *Askaris* Are Family Men: Sex, Domesticity and Discipline in the King's African Rifles, 1902–1964," in Killingray and Omissi, *Guardians of Empire*.

11. Myles Osborne, *Ethnicity and Empire in Kenya: Loyalty and Martial Race among the Kamba, c. 1800 to the Present* (Cambridge: Cambridge University Press, 2014); Heather Streets-Salter, *Martial Races: The Military, Race, and Masculinity in British Imperial Culture, 1857–1914* (Manchester: Manchester University Press, 2004), 10–11; Gregory Mann, "Old Soldiers, Young Men: Masculinity, Islam, and Military Veterans in late 1950s Soudan Français (Mali)," in *Men and Masculinities in Modern Africa*, ed. Lisa A. Lindsay and Stephan F. Miescher (Portsmouth, NH: Heinemann, 2003); Joe Lunn, "'Les Races Guerrières': Racial Preconceptions in the French Military about West African Soldiers during the First World War," *Journal of Contemporary History* 34, no. 4 (October 1999): 517–36.

12. Gregory Mann, *Native Sons: West African Veterans and France in the Twentieth Century* (Durham, NC: Duke University Press, 2006).

13. Michelle Moyd, *Violent Intermediaries: African Soldiers, Conquest, and Everyday Colonialism in German East Africa* (Athens: Ohio University Press, 2014), 126.

14. Alicia C. Decker, *In Idi Amin's Shadow: Women, Gender, and Militarism in Uganda* (Athens: Ohio University Press, 2014); Ruth Ginio, "'Cherchez la femme': African Gendarmes, Quarrelsome Women, and French Commanders in French West Africa, 1945–1960," *International Journal of African Historical Studies* 47, no. 1 (2014): 37–53.

15. Jennie E. Burnet, *Genocide Lives in Us: Women, Memory, and Silence in Rwanda* (Madison: University of Wisconsin Press, 2012); Danny Hoffman, *The War Machines: Young Men and Violence in Sierra Leone and Liberia* (Durham, NC: Duke University Press, 2011); Chris Coulter, *Bush Wives and Girl Soldiers: Women's Lives through War and Peace in Sierra Leone* (Ithaca, NY: Cornell University Press, 2009); Tanya Lyons, *Guns and Guerilla Girls: Women in the Zimbabwean National Liberation Struggle* (Trenton, NJ: Africa World Press, 2004).

16. Sjoberg and Via, *Gender, War, and Militarism*, 3.

17. Jennine Hurl-Eamon's work problematizes this binary, while historicizing the gradual removal of soldiers' wives from the British army in the eighteenth century, in *Marriage and the British Army in the Long Eighteenth Century: "The Girl I Left behind Me"* (Oxford: Oxford University Press, 2014).

18. John A. Lynn II, *Women, Armies, and Warfare in Early Modern Europe* (Cambridge: Cambridge University Press, 2008); Holly A. Mayer, *Belonging to the Army: Camp Followers and Community during the American Revolution* (Columbia: University of South Carolina Press, 1996), 3–4; Patricia Y. Stallard, *Glittering Misery: Dependents of the Indian Fighting Army* (San Rafael, CA: Presidio, 1978), 53.

19. Thomas Cardoza, *Intrepid Women: Cantinières and Vivandières of the French Army* (Bloomington: Indiana University Press, 2010), 3.

20. Rogers Brubaker, *Citizenship and Nationhood in France and Germany* (Cambridge, MA: Harvard University Press, 1992), 14. Women challenged these ideas during World War I; see Nicoletta F. Gullace, *"The Blood of Our Sons": Men, Women, and the Renegotiation of British Citizenship during the Great War* (New York: Palgrave Macmillan, 2002).

21. Myna Trustram, *Women of the Regiment: Marriage and the Victorian Army* (Cambridge: Cambridge University Press, 1984), 201.

22. Barton C. Hacker, "Women and Military Institutions in Early Modern Europe: A Reconnaissance," *Signs* 6, no. 4 (Summer 1981): 645.

23. Annie Bunting, Benjamin N. Lawrance, and Richard Roberts, eds., *Marriage by Force? Contestation over Consent and Coercion in Africa* (Athens: Ohio University Press, 2016); Jody Sarich, Michele Olivier, and Kevin Bales, "Forced Marriage, Slavery, and Plural Legal Systems: An African Example," *Human Rights Quarterly* 38, no. 2 (May 2016): 450–76; Annie Bunting, "'Forced Marriage' in Conflict Situations: Researching and Prosecuting Old Harms and New Crimes," *Canadian Journal of Human Rights* 1, no. 1 (Spring 2012): 165–85; James Giblin, "The Victimization of Women in Late Precolonial and Early Colonial Warfare in Tanzania," in *Sexual Violence in Conflict Zones: From the Ancient World to the Era of Human Rights*, ed. Elizabeth D. Heineman (Philadelphia: University of Pennsylvania Press, 2011); Aisha K. Gill and Sundari Anitha, eds., *Forced Marriage: Introducing a Social Justice and Human Rights Perspective* (New York: Zed Books, 2011); Bridgette A. Toy-Cronin, "What is Forced Marriage? Towards a Definition of Forced Marriage as a Crime against Humanity," *Columbia Journal of Gender and Law* 19, no. 2 (2010): 539–90; John Laband, ed., *Daily Lives of Civilians in Wartime Africa: From Slavery Days to Rwandan Genocide* (Westport, CT: Greenwood Press, 2006).

24. Cynthia Enloe, *Globalization and Militarism: Feminists Make the Link*, 2nd ed. (Lanham, MD: Rowman & Littlefield, 2016); Mary Louise Roberts, *What Soldiers Do: Sex and the American GI in World War II France* (Chicago: University of Chicago Press, 2013).

25. Marcia Wright, *Strategies of Slaves and Women: Life-Stories from East/Central Africa* (New York: Lilian Barber, 1993); Marie Rodet, "Continuum of Gendered Violence: The Colonial Invention of Female Desertion as a Customary Criminal Offense, French

Soudan, 1900–1949," in *Domestic Violence and the Law in Colonial and Postcolonial Africa*, ed. Emily S. Burrill, Richard L. Roberts, and Elizabeth Thornberry (Athens: Ohio University Press, 2010).

26. Isabelle Tracol-Huynh, "Between Stigmatisation and Regulation: Prostitution in Colonial Northern Vietnam," *Culture, Health, and Sexuality* 12, no. S1 (August 2010): S73–S87; Michel Serge Hardy, *De la morale au moral des troupes ou l'histoire des B.M.C., 1918–2004* (Panazol, France: Lavauzelle, 2004); Christelle Taraud, *La prostitution coloniale: Algérie, Tunisie, Maroc (1830–1962)* (Paris: Payot, 2003); Philippa Levine, *Prostitution, Race, and Politics: Policing Venereal Disease in the British Empire* (New York: Routledge, 2003).

27. Kamari Maxine Clarke, *Fictions of Justice: The International Criminal Court and the Challenge of Legal Pluralism in Sub-Saharan Africa* (Cambridge: Cambridge University Press, 2009), 75–76, 189–92.

28. Carole Pateman, "Women and Consent," *Political Theory* 8, no. 2 (May 1980): 149–68.

29. Elizabeth Thornberry, *Colonizing Consent: Rape and Governance in South Africa's Eastern Cape* (Cambridge: Cambridge University Press, 2019); Jean Allman and Victoria Tashjian, *"I Will Not Eat Stone": A Women's History of Colonial Asante* (Portsmouth, NH: Heinemann, 2000); Diana Jeater, *Marriage, Perversion, and Power: The Construction of Moral Discourse in Southern Rhodesia, 1894–1930* (Oxford: Clarendon, 1993).

30. Susan Zeiger, *Entangling Alliances: Foreign War Brides and American Soldiers in the Twentieth Century* (New York: New York University Press, 2010), 5–6.

31. Enloe, *Maneuvers*, 51.

32. Lynn M. Thomas, *Politics of the Womb: Women, Reproduction, and the State in Kenya* (Berkeley: University of California Press, 2003), 4.

33. Nancy F. Cott, *Public Vows: A History of Marriage and the Nation* (Cambridge, MA: Harvard University Press, 2000), 1.

34. Martin Chanock, *Law, Custom, and Social Order: The Colonial Experience in Malawi and Zambia* (Cambridge: Cambridge University Press, 1985), 9.

35. Terence Ranger, "The Invention of Tradition in Colonial Africa," in *The Invention of Tradition*, ed. Eric Hobsbawm and Terence Ranger (Cambridge: Cambridge University Press, 1983); Leroy Vail, *The Creation of Tribalism in Southern Africa* (Berkeley: University of California Press, 1989); Sara Berry, *No Condition is Permanent: The Social Dynamics of Agrarian Change in Sub-Saharan Africa* (Madison: University of Wisconsin Press, 1993); Mahmood Mamdani, *Citizen and Subject: Contemporary Africa and the Legacy of Late Colonialism* (Princeton, NJ: Princeton University Press, 1996); Carolyn Hamilton, *Terrific Majesty: The Powers of Shaka Zulu and the Limits of Historical Invention* (Cambridge, MA: Harvard University Press, 1998).

36. Chanock, *Law, Custom, and Social Order*, chaps. 10 and 11.

37. Margaret Jean Hay and Marcia Wright, eds., *African Women and the Law: Historical Perspectives* (Boston: Boston University African Studies Center, 1982); Kristin Mann and Richard Roberts, eds. *Law in Colonial Africa* (Portsmouth, NH: Heinemann, 1991); Jean Allman, "Rounding up Spinsters: Gender Chaos and Unmarried Women

in Colonial Asante," *Journal of African History* 37, no. 2 (July 1996): 195–214; Richard Roberts, *Litigants and Households: African Disputes and Colonial Courts in the French Soudan, 1895–1912* (Portsmouth, NH: Heinemann, 2005); Emily Lynn Osborn, *Our New Husbands Are Here: Households, Gender, and Politics in a West African State from the Slave Trade to Colonial Rule* (Athens: Ohio University Press, 2011); Elizabeth Thornberry, "Sex, Violence, and Family in South Africa's Eastern Cape," in *Domestic Violence and the Law in Colonial and Postcolonial Africa*, ed. Emily S. Burrill, Richard L. Roberts, and Elizabeth Thornberry (Athens: Ohio University Press, 2010).

38. Emily Burrill, *States of Marriage: Gender, Justice, and Rights in Colonial Mali* (Athens: Ohio University Press, 2015), 4–5.

39. I discuss this in greater detail in the following chapter, but for some relevant literature see Barbara Cooper, *Marriage in Maradi: Gender and Culture in a Hausa Society in Niger, 1900–1989* (Oxford: James Currey, 1997); Sarah Mirza and Margaret Strobel, *Three Swahili Women: Life Histories from Mombasa, Kenya* (Bloomington: Indiana University Press, 1989); Kristin Mann, *Marrying Well: Marriage, Status and Social Change among the Educated Elite in Colonial Lagos* (Cambridge: Cambridge University Press, 1985).

40. Napoleon's Civil Code of 1804 and the French Family Code of 1939 shaped the boundaries of families in France. See Camille Robcis, *The Law of Kinship: Anthropology, Psychoanalysis, and the Family in France* (Ithaca, NY: Cornell University Press, 2013), 1–14; Kristen Stromberg Childers, *Fathers, Families, and the State in France, 1914–1945* (Ithaca, NY: Cornell University Press, 2003), 12–41; Jean Elisabeth Pedersen, *Legislating the French Family: Feminism, Theater, and Republican Politics, 1870–1920* (New Brunswick, NJ: Rutgers University Press, 2003).

41. George Brooks, *Eurafricans in Western Africa: Commerce, Social Status, Gender and Religious Observance from the Sixteenth to the Eighteenth Century* (Athens: Ohio University Press, 2003).

42. Owen White, *Children of the French Empire: Miscegenation and Colonial Society in French West Africa, 1895–1960* (Oxford: Clarendon, 1999), 12.

43. Legitimate marriages replaced temporary conjugal arrangements by the late nineteenth century. See Hilary Jones, "From *Mariage à la Mode* to Weddings at Town Hall: Marriage, Colonialism, and Mixed-Race Society in Nineteenth-Century Senegal," *International Journal of African Historical Studies* 38, no. 1 (2005): 27–48. For other important works dealing with race, marriage, and legitimacy in empire, see Carina E. Ray, *Crossing the Color Line: Race, Sex, and the Contested Politics of Colonialism in Ghana* (Athens: Ohio University Press, 2015); Ann Laura Stoler, "Making Empire Respectable: The Politics of Race and Sexual Morality in 20th-Century Colonial Cultures," *American Ethnologist* 16, no. 4 (November 1989): 634–60; Julia Clancy-Smith and Frances Gouda, eds., *Domesticating the Empire: Race, Gender, and Family Life in French and Dutch Colonialism* (Charlottesville: University of Virginia Press, 1998).

44. For a contemporary parallel, see Stacey Hynd, "'To Be Taken as a Wife Is a Form of Death': The Social, Military and Humanitarian Dynamics of Forced Marriage and Girl Soldiers in African Conflicts, c. 1999–2010," in *Marriage by Force? Contestation over*

Consent and Coercion in Africa, ed. Annie Bunting, Benjamin N. Lawrance, and Richard Roberts (Athens: Ohio University Press, 2016), 293.

45. Parsons, "All *Askari* Are Family Men."

46. Yaël Simpson Fletcher, "Unsettling Settlers: Colonial Migrants and Racialised Sexuality in Interwar Marseilles," in *Gender, Sexuality, and Colonial Modernities*, ed. Antoinette Burton (New York: Routledge, 1999).

47. Lisa A. Lindsay, "Domesticity and Difference: Male Breadwinners, Working Women, and Colonial Citizenship in the 1945 Nigerian General Strike," *American Historical Review* 104, no. 3 (June 1999): 783–812.

48. Robcis, *Law of Kinship*, 42–43; Susan Pedersen, *Family, Dependence, and the Origins of the Welfare State: Britain and France, 1914–1945* (Cambridge: Cambridge University Press, 1993); Dorit Geva, *Conscription, Family, and the Modern State: A Comparative Study of France and the United States* (Cambridge: Cambridge University Press, 2013); Elisa Camiscioli, *Reproducing the French Race: Immigration, Intimacy, and Embodiment in the Early Twentieth Century* (Durham, NC: Duke University Press, 2009).

49. Frederick Cooper, "From Free Labor to Family Allowances: Labor and African Society in Colonial Discourse," *American Ethnologist* 16, no. 4 (November 1989): 745–65.

50. Jennifer Mittelstadt, *The Rise of the Military Welfare State* (Cambridge, MA: Harvard University Press, 2015), 4–5.

51. Enloe, *Maneuvers*, 156.

52. Gregory Mann, *Native Sons*, 4–8.

53. Judith A. Byfield et al., eds., *Africa and World War II* (Cambridge: Cambridge University Press, 2015); Eric T. Jennings, *Free French Africa in World War II: The African Resistance* (Cambridge: Cambridge University Press, 2015); Catherine Akpo-Vaché, *L'AOF et la Seconde Guerre mondiale: La vie politique (septembre 1939–octobre 1945)* (Paris: Karthala, 1996); Charles Onana, *1940–1945: Noirs, blancs, beurs: Libérateurs de la France* (Paris: Duboiris, 2006); Raffael Scheck, *Hitler's African Victims: The German Army Massacre of Black French Soldiers in 1940* (Cambridge: Cambridge University Press, 2006); Joe Lunn, *Memoirs of the Maelstrom: A Senegalese Oral History of the First World War* (Portsmouth, NH: Heinemann, 1999); Nancy Ellen Lawler, *Soldiers of Misfortune: Ivoirien Tirailleurs of WW II* (Athens: Ohio University Press, 1992); David Killingray and Richard Rathbone, eds., *Africa and the Second World War* (London: Macmillan, 1986); Myron Echenberg, "'Morts pour la France': The African Soldier in France during the Second World War," *Journal of African History* 26, no. 4 (1985): 363–80; Marc Michel, *L'appel à l'Afrique: Contributions et réactions à l'effort de guerre en A.O.F. (1914–1919)* (Paris: Publications de la Sorbonne, 1982).

54. Martin Mourre, *Thiaroye 1944: Histoire et mémoire d'un massacre colonial* (Rennes, France: Presses Universitaires de Rennes, 2017); Armelle Mabon, *Prisonniers de guerre indigènes: Visages oubliés de la France occupée* (Paris: La Découverte, 2010); Dana S. Hale, *Races on Display: French Representations of Colonized Peoples, 1886–1940* (Bloomington: Indiana University Press, 2008), 91–117; Gregory Mann, "Immigrants and Arguments in France and West Africa," *Comparative Studies in Society and History* 45, no. 2 (April 2003): 362–85; Anne Donadey, "'Y'a bon Banania': Ethics and Cultural Criticism

in the Colonial Context," *French Cultural Studies* 11, no. 31 (2000): 9–29; Laura Rice, "African Conscripts/European Conflicts: Race, Memory, and the Lessons of War," *Cultural Critique* 45 (Spring 2000): 109–49; Myron Echenberg, "Tragedy at Thiaroye: The Senegalese Soldiers' Uprising of 1944," in *African Labor History*, ed. Peter C. W. Gutkind, Robin Cohen, and Jean Copans (London: Sage, 1978).

55. Ruth Ginio, *The French Army and Its African Soldiers: The Years of Decolonization* (Lincoln: University of Nebraska Press, 2017); Ba, *Les "Sénégalais"*; Gregory Mann, *Native Sons*.

56. Ann Laura Stoler and Frederick Cooper, "Between Metropole and Colony: Rethinking a Research Agenda," in *Tensions of Empire: Colonial Cultures in a Bourgeois World*, ed. Cooper and Stoler (Berkeley: University of California Press, 1997), 18; Henri Brunschwig, *Noirs et blancs dans l'Afrique noire française, ou, comment le colonisé deviant le colonisateur (1870–1914)* (Paris: Flammarion, 1983).

57. Benjamin N. Lawrance, Emily Lynn Osborn, and Richard L. Roberts, "Introduction: African Intermediaries and the 'Bargain' of Collaboration," in *Intermediaries, Interpreters, and Clerks: African Employees in the Making of Colonial Africa*, ed. Lawrance, Osborn, and Roberts (Madison: University of Wisconsin Press, 2006), 7.

58. Joël Glasman, "Penser les intermédiaires coloniaux: Note sur les dossiers de carrière de la police du Togo," *History in Africa* 37 (2010): 75–76.

59. Frederick Cooper, "Conflict and Connection: Rethinking Colonial African History," *American Historical Review* 99, no. 5 (December 1994): 1544.

60. Elizabeth A. Foster, *Faith in Empire: Religion, Politics, and Colonial Rule in French Senegal, 1880–1940* (Stanford, CA: Stanford University Press, 2013); Alice L. Conklin, "Colonialism and Human Rights, a Contradiction in Terms? The Case of France and West Africa, 1895–1914," *American Historical Review* 103, no. 2 (April 1998): 419–42; Mamadou Diouf makes a similar argument about the limits of assimilation in "The French Colonial Policy of Assimilation and the Civility of the Originaires of the Four Communes (Senegal): A Nineteenth Century Globalization Project," *Development and Change* 29, no. 4 (October 1998): 671–96.

61. Marie Rodet, *Les migrantes ignorées du Haut-Sénégal (1900–1946)* (Paris: Karthala, 2009).

62. See Madhavi Kale's observations on coolie labor migration in postemancipation British Empire in *Fragments of Empire: Capital, Slavery, and Indian Indentured Labor Migration in the British Caribbean* (Philadelphia: University of Pennsylvania Press, 1998), 171.

63. Gregory Mann, *Native Sons*, 146–49.

64. Adele Perry, *Colonial Relations: The Douglas-Connolly Family and the Nineteenth-Century Imperial World* (Cambridge: Cambridge University Press, 2015); Elizabeth Buettner, *Empire Families: Britons and Late Imperial India* (Oxford: Oxford University Press, 2004); Tony Ballantyne and Antoinette Burton argue that colonizers do not hold the monopoly on migration in empire in their introduction to *Moving Subjects: Gender, Mobility, and Intimacy in an Age of Global Empire* (Urbana: University of Illinois Press, 2009), 5–6.

65. Stoler and Cooper, "Between Metropole and Colony."

66. Joel Quirk and Darshan Vigneswaran, "Mobility Makes States," in *Mobility Makes States: Migration and Power in Africa*, ed. Vigneswaran and Quirk (Philadelphia: University of Pennsylvania Press, 2015), 23.

67. Cynthia Enloe, *Bananas, Beaches, and Bases: Making Feminist Sense of International Politics*, 2nd ed. (Berkeley: University of California Press, 2014), 141.

68. Dinah Hannaford, *Marriage without Borders: Transnational Spouses in Neoliberal Senegal* (Philadelphia: University of Pennsylvania Press, 2017); Cati Coe, *The Scattered Family: Parenting, African Migrants, and Global Inequality* (Chicago: University of Chicago Press, 2014); Beth Buggenhagen, *Muslim Families in Global Senegal: Money Takes Care of Shame* (Bloomington: Indiana University Press, 2012).

69. Ray, *Crossing the Color Line*; Rachel Jean-Baptiste, *Conjugal Rights: Marriage, Sexuality, and Urban Life in Colonial Libreville, Gabon* (Athens: Ohio University Press, 2014); Hilary Jones, *The Métis of Senegal: Urban Life and Politics in French West Africa* (Bloomington: Indiana University Press, 2013); Durba Ghosh, *Sex and the Family in Colonial India: The Making of Empire* (Cambridge: Cambridge University Press, 2006); Ann Laura Stoler, *Race and the Education of Desire: Foucault's History of Sexuality and the Colonial Order of Things* (Durham, NC: Duke University Press, 1995); Stoler, *Carnal Knowledge and Imperial Power: Race and the Intimate in Colonial Rule* (Berkeley: University of California Press, 2002).

70. Christina E. Firpo, *The Uprooted: Race, Children, and Imperialism in French Indochina, 1890–1980* (Honolulu: University of Hawai'i Press, 2016); Emmanuelle Saada, *Empire's Children: Race, Filiation, and Citizenship in the French Colonies* (Chicago: University of Chicago Press, 2012); Owen White, *Children of the French Empire*.

71. Michel Foucault, *The History of Sexuality: An Introduction*, trans. Robert Hurley (New York: Vintage, 1990), 103.

72. Christopher J. Lee, *Unreasonable Histories: Nativism, Multiracial Lives, and the Genealogical Imagination in British Africa* (Durham, NC: Duke University Press, 2014), 6–7.

73. Michel Foucault, "Nietzsche, Genealogy, History," in *The Foucault Reader*, ed. Paul Rabinow (New York: Pantheon Books, 1984), 76.

74. Joan Wallach Scott, *Gender and the Politics of History*, rev. ed. (New York: Columbia University Press, 1999), 6.

75. Michel-Rolphe Trouillot, *Silencing the Past: Power and the Production of History* (Boston: Beacon Press, 1995), 52–53.

76. Ann Laura Stoler, *Along the Archival Grain: Epistemic Anxieties and Colonial Common Sense* (Princeton, NJ: Princeton University Press, 2009), 47–50.

77. Bakary Diallo, *Force-Bonté* (Paris: F. Reider, 1926); Joseph Issoufou Conombo, *Souvenirs de guerre d'un "tirailleurs sénégalais"* (Paris: Harmattan, 1989); Anne-Marie Niane, *L'étrangère* (Paris: Hatier International, 2002); Marc Guèye, *Un tirailleur sénégalais dans la guerre d'Indochine, 1953–1955* (Dakar: Presses Universitaires de Dakar, 2007); Joe Lunn, "Male Identity and Martial Codes of Honor: A Comparison of the War Memoirs of Robert Graves, Ernst Jünger, and Kande Kamara," *Journal of Military History* 69, no. 3 (July 2005): 713–35; Lunn, "Kande Kamara Speaks: An Oral History of the West

African Experience in France, 1914–18," in *Africa and the First World War*, ed. Melvin E. Page and Andy McKinlay (London: Macmillan, 1987).

78. Antoinette Burton argues that memoirs should be included in archives, in *Dwelling in the Archive: Women Writing House, Home, and History in Late Colonial India* (Oxford: Oxford University Press, 2003), 4–5.

79. The former ENS (Dakar) is now the Faculté des Sciences et Technologies de l'Éducation et de la Formation (FASTEF).

80. These crescendos included the *"sans papiers"* movement, the release of critical films, and veterans' legislation passed by French presidents Jacques Chirac and Nicholas Sarkozy. See Gregory Mann, "Immigrants and Arguments"; Rachid Bouchareb, dir., *Indigènes* (Paris: Tessalit Productions, 2007).

81. Elizabeth Tonkin, *Narrating Our Pasts: The Social Construction of Oral History* (Cambridge: Cambridge University Press, 1992); James Giblin, "Passages in a Struggle over the Past: Stories of Maji Maji in Njombe, Tanzania," in *Sources and Methods in African History: Spoken, Written, Unearthed*, ed. Toyin Falola and Christian Jennings (Rochester, NY: University of Rochester Press, 2003), 296–97.

82. For more on discretion in Senegal, see Ivy Mills, "Sutura: Gendered Honor, Social Death, and the Politics of Exposure in Senegalese Literature and Popular Culture" (PhD diss., University of California, Berkeley, 2011).

83. Trouillot, *Silencing the Past*, 26.

84. Richard Roberts, "History and Memory: The Power of Statist Narratives," *International Journal of African Historical Studies* 33, no. 3 (2000): 516–17; see also Thaddeus Sunseri, "Statist Narratives and Maji Maji Ellipses," *International Journal of African Historical Studies* 33, no. 3 (2000): 567–84.

85. Jamie Monson, "*Maisha*: Life History and the History of Livelihood along the TAZARA Railway in Tanzania," in *Sources and Methods in African History: Spoken, Written, Unearthed*, ed. Toyin Falola and Christian Jennings (Rochester, NY: University of Rochester Press, 2003), 313.

86. Pierre Nora, "General Introduction: Between Memory and History," in *Realms of Memory: Rethinking the French Past*, vol. 1, *Conflicts and Divisions*, ed. Pierre Nora, English-language edition ed. Lawrence D. Kritzman, trans. Arthur Goldhammer (New York: Columbia University Press, 1996), 8–12.

87. Joe Lunn, "Remembering the *Tirailleurs Sénégalais* and the Great War: Oral History as a Methodology of Inclusion in French Colonial Studies," *French Colonial History* 10 (2009): 125–49; Luise White, Stephan F. Miescher, and David William Cohen, eds., *African Words, African Voices: Critical Practices in Oral History* (Bloomington: Indiana University Press, 2001), 3; Jan Vansina, *Oral Tradition as History* (Madison: University of Wisconsin Press, 1985).

88. Steve Feierman, "Colonizers, Scholars, and the Creation of Invisible History," in *Beyond the Cultural Turn: New Directions in the Study of Society and Culture*, ed. Victoria E. Bonnell and Lynn Hunt (Berkeley: University of California Press, 1999), 183; Dipesh Chakrabarty, "Postcoloniality and the Artifice of History: Who Speaks for 'Indian' Pasts?," *Representations*, no. 37 (Winter 1992): 21.

89. Arjun Appadurai, "The Past as a Scarce Resource," *Man*, n.s., 16, no. 2 (June 1981): 217; Thomas Spear, "Neo-Traditionalism and the Limits of Invention in British Colonial Africa," *Journal of African History* 44, no. 1 (2003): 3–27; Hamilton, *Terrific Majesty*.

90. Echenberg, *Colonial Conscripts*, 3.

91. Foster, *Faith in Empire*, 5–7; Gary Wilder, *The French Imperial Nation-State: Negritude and Colonial Humanism between the Two World Wars* (Chicago: University of Chicago Press, 2005); Alice L. Conklin, *A Mission to Civilize: The Republican Idea of Empire in France and West Africa, 1895–1930* (Stanford: Stanford University Press, 1997).

92. *Nègre* is a racially charged term. During the Atlantic slave trade, "nègre" was interchangeable with "slave." In contemporary France, this word has pejorative connotations. In the Moroccan context, I translate "nègre" as "black."

CHAPTER 1: MARRYING INTO THE MILITARY

1. J. Malcolm Thompson, "Colonial Policy and the Family Life of Black Troops in French West Africa, 1817–1904," *International Journal of African Historical Studies* 23, no. 3 (1990): 423–53; Emily Lynn Osborn, *Our New Husbands Are Here: Households, Gender, and Politics in a West African State from the Slave Trade to Colonial Rule* (Athens: Ohio University Press, 2011).

2. On military and political power in West Africa, see Alexander S. Kanya-Forstner, *The Conquest of Western Sudan: A Study in French Military Imperialism* (London: Cambridge University Press, 1969); Anthony Clayton, *France, Soldiers, and Africa* (London: Brassey's Defence Publishers, 1988). For historical studies employing these troublesome dichotomies, see Terence O. Ranger, *Revolt in Southern Rhodesia, 1896–97: A Study in African Resistance* (London: Heinemann, 1967); Michael Crowder, ed. *West African Resistance: The Military Response to Colonial Occupation* (London: Hutchinson, 1971); Allen Isaacman and Barbara Isaacman, "Resistance and Collaboration in Southern and Central Africa, c. 1850–1920," *International Journal of African Historical Studies* 10, no. 1 (1977): 31–62; Charles John Balesi, *From Adversaries to Comrades-in-Arms: West Africans in the French Military, 1885–1918* (Waltham, MA: Crossroads, 1979). For critiques of these dichotomies, see Benjamin N. Lawrance, Emily Lynn Osborn, and Richard L. Roberts, "Introduction: African Intermediaries and the 'Bargain' of Collaboration," in *Intermediaries, Interpreters, and Clerks: African Employees in the Making of Colonial Africa*, ed. Lawrance, Osborn, and Roberts (Madison: University of Wisconsin Press, 2006); Frederick Cooper, "Conflict and Connection: Rethinking Colonial African History," *American Historical Review* 99, no. 5 (December 1994): 1516–45.

3. Michelle Moyd, *Violent Intermediaries: African Soldiers, Conquest, and Everyday Colonialism in German East Africa* (Athens: Ohio University Press, 2014), chaps. 3 and 4. Other recent works have included African women in histories of conquest, but without explicit gendered analysis. See Ronald Lamothe, *Slaves of Fortune: Sudanese Soldiers and the River War, 1896–1898* (Rochester, NY: James Currey, 2011), 72–120; Alicia C. Decker, "What Does a Feminist Curiosity Bring to African Military History? An Analysis and an Intervention," *Journal of African Military History* 1, no. 1 (2017): 93–111.

4. Many of French West Africa's early administrators were military men. Once the federated colony shifted to civilian rule in 1905, many high- and low-level administrators continued to be military men or veterans.

5. Pamela Scully, "Gender, History, and Human Rights," in *Gender and Culture at the Limit of Rights*, ed. Dorothy L. Hodgson (Philadelphia: University of Pennsylvania Press, 2011), 22–23; Scully, *Liberating the Family? Gender and British Slave Emancipation in the Rural Western Cape, South Africa, 1823–1853* (Portsmouth, NH: Heinemann, 1997), 4.

6. Diana Paton and Pamela Scully, "Introduction: Gender and Slave Emancipation in Comparative Perspective," in *Gender and Slave Emancipation in the Atlantic World*, ed. Scully and Paton (Durham, NC: Duke University Press, 2005), 3.

7. *Mesdames tirailleurs* (sing. *madame tirailleur*) was a moniker used by French observers to recognize women affiliated with West African colonial troops.

8. Anthony Clayton and David Killingray describe a similar phenomenon among Nigerian West African fighting forces in *Khaki and Blue: Military and Police in British Colonial Africa* (Athens: Ohio University Press, 1989), 187–89.

9. Klein, *Slavery and Colonialism*, 74–104.

10. Myron Echenberg, "Slaves into Soldiers: Social Origins of the Tirailleurs Senegalais," in *Africans in Bondage: Studies in Slavery and the Slave Trade*, ed. Paul E. Lovejoy (Madison: African Studies Program, University of Wisconsin–Madison, 1986); Echenberg, *Colonial Conscripts: The Tirailleurs Sénégalais in French West Africa, 1857–1960* (Portsmouth, NH: Heinemann, 1991), 7–24. For a parallel example, see Lamothe, *Slaves of Fortune*.

11. Igor Kopytoff and Suzanne Miers, "African 'Slavery' as an Institution of Marginality," in *Slavery in Africa: Historical and Anthropological Perspectives*, ed. Miers and Kopytoff (Madison: University of Wisconsin Press, 1977); Claude Meillassoux, *The Anthropology of Slavery: The Womb of Iron and Gold* (Chicago: University of Chicago Press, 1991).

12. Report on slavery from Medina, 1894, K14, ANS.

13. Parfait-Louis Monteil, *De St. Louis à Tripoli par le Lac Tchad* (Paris: Félix Alcan, 1895), 289.

14. For a more in-depth explanation of Senegambian military practices, see Sarah Davis Westwood, "Military Culture in Senegambia and the Origins of the *Tirailleur Sénégalais* Army, 1750–1910" (PhD diss., Boston University, 2018).

15. Edna G. Bay, *Wives of the Leopard: Gender, Politics, and Culture in the Kingdom of Dahomey* (Charlottesville: University of Virginia Press, 1998); Robert B. Edgerton, *Warrior Women: The Amazons of Dahomey and the Nature of War* (Boulder, CO: Westview Press, 2000); Stanley B. Alpern, *Amazons of Black Sparta: The Women Warriors of Dahomey* (New York: New York University Press, 1998).

16. Richard Roberts, *Warriors, Merchants, and Slaves: The State and the Economy in the Middle Niger Valley, 1700–1914* (Stanford, CA: Stanford University Press, 1987), 27–43; Kanya-Forstner, *Conquest of Western Sudan*; Balesi, *From Adversaries to Comrades-in-Arms*.

17. James F. Searing, "Aristocrats, Slaves, and Peasants: Power and Dependency in the Wolof States, 1700–1850," *International Journal of African Historical Studies* 21, no. 3 (1988): 480.

Notes to Pages 33–36

18. Sofas were Samory's soldiers. Martin Legassick, "Firearms, Horses and Samorian Army Organization 1870–1898," *Journal of African History* 7, no. 1 (1966): 96. For more on Samory and wars of conquest, see Brian J. Peterson, "History, Memory, and the Legacy of Samori in Southern Mali, c. 1880–1898," *Journal of African History* 49, no. 2 (2008): 261–79; Yves Person, *Samori: Une revolution Dyula*, 3 vols. (Dakar: IFAN, 1968–75).

19. Martin A. Klein, "Sexuality and Slavery in the Western Sudan," in *Sex, Power, and Slavery*, ed. Gwyn Campbell and Elizabeth Elbourne (Athens: Ohio University Press, 2015), 68.

20. Raymonde Bonnetain, *Une française au Soudan: Sur la route de Tombouctou, du Sénégal au Niger* (Paris: Librairies-Imprimeries Réunies, 1894), 77.

21. Marie Rodet, "Le sous-lieutenant Mansouka (c. 1860–1920): Un parcours d'esclave affranchi entre rébellion et allégeance au temps de la conquête coloniale française en Afrique," in *Résistances et mémoires des esclavages: Espaces arabo-musulmans et transatlantiques*, ed. Olivier Leservoisier and Salah Trabeisi (Paris: Karthala, 2014), 86.

22. J. Malcolm Thompson, "In Dubious Service: The Recruitment and Stabilization of West African Maritime Labor by the French Colonial Military, 1659–1900" (PhD diss., University of Minnesota, 1989).

23. François Manchuelle, "The 'Patriarchal Ideal' of Soninke Labor Migrants: From Slave Owners to Employers of Free Labor," *Canadian Journal of African Studies* 23, no. 1 (1989): 111.

24. J. Malcolm Thompson, "Colonial Policy."

25. Echenberg describes the rachat system in *Colonial Conscripts*, 8–11.

26. Bonnetain, *Une française*, 66–67.

27. Confidential circular in Saint-Louis, 14 November 1857, K11, ANS.

28. Note from 7 August 1885, in "Bakel Correspondance départ 1885," 13G185, ANS. There is also evidence to suggest that rachat was used to recruit tirailleurs sénégalais until 1899. Kaedi, 30 April 1899, 4D97, ANS.

29. Francois Renault, *Libération d'esclaves et nouvelle servitude* (Dakar: Nouvelles Éditions Africaines, 1976), 121.

30. Andrew F. Clark, "Freedom Villages in the Upper Senegal Valley, 1887–1910: A Reassessment," *Slavery and Abolition* 16, no. 3 (December 1995): 311–30; Denise Bouche, *Les villages de liberté en Afrique noire française, 1887–1910* (Paris: Mouton, 1968).

31. François Manchuelle, *Willing Migrants: Soninke Labor Diasporas, 1848–1960* (Athens: Ohio University Press, 1997), 130–31.

32. General Order no. 15, 1891, 15G156, ANS.

33. Report on captivity from Nioro, 20 March 1894, K14, ANS; Captain Frement at Kita to the governor of Soudan in Kayes, 6 March 1894, K14, ANS.

34. Letter from Captain Frement, commander of the Kita Cercle, to the governor of Soudan in Kayes, 6 March 1894, K14, ANS.

35. Richard Roberts, "The Case of Faama Mademba Sy and the Ambiguities of Legal Jurisdiction in Early Colonial French Soudan," in *Law in Colonial Africa*, ed. Kristin Mann and Richard Roberts (Portsmouth, NH: Heinemann, 1991). Faama Mademba

Sy was the brother of the first indigenous officer in the tirailleurs sénégalais, Mamadou Racine Sy. Another example is the fabled Wangrin, in Amadou Hampaté Bâ, *The Fortunes of Wangrin*, trans. Aina Pavolini Taylor (Bloomington: Indiana University Press, 1999).

36. Letter from Captain Frement, commander of the Kita Cercle, to the governor of Soudan in Kayes, 6 March 1894, K14, ANS.

37. There is evidence for this throughout a colony-wide survey conducted in French Soudan in 1894, K14, ANS; Report on Captivity from Nioro, 20 March 1894, K14, ANS; Joseph-Simon Gallieni, *Deux campagnes au Soudan français, 1886–1888* (Paris: Hachette, 1891), 429.

38. Allman and Tashjian, "I Will Not Eat Stone," xxxiv–xxxv.

39. Guide to captivity in Siguiri, 1894, K14, ANS.

40. Recent texts that illustrate this point for civilian African households include Emily S. Burrill, *States of Marriage: Gender, Justice, and Rights in Colonial Mali* (Athens: Ohio University Press, 2015); Elizabeth McMahon, *Slavery and Emancipation in Islamic East Africa: From Honor to Respectability* (Cambridge: Cambridge University Press, 2013); Trevor R. Getz and Liz Clarke, *Abina and the Important Men: A Graphic History* (New York: Oxford University Press, 2012); Marie Rodet, *Les migrantes ignorées du Haut-Sénégal (1900–1946)* (Paris: Karthala, 2009); Paton and Scully, "Introduction: Gender and Slave Emancipation"; Trevor R. Getz, *Slavery and Reform in West Africa: Toward Emancipation in Nineteenth-Century Senegal and the Gold Coast* (Athens: Ohio University Press, 2004).

41. Captain Frement in Kita to the governor of Soudan in Kayes, 6 March 1894, K14, ANS. Tera W. Hunter addresses the emancipation of African American soldiers' families in the Civil War in *Bound in Wedlock: Slave and Free Black Marriage in the Nineteenth Century* (Cambridge, MA: Belknap Press of Harvard University Press, 2017), 166–72.

42. Claire C. Robertson and Martin A. Klein, "Women's Importance in African Slave Systems," in *Women and Slavery in Africa*, ed. Robertson and Klein (Portsmouth, NH: Heinemann, 1997).

43. An excellent example comes from Marie Étienne Péroz, *Au Soudan français: Souvenirs de guerre et de mission* (Paris: Callman Lévy, 1891), 125–26.

44. Paton and Scully, "Introduction: Gender and Slave Emancipation," 3.

45. Martin A. Klein and Richard Roberts, "Gender and Emancipation in French West Africa," in *Gender and Slave Emancipation in the Atlantic World*, ed. Pamela Scully and Diana Paton (Durham, NC: Duke University Press, 2005), 171.

46. Marie Rodet, "Continuum of Gendered Violence: The Colonial Invention of Female Desertion as a Customary Criminal Offense, French Soudan, 1900–1949," in *Domestic Violence and the Law in Colonial and Postcolonial Africa*, ed. Emily S. Burrill, Richard L. Roberts, and Elizabeth Thornberry (Athens: Ohio University Press, 2010).

47. Oyèrónkẹ́ Oyěwùmí, *The Invention of Women: Making an African Sense of Western Gender Discourses* (Minneapolis: University of Minnesota Press, 1997), 151–52.

48. Osborn, *Our New Husbands*; Susan Pedersen, *Family, Dependence, and the Origins of the Welfare State: Britain and France, 1914–1945* (Cambridge: Cambridge

University Press, 1993); Lisa A. Lindsay, "Domesticity and Difference: Male Breadwinners, Working Women, and Colonial Citizenship in the 1945 Nigerian General Strike," *American Historical Review* 104, no. 3 (June 1999): 783–812.

49. Richard Roberts, "Long Distance Trade and Production: Sinsani in the Nineteenth Century," *Journal of African History* 21, no. 2 (1980): 169–88.

50. Péroz, *Au Soudan français*, 224. See also Gracia Clark, *Onions Are My Husband: Survival and Accumulation by West African Market Women* (Chicago: University of Chicago Press, 1994).

51. Gallieni, *Deux campagnes*, 121–22. The image of this distribution of wives is reproduced on the cover of Klein, *Slavery and Colonial Rule*.

52. Henri Frey, *Campagne dans le haut Sénégal et dans le haut Niger (1885–1886)* (Paris: Librairie Plon, 1888), 392.

53. Gallieni, *Deux campagnes*, 122.

54. Report from Nioro on captivity, 20 March 1894, K14, ANS.

55. Klein, *Slavery and Colonial Rule*, 104.

56. Report authored by Gallieni in Bafoulabé, 10 May 1888, 1D92, ANS.

57. Nwando Achebe identified exceptions in *The Female King of Colonial Nigeria: Ahebi Ugbabe* (Bloomington: Indiana University Press, 2011). Divorce occurred more often for Muslim women in urban spaces than rural spaces. Barbara Cooper, *Marriage in Maradi: Gender and Culture in a Hausa Society in Niger, 1900–1989* (Oxford: James Currey, 1997), 24; Sarah Mirza and Margaret Strobel, *Three Swahili Women: Life Histories from Mombasa, Kenya* (Bloomington: Indiana University Press, 1989), 10.

58. Kopytoff and Miers, "African 'Slavery' as an Institution of Marginality"; Jane I. Guyer and Samuel M. Eno Belinga, "Wealth in People as Wealth in Knowledge: Accumulation and Composition in Equatorial Africa," *Journal of African History* 36, no. 1 (March 1995): 91–120.

59. Barbara Cooper, "Women's Worth and Wedding Gift Exchange in Maradi, Niger, 1907–1989," *Journal of African History* 36, no. 1 (1995): 121–40.

60. Benedetta Rossi, "Introduction: Rethinking Slavery in West Africa," in *Reconfiguring Slavery: West African Trajectories* (Liverpool: Liverpool University Press, 2009), 7–8.

61. Paul E. Lovejoy, "Concubinage and the Status of Women Slaves in Early Colonial Northern Nigeria," *Journal of African History* 29, no. 2 (1988): 245–66; Timothy Cleaveland, "Reproducing Culture and Society: Women and the Politics of Gender, Age, and Social Rank in Walāta," *Canadian Journal of African Studies* 34, no. 2 (2000): 196; Mohammed Ennaji, *Serving the Master: Slavery and Society in Nineteenth-Century Morocco*, trans. Seth Graebner (London: Macmillan, 1999), 31–42.

62. Frey, *Campagne*, 128, 391–93, 407; Gallieni, *Deux campagnes*, 121–22, 430.

63. I address mariage à la mode du pays in the introduction.

64. Getz and Clarke, *Abina and the Important Men*; Burrill, *States of Marriage*, chap. 2; Richard Roberts, *Litigants and Households: African Disputes and Colonial Courts in the French Soudan, 1895–1912* (Portsmouth, NH: Heinemann, 2005), 99–148; Marie Rodet,

"Sexualité, mariage, et esclavage au Soudan français à la fin du XIXe siècle," *CLIO: Femmes, Genre, Histoire*, no. 33 (2011): 45–64.

65. Osborn, *Our New Husbands*, 92–140.

66. Burrill, *States of Marriage*, 70–75.

67. Ciraïa Aminata's history is in Gallieni, *Deux campagnes*, 429–30.

68. Gallieni, 430.

69. Guide to captivity in Siguiri, 1894, K14, ANS. Siguiri received many refugees from Samory's wars on the right bank of the Niger River.

70. Marcia Wright, *Strategies of Slaves and Women: Life-Stories from East/Central Africa* (New York: Lilian Barber, 1993); Rodet, *Migrantes ignorées*.

71. Many administrators across French Soudan shared this view in 1894, K14, ANS.

72. For a useful discussion on elopement and abduction in marital rites, see Brett Shadle, *"Girl Cases": Marriage Disputes and Colonialism in Gusiiland, Kenya, 1890–1970* (Portsmouth, NH: Heinemann, 2006), 131–40.

73. Colonel Frey, quoted in J. Malcolm Thompson, "Colonial Policy," 441.

74. Lynn M. Thomas and Jennifer Cole, "Thinking through Love in Africa," in *Love in Africa*, ed. Cole and Thomas (Chicago: University of Chicago Press, 2009).

75. Paul Vigné d'Octon, *Journal d'un marin: Premiers feuillets: Sur la route d'exil* (Paris: Flammarion, 1897), 161.

76. Émile Dussaulx, *Journal du Soudan (1894–1898)*, ed. Sophie Dulucq (Paris: Harmattan, 2000), 155; J. Sarzeau [pseud.], *Les Français aux colonies: Sénégal et Soudan français, Dahomey, Madagascar, Tunisie* (Paris: Bloud et Barral, 1897), 20.

77. Frey, *Campagne*, 47–48.

78. Gallieni, *Deux campagnes*, 387; Charles Guilleux, *Journal de route d'un caporal de tirailleurs de la mission saharienne (mission Foureau-Lamy), 1898–1900* (Belfort, France: Schmitt, 1904), 114.

79. Guilleux, 190.

80. Frey, *Campagne*, 47–48.

81. Gallieni, *Deux campagnes*, 10; Frey, *Campagne*, 47–48.

82. Vigné d'Octon, *Journal d'un marin*, 162; François Descostes, *Au Soudan (1890–1891): Souvenirs d'un tirailleur sénégalais, d'après sa correspondance intime* (Paris: Picard, 1893), 29.

83. Frey, *Campagne*, 79; James F. Searing, *West African Slavery and Atlantic Commerce: The Senegal River Valley, 1700–1860* (Cambridge: Cambridge University Press, 1993), 122; Balesi, *From Adversaries to Comrades-in-Arms*, 43; Andrew F. Clark, *From Frontier to Backwater: Economy and Society in the Upper Senegal Valley (West Africa), 1850–1920* (Lanham, MD: University Press of America, 1999), 112–13.

84. Hippolyte Marceau, *Le tirailleur soudanais* (Paris: Berger-Levrault, 1911), 43.

85. Gaston Lautour, *Journal d'un spahi au Soudan, 1897–99* (Paris: Perrin, 1909), 138–39.

86. Dussaulx, *Journal du Soudan*, 41; Bonnetain, *Une française*, 67, 73.

87. Frey, *Campagne*, 391–92.

88. Gallieni, *Deux campagnes*, 158.
89. Gallieni, 10.
90. Lautour, *Journal d'un spahi*, 81.
91. Jean-François Arsène Klobb, *Dernier carnet de route: Au Soudan français: Rapport officiel de M. le gouverneur Bergès sur la fin de la mission Klobb* (Paris: Ernest Flammarion, 1905), 82.
92. Henri Joseph Eugène Gouraud, *Souvenirs d'un africain*, vol. 1, *Au Soudan* (Paris: Pierre Tisné, 1939), 80.
93. Klobb, *Dernier carnet*, 102.
94. Péroz, *Soudan français*, 197.
95. Guilleux, *Journal de route*, 211–12.
96. Marceau, *Le tirailleur soudanais*, 35.
97. Guilleux, *Journal de route*, 115.
98. Gallieni, *Deux campagnes*, 415.
99. J. Malcolm Thompson, "Colonial Policy," 436.
100. Marabouts are religious leaders, predominantly affiliated with Sufi sects, in West Africa.
101. Péroz, *Au Soudan français*, 144–46.
102. Report on captivity from Bafoulabé, 15 May 1894, K14, ANS.
103. Gallieni, *Deux campagnes*, 158; Marceau, *Le tirailleur soudanais*, 58.
104. Gouraud, *Souvenirs d'un africain*, 170.
105. Marceau, *Le tirailleur soudanais*, 38.
106. Frey, *Campagne*, 393.
107. Guilleux, *Journal de route*, 201, 219, 212.
108. Correspondence from Bakel to Kayes, 10 June 1885, 13G185, ANS.
109. General Order no. 21, Kayes, 22 July 1891, 15G156, ANS.
110. Marceau, *Le tirailleur soudanais*, 35.

CHAPTER 2: COLONIAL CONQUEST "EN FAMILLE"

1. Governor-general of FWA to the minister of the colonies, Saint-Louis, 26 July 1899, FM-SG-SEN-XIV-28, ANOM.
2. Exceptions for French Congo include Bruce Whitehouse, *Migrants and Strangers in an African City: Exile, Dignity, Belonging* (Bloomington: Indiana University Press, 2012), 25–57; Phyllis M. Martin, *Leisure and Society in Colonial Brazzaville* (Cambridge: Cambridge University Press, 1995), 26–27; Catherine Coquery-Vidrovitch, *Brazza et la prise de possession du Congo: La mission de l'ouest africain, 1883–1885* (Paris: Mouton, 1969). Exceptions for Madagascar include Amadou Ba, *Les "Sénégalais" à Madagascar: Militaires ouest-africains dans la conquête et la colonisation de la Grande-Île (1895–1960)* (Paris: Harmattan, 2012).
3. Achille Mbembe, "African Modes of Self-Writing," trans. Steven Rendall, *Public Culture* 14, no. 1 (Winter 2002): 264.
4. Carina E. Ray, *Crossing the Color Line: Race, Sex, and the Contested Politics of Colonialism in Ghana* (Athens: Ohio University Press, 2015); Christopher J. Lee, *Unreasonable*

Histories: Nativism, Multiracial Lives, and the Genealogical Imagination in British Africa (Durham, NC: Duke University Press, 2014); Rachel Jean-Baptiste, *Conjugal Rights: Marriage, Sexuality, and Urban Life in Colonial Libreville, Gabon* (Athens: Ohio University Press, 2014).

5. General of division to the colonel, Paris, 18 May 1867, FM-SG-SEN-XVI-25b, ANOM.

6. Christina E. Firpo, *The Uprooted: Race, Children, and Imperialism in French Indochina, 1890–1980* (Honolulu: University of Hawai'i Press, 2016), 17–22. This was further evidenced by the rise in interracial children (métis) in French Indochina; Emmanuelle Saada, *Empire's Children: Race, Filiation, and Citizenship in the French Colonies* (Chicago: University of Chicago Press, 2012).

7. Governor-general of Indochina to the governor-general of FWA, 12 January 1903, 4D96, ANS.

8. Report on the employment of tirailleurs sénégalais in Cochinchine in 1867, FM-SG-SEN-XVI-25b, ANOM.

9. Henri Frey, *Campagne dans le haut Sénégal et dans le haut Niger (1885–1886)* (Paris: Librairie Plon, 1888), 47–48.

10. Coquery-Vidrovitch, *Brazza*; Catherine Coquery-Vidrovitch, *Le Congo au temps des grandes compagnies concessionnaires, 1898–1930* (Paris: Mouton, 1972).

11. Charles de Chavannes, *Avec Brazza: Souvenirs de la mission de l'ouest-africain (mars 1883–janvier 1886)* (Paris: Plon, 1935), 33–41.

12. Albert Veistroffer, *Vingt ans dans la brousse africaine: Souvenirs d'un ancien membre de la mission Savorgnan de Brazza dans l'ouest africain (1883–1903)* (Lille: Mercure de Flandre, 1883), 18.

13. Jeremy Rich, "Where Every Language is Heard: Atlantic Commerce, West African and Asian Migrants, and Town Society in Libreville, ca. 1860–1914," in *African Urban Spaces in Historical Perspective*, ed. Steven J. Salm and Toyin Falola (Rochester, NY: University of Rochester Press, 2005), 194–200; Whitehouse, *Migrants and Strangers*, 26.

14. Léon Guiral, *Le Congo français du Gabon à Brazzaville* (Paris: Plon, 1889), 230, n1.

15. Christopher Gray, *Colonial Rule and Crisis in Equatorial Africa: Southern Gabon, ca. 1850–1940* (Rochester, NY: University of Rochester Press, 2002), 85, 100–101.

16. Veistroffer, *Vingt ans*, 174.

17. Albert Baratier, *Au Congo: Souvenirs de la mission Marchand* (Paris: Arthème Fayard, 1914), 76.

18. M. Laplène was suspected of recruiting laborers from Senegal through métis intermediaries. "Verbal Process," signed by Blanckeman in Saint-Louis, 13 August 1896, FM-SG-SEN-XIV-28, ANOM. See also François Zuccarelli, "Le recrutement de travailleurs sénégalais par l'État indépendant du Congo (1888–1896)," *Revue française d'histoire d'outre-mer* 47, no. 168/169 (1960): 475–81.

19. "Government Notice: Emigration to Congo Free State," *Weekly News*, 6 July 1894 (348), 5. See also the confessions of Senegalese recruits found in FM-SG-SEN-XIV-26, ANOM.

20. The French Congo was divided into forty concessionary companies in 1898. See Coquery-Vidrovitch, *Le Congo.*

21. Henri Brunschwig, *Brazza explorateur: L'Ogooué, 1875–1879* (Paris: Mouton, 1966), 29–33.

22. Guiral, *Le Congo français*, 91, 193.

23. Telegram from Dakar, 5 October 1892, 4D98, ANS.

24. Colonel Houry to the governor of Senegal, 25 June 1894, 4D98, ANS. It is unclear if the colonial state funded this proposal.

25. Martin, *Leisure and Society*, 27, 33.

26. Whitehouse, *Migrants and Strangers*, 25–57, 176.

27. Governor-general of FWA to the general commissioner in Brazzaville, 15 September 1906, 4D96, ANS.

28. Lieutenant Colonel Mordrelle to governor of Congo-Brazzaville, 1 December 1909, 4D96, ANS.

29. The French imposed a protectorate over the island in 1882, which remained unenforced for more than a decade. Gwyn Campbell, *An Economic History of Imperial Madagascar, 1750–1895: The Rise and Fall of an Island Empire* (New York: Cambridge University Press, 2005), 331.

30. Calixte Savaron, *Mes souvenirs à Madagascar avant et après la conquête (1885–1898)* (Tananarive: G. Pitot, 1932), 317.

31. Solofo Randrianja and Stephen Ellis, *Madagascar: A Short History* (Chicago: University of Chicago Press, 2009), 155.

32. So-called haoussa recruits came from Yoruba-speaking regions of eastern Nigeria. Report on the military situation of Dahomey, 20 December 1894, FM-SG-DAHO-XVI-1-8, ANOM; Louis-Jules-Albin Obissier, *Notice sur les tirailleurs sénégalais (races, caractères, moeurs et coutumes)* (Antananarivo, Madagascar: Typographie de l'Etat-Major, 1903), 18–19.

33. Whitehouse, *Migrants and Strangers*, 37.

34. For further nuance and detail, see Sarah Davis Westwood, "Military Culture in Senegambia and the Origins of the *Tirailleur Sénégalais* Army, 1750–1910" (PhD diss., Boston University, 2018), 252–91.

35. Étienne Grosclaude, *Un parisien à Madagascar* (Paris: Hachette, 1898), 76.

36. Henri Galli, *La guerre à Madagascar: Histoire anecdotique des expeditions françaises de 1885 à 1895* (Paris: Garnier, 1897), 869–70.

37. Campbell, *An Economic History*, 336.

38. Randrianja and Ellis, in *Madagascar* (157), estimated a half-million slaves; Philip M. Allen estimated one million in *Madagascar: Conflicts of Authority in the Great Island* (Boulder, CO: Westview, 1995), 36.

39. Stephen Ellis, *The Rising of the Red Shawls: A Revolt in Madagascar 1895–1899* (Cambridge: Cambridge University Press, 1985), 153; Solofo Randrianja, *Société et luttes anticoloniales à Madagascar de 1896 à 1946* (Paris: University of Chicago Press, 2001), 98.

40. Ba, *Les "Sénégalais,"* 97; Grosclaude, *Un parisien*, 35, 127–28.

41. Battalions containing hundreds of men arrived in Madagascar in 1896, 1897, 1899, and 1900. Ba, *Les "Sénégalais,"* 97.

42. Joseph-Simon Gallieni, *Neuf ans à Madagascar* (Paris: Hachette, 1908), 19–20.

43. Minister of the marines to the commander of troops in Dahomey, Paris, 18 July 1896, FM-SG-DAHO-XVI-1-8, ANOM.

44. Grosclaude, *Un parisien*, 128–29.

45. Edna G. Bay, *Wives of the Leopard: Gender, Politics, and Culture in the Kingdom of Dahomey* (Charlottesville: University of Virginia Press, 1998); Robin Law, "The 'Amazons' of Dahomey," *Paideuma: Mitteilungen zur Kulturkunde* 39 (1993): 245–46.

46. This translates to the neighborhood of Senegalese wives. Ba, *Les "Sénégalais,"* 240.

47. Conductor's death notice, 11 March 1897, 4D97, ANS.

48. Brigadier General Boilève to the governor-general in Saint-Louis, 7 July 1896, 4D97, ANS.

49. Report on the marching operation of the two companies from Majunga to Tananarive, 1896, 8H106, SHD-T.

50. Galli, *La guerre à Madagascar*, 869–70.

51. Chantal Valensky, *Le soldat occulté: Les malgaches de l'armée française, 1884–1920* (Paris: Harmattan, 1995), 39.

52. Elisabeth Rabut, *Brazza, commissaire général: Le Congo français 1886–1897* (Paris: Éditions de l'École des Hautes Études en Sciences Sociales, 1989), 25.

53. "La transportation des sénégalais," *Lanterne*, 28 May 1901, FM-SG-SEN-XVIII-31, ANOM.

54. Combes, in Kayes to the governor-general in Saint-Louis, 29 December 1899, 4D97, ANS.

55. Obissier, *Notice*, 18.

56. De Brazza to Goujon in Upper Sangha, 15 September 1894, ANOM, found in Rabut, *Brazza, commissaire général*, 252.

57. Ba, *Les "Sénégalais,"* 221–23.

58. Jean Boutonne, "L'expérience de colonisation militaire à Madagascar au temps de Gallieni," *Omaly sy anio: Hier et aujourd'hui* 12 (1980): 17.

59. Ferras, a copy (no. 239), 18 June 1896, 4D97, ANS.

60. Brigadier General Boilève to the governor-general of FWA, 18 June 1896, 4D97, ANS.

61. Obissier, *Notice*, 21.

62. Partial charter for the transport of conductors and tirailleurs sénégalais from Dakar to Majunga, 13 April 1900, 4D97, ANS.

63. Obissier, *Notice*, 20.

64. In a regiment preparing for departure to Madagascar in 1900, 518 tirailleurs sénégalais were accompanied by 108 wives and 14 children. The percentage of West African women accompanying their soldiering husbands rarely exceeded 25 percent; Colonel Combes to the governor-general of FWA, 29 May 1900, 4D97, ANS.

65. Savaron, *Mes souvenirs*, 319.

66. Hippolyte Marceau, *Le tirailleur soudanais* (Paris: Berger-Levrault, 1911); Savaron, *Mes souvenirs*, 320–21; Grosclaude, *Un parisien*, 128.

67. After the battle of Sikasso in West Africa, one observer claimed that each tirailleur acquired three women. Paul Vigné d'Octon, *La gloire du sabre* (Paris: Flammarion, 1900), 131.

68. Savaron, *Mes souvenirs*, 319–21.

69. De Brazza to Goujon, 15 September 1894, ANOM, found in Rabut, *Brazza, commissaire général*, 251–52.

70. Veistroffer, *Vingt ans*, 193. Taouré is likely the common West African patronym Traoré.

71. Léon Lejeune, *Au Congo: La femme et la famille* (Paris: A. Challamel, 1900), 14.

72. Alexandre Le Roy, "Comment-on civilise les races primitives," *Univers*, 15 December 1899.

73. "La civilization au Congo," *Le journal de Bambane*, 2 February 1900, found in FM-SG-SEN-XIV-28b, ANOM.

74. Le Roy, "Comment-on civilise."

75. Letters reproduced in Lejeune, *Au Congo*, 16–17.

76. Grosclaude, *Un parisien*, 127.

77. Lieutenant Colonel Mordrelle to the governor of Congo Brazzaville, signed on 1 December 1909, 4D96, ANS.

78. N. Ballay, report on the political situation in French Congo, 18 December 1888, ANOM. Found in Rabut, *Brazza, commissaire général*, 87.

79. Jean-Baptiste, *Conjugal Rights*, 40.

80. Lejeune, *Au Congo*, 13–14.

81. Lieutenant-governor of French Congo to the minister of the colonies, Libreville, 19 March 1900, FM-SG-SEN-XIV-28b, ANOM.

82. Veistroffer, *Vingt ans*, 162.

83. Lejeune, *Au Congo*, 11–13. Rachel Jean-Baptiste describes how colonialism created the context for congolaises to engage in prostitution in *Conjugal Rights*, 63.

84. Lieutenant-governor of French Congo to the minister of the colonies, 1 March 1900, FM-SG-SEN-XIV-28b, ANOM.

CHAPTER 3: *MESDAMES TIRAILLEURS* AND BLACK VILLAGES

1. Moshe Gershovich, *French Military Rule in Morocco: Colonialism and Its Consequences* (London: Frank Cass, 2000), 50; Jonathan G. Katz, "The 1907 Mauchamp Affair and the French Civilizing Mission in Morocco," *Journal of North African Studies* 6, no. 1 (Spring 2001): 143–66.

2. *Troupes noires* translates to "black troops." Joe Lunn, "'Les Races Guerrières': Racial Preconceptions in the French Military about West African Soldiers during the First World War," *Journal of Contemporary History* 34, no. 4 (October 1999): 523.

3. For an important assessment of racial difference across the Sahara, see Bruce S. Hall, "The Question of 'Race' in the Pre-colonial Southern Sahara," *Journal of North*

African Studies 10, no. 3/4 (2005): 339–67; Hall, *A History of Race in Muslim West Africa, 1600–1960* (Cambridge: Cambridge University Press, 2011).

4. For French colonial ideas on race and slavery, see William B. Cohen, *The French Encounter with Africans: White Response to Blacks, 1530–1880* (Bloomington: Indiana University Press, 2000); Andrew S. Curran, *The Anatomy of Blackness: Science and Slavery in the Age of Enlightenment* (Baltimore: Johns Hopkins University Press, 2011); Sue Peabody, *There Are No Slaves in France: The Political Culture of Race and Slavery in the Ancien Régime* (New York: Oxford University Press, 1996); Christopher L. Miller, *Blank Darkness: Africanist Discourse in French* (Chicago: University of Chicago Press, 1985).

5. For further work on trans-Saharan relations and Moroccan social hierarchies related to slavery and its legacies, see E. Ann McDougall, "Discourse and Distortion: Critical Reflections on Studying the Saharan Slave Trade," *Outre-mers: Revue d'histoire* 89, no. 336/337 (2002): 195–227; Mohammed Ennaji, *Serving the Master: Slavery and Society in Nineteenth-Century Morocco*, trans. Seth Graebner (London: Macmillan, 1999); Chouki El Hamel, "Blacks and Slavery in Morocco: The Question of the Haratin at the End of the Seventeenth Century," in *Diasporic Africa: A Reader*, ed. Michael A. Gomez (New York: New York University Press, 2006); El Hamel, *Black Morocco: A History of Slavery, Race, and Islam* (Cambridge: Cambridge University Press, 2013).

6. Edmund Burke III, *The Ethnographic State: France and the Invention of Moroccan Islam* (Berkeley: University of California Press, 2014), 8–9.

7. For the term "Black Villages," see note 92 to page 25 in the introduction.

8. Letter from Angoulvant to Lyautey, 2 November 1918, 4D3V81, ANS.

9. *Force noire* translates to "black strength" or "black manpower." Charles Mangin, *La force noire* (Paris: Hachette, 1910).

10. Aboulqasem Ben Ahmed Al-Ezzaini, *Le Maroc de 1631 à 1812*, trans. Octave V. Houdas (Amsterdam: Philo Press, 1969), 29. Houdas was a well-known French orientalist and this translation was first published in 1886.

11. El Hamel, *Black Morocco*, 163.

12. Ezzaini, *Le Maroc*, 30.

13. Lansine Kaba, "Archers, Musketeers, and Mosquitos: The Moroccan Invasion of the Sudan and the Songhay Resistance (1591–1612)," *Journal of African History* 22 (1981): 461; Richard L. Smith, *Ahmad al-Mansur: Islamic Visionary* (New York: Pearson Longman, 2006), 100–108; El Hamel, *Black Morocco*, 146–49.

14. Mangin, *La force noire*, 105.

15. Variations on this method of emancipation are described by Igor Kopytoff and Suzanne Miers, "African 'Slavery' as an Institution of Marginality," in *Slavery in Africa: Historical and Anthropological Perspectives*, ed. Miers and Kopytoff (Madison: University of Wisconsin Press, 1977); Beverley B. Mack, "Women and Slavery in Nineteenth-Century Hausaland," in *The Human Commodity: Perspectives on the Trans-Saharan Slave Trade*, ed. Elizabeth Savage (Portland, OR: Frank Cass, 1992); and E. Ann McDougall, "A Sense of Self: The Life of Fatma Barka," *Canadian Journal of African Studies* 32, no. 2 (1998): 285–315.

16. A population in Morocco known as *haratin* came to exemplify racialized servitude. El Hamel, *Black Morocco*, 160–66; Chouki El Hamel, "'Race,' Slavery, and Islam in Maghrebi Mediterranean Thought: The Question of the *Haratin* in Morocco," *Journal of North African Studies* 7, no. 3 (2002): 29–52.

17. R. David Goodman, "Expediency, Ambivalence, and Inaction: The French Protectorate and Domestic Slavery in Morocco, 1912–1956," *Journal of Social History* 47, no. 1 (Fall 2013): 101–31; El Hamel, "Blacks and Slavery in Morocco," 194; Ennaji, *Serving the Master*.

18. Mangin, *La force noire*, 79–128.

19. Mangin, 245. See Michael A. Osborne and Richard F. Fogarty, "Views from the Periphery: Discourses of Race and Place in French Military Medicine," *History and Philosophy of Life Sciences* 25, no. 3 (2003): 374–75.

20. For a disambiguation of racial science and scientific racism, see Alice L. Conklin, *In the Museum of Man: Race, Anthropology, and Empire in France, 1850–1860* (Ithaca, NY: Cornell University Press, 2013), 5–6.

21. Mangin, *La force noire*, 111–28.

22. Lunn, "Les Races Guerrières," 521. For further reading on colonialism and martial races see Heather Streets-Salter, *Martial Races: The Military, Race, and Masculinity in British Imperial Culture, 1857–1914* (Manchester: Manchester University Press, 2004); Myles Osborne, *Ethnicity and Empire in Kenya: Loyalty and Martial Race among the Kamba, c. 1800 to the Present* (New York: Cambridge University Press, 2014); Cynthia H. Enloe, *Ethnic Soldiers: State Security in Divided Societies* (Athens: University of Georgia Press, 1980).

23. See Lawrence C. Jennings, *French Anti-Slavery: The Movement for the Abolition of Slavery in France, 1802–1848* (Cambridge: Cambridge University Press, 2000), 142–64. In reference to West Africa, see Elizabeth A. Foster, *Faith in Empire: Religion, Politics, and Colonial Rule in French Senegal, 1880–1940* (Stanford, CA: Stanford University Press, 2013), 11–12; Alice L. Conklin, *A Mission to Civilize: The Republican Idea of Empire in France and West Africa, 1895–1930* (Stanford, CA: Stanford University Press, 1997), 94–102.

24. Edward Berenson, *Heroes of Empire: Five Charismatic Men and the Conquest of Africa* (Berkeley: University of California Press, 2011), 229.

25. Michael P. M. Finch, *A Progressive Occupation? The Gallieni-Lyautey Method and Colonial Pacification in Tonkin and Madagascar, 1885–1900* (Oxford: Oxford University Press, 2013), 190–92.

26. Daniel Rivet, *Lyautey et l'institution du protectorat français au Maroc, 1912–1925*, vol. 2 (Paris: Harmattan, 1988), 17.

27. "Note sur le recrutement des Troupes Noires en Afrique Occidentale Française," signed by William Ponty, 1910, 10N104, ANS; Myron Echenberg, "Slaves into Soldiers: Social Origins of the Tirailleurs Senegalais," in *Africans in Bondage: Studies in Slavery and the Slave Trade*, ed. Paul E. Lovejoy (Madison: African Studies Program, University of Wisconsin–Madison, 1986); Klein, *Slavery and Colonial Rule*, 104.

28. Correspondence from the lieutenant-governor of French Guinea to the governor-general of FWA, William Ponty, 19 October 1907, 4D30, ANS.

29. Charles Mangin, "Sommaire" for William Ponty, in a folder dated 1909–1910, 4D31, ANS.

30. Rita Aouad Badoual, "'Esclavage' et situation des 'noirs' au Maroc dans la première moitié du XXe siècle," in *Les relations transsahariennes á l'époque contemporaine: Un espace en constante mutation*, ed. Laurence Marfaing and Steffen Wippel (Paris: Karthala, 2004), 353; Salim Khiat, "De la négrophobie en Algérie: Autopsie des mots qui disent le Mal en couleurs," in *Noirs au Maghreb: Enjeux identitaires*, ed. Stéphanie Pouessel (Paris: Karthala, 2012), 64.

31. Allan R. Meyers, "Class, Ethnicity, and Slavery: The Origins of the Moroccan 'Abid," *International Journal of African Historical Studies* 13, no. 3 (1997): 427–42.

32. Louis Arnaud, "Étude anthropologique de la Garde Noire des sultans du Maroc," *Bulletin de l'Institut d'Hygiène du Maroc* 10 (1940): 44.

33. Civilian Moroccans committed a range of aggressions against off-duty tirailleurs sénégalais throughout the protectorate period. See "La nuit rouge: 63 morts, 118 blessés graves," *L'écho du Maroc*, April 9, 1947; and files 3H465, 7U2829, 7U2834, 7U2840 at SHD-T.

34. Charles J. A. Cornet, *À la conquête du Maroc sud avec la colonne Mangin, 1912–1913* (Paris: Plon-Nourrit, 1914), 77–78.

35. Stephanie E. Smallwood describes a similar process in *Saltwater Slavery: A Middle Passage from Africa to American Diaspora* (Cambridge, MA: Harvard University Press, 2007), 151–52.

36. "Note pour l'état-majeur de l'armée," 5 November 1909, 7N80, SHD-T.

37. Report from Lieutenant Dardignac of Casbah Tadla to general-commandant in Casablanca, 18 November 1913, 3H692, SHD-T.

38. "État des militaires des unités sénégalaises condamnées par le 1ère conseil de guerre des T2H0 du 1er janvier au 30 juin 1913," Casablanca 1913, 3H692, SHD-T.

39. Chef de bataillon Mouveaux to the governor-general of FWA, Colomb-Béchar, 1 December 1910, 4D32, ANS.

40. "Rapport au ministre sur l'utilisation des troupes noires en 1910–1911," Casablanca, 22 September 1911, 3H152, SHD-T.

41. Report from Colonel Bulleux, commander of the 5th Mixed Colonial Regiment in Fez, 25 October 1913, 3H92, SHD-T.

42. General Lyautey to the minister of war, 14 November 1914, 3H92, SHD-T. This military practice became known as *hivernage*—wintering African troops at lower elevations and warmer latitudes.

43. "Rapport du chef de bataillon Billotte," Fez, 27 January 1915, 3H92, SHD-T.

44. "Sur les troupes sénégalaises du Maroc Occidental," Franchet d'Esperey, September 1913, 3H692, SHD-T.

45. "Les troupes noires: Le parlement: Rapports, commissions, séances," *L'armée coloniale* (May 1911): 42.

46. "Rapport au ministre sur l'utilisation des troupes noires en 1910–1911," Casablanca, 22 September, 3H152, SHD-T.

47. Marc Epprecht, *Heterosexual Africa? The History of an Idea from the Age of Exploration to the Age of AIDS* (Athens: Ohio University Press, 2008), 33–35.

48. Jacobus X, *L'amour aux colonies: Singularités physiologiques et passionelles observées durant trente années de séjour dans les colonies françaises, Cochinchine, Tonkin, Cambodge, Guyane et Martinique, Sénégal et Rivières du Sud, Nouvelle-Calédonie, Nouvelles-Hébrides et Tahiti* (Paris: Isidore Liseux, 1893), 258.

49. Maurice Delafosse was a key figure at the French School of Oriental Languages and the French Colonial School. Delafosse, *Haut-Sénégal-Niger (Soudan français)* (Paris: E. Larose, 1912), 3:92.

50. Robert Aldrich refers to a colloquial phrase, "faire passer son brevet colonial," which meant to initiate colonial employees into sodomy during their first assignment in North Africa. *Colonialism and Homosexuality* (New York: Routledge, 2002), 1; Epprecht, *Heterosexual Africa*, 48.

51. Robert Aldrich, "Homosexuality in the French Colonies," *Journal of Homosexuality* 41, no. 3/4 (2002): 207.

52. Houdas, *Le Maroc*, 30–31; Mangin, *La force noire*, 107.

53. El Hamel, *Black Morocco*, 203.

54. El Hamel, 190.

55. "Sur les troupes sénégalaises du Maroc Occidental," Franchet d'Esperey, September 1913, 3H692, SHD-T; "Extraits et commentaires de la 'force noire' du colonel Mangin," by Capitaine Voland, undated, 4D31, ANS.

56. Report from capitaine Causette in Casablanca, 1 September 1911, 3H692, SHD-T.

57. Postcard entitled "Casablanca.–Au Camp Sénégalais: Les Futurs Tirailleurs," 2K 148 Michat Album Maroc/Algésiras/Chaouia/Casablanca 32, SHD-SI.

58. Tirailleurs sénégalais deployed to Algeria in small numbers during the first decades of the twentieth century. Louis Joseph Gilles de Torcy, *La question des troupes noires en Algérie* (Paris: Augustin Challamel, 1911), 21.

59. Thomas Cardoza, *Intrepid Women: Cantinières and Vivandières of the French Army* (Bloomington: Indiana University Press, 2010), 166–215; Barton C. Hacker, "Women and Military Institutions in Early Modern Europe: A Reconnaissance," *Signs* 6, no. 4 (Summer 1981): 645; Myna Trustram, *Women of the Regiment: Marriage and the Victorian Army* (Cambridge: Cambridge University Press, 1984).

60. For further information on tirailleurs sénégalais and citizenship/political belonging, see Richard S. Fogarty, *Race and War in France: Colonial Subjects in the French Army, 1914–1918* (Baltimore: Johns Hopkins University Press, 2008), 230–69; Gregory Mann, *Native Sons: West African Veterans and France in the Twentieth Century* (Durham, NC: Duke University Press, 2006), 7–9.

61. Letter from head of the military office in Bofosso, Guinea, 3 February 1910, 3N44, ANG; "Sur les troupes sénégalaises du Maroc Occidental," Franchet d'Esperey, September 1913, 3H692, SHD-T.

62. Chief of battalion Mouveaux in Colomb-Béchar, Algeria, to the governor-general of FWA, 1 December 1910, 4D32, ANS.

63. Commandant Mouveaux, quoted in "Les troupes noires," *Bulletin du Comité de l'Afrique française* 4 (April 1912): 124–30.

64. "Avantages et inconvénients que comporte la presence des familles noires auprès des unités detachées au Maroc," 22 September 1911, 3H152, SHD-T.
65. Bakary Diallo, *Force-bonté* (Paris: F. Reider, 1926), 98.
66. General Amade to the minister of war, 3 August 1908, 3H152, SHD-T.
67. "Troupes noires," *L'Afrique française: Bulletin mensuel du Comité de l'Afrique française et du Comité du Maroc* 8 (August 1909): 274–78.
68. "Sur l'utilisation des troupes noires en 1910–1911," 22 September 1911, 3H152, SHD-T.
69. Report from Lieutenant Colonel Reuf, 24 November 1912, 3H692, SHD-T.
70. Health report from Doctor Casanove at Colomb-Béchar, 8 January 1911, 7N80, SHD-T.
71. Letter from Mouveaux to the governor-general of FWA, 1 December 1910, 4D32, ANS.
72. "Sur les troupes sénégalaises du Maroc Occidental," Franchet d'Esperey, September 1913, 3H692, SHD-T.
73. "Sur les troupes sénégalaises du Maroc Occidental," Franchet d'Esperey, September 1913, 3H692, SHD-T.
74. "Pour les moussous sénégalais," *La vigie marocaine*, 23 March 1913.
75. "Pour les familles des tirailleurs sénégalais au Maroc," *La dépêche marocaine*, 6 May 1913.
76. Report to the minister on the use of troupes noires in 1910–1911, Casablanca, 22 September 1911, 3H152, SHD-T.
77. Resident general to the minister of war, 25 February 1913, ProMarocint6–1-1931, ADN.
78. "Avantages et inconvénients que comporte la présence des familles noires auprès des unités detachées au Maroc," 22 September 1911, 3H152, SHD-T.
79. Postcards from the Moroccan campaign available in the 2K series at SHD-SI and the 1A series at Établissement de Communication et de Production Audiovisuelle de la Défense (Ivry-sur-Seine, France).
80. Jane Turrittin, "Colonial Midwives and Modernizing Childbirth in French West Africa," in *Women in African Colonial Histories*, ed. Jean Allman, Susan Geiger, and Nakanyike Musisi (Bloomington: Indiana University Press, 2002).
81. Sarah Zimmerman, "*Mesdames Tirailleurs* and Indirect Clients: West African Women and the French Colonial Army, 1908–1918," *International Journal of African Historical Studies* 44, no. 2 (2011): 299–322.
82. "Enquête sur la famille des fonçailles et le mariage en Guinée française 1910," 1G338, ANS.
83. Letter addressed to the governor-general's military cabinet, 2 May 1911, 4D32, ANS.
84. For more information on French colonial interpretations of bridewealth in West Africa, see Richard Roberts, *Litigants and Households: African Disputes and Colonial Courts in the French Soudan, 1895–1912* (Portsmouth, NH: Heinemann, 2005), 149–78; Emily S. Burrill, *States of Marriage: Gender, Justice, and Rights in Colonial Mali* (Athens: Ohio University Press, 2015), 61–68.

85. Letter from the chief of the military cabinet to the governor-general, Dakar, 2 May 1911, 4D32, ANS.

86. Report from Lieutenant Colonel Mazillier, West African Regiment in Ciflez, Morocco, 5 August 1911, 3H692, SHD-T.

87. Letter from Lombard to the general commandant superior in FWA, 22 March 1911, 4D32, ANS.

88. Owen White, *Children of the French Empire: Miscegenation and Colonial Society in French West Africa, 1895–1960* (Oxford: Clarendon, 1999), 9; Hilary Jones, "From *Mariage à la Mode* to Weddings at Town Hall: Marriage, Colonialism, and Mixed-Race Society in Nineteenth-Century Senegal," *International Journal of African Historical Studies* 38, no. 1 (2005): 34–39.

89. Letter by Franchet d'Esperey, 30 April 1913, 3H152, SHD-T. See Cardoza, *Intrepid Women*; and Cynthia Enloe, *Maneuvers: The International Politics of Militarizing Women's Lives* (Berkeley: University of California Press, 2000), 35–48.

90. Pierre Khorat, *Scènes de la pacification marocaine* (Paris: Perrin, 1914), 179–80. Pierre Khorat is a pseudonym for Pierre Ibos, who spent the majority of his military career in Morocco.

91. Letter from General Moinier to the minister of war, 12 November 1909, 3H152, SHD-T.

CHAPTER 4: DOMESTIC AFFAIRS IN THE GREAT WAR

1. Bakary Diallo, *Force-bonté* (Paris: F. Reider, 1926), 109.

2. Anthony Clayton, *France, Soldiers, and Africa* (London: Brassey's Defence Publishers, 1988), 95; Éric Deroo and Antoine Champeaux, *La force noire: Gloire et infortunes d'une légende coloniale* (Paris: Tallandier, 2006), 50. Each battalion had roughly six hundred men.

3. Communities responded to conscription with revolt and migration. In 1918, it was estimated that nearly a hundred thousand people had migrated to foreign territories to avoid conscription. Note from the minister of war's council to the minister of the colonies, 12 January 1918, 4D3V81, ANS.

4. "Au sujet des troupes noires," signed by Lieutenant Lautrou, 29 August 1913, 3H692, SHAT.

5. Joe Lunn, *Memoirs of the Maelstrom: A Senegalese Oral History of the First World War* (Portsmouth, NH: Heinemann, 1999); Myron Echenberg, "'Morts pour la France': The African Soldier in France during the Second World War," *Journal of African History* 26, no. 4 (1985): 363–80; Marc Michel, *L'appel à l'Afrique: Contributions et réactions à l'effort de guerre en A.O.F. (1914–1919)* (Paris: Publications de la Sorbonne, 1982); Michel, *L'Afrique dans l'engrenage de la Grande Guerre, 1914–1918* (Paris: Karthala, 2013); Iba Der Thiam, *Le Sénégal dans la guerre 14–18 ou le prix du combat pour l'égalité* (Dakar: Nouvelles Éditions Africaines du Sénégal, 1992).

6. Richard S. Fogarty, *Race and War in France: Colonial Subjects in the French Army, 1914–1918* (Baltimore: Johns Hopkins University Press, 2008); Michael Adas, "Contested Hegemony: The Great War and the Afro-Asian Assault on the Civilizing Mission

Ideology," *Journal of World History* 15, no. 1 (March 2004): 31–63; Yaël Simpson Fletcher, "Unsettling Settlers: Colonial Migrants and Racialized Sexuality in Interwar Marseilles," in *Gender, Sexuality, and Colonial Modernities*, ed. Antoinette Burton (New York: Routledge, 1999); Tyler Stovall, "Love, Labor, and Race: Colonial Men and White Women in France during the Great War," in *French Civilization and Its Discontents: Nationalism, Colonialism, Race*, ed. Tyler Stovall and Georges Van Den Abbeele (Lanham, MD: Lexington Books, 2003); Jean-Loup Saletes, "Les tirailleurs sénégalais dans la Grande Guerre et la codification d'un racisme ordinaire," *Guerres mondiales et conflits contemporains*, no. 244 (December 2011): 129–40.

7. Jacqueline Woodfork, "'It is a Crime to be a Tirailleur in the Army': The Impact of Senegalese Civilian Status in the French Colonial Army during the Second World War," *Journal of Military History* 77, no. 1 (2013): 115–39.

8. Richard Roberts, *Litigants and Households: African Disputes and Colonial Courts in the French Soudan, 1895–1912* (Portsmouth, NH: Heinemann, 2005), 35–70.

9. "Circulaire relative à l'étude des coutumes indigènes," signed by Clozel, 12 January 1909. Found in Maurice Delafosse, *Haut-Sénégal-Niger (Soudan français)* (Paris: E. Larose, 1912), 1:18.

10. Decree of 7 February 1912, *Journal officiel de la République française*, 10 February 1912, 1347–48; Charles Mangin, *La force noire* (Paris: Hachette, 1910).

11. These ambiguities are evidenced in the letters exchanged between soldiers during World War I. See the letter from Alioune Marius N'Doye to Diawar Sarr on 24 December 1914, in Guy Thilmans and Pierre Rosière, *Les sénégalais et la Grande Guerre: Lettres de tirailleurs et recrutement (1912–1919)* (Dakar: Musée Historique du Sénégal (Gorée), 2012), 84.

12. Mamadou Diouf, "The French Colonial Policy of Assimilation and the Civility of the Originaires of the Four Communes (Senegal): A Nineteenth Century Globalization Project," *Development and Change* 29, no. 4 (October 1998): 672–73; Karen Amanda Sackur, "The Development of Creole Society and Culture in Saint-Louis and Gorée, 1719–1817" (PhD diss., School of Oriental and African Studies, University of London, 1999), 219–21; Michael David Marcson, "European-African Interaction in the Precolonial Period: Saint Louis, Senegal, 1758–1854" (PhD diss., Princeton University, 1976), 219–41.

13. Sarah Zimmerman, "Citizenship, Military Service and Managing Exceptionalism: *Originaires* in World War I," in *Empires in World War I: Shifting Frontiers and Imperial Dynamics in a Global Conflict*, ed. Andrew Tait Jarboe and Richard S. Fogarty (London: I. B. Tauris, 2014), 219–20.

14. Raymond Betts, *Assimilation and Association in French Colonial Theory, 1890–1914* (New York: Columbia University Press, 1961); Michael Crowder, *Senegal: A Study in French Assimilation Policy* (London: Methuen, 1967); Diouf, "French Colonial Policy of Assimilation."

15. Allan Christelow finds that the entanglement of colonial electoral politics and the development of Muslim courts influenced this disparity, in "The Muslim Judge and Municipal Politics in Colonial Algeria and Senegal," *Comparative Studies in Society and*

History 24, no. 1 (January 1982): 3–24. For debates concerning enfranchising Algerian Muslims during the nineteenth century, see Patrick Weil, *How to Be French: Nationality in the Making since 1789*, trans. Catherine Porter (Durham, NC: Duke University Press, 2008), 207–19.

16. Rebecca Shereikis, "From Law to Custom: The Shifting Legal Status of Muslim Originaires in Kayes and Medine, 1903–13," *Journal of African History* 42, no. 2 (2001): 275–76.

17. G. Wesley Johnson Jr., *The Emergence of Black Politics in Senegal: The Struggle for Power in the Four Communes, 1900–1920* (Stanford, CA: Stanford University Press, 1971), 179.

18. "Law Extending the Dispositions of the Military Law of 19 October 1915 to the Descendants of Originaires," 29 September 1916, *Journal officiel de la République française*, 1 October 1916, 8667–68.

19. Hilary Jones has taken up this question in "Originaire Women and Political Life in Senegal's Four Communes," in *Black French Women and the Struggle for Equality, 1848–2016*, ed. Félix Germain and Silyane Larcher (Lincoln: University of Nebraska Press, 2018), 3–18.

20. Thilmans and Rosière, *Les sénégalais*.

21. Mahmood Mamdani, *Citizen and Subject: Contemporary Africa and the Legacy of Late Colonialism* (Princeton, NJ: Princeton University Press, 1996).

22. Governor-general of FWA to the minister of the colonies, 9 December 1915, 4D23, ANS.

23. Attorney general of the Judicial Service of FWA to governor-general's Service for Civil and Muslim Affairs, 8 March 1916, 4D26, ANS.

24. Le Herisse in Thiès to the lieutenant-governor of Senegal in Saint-Louis, 12 December 1915, 4D26, ANS.

25. Benjamin N. Lawrance, Emily Lynn Osborn, and Richard L. Roberts, eds., *Intermediaries, Interpreters, and Clerks: African Employees in the Making of Colonial Africa* (Madison: University of Wisconsin Press, 2006).

26. Letter signed by Angoulvant, October 1916, 4D27, ANS.

27. Letter signed by Clozel, 23 March 1916, 4D26, ANS.

28. Raphael Antonetti to Governor-General Clozel, 18 November 1915, 4D25, ANS.

29. See Gregory Mann, "What's in an Alias? Family Names, Individual Histories, and Historical Method in the Western Sudan," *History in Africa* 29 (2002): 309–20.

30. Lieutenant-governor of Saint-Louis to the governor-general of FWA, 10 February 1916, 4D26, ANS.

31. Lieutenant-governor of Senegal to the governor-general of FWA, 19 December 1916, 4D23, ANS.

32. Letter concerning the application of the law of September 1916, signed by Clozel, December 1916, 4D23, ANS. Dahomey is currently Benin. Neighboring territories included British Gambia, Sierra Leone, Gold Coast, and Nigeria, as well as Portuguese Guinea and independent Liberia.

33. Lieutenant-governor of Senegal to the governor-general of FWA, 6 January 1916, 4D28, ANS.

34. Governor-general Clozel to the lieutenant-governor of Senegal, 14 December 1915, 4D28, ANS.

35. Lieutenant-governor of Senegal to the governor-general of FWA, 6 January 1916, 4D28, ANS.

36. Governor-general Clozel to the lieutenant-governor of Senegal, 5 January 1916, 4D28, ANS.

37. Extract from the register of sectional deliberations meeting, 4 November 1924, 4D61V89, ANS.

38. This soldier was referred to as Ali and Aly throughout the documents related to this matter.

39. Verbal proceedings of the commission convened to manage allocations, 8 January 1917, 4D28, ANS.

40. Attorney general of FWA to the governor-general, 24 January 1917, 4D28, ANS.

41. Governor-general to the attorney general of FWA, 6 February 1917, 4D28, ANS.

42. *Militaire* means an active member of the French military. Head of the Service for Muslim and Civil Affairs to military cabinet, 8 October 1915, 4D3V81, ANS.

43. Decorated ex-tirailleur Lamine Senghor took the witness stand in a libel trial involving Blaise Diagne in Paris in 1924. Senghor used this stage to denounce the division among West African soldiers. Alice L. Conklin, "Who Speaks for Africa? The René Maran–Blaise Diagne Trial in 1920s Paris," in *The Color of Liberty: Histories of Race in France*, ed. Sue Peabody and Tyler Stovall (Durham, NC: Duke University Press, 2003), 308. Veterans of the tirailleurs sénégalais complained about how subjecthood affected their pensions in the twenty-first century: A. Mbodj, interview, Dakar, 31 December 2007; S. Mansaly, interview, Ziguinchor, 5 March 2008.

44. Catherine Coquery-Vidrovitch cites one exception in "Nationalité et citoyenneté en Afrique occidentale français: Originaires et citoyens dans le Sénégal colonial," *Journal of African History* 42, no. 2 (July 2001): 291.

45. "Comparison entre la situation militaire des originaires et celle des indigenes," undated and unsigned, 17G233V108, ANS.

46. Thilmans and Rosière, *Les sénégalais*, 215.

47. Letter from Mourin in Zinder to the governor-general of FWA, 8 November 1915, 4D71, ANS.

48. Circulaire no. 31, 27 April 1918, 4D88, ANS.

49. Also referred to as Mme Ousitou N. Diaye in these documents.

50. The direct exchange of bridewealth between conjugal partners may have resulted from urbanization. In most cases, conjugal partners' families were involved in these prenuptial processes.

51. Governor-general of FWA to the minister of the colonies, 6 March 1919, 4D71, ANS.

52. Minister of the colonies to the governor-general of FWA, 29 October 1918, 4D71, ANS.

53. Judith Byfield examines marital disputes brought before the British Railway Commission in colonial Abeokuta in "Women, Marriage, Divorce and the Emerging

Colonial State in Abeokuta (Nigeria) 1892–1904," *Canadian Journal of African Studies* 30, no. 1 (1996): 32–51.

54. Emily S. Burrill, *States of Marriage: Gender, Justice, and Rights in Colonial Mali* (Athens: Ohio University Press, 2015), 99.

55. Marie Rodet, "Continuum of Gendered Violence. The Colonial Invention of Female Desertion as a Customary Criminal Offense, French Soudan, 1900–1949," in *Domestic Violence and the Law in Colonial and Postcolonial Africa*, ed. Emily S. Burrill, Richard L. Roberts, and Elizabeth Thornberry (Athens: Ohio University Press, 2010); Roberts, *Litigants and Households*, 99–124.

56. Barbara Cooper, *Marriage in Maradi: Gender and Culture in a Hausa Society in Niger, 1900–1989* (Oxford: James Currey, 1997), 24.

57. Ghislaine Lydon, "Droit islamique et droits de la femme d'après les registres du Tribunal Musulman de Ndar (Saint-Louis du Sénégal)," *Canadian Journal of African Studies* 41, no. 2 (2007): 289–307.

58. In one fascinating case, a woman named Mariama reimbursed her own bridewealth in order to divorce and then marry a tirailleur sénégalais. Cited in Odile Goerg, "Femmes adultères, hommes voleurs? La 'justice indigène' en Guinée," *Cahiers d'études africaines* 47, no. 187/188 (2007): 512–13.

59. Marie Rodet, "'Le délit d'abandon de domicile conjugal' ou l'invasion du pénal colonial dans les jugements des 'tribunaux indigènes' au Soudan français, 1900–1947," *French Colonial History* 10 (2009): 151–69.

60. Attorney general to the head of the Judiciary Services of FWA, 10 December 1915, 4D71, ANS.

61. Lieutenant-governor of Dahomey to the governor-general of FWA, 14 November 1915, 4D71, ANS.

62. Report from Bamako, from the lieutenant-governor of Haut-Sénégal-Niger to the governor-general of FWA, 12 October 1915, 4D71, ANS.

63. These types of measures ignored the legacies of forced conjugal association and concubinage in tirailleurs sénégalais' conjugal traditions. During and prior to the Great War, many military households formed without the exchange of bridewealth—making divorce difficult.

64. Letter, 11 October 1918, 4D71, ANS.

65. Marie Rodet, *Les migrantes ignorées du Haut-Sénégal (1900–1946)* (Paris: Karthala, 2009), 107–26; Marcia Wright, *Strategies of Slaves and Women: Life-Stories from East/Central Africa* (New York: Lilian Barber, 1993), 1–16.

66. Klein, *Slavery and Colonial Rule*, 74–75, 80–81; J. Malcolm Thompson, "Colonial Policy and the Family Life of Black Troops in French West Africa, 1817–1904," *International Journal of African Historical Studies* 23, no. 3 (1990): 423–53.

67. Colonel Hérisson report, 17 August 1916, 11N6, ANS.

68. Letter from the inspector general of Health and Medical Services, 12 May 1917, 4D71, ANS.

69. Saheed Aderinto, *When Sex Threatened the State: Illicit Sexuality, Nationalism, and Politics in Colonial Nigeria, 1900–1958* (Urbana: University of Illinois Press, 2015);

Rachel Jean-Baptiste, *Conjugal Rights: Marriage, Sexuality, and Urban Life in Colonial Libreville, Gabon* (Athens: Ohio University Press, 2014), 44–72; Luise White, *The Comforts of Home: Prostitution in Colonial Nairobi* (Chicago: University of Chicago Press, 1990).

70. Michel Serge Hardy, *De la morale au moral des troupes ou l'histoire des B.M.C, 1918–2004* (Panazol, France: Lavauzelle, 2004); Christelle Taraud, *La prostitution coloniale: Algérie, Tunisie, Maroc (1830–1962)* (Paris: Payot, 2003), 340–51.

71. Colonel Hérisson report, 17 August 1916, 4D71, ANS.

72. For parallel examples, see Steven Pierce, "Farmers and 'Prostitutes': Twentieth-Century Problems of Female Inheritance in Kano Emirate, Nigeria," *Journal of African History* 44, no. 3 (2003): 463–86; Jean-Baptiste, *Conjugal Rights*, 135–62.

73. General inspector of Health and Medical Services correspondence, May 1917, 4D71, ANS.

74. Colonel Hérisson report, 17 August 1916, 10N109, ANS.

75. Pinneau to the minister of the colonies, 7 February 1916, 4D71, ANS.

76. Johnson, *Emergence of Black Politics*, 194.

CHAPTER 5: CHALLENGING COLONIAL ORDER

1. Response to a questionnaire distributed by General Charles Mangin, from Dakar, 17 September 1921, 5D17V14, ANS. This report does not include West African men stationed in Madagascar.

2. *Rif* means "countryside." The "Rif War" refers to the conflict in the northern mountainous region that served as the border between the Spanish and French protectorates in Morocco. *Djebel* in Arabic means "mountains"; this region is located in southern Syria near the border with Jordan.

3. Report from the general commandant of Troupes du Groupes de l'AOF, report by Freydenberg, 28 February 1933, 5D57V89, ANS; Report on the Rif, 25 March 1925, FMcote74, ANOM.

4. Myron Echenberg, *Colonial Conscripts: The Tirailleurs Sénégalais in French West Africa, 1857–1960* (Portsmouth, NH: Heinemann, 1991), 61; Babacar Fall, *Le travail forcé en Afrique occidentale française, 1900–1946* (Paris: Karthala, 1993).

5. Ministerial circular, 6 March 1920, 4D64V89, ANS.

6. Minister of the colonies to the general governments of French Empire, 16 April 1923, 4D64V89, ANS.

7. Oyèrónkẹ́ Oyěwùmí, *The Invention of Women: Making an African Sense of Western Gender Discourses* (Minneapolis: University of Minnesota Press, 1997), 151–52; Stephan Miescher, *Making Men in Ghana* (Bloomington: Indiana University Press, 2005), 84–114; Lisa Lindsay and Stephan Miescher, eds. *Men and Masculinities in Modern Africa* (Portsmouth: Heinemann, 2003); Lisa A. Lindsay, *Working with Gender: Wage Labor and Social Change in Southwestern Nigeria* (Portsmouth, NH: Heinemann, 2003).

8. Napoleon created the French Civil Code in 1804. This set of statutes protected personal rights and contracts and established family law. During the French Third Republic (1871–1940), the French National Assembly added hundreds of amendments to the Civil Code.

9. Cases of Soulaymane Diallo and Demba N'Dao during 1922–25, 11N15, ANS.

10. For literature on the expansion of social welfare for French families, see Susan Pedersen, *Family, Dependence, and the Origins of the Welfare State: Britain and France, 1914–1945* (Cambridge: Cambridge University Press, 1993); Paul V. Dutton, *Origins of the French Welfare State: The Struggle for Social Reform in France, 1914–1947* (Cambridge: Cambridge University Press, 2002); Kristen Stromberg Childers, *Fathers, Families, and the State in France, 1914–1945* (Ithaca, NY: Cornell University Press, 2003); Camille Robcis, *The Law of Kinship: Anthropology, Psychoanalysis, and the Family in France* (Ithaca, NY: Cornell University Press, 2013); Dorit Geva, *Conscription, Family, and the Modern State: A Comparative Study of France and the United States* (Cambridge: Cambridge University Press, 2013).

11. Villain to the governor-general of FWA, 2 March 1936, 4D68V89, ANS.

12. Minister of the colonies to the governor-general of FWA, 27 July 1923, 4D64V89, ANS.

13. Telegram signed by Camille Maille, 16 September 1926, 11N15, ANS.

14. Governor-general to the superior commandant of the troops of FWA, 15 April 1933, 4D68V89, ANS.

15. Inspector of administrative affairs to lieutenant-governor of Côte d'Ivoire, Bouaké, 6 August 1935, 4D68V89, ANS. Bobo Dioulasso and Tiefoura were in Côte d'Ivoire in the 1930s and are now in Burkina Faso.

16. Official instructions for 588CM for the 2 September 1933 modification of the indemnité de séparation, signed by Fournier, 4D64V89, ANS.

17. Article 7 of an undated decree, 4D61V89, ANS.

18. Historians have addressed child marriage at the intersection of customary rites and colonial interventions. Elke Stockreiter, "Child Marriage and Domestic Violence: Islamic and Colonial Discourses on Gender Relations and Female Status in Zanzibar, 1900–1950s," in *Domestic Violence and the Law in Colonial and Postcolonial Africa*, ed. Emily S. Burrill, Richard L. Roberts, and Elizabeth Thornberry (Athens: Ohio University Press, 2010); Jessica Cammaert, *Undesirable Practices: Women, Children, and the Politics of the Body in Northern Ghana, 1930–1972* (Lincoln: University of Nebraska Press, 2016), 117–62.

19. Governor-general to the lieutenant-governors of FWA, 26 February 1934, 4D64V89, ANS.

20. Governor-general of FWA to the minister of the colonies, 12 July 1934, 4D64V89, ANS.

21. Administrator in Man to the governor of Côte d'Ivoire, 5 September 1922, 4D68V89, ANS.

22. Echenberg, *Colonial Conscripts*, 88.

23. Ruth Ginio, *French Colonialism Unmasked: The Vichy Years in French West Africa* (Lincoln: University of Nebraska Press, 2006); Cristophe Capuano, *Vichy et la famille: Réalités et faux-semblants d'une politique publique* (Rennes, France: Presses Universitaires de Rennes, 2009); Eric T. Jennings, *Vichy in the Tropics: Pétain's National Revolution in Madagascar, Guadeloupe, and Indochina, 1940–1944* (Stanford, CA: Stanford University

Notes to Pages 147–154

Press, 2001); Miranda Pollard, *Reign of Virtue: Mobilizing Gender in Vichy France* (Chicago: University of Chicago Press, 1998).

24. Decree for the allocation of urgent assistance to the families of dead or missing soldiers, Paris, 15 May 1940, 4D68V89, ANS.

25. Barrau to military cabinet of the governor-general of FWA, 3 July 1941, 4D68V89, ANS; Commodore Platon to the high commissioner of French Africa, 23 June 1941, 4D68V89, ANS.

26. Marc Michel, "L'armée colonial en Afrique occidentale française," in *L'Afrique occidentale au temps des Français: Colonisateurs et colonisés*, ed. Catherine Coquery-Vidrovitch (Paris: La Découverte, 1992), 73.

27. Barbara Bush, "Gender and Empire: The Twentieth Century," in *Gender and Empire*, ed. Philippa Levine (Oxford: Oxford University Press, 2004), 77; Jennifer Anne Boittin, Christina Firpo, and Emily Musil Church, "Hierarchies of Race and Gender in the French Colonial Empire, 1914–1946," *Historical Reflections / Réflexions historiques* 37 (2011): 60–90.

28. Report addressing "projet de réglementation de l'émigration et de la circulation des indigènes de l'Afrique Occidentale Française," 12 November 1925, 4D61V89, ANS.

29. Jean Boutonne, "L'expérience de colonisation militaire à Madagascar au temps de Gallieni," *Omaly sy anio: Hier et aujourd'hui* 12 (1980): 17.

30. Amadou Ba, *Les "Sénégalais" à Madagascar: Militaires ouest-africains dans la conquête et la colonisation de la Grande-Île (1895–1960)* (Paris: Harmattan, 2012), 93–116, 177–92.

31. Correspondence between Fatamata Bambara, the governor-general of Madagascar, and the governor-general of FWA, September 1926 to April 1927, 4D61V89, ANS.

32. Gregory Mann, "What's in an Alias? Family Names, Individual Histories, and Historical Method in the Western Sudan," *History in Africa* 29 (2002): 309–20; B. Marie Perinbam, *Family Identity and the State in the Bamako Kafu, c. 1800–c. 1900* (Boulder, CO: Westview Press, 1997).

33. Handwritten note on tirailleurs sénégalais demobilized outside of FWA, undated, 4D61V89, ANS.

34. Governor-general of FWA to governor-general of Madagascar, April 1927, 4D61V89, ANS.

35. In French Gabon, bridewealth determined child custody. Rachel Jean-Baptiste, *Conjugal Rights: Marriage, Sexuality, and Urban Life in Colonial Libreville, Gabon* (Athens: Ohio University Press, 2014), 158–61.

36. Director of military services in Paris, Fourier, 21 December 1925, 4D61V89, ANS.

37. Correspondence between the lieutenant-governors and the governor-general of FWA, January and February 1926, 4D61V89, ANS.

38. Governor-general of FWA to the governor-general of Madagascar, 10 March 1926; administrative chief to the governor-general of FWA, 11 May 1926[?], 4D61V89, ANS.

39. Moshe Gershovich, *French Military Rule in Morocco: Colonialism and Its Consequences* (London: Frank Cass, 2000), 80–81.

40. General commandant of the Troupes du Groupes de l'AOF, report by Freydenberg, 28 February 1933, 5D57V89, ANS.

41. Letter to resident-general of the French Republic in Morocco, 21 May 1926, 4D61V89, ANS.

42. "Repatriation of Saida Mint Saloum," 2 October 1919–30 December 1919, H273, ANS.

43. Lieutenant-governor of Mauretania to the governor-general of FWA, 25 August 1923, 4D61V89, ANS.

44. Minister of war and pensions to the heads of colonial territories, 12 January 1923, 4D61V89, ANS.

45. See chapter 3 for further details.

46. "Grave incidents entre Sénégalais et Marocains," *L'écho du Maroc*, 8 April 1947.

47. *Journal de Marche* of the 5th regiment of tirailleurs sénégalais, Dossier 1, 8 April 1947, 7U2827, SHD-T.

48. Conclusion drawn from my observations of the French military archives and many interviews with West African veterans. Letter from General Breuillac in Algiers, 27 April 1945, and letter from Lieutenant Mercadal, 3 April 1945, in 1K294, ANOM.

49. Minister of overseas France to the governor-general of FWA, 7 November 1946, 4D61V89, ANS.

50. James L. Gelvin, *Divided Loyalties: Nationalism and Mass Politics in Syria at the Close of Empire* (Berkeley: University of California Press, 1998).

51. "The Levant" refers to the region along the eastern seaboard of the Mediterranean that extends into the interior until reaching Iraq's border. Soldiers garrisoned in Syria and Lebanon in the interwar period made up the Armée du Levant. Maurice Albord, *L'armée française et les états du Levant, 1936–1946* (Paris: CNRS Éditions, 2000), 26.

52. Michael Provence, *The Great Syrian Revolt and the Rise of Arab Nationalism* (Austin: University of Texas Press, 2005); Philip Shukry Khoury, *Syria and the French Mandate: The Politics of Arab Nationalism, 1920–1945* (Princeton, NJ: Princeton University Press, 1987), 20.

53. Elizabeth Thompson, *Colonial Citizens: Republican Rights, Paternal Privilege, and Gender in French Syria and Lebanon* (New York: Columbia University Press, 2000), 49.

54. Report from Captain Massa, officer of the special forces station in Homs, 12 February 1942, 4H369, SHD-T.

55. Elizabeth Thompson, *Colonial Citizens*, 233.

56. Edward Spears, *Fulfillment of a Mission: The Spears Mission to Syria and Lebanon, 1941–44* (London: Leo Cooper, 1977), 110, 230, 237–39.

57. Governor-general of FWA to minister of the colonies, 21 November 1922, 4D61V89, ANS.

58. Lieutenant-governor of Côte d'Ivoire to governor-general of FWA, 12 September 1923, 4D61V89, ANS. This letter and surrounding correspondence also refer to Fadona Selim El Thomi and Sekou Maiga.

59. Correspondence concerning Aminé ben Mohamed el Abel from 1922 to 1927, in 11N15, ANS. This correspondence uses multiple spellings for the people involved: Soulayman Diallo (or Suleiman N'Diallo), Amine Ben Mohamed (or Mahmoud) el Abel, and Madame Della Mangassa (or N'Della Magassa).

60. "Introduction," in Alice L. Conklin, *A Mission to Civilize: The Republican Idea of Empire in France and West Africa, 1895–1930* (Stanford: Stanford University Press, 1997).

61. Michael Adas, "Contested Hegemony: The Great War and the Afro-Asian Assault on the Civilizing Mission Ideology," *Journal of World History* 15, no. 1 (March 2004): 63.

62. Richard S. Fogarty, *Race and War in France: Colonial Subjects in the French Army, 1914–1918* (Baltimore: Johns Hopkins University Press, 2008), 228; Yaël Simpson Fletcher, "Unsettling Settlers: Colonial Migrants and Racialized Sexuality in Interwar Marseilles," in *Gender, Sexuality, and Colonial Modernities*, ed. Antoinette Burton (New York: Routledge, 1999); Tyler Stovall, "Love, Labor, and Race: Colonial Men and White Women in France during the Great War," in *French Civilization and Its Discontents: Nationalism, Colonialism, Race*, ed. Tyler Stovall and Georges Van Den Abbeele (Lanham, MD: Lexington Books, 2003).

63. *Marraine de guerre* means "godmother of war." During the Great War, this was an institutionally encouraged relationship, akin to "pen pals," where French women corresponded with and sent presents to French forces, including colonial troops.

64. Lucie Cousturier, *Des inconnus chez moi* (Paris: La Sirène, 1920), 74–75, 194–96.

65. Cousturier, 18–19.

66. Lieutenant-governor of Côte d'Ivoire to the governor-general of FWA, 22 August 1920, 5D6V14, ANS.

67. "L'état de l'armée de l'Afrique occidentale française," p. 8, 25 March 1925, FM-COTE74, ANOM.

68. Lieutenant-governor of Upper-Senegal-Niger to governor-general of FWA, 23 March 1920, 5D6V14, ANS.

69. Elisa Camiscioli, *Reproducing the French Race: Immigration, Intimacy, and Embodiment in the Early Twentieth Century* (Durham, NC: Duke University Press, 2009), 75–83.

70. Echenberg, *Colonial Conscripts*, 88.

71. Raffael Scheck, *Hitler's African Victims: The German Army Massacre of Black French Soldiers in 1940* (Cambridge: Cambridge University Press, 2006).

72. Fabrice Virgili, *Shorn Women: Gender and Punishment in Liberation France*, trans. John Flower (Oxford: Berg, 2002); Hanna Diamond, *Women and the Second World War in France, 1939–1948: Choices and Constraints* (London: Pearson, 1999); Mary Louise Roberts, *What Soldiers Do: Sex and the American GI in World War II France* (Chicago: University of Chicago Press, 2013).

73. Ruth Ginio, "African Soldiers, French Women, and Colonial Fears during and after World War II," in *Africa and World War II*, ed. Byfield et al. (Cambridge: Cambridge University Press, 2015).

74. Other imperial regimes also moved to restrict the mobility and existence of interracial sexual relationships in the colonies through interracial marriage bans. See the example of Mtoro Bakari and Bertha Hilske in Lora Wildenthal, *German Women for Empire, 1884–1945* (Durham, NC: Duke University Press, 2001), 107–21.

75. This law awarded West African soldiers the "quality of citizen," but not citizenship. See further discussion of the Lamine Guèye law in chapter 6 hereof. See also

Frederick Cooper, *Citizenship between Empire and Nation: Remaking France and French Africa, 1945–1960* (Princeton, NJ: Princeton University Press, 2014), 124–64.

76. Minister of overseas France to the high commissioner of FWA, 13 June 1946, 4D68V89, ANS.

77. Lieutenant Sekou Koné's report regarding tirailleurs sénégalais encampments, 17–26 September 1946, FM14SLOTFOM-2, ANOM.

78. Lieutenant Philippe Aho's report on tirailleurs sénégalais encampments in southwest France, 10 September 1945, FM14SLOTFOM-2, ANOM.

79. High commissioner of FWA to minister of overseas France, 3 September 1946, 4D61V89, ANS.

80. Minister of the colonies to the governor-general of FWA, 2 August 1946, 4D61V89, ANS.

81. See discussion around the 1927 nationality law in Patrick Weil, *How to Be French: Nationality in the Making since 1789*, trans. Catherine Porter (Durham, NC: Duke University Press, 2008), 202–7; Camiscioli, *Reproducing the French Race*, 129–59.

82. Administrative Service Note, 25 January 1947, 4D64V89, ANS.

83. "Decree 47–2163 of 10 November 1947," *Journal officiel de l'Afrique occidentale française*, 6 December 1947.

84. Minister of overseas France to the prefect of Var, 25 October 1946, regarding Tiemoko Cissé, 14SLOTFOM2, ANOM; corresponding documents from January 1946, in 4D61V89, ANS.

85. Minister of overseas France to the governor-general of FWA, 21 October 1946, 14SLOTFOM2, ANOM.

86. Governor-general of FWA to the minister of overseas France, 27 July 1946, 4D61V89, ANS.

87. Governor-general of FWA to the minister of overseas France, 18 November 1946, 4D61V89, ANS.

88. Commissioner of police in the Medina, GRESSE, report, 9 April 1946, 4D61V89, ANS.

89. Lora Wildenthal similarly outlines the extralegal means used by colonial officials in Tanganyika to prohibit an interracial married couple—made up of a German woman and an East African man—from disembarking at any German East African ports in 1905. Wildenthal, *German Women for Empire*, 113–17.

90. Official decree on 14 September 1946, 4D61V89, ANS.

91. Minister of overseas France to Mademoiselle Hugette Pernot, 9 October 1946, 14SLOTFOM, ANOM.

92. General Secretariat of Political Affairs, 13 June 1945, 4D61V89, ANS.

93. Documents dating from 27 November 1945 to 10 April 1948, in 4D61V89, ANS.

CHAPTER 6: AFRO-VIETNAMESE MILITARY HOUSEHOLDS IN
FRENCH INDOCHINA AND WEST AFRICA, 1930–56

1. Telegram from A. Beraud to the governor-general of FWA, 5 October 1950, 13G94V180, ANS.

2. Emmanuelle Saada, *Empire's Children: Race, Filiation, and Citizenship in the French Colonies* (Chicago: University of Chicago Press, 2012); Owen White, *Children of the French Empire: Miscegenation and Colonial Society in French West Africa, 1895–1960* (Oxford: Clarendon, 1999).

3. French military sources refer to these children as "Africasian." Throughout this chapter, I employ "Afro-Vietnamese" or "Afro-Laotian" to describe these children.

4. Similarly, Maria Höhn finds that African American GIs experienced greater racial freedoms in post–World War II Germany than at home. *GIs and Fräuleins: The German-American Encounter in 1950s West Germany* (Chapel Hill: University of North Carolina Press, 2002), 13.

5. Nancy R. Hunt, "The Affective, the Intellectual, and Gender History," *Journal of African History* 55, no. 3 (November 2014): 335–38; Jennifer Cole and Lynn M. Thomas, eds., *Love in Africa* (Chicago: University of Chicago Press, 2009); Patricia Ticineto Clough, ed., *The Affective Turn: Theorizing the Social* (Durham, NC: Duke University Press, 2007); Matt K. Matsuda, *Empire of Love: Histories of France and the Pacific* (Oxford: Oxford University Press, 2005).

6. As seen in the case of Vuti Chat that opened this book. See also Christina E. Firpo, *The Uprooted: Race, Children, and Imperialism in French Indochina, 1890–1980* (Honolulu: University of Hawai'i Press, 2016), chap. 6. The rejection of interracial relationships and the recovery of interracial military children occurred in many contexts. The US government embarked on similar projects, such as "Operation Babylift," after 1975; Susan Zeiger, *Entangling Alliances: Foreign War Brides and American Soldiers in the Twentieth Century* (New York: New York University Press, 2010), 230. In the case of Afro-German children in the post–World War II American occupation of Germany, see Heide Fehrenbach, "Black Occupation Children and the Devolution of the Nazi Racial State," in *After the Nazi Racial State: Difference and Democracy in Germany and Europe*, ed. Rita Chin et al. (Ann Arbor: University of Michigan Press, 2009), 45.

7. Cati Coe, *The Scattered Family: Parenting, African Migrants, and Global Inequality* (Chicago: University of Chicago Press, 2014), chap. 2.

8. "Note sur les éffectifs necessaires en Indochine," 9 December 1945, 15H113, CHETOM.

9. Daily journal of 28th Bataillon de Marche de Tirailleurs Sénégalais, 16 November 1948, 16H342, CHETOM.

10. Myron Echenberg, *Colonial Conscripts: The Tirailleurs Sénégalais in French West Africa, 1857–1960* (Portsmouth, NH: Heinemann, 1991), 108–10.

11. The number of Africans serving in Indochina rose from 2,260 in 1948 to 19,731 in 1954. "French Land Forces in the Far East," 15H113, CHETOM.

12. Michel Bodin, *La France et ses soldats: Indochine, 1945–1954* (Paris: Harmattan, 1996), 49; Bodin, *Les africains dans la guerre d'Indochine, 1947–1954* (Paris: Harmattan, 2000).

13. Michael G. Vann, "Sex and the Colonial City: Mapping Masculinity, Whiteness, and Desire in French Occupied Hanoi," *Journal of World History* 28, no 3/4 (December 2017): 395–435; Isabelle Tracol-Huynh, "Between Stigmatisation and Regulation:

Prostitution in Colonial Northern Vietnam," *Culture, Health, and Sexuality* 12, no. S1 (August 2010): S73–S87; Tracol-Huynh, "La prostitution au Tonkin colonial, entre races et genres," *Genre, Sexualité, et Société*, no. 2 (Autumn 2009): 1–19.

14. Helle Rydstrom, "The Politics of Colonial Violence: Gendered Atrocities in French Occupied Vietnam," *European Journal of Women's Studies* 22, no. 2 (May 2015): 191–207; Nicola Cooper, *France in Indochina: Colonial Encounters* (Oxford: Berg, 2001).

15. Micheline Lessard, *Human Trafficking in Colonial Vietnam* (New York: Routledge, 2015); Vũ Trọng Phụng, *Lục Xì: Prostitution and Venereal Disease in Colonial Hanoi*, trans. Shaun Kingsley Malarney (Honolulu: University of Hawai'i Press, 2011).

16. U. Diagne, interview, Dakar, 6 February 2008.

17. For France, see Joe Lunn, "'*Bon Soldats*' and '*Sales Nègres*': Changing French Perceptions of West African Soldiers during the First World War," *French Colonial History* 1 (2002): 1–16. For Germany, see Lisa M. Todd, *Sexual Treason in Germany during the First World War* (Cham, Switzerland: Palgrave Macmillan, 2017); Iris Wigger, *The "Black Horror on the Rhine": Intersections of Race, Nation, Gender and Class in 1920s Germany* (London: Palgrave Macmillan, 2017); Dick van Galen Last, *Black Shame: African Soldiers in Europe, 1914–1922*, trans. Marjolijn de Jager (New York: Bloomsbury Academic, 2015); Julia Roos, "Nationalism, Racism and Propaganda in Early Weimar Germany: Contradictions in the Campaign against the 'Black Horror on the Rhine,'" *German History* 30, no. 1 (2012): 45–74; Tina Campt, *Other Germans: Black Germans and the Politics of Race, Gender, and Memory in the Third Reich* (Ann Arbor: University of Michigan Press, 2004); Keith L. Nelson, "The 'Black Horror on the Rhine': Race as a Factor in Post-World War I Diplomacy," *Journal of Modern History* 42, no. 4 (December 1970): 606–27.

18. Authored by an anonymous lieutenant, "À la recherché de Barnavaux: Le divorce de Thémélius Saint-Afrique," *Journal des Coloniaux*, 1926, private collection of Colonel M. Rives. Similar racialized ribald humor was used in Stanley Kubrick's *Full Metal Jacket* (1987).

19. Colonel M. Rives, interview, Paris, 16 June 2008.

20. "Note sur les éffectifs necessaries en Indochine," 9 December 1945, 15H113, CHETOM.

21. Sébastien Verney, *L'Indochine sous Vichy: Entre révolution nationale, collaboration et identités nationales, 1940–1945* (Paris: Riveneuve, 2012). For details of this Japanese military maneuver, see Michel Huguier, *De Gaulle, Roosevelt et l'Indochine de 1940 à 1945* (Paris: Harmattan, 2010), chap. 8.

22. N. Beye and her adult children Marie, Awa, Bathio, and Massitou, interview, Dakar, 27 February 2008.

23. J. Gomis, interview, Dakar, 9 February 2009.

24. J. Gomis, interview, Dakar, 25 January 2011. See Eric T. Jennings, *Vichy in the Tropics: Pétain's National Revolution in Madagascar, Guadeloupe, and Indochina, 1940–1944* (Stanford, CA: Stanford University Press, 2001), 130–98.

25. Anne Raffin, *Youth Mobilization in Vichy Indochina and Its Legacies* (Lanham, MD: Lexington Books, 2005).

26. Ruth Ginio, *French Colonialism Unmasked: The Vichy Years in French West Africa* (Lincoln: University of Nebraska Press, 2006), 33–58.

27. Frederick Cooper, *Citizenship between Empire and Nation: Remaking France and French Africa, 1945–1960* (Princeton, NJ: Princeton University Press, 2014), 126.

28. Private photograph collection of S. Diagne, consulted during interview, Dakar, 8 December 2007. Anne-Marie Niane in *L'étrangère* (Paris: Hatier International, 2002) also describes this type of church wedding.

29. S. Diagne, interviews, Dakar, 13 and 19 March 2008.

30. French officers opened fire on demobilizing tirailleurs sénégalais, the majority of whom were repatriating German prisoners of war, in a military camp in Thiaroye, Senegal. These men had demanded back pay and compensation for internment and refused to return to their villages prior to payment. In total, thirty-five soldiers died. Martin Mourre, *Thiaroye 1944: Histoire et memoire d'un massacre colonial* (Rennes, France: Presses Universitaires de Rennes, 2017); Julien Fargettas, "La révolte des tirailleurs sénégalais de Thiaroye: Entre reconstructions mémorielles et histoire," *Vingtième siècle: Revue d'histoire*, no. 92 (2006): 117–30; Armelle Mabon, "La tragédie de Thiaroye, symbole du déni d'égalité," *Hommes et Migrations*, no. 1235 (January–February 2002): 86–95; Ousmane Sembène and Thierno Faty Sow, dirs., *Camp de Thiaroye* (New York: New Yorker Films, 1988); Myron Echenberg, "Tragedy at Thiaroye: The Senegalese Soldiers' Uprising of 1944," in *African Labor History*, ed. Peter C. W. Gutkind, Robin Cohen, and Jean Copans (London: Sage, 1978).

31. Allasane Fall, "Itinéraire d'un ancien combattant de la guerre d'Algérie, Amady Moutar Gaye" (thesis, École Normale Supérieure du Sénégal, 2005).

32. O. Diop, interview, Thiès, 12 December 2007.

33. Handwritten letter concerning a wife named Koué Salamatou Diallo authored in Zourame (lower Senegal), 9 February 1954, 11N51, ANS. For the latter point, O. Diop, interview, Thiès, 12 December 2007; and S. Diagne, interview, Dakar, 8 December 2008.

34. List by territory of the African military men embarking to Marseille, 26 September 1949, on the *Pasteur*, 11D1/380, SHD-T.

35. List of emergency contacts for servicemen from Senegal, 16 March 1949, 11D1-380, ANS.

36. Questionnaires for soldiers liberated by the Viet Minh, 1954, 10H445, SHD-T.

37. Home-front wives in long-distance African relationships share characteristics with the "jabaaru immigré" in present-day Senegal. See Dinah Hannaford, *Marriage without Borders: Transnational Spouses in Neoliberal Senegal* (Philadelphia, PA: University of Pennsylvania Press, 2017), 1, 42–44.

38. See description of runaway bride, Emily S. Burrill, *States of Marriage: Gender, Justice, and Rights in Colonial Mali* (Athens: Ohio University Press, 2015), 99–103.

39. Minister of overseas France to the high commissioner of the republic in FWA, in a folder labeled "Assistance for Families," 1948–1955, 4D76V100, ANS.

40. Correspondence between the head of the subdivision in Saint Louis to the colonel commanding the 1st Régiment de Tirailleurs Sénégalais, 26 November 1953, 11N51, ANS.

Notes to Pages 181–186

41. Telegram signed by R. Guhalde, 4 February 1949, 11D1-380, ANS.

42. Reference to the morale of tirailleurs sénégalais serving in the Far East, from the governor of Niger to the governor-general of FWA, 13 December 1948, 4D76V100, ANS.

43. French West Africa contained an area of 1,810,000 square miles and more than twenty million people in the 1950s. Instructions for paying family benefits, 7 November 1956, 11D1-903, ANS.

44. Summary on the morale of African military men in the French Corps of the Far East, signed by Lieutenant Boubakar, 30 September 1955, 10H420, SHD-T.

45. Cynthia Enloe, *The Morning After: Sexual Politics at the End of the Cold War* (Berkeley: University of California Press, 1993), 145, found in Levine, *Prostitution*, 270.

46. Frank Proschan, "'Syphilis, Opiomania, and Pederasty': Colonial Constructions of Vietnamese (and French) Social Diseases," *Journal of the History of Sexuality* 11, no. 4 (October 2002): 614; Michael G. Vann, "The Good, the Bad, and the Ugly: Variation and Difference in French Racism in Colonial *Indochine*," in *The Color of Liberty: Histories of Race in France*, ed. Sue Peabody and Tyler Stovall (Durham, NC: Duke University Press, 2003), 191.

47. Marc Guèye, *Un tirailleur sénégalais dans la guerre d'Indochine, 1953–1955* (Dakar: Presses Universitaires de Dakar, 2007), 18–23.

48. Guèye, 19; and J. Gomis, interview, Dakar, 2 February 2009.

49. Lessard, *Human Trafficking*.

50. Michel Serge Hardy, *De la morale au moral des troupes ou l'histoire des B.M.C, 1918–2004* (Panazol, France: Lavauzelle, 2004), 121.

51. Circumstantial report from sub-lieutenant Baba Famory, African officer of the 27th Bataillon de Marche de Tirailleurs Sénégalais, regarding events occurring from 21 April to 1 May 1951, 10H420, SHD-T.

52. "Incident entre les elements viet-namiens et africains," signed by Soglo, 8 June 1954, 10H420, SHD-T.

53. Morale report from the subsector of Phu-Lang-Thuong, signed by Mouret of the 26th Bataillon de Marche de Tirailleurs Sénégalais, 4 December 1952, 10H363, SHD-T.

54. Y. Danfa, interview, Ziguinchor, 6 March 2008. The Viet Minh were members of the nationalist movement fighting for independence.

55. *Journal de Marche et Opérations* of the 32nd Bataillon de Marche de Tirailleurs Sénégalais in the subsector of Phu-Lo, 1 April–30 June 1954, 10H363, SHD-T.

56. S. Diba, interview, Thiès, 12 December 2007.

57. These types of images were available to soldiers in propaganda posters, 10H424, SHD-T.

58. Report from Captain Drabo, 16 December 1954, 10H420, SHD-T.

59. Pseudonym used. A. Sall, interview, Dakar, 1 February 2008.

60. Frederick Cooper, "From Imperial Inclusion to Republican Exclusion? France's Ambiguous Postwar Trajectory," in *Frenchness and the African Diaspora: Identity and Uprising in Contemporary France*, ed. Charles Tshimanga, Didier Gondola, and Peter J. Bloom (Bloomington: Indiana University Press, 2009), 100.

61. Shawn McHale deals with Vietnamese racial stereotypes concerning West African and North African soldiers in "Understanding the Fanatic Mind? The Việt Minh and Race Hatred in the First Indochina War (1945–1954), *Journal of Vietnamese Studies* 4, no. 3 (Fall 2009): 98–138.

62. Colonel M. Rives, interview, Paris, 16 June 2008.

63. Interviews with H. N'Diaye, Dakar, 22 February 2008; A. Bâ, Dakar, 2 February 2008; N. Beye, Dakar, 27 February 2008.

64. Niane, *L'étrangère*, 9.

65. Jacques Dalloz, *The War in Indo-China, 1945–54*, trans. Josephine Bacon (Dublin: Gill and Macmillan, 1990), 300.

66. "BQR NVN no. 15h/RG du 10 juillet 1954, 'Évacuation Delta,'" 10 July 1954, Spce74, ANOM.

67. Note on the subject of mixed African-Indochinese children, April 1951, 13G94V180, ANS.

68. Note from the Rufisque police commissioner, Mesureur, 28 February 1951, 13G94V180, ANS.

69. Camille Bailly forwarded Senghor's request regarding the social institutions that could support Afro-Vietnamese children to the governor-general of FWA, 18 July 1950, 13G94V180, ANS.

70. List of African military men accompanied by children on Champollion, departed Saigon 14 August 1950, and list of African military men repatriating on Cap Tourane, departed Saigon 24 November 1950, 13G94V180, ANS.

71. Chambon to the governor-general of FWA, 11 August 1950, 13G94V180, ANS.

72. A. Sow, interview, Saint-Louis, 23 January 2008. These obstacles are also described in Nadine Bari and Laby Camara, *L'enfant de Seno* (Paris: Harmattan, 2011).

73. Report from Captain Drabo, 16 December 1954, 10H420, SHD-T.

74. A. Sow, interview, Saint-Louis, 15 January 2008; B. Bieye, interview, Ziguinchor, 6 March 2008.

75. Brian Titley, *Dark Age: The Political Odyssey of Emperor Bokassa* (Montreal: McGill-Queen's University Press, 1997), 51–60; Firpo, *Uprooted*, 156.

76. Report on morale, signed by Soglo, 7 January 1954, 10H420, SHD-T; A. Sall, interview, Dakar, 1 February 2008.

77. B. Bieye, interview, Ziguinchor, 6 March 2008. There are similar stories for North African soldiers in Nelcya Delanoë, *Poussières d'empires* (Paris: Presses Universitaires de France, 2002).

78. U. Diagne, interview, Dakar, 6 February 2008.

79. Captain Soglo and Lieutenant Aho, both BAA agents, adopted five and four Afro-Vietnamese children, respectively; found in a summary of morale reports from the first semester of 1955, 10H420, SHD-T. The Lam family adopted two orphaned children in addition to their six biological Afro-Vietnamese children at the conclusion of World War II; letter to the delegate of the governor of Senegal, 6 February 1951, 13G94V180.

80. The repercussions of this are addressed in two documentaries: Laurence Gavron, dir., *Si loin du Vietnam* (Senegal: Mbokki Mbaar Productions, 2016); Idrissou Mora-Kpai, dir., *Indochine, sur les traces d'une mère* (France: MKJ Films, 2011).

81. U. Diagne, interview, Dakar, 26 February 2008.

82. Ibrahima Ndour, "Itinéraire d'un ancien combattant" (thesis, École Normale Supérieure du Sénégal, 2006).

83. Niane, *L'étrangère*, 12.

84. H. N'Diaye, interview, Dakar, 22 February 2008; N. Beye, interview, Dakar, 27 February 2008.

85. U. Diop, interview, Dakar, 16 February 2008.

86. In a related example, an Afro-Vietnamese orphan, Laby Camara, found a civic association for Guinean-Vietnamese people (Association des métis guinéen-vietnamiens en Guinée) when he visited Conakry in 2008. Bari and Camara, *L'enfant de Seno*, 37.

87. N. Beye, interview, Dakar, 27 February 2008; Niane, *L'étrangère*.

88. See file 13G94V180, ANS.

89. Niane, *L'étrangère*, 6, 21.

90. Niane, *L'étrangère*; H. N'Diaye, interview, Dakar, 22 February 2008; A-M. Niane and Félicité, interview, Dakar, 25 February 2008.

91. J. Gomis, interview, Dakar, 25 January 2011.

92. Captain Diop, interview, Veterans' Bureau, Dakar, February 2008.

93. Nellie Peyton, "How Spring Rolls Got to Senegal," Roads and Kingdoms, 6 November 2016, accessed 21 May 2017, https://roadsandkingdoms.com/2016/spring-rolls-got-senegal.

EPILOGUE: DECOLONIZATION, ALGERIA, AND LEGACIES

1. Martin Thomas, "From Sétif to Moramanga: Identifying Insurgents and Ascribing Guilt in the French Colonial Post-war," *War in History* 25, no. 2 (2018): 227–53; Yves Benot, *Massacres coloniaux, 1944–1950: La IVe République et la mise au pas des colonies françaises* (Paris: La Découverte, 2001).

2. Benjamin Stora, *Messali Hadj, 1898–1974* (Paris: Sycomore, 1982).

3. Dramatized in Rachid Bouchareb, dir., *Hors-la-loi* (Paris: Tessalit Productions, 2010).

4. Charles-Robert Ageron, "Les troubles du nord-constantinois en mai 1945: Une tentative insurrectionnelle?" *Vingtième siècle: Revue d'histoire*, no. 4 (October 1984): 36; Jean-Louis Planche, *Sétif 1945: Histoire d'un massacre annoncé* (Paris: Perrin, 2006), chapter entitled, "Les massacres du 8 mai"; file 16H333 at CHETOM.

5. Jeffrey James Byrne, *Mecca of Revolution: Algeria, Decolonization, and the Third World Order* (New York: Oxford University Press, 2016), 31–64.

6. Rapport d'ensemble sur les événements de Madagascar, undated, FMCOTE74, ANOM.

7. Report signed by Pellet, the director of military affairs, 29 May 1947, FMCOTE74, ANOM.

8. Martin Thomas, "From Sétif to Moramanga," 251.

9. Jennifer Cole, "Narratives and Moral Projects: Generational Memories of the Malagasy 1947 Rebellion," *Ethos* 31, no. 1 (March 2003): 95–126; introduction to Amadou Ba, *Les "Sénégalais" à Madagascar: Militaires ouest-africains dans la conquête et la colonisation de la Grande-Île (1895–1960)* (Paris: Harmattan, 2012).

10. Ruth Ginio, *The French Army and Its African Soldiers: The Years of Decolonization* (Lincoln: University of Nebraska Press, 2017), 41, 79–81.

11. Mouloud Feraoun, *Journal, 1955–1962: Reflections on the French-Algerian War*, trans. Mary E. Wolf and Claude Fouillade (Lincoln: University of Nebraska Press, 2000).

12. A. Kamara, interview, Dakar, 27 June 2006.

13. Gillo Pontecorvo's film *The Battle of Algiers* (*La battaglia di Algeri*, 1966) vividly portrays Massu's assault on Algiers.

14. Y. Sow, "Itinéraire d'un ancien combattant aux guerres d'Indochine et d'Algérie: Djigal Faye né en 1926" (thesis, École Normale Supérieure du Sénégal, 2006).

15. Report from Orsini, 9 May 1956, 1H2454, SHD-T.

16. A. Sow, interview, Saint-Louis, 23 January 2008.

17. Document concerning the Psychological Bureau for the Chief of Headquarters, 5 November 1955, 1H2454, SHD-T.

18. Frantz Fanon, *The Wretched of the Earth*, trans. Constance Farrington (New York: Grove Press, 1968), 269.

19. "L'Afrique noire face au colonialism français," *El moudjahid* 18, 15 February 1958. For reference to Fanon's ideological development and contributions to *El moudjahid*, see Alice Cherki, *Frantz Fanon: A Portrait*, trans. Nadia Benabid (Ithaca, NY: Cornell University Press, 2006), 106–10; Christopher J. Lee, *Frantz Fanon: Toward a Revolutionary Humanism* (Athens: Ohio University Press, 2015), 123–31.

20. "Le conflit algérien et l'anticolonialisme africain," *El moudjahid* 11, 1 November 1957. *Moudjahidine* is an Arabic term that means freedom fighter. *Maquis* was a French word used to describe these people. During World War II, *maquis* was a neologism for the French resistance to German occupation. Originally, *maquis* meant scrub brush.

21. West African servicemen were concerned for their safety while attending daily prayers in Algeria. Youssouf à Lô, interview, Dakar, 20 November 2007.

22. Most military records regarding the French-Algerian War are sealed and require special permissions. This observation comes from the few accessible files in Vincennes and archival sources available in Dakar and Fréjus.

23. Letter from Laporte, 1/3ème Régiment d'Infanterie Coloniale, 7 May 1956, 1H2454, SHD-T; morale report from Tiecoura, 28 November 1959, 1H2455Bis, SHD-T.

24. K. A. Jamil, interview, Aix-en-Provence, August 2013; S. Diagne, interview, Dakar, 26 February 2008.

25. P. S. Gueye, "Itinéraire d'un ancien combattant: La parcours de Samba Ndiaga Diop tirailleur de la guerre d'Algérie (1954–62)" (thesis, École Normale Supérieure du Sénégal, 2006).

26. Djamila Amrane, "Les combattantes de la guerre d'Algérie," *Matériaux pour l'histoire de notre temps*, no. 26 (January–March 1992): 59.

27. Raphaëlle Branche, "Des viols pendant la guerre d'Algérie," *Vingtième siècle: Revue d'histoire*, no. 75 (July–September 2002): 125–28.

28. Simone de Beauvoir and Gisèle Halimi, *Djamilla Boupacha* (Paris: Gallimard, 1962); Georges Arnaud and Jacques Vergès, *Pour Djamila Bouhired* (Paris: Minuit, 1957).

29. Gregory Mann, "What Was the *Indigénat*? The 'Empire of Law' in French West Africa," *Journal of African History* 50, no. 3 (2009): 333–34.

30. Anthony Clayton, *France, Soldiers, and Africa* (London: Brassey's Defence Publishers, 1988), 359.

31. For details on the *deuxième portion*, see Myron Echenberg, "Les migrations militaires en Afrique occidentale française, 1900–1945," *Canadian Journal of African Studies* 14, no. 3 (1980): 437; and Frederick Cooper, *Decolonization and African Society: The Labor Question in French and British Africa* (Cambridge: Cambridge University Press, 1996), 38–40, 88–91.

32. Ruth Morgenthau, *Political Parties in French-Speaking West Africa* (Oxford: Clarendon, 1964), 49–50; Frederick Cooper, *Citizenship between Empire and Nation: Remaking France and French Africa, 1945–1960* (Princeton, NJ: Princeton University Press, 2014), 121–23.

33. Ginio, *French Army*, 48–60.

34. Myron Echenberg, *Colonial Conscripts: The Tirailleurs Sénégalais in French West Africa, 1857–1960* (Portsmouth, NH: Heinemann, 1991), 123.

35. Frederick Cooper, "Conflict and Connection: Rethinking Colonial African History," *American Historical Review* 99, no. 5 (December 1994): 1544.

36. Alice L. Conklin, Sarah Fishman, and Robert Zaretsky, eds., *France and Its Empire since 1870* (New York: Oxford University Press, 2011), 274–79; Matthew Connelly, *A Diplomatic Revolution: Algeria's Fight for Independence and the Origins of the Post–Cold War Era* (Oxford: Oxford University Press, 2002), 173–80.

37. Frederick Cooper, *Citizenship*, 354–55.

38. Evidenced throughout the 16H series at CHETOM, but one specific reference is the *Journal de Marche et Opérations* of the 2nd Battalion of the 5th Régiment de Tirailleurs Sénégalais from 1 July to 10 September 1958, 29 September 1958, 16H329, CHETOM.

39. Tony Chafer, *The End of French Empire in French West Africa: France's Successful Decolonization?* (Oxford: Berg, 2002), 179; Elizabeth Schmidt, "Anticolonial Nationalism in French West Africa: What Made Guinea Unique?" *African Studies Review* 52, no. 2 (September 2009): 1–34.

40. Sarah Zimmerman, "Apatridie et décolonisation: Les tirailleurs sénégalais guinéens et la Guinée de Sékou Touré," *Les temps modernes*, no. 693/694 (April–July 2017): 111–45.

41. K. Kourouma, interview, Dakar, 13 November 2007; Camille DuParc, "Les femmes des tirailleurs Sénégalais de 1857 à nos jours" (master's thesis, Université du Havre, 2009), 2:46.

42. For a parallel example of the militarization of male colonial employees and how it relates to masculinity in the Gold Coast, see Stephan Miescher, *Making Men in Ghana* (Bloomington: Indiana University Press, 2005), 91–99.

Notes to Pages 205–207

43. Communication from the governor-general of French West Africa, 3rd Military Cabinet, n.d., 4D78V100, ANS.

44. O. Mbaye, "Itinérarie d'un ancien combattant de l'armée française: Koly Kourouma," (masters' thesis, École Normale Superieure du Sénégal, 2006).

45. "Point de vue du SSDNFA/G X°RM sur l'évolution du morale et de l'état d'esprit au course de l'année 1958," 16 December 1958, 1H2413, SHD-T; Echenberg also found evidence of these sentiments, *Colonial Conscripts*, 163.

46. T. Conté, interview, Conakry, 23 February 2009.

47. For recent publications exploring "intermediary concepts," see Michelle Moyd, *Violent Intermediaries: African Soldiers, Conquest, and Everyday Colonialism in German East Africa* (Athens: Ohio University Press, 2014); Joël Glasman, "Penser les intermédiaires coloniaux: Note sur les dossiers de carrière de la police du Togo," *History in Africa* 37 (2010): 51–81; Benjamin N. Lawrance, Emily Lynn Osborn, and Richard L. Roberts, eds., *Intermediaries, Interpreters, and Clerks: African Employees in the Making of Colonial Africa* (Madison: University of Wisconsin Press, 2006).

48. Mbaye, "Itineraire.'

49. Note to the attention of the general of the army, signed by Colonel Radix, n.d., AncColAOF-43–58, ADN.

50. "Évolution de la situation en Guinée du 29 septembre au 30 novembre," 4, AncColAOF-232, ADN.

51. Expedited message signed by General Raoul Salan, 30 September 1958, 1H1398, SHD-T.

52. "Évolution de la situation en Guinée du 29 septembre au 30 novembre," 4, AncColAOF-232, ADN.

53. M. Diallo, M. Kourouma, and Y. Camara, interview, Conakry, 24 February 2009.

54. T. Conté, interview, Conakry, 23 February 2009.

55. M. Diallo, M. Kourouma, and Y. Camara, interview, Conakry, 24 February 2009. 56. Note to the attention of the general of the army, signed by Colonel Radix, n.d., AncColAOF-43–58, ADN.

57. Amadou Ba, "Madagascar: Les tirailleurs 'sénégalais' et leurs enfants," RFI, 23 July 2010, accessed 28 October 2018, https://www.rfi.fr/afrique/20100723-madagascar-tirailleurs-senegalais-leurs-enfants.

58. Clayton, *France, Soldiers*, 6–19.

59. Christian Koller, "Recruitment Policies and Recruitment Experiences in the French Foreign Legion," in *Transnational Soldiers: Foreign Military Enlistment in the Modern Era*, ed. Nir Arielli and Bruce Collins (New York: Palgrave Macmillan, 2013); Patrick Weil, *How to Be French: Nationality in the Making since 1789*, trans. Catherine Porter (Durham, NC: Duke University Press, 2008), 235.

60. Letter from the overseas minister to the high commissioner of French West Africa, 23 October 1958, AncColAOF-43, ADN.

61. Telegram signed by Bonjean in Constantine, 1 October 1958, 1H398, SHD-T.

62. Frederick Cooper, *Citizenship*, 349–65.

63. Mariane Ferme addresses the arbitrary ways in which decolonizing states revoked imperial citizenship and deterritorialized former colonial subjects. "Deterritorialized Citizenship and the Resonances of the Sierra Leonean State," in *Anthropology in the Margins of the State*, ed. Veena Das and Deborah Poole (Santa Fe: School of American Research Press, 2004), 102–5.

64. DuParc, "Les femmes," 2:45–49.

65. Gregory Mann, *Native Sons: West African Veterans and France in the Twentieth Century* (Durham, NC: Duke University Press, 2006), 142.

66. M. Diallo, M. Kourouma, and Y. Camara, interview, Conakry, 24 February 2009.

67. "Notes de Service no. 7 256 en date du 4 octobre 1958, relative à la situation dans la Métropole ou en Afrique du Nord," 2 November 1958, 1H1398, SHD-T.

68. Note signed by Brebisson and Carles, 4 October 1958, 1H1398, SHD-T.

69. John F. Straussberger, "The 'Particular Situation' in Futa Jallon: Ethnicity, Region, and Nation in Twentieth-Century Guinea" (PhD diss., Columbia University, 2015), 313–14.

70. "Compte rendu," stamped by the général adjoint d'outre-mer, 30 November 1960, 5H61, SHD-T.

71. Morgenthau, *Political Parties*, 332; Frederick Cooper, *Citizenship*, 338.

72. Mbaye, "Itinéraire"; interview with Marc Guèye, Dakar, 17 July 2008.

73. Patrick Pesnot, *Les dessous de la Françafrique: Les dossiers secrets de Monsieur X* (Paris: Nouveau Monde, 2014), 125.

74. By 1963, rumors of conspiracy and political intrigue in Guinea were common. Historians question the degree to which Sékou Touré manipulated these threats toward the use of emergency state powers. Lansiné Kaba, "From Colonialism to Autocracy: Guinea under Sékou Touré, 1957–1984," in *Decolonization and African Independence: The Transfers of Power, 1960–1980*, ed. Prosser Gifford and Wm. Roger Louis (New Haven: Yale University Press, 1988); Sidiki Kobélé Kéïta, *Des complots contre la Guinée de Sékou Touré (1958–1984)* (Conakry: Les Classiques Guinéens, 2002); Mohamed Saliou Camara, *Political History of Guinea since World War Two* (New York: Peter Lang, 2014), 122.

75. K. Kourouma, interview, Dakar, 10 February 2009.

76. Decree 72.875 of the Republic of Senegal, 17 July 1972, ANS.

77. Duparc, "Les femmes," 2:43; Bronwyn Manby, *Citizenship Law in Africa: A Comparative Study*, 2nd ed. (New York: Open Society Foundations, 2010), 41.

78. "Note pour l'ambassador de l'ambassade de France, consulat général de Dakar," 27 December 1963, ADP-Dakar 482, AND.

79. "Compte-rendu," 30 November 1960, 5H61, SHD-T.

80. Gregory Mann, *Native Sons*, 142.

81. Veteran A. Wade made these allegations, interview, Dakar, 23 January 2008. He specifically mentioned Valdiodio Ndiaye (former minister of the interior for colonial Senegal) as having signed the legislation.

82. Pierre Nora, "Between Memory and History: Les Lieux de Mémoire," *Representations*, no. 26 (Spring 1989): 7–24.

83. Eric T. Jennings, *Free French Africa in World War II: The African Resistance* (Cambridge: Cambridge University Press, 2015); Joe Lunn, *Memoirs of the Maelstrom: A Senegalese Oral History of the First World War* (Portsmouth, NH: Heinemann, 1999).

84. On 23 February 2005, the French National Assembly passed a law on teaching the "positive values" of colonialism. Robert Aldrich, "Colonial Past, Post-colonial Present: History Wars French Style," *History Australia* 3, no. 1 (June 2006): 14.1–14.10; Gregory Mann, "Immigrants and Arguments in France and West Africa," *Comparative Studies in Society and History* 45, no. 2 (April 2003): 362–85; Trica Danielle Keaton, T. Denean Sharpley-Whiting, and Tyler Stovall, "Introduction: Black Matters, Blackness Made to Matter," in *Black France / France Noire: The History and Politics of Blackness*, ed. Keaton, Sharpley-Whiting, and Stovall (Durham, NC: Duke University Press, 2012).

85. Awa Ndiaye and Mbaye Gana Kébé, *Un president au service des tirailleurs* (Dakar: Maguilen, 2007), celebrates former Senegalese president Abdoulaye Wade, whose administration increased the visibility of veterans.

86. Armelle Mabon, *Prisonniers de guerre indigènes: Visages oubliés de la France occupée* (Paris: La Découverte, 2010); Raffael Scheck, *Hitler's African Victims: The German Army Massacres of Black French Soldiers in 1940* (Cambridge: Cambridge University Press, 2006); Charles Onana, *1940–1945: Noirs, blancs, beurs: Libérateurs de la France* (Paris: Duboiris, 2006); Maurice Rives and Robert Dietrich, *Héros méconnus, 1914–1918, 1939–1945: Mémorial des combattants d'Afrique noire et de Madagascar* (Paris: Association Française Frères d'Armes, 1990).

87. Pierre Bouvier, *La longue marche des tirailleurs sénégalais: De la Grande Guerre aux indépendances* (Paris: Belin, 2018).

88. A. Mbodj, interview, Paris, 21 June 2008. See file ADP Dakar 482, ADN.

89. Tanguy Berthemet, "Pensions militaires: Français et africains enfin à égalité," *Le Figaro*, 12 July 2010, accessed 28 October 2018, https://www.lefigaro.fr/international/2010/07/12/01003-20100712ARTFIG00628-pensions-militaires-francais-et-africains-enfin-a-egalite.php.

90. Philippe Douroux, "Aïssata Seck, Marianne Noire," *Libération*, 11 June 2017, accessed 29 October 2018, https://www.liberation.fr/debats/2017/06/11/aissata-seck-marianne-noire_1576018.

91. "Hollande naturalise 28 anciens tirailleurs sénégalais," *Ouest-France*, 15 April 2017, accessed 28 October 2018, https://www.ouest-france.fr/culture/histoire/d-anciens-tirailleurs-senegalais-naturalises-francais-4931136.

92. New research addresses the postcolonial psychological health of former Moroccan tirailleurs. Aziza Doudou, "Fragmentations identitaires des soldats marocains durant la guerre d'Indochine" (paper presented at the annual meeting of the French Colonial Historical Society, Seattle, Washington, 30 May–2 June 2018).

Bibliography

INTERVIEWS CONDUCTED BY THE AUTHOR

Bâ, Asstou. Dakar, 2 February 2008. Vietnamese widow.
Beye, Ninh, and her children Marie, Awa, Bathio, and Massitou. Dakar, 27 February 2008. Vietnamese widow of an *originaire* soldier. Her first two children were born in Indochina.
Camara, Yaya. Conakry, 24 and 25 February 2009. Veteran.
Conté, El Hadj Thierno, Mr. Diallo, and Mr. Kourouma. Conakry, 23 February 2009. Veterans.
Danfa, Yaya, and El Hajj Bakary Biaye. Ziguinchor, 6 March 2008. Veterans.
Diagne, Sophie. Dakar, 8 December 2007; 19 March 2008. Daughter of *originaire* veteran. She was born in Indochina.
Diagne, Sophie, and Urbain Diop. Dakar, 26 February 2008; 13 March 2008. Daughter and *originaire* veteran.
Diagne, Urbain. Dakar, 30 December 2007; 6 February 2008. Veteran.
Diop, Omar, Samba Diba, and Demba Sao. Thiès, 12 December 2007. Veterans.
Diop, Urbain. Dakar, 16 February 2008. Son of Afro-Vietnamese couple.
Fall, El Hadj Alioune. Thiès, 13 December 2007. Veteran.
Faye, Djibi (Vieux Faye). Saint-Louis, 18 December 2007. Veteran.
Gomis, Jean. Dakar, 9 February 2009; 25 January 2011. Son of Afro-Vietnamese couple and veteran of French Indochina War.
Hane, Baby. Podor, 12 February 2008. Veteran.
Jamil, K. A. Aix-en-Provence, August 2013. Relative.
Kamara, Alioune. Dakar, 27 June 2006; 3 December 2007. Veteran.
Kourouma, Koly. Dakar, 13 November 2007; 17 July 2008; 10 February 2009. Guinean veteran residing in Dakar.
Lô, Youssouf à. Dakar, 14, 20, and 30 November 2007; 8 January 2008; 27 February 2008; 28 March 2008; January 2011. Veteran and historian.
Mbodj, Aliou. Dakar, 31 December 2007; Paris, 21 June 2008; Dakar, 12 February 2009. Veteran.

Mbow, Amadou Mahtar. Dakar, 18 March 2008; 27 January 2011. Veteran and politician/scholar.
N'Diaye, Hélène. Dakar, 22 February 2008. Daughter of Afro-Vietnamese couple. Left Saigon for Dakar at age eighteen.
Niane, Anne-Marie, and Félicité. Dakar, 25 February 2008. Daughters of an Afro-Vietnamese couple.
Rives, Maurice. Paris, 16 June 2008. Former French commander of *tirailleurs sénégalais* in Indochina.
Sadio, Kéba. Ziguinchor, 6 March 2008. Veteran.
Sall, Amadou. Dakar, 22 November 2007; 5 December 2007; 1 February 2008. Veteran.
Samb, Sanga. Saint-Louis, 16 February 2008. Veteran.
Sao, Demba. Thiès, 18 and 19 December 2008. Veteran.
Solabé, Massaly. Ziguinchor, 5 March 2008. Veteran.
Sow, Alioune. Saint-Louis, 14, 15, 20, and 22 January 2008. Veteran.
Traoré, Mamadou. Thiès, 12 December 2007. Veteran.
Touré, Colonel Lamdou. Dakar, 1 February 2008. Former colonel in Senegalese Army.
Touré, Kéba. Ziguinchor, 7 March 2008. Veteran.
Touré, Kéba, Yaya Danfa, Massaly Solabé, and El Hajj Bakary Biaye. Ziguinchor, 5 March 2008. Veterans.
Wade, Allassane. Dakar, 8 and 23 January 2008; 4 February 2008; 16 July 2008. Veteran.

ARCHIVES AND LIBRARIES CONSULTED
(BY COUNTRY)

Archives de Préfecture de Dakar (APD), Senegal
Archives Nationales du Sénégal (ANS), Dakar, Senegal
Bibliothèque du Musée des Forces Armées, Dakar, Senegal
Centre National des Recherches et Sciences (CNRS), Saint-Louis, Senegal
Institut Fondamental d'Afrique Noire, Dakar, Senegal
Archives Diplomatiques de Nantes (ADN), France
Archives Nationales de France, Paris, France
Archives Nationales d'Outre-Mer (ANOM), Aix-en-Provence, France
Centre d'Histoire et d'Études des Troupes d'Outre-Mer (CHETOM), Fréjus, France
Établissement de Communication et de Production Audiovisuelle de la Défense (ECPA-D), Ivry-sur-Seine, France
Service Historique de la Défense, Service Iconographique (SHD-SI), Vincennes, France
Service Historique de la Défense, Terre (SHD-T), Vincennes, France
Archives Nationales de Guinée (ANG), Conakry, Guinea
Bibliothèque de la Source, Rabat, Morocco
Bibliothèque Nationale du Royaume du Maroc, Rabat, Morocco
Centre des Archives Nationales de l'Algérie, Algiers, Algeria
Bancroft Library at University of California, Berkeley, United States
Hoover Institution at Stanford University, United States

Bibliography

NEWSPAPERS AND PERIODICALS

L'Afrique française: Bulletin mensuel du Comité de l'Afrique française et du Comité du Maroc
Bulletin du Comité de l'Afrique française
Dépêche coloniale
L'écho du Maroc
El-Moudjahidine
Le Figaro
Journal officiel de l'Afrique occidentale française
Journal officiel de la République du Sénégal
Journal officiel de la République française
Libération
Liberté
La vigie marocaine
Ouest-France

UNPUBLISHED THESES FROM ÉCOLE NORMALE SUPÉRIEURE DU SÉNÉGAL (NOW FACULTÉ DES SCIENCES ET TECHNOLOGIES DE L'ÉDUCATION ET DE LA FORMATION)

Ba, Coumba. "Itinéraire d'un ancien combattant: L'exemple de Oumar Ngalla Diene." 2006.
Ba, Loba. "Itinéraires des anciens combattants: Souleyemane Hanne, Aliou Sarr, et Ousmane Sarr." 2003.
Cissé, Ouseynou. "Itinéraire d'un ancien combattant de la Deuxième Guerre mondiale." 2005.
Cissokho, Papa Fily Gueye. "Itinéraire d'un ancien tirailleur sénégalais de l'armée coloniale française: Mamadou Ba." 2006.
Coly, Younousse. "L'itinéraire d'un ancien combattant de la guerre d'Algérie, Bassirou Dieme." 2005.
Dia, Mohammadou. "Itinéraire d'un ancien combattant de la guerre d'Algérie: Djibril Dieng 1954–1960." 2005.
Diallo, Mamadou Sellou. "Itinéraire d'un ancien combattant de la Deuxième Guerre mondiale, de la guerre d'Indochine et de la guerre d'Algérie." 2004.
Diedhiou, Mariama Sene. "Itinéraire d'un ancien combattant de la guerre d'Algérie: Sagna Ousmane." 2005.
Dieng, Fatou. "Itinéraire d'un ancien combattant." 2005.
Diop, Alimata. "Itinéraire d'un ancien combattant: Mass Top." 2005.
Diop, Alioune. "Itinéraire d'un ancien combattant de la guerre d'Algérie: Boubacar Baldé." 2005.
Fall, Allasane. "Itinéraire d'un ancien combattant de la guerre d'Algérie, Amady Moutar Gaye." 2005.
Gueye, Papa Samba. "Itinéraire d'un ancien combattant: La parcours de Samba Ndiaga Diop tirailleur de la guerre d'Algérie (1954–62)." 2006.
Kane, Aly Bocar. "Itinéraire d'un tirailleur sénégalais en Algérie: Saïdou Seye Sy de Dabia Odédji." 2004.
Kébé, Djibril. "Itinéraire de Ndiaga Gueye de la guerre d'Indochine (1946–1954)." 2003.

Mbaye, Oumar. "Itinéraire d'un ancien combattant de l'armée française: Koly Kourouma." 2006.
Ndao, Aboulaye Faye. "Itinéraire d'un ancien combattant de la guerre d'Algérie, Charles Gomis." 2005.
Ndiaye, Mamdou Bernard. "Itinéraire d'un ancien combattant de la guerre d'Indochine, 1954–1962. 2006.
Ndiaye, Sidy Al Moctar. "Itinéraire d'un ancien combattant: Colonel Bamba Ndiaye." 2006.
Ndioné, Cécile. "Itinéraire d'un ancien combattant: Mamdou Diallo." 2006.
Ndour, Ibrahima. "Itinéraire d'un ancien combattant." 2006.
Niang, Malick. "Itinéraire d'un ancien combattant pendant la guerre d'Algérie: Keba Touré." 2005.
Sagna, Clara. "Itinéraire d'un ancien combattant de la guerre d'Indochine: L'exemple de Ousmane Kassé." 2006.
Sambou, Léopold. "Boubacar Diop Indochine." 2005.
Sandou, Djiby. "Abdoul Botol Ba: Ancien combattant des guerres d'Algérie et d'Indochine." 2005.
Sow, Yoro. "Itinéraire d'un ancien combattant aux guerres d'Indochine et d'Algérie: Djigal Faye né en 1926." 2006.
Tall, Salamata Bâ. "Itinéraire de Khadim Ndiaye, ancien combattant 1946–1954." 2003.

BOOKS, ARTICLES, DISSERTATIONS, PRESENTATIONS

Achebe, Nwando. *The Female King of Colonial Nigeria: Ahebi Ugbabe.* Bloomington: Indiana University Press, 2011.
Adas, Michael. "Contested Hegemony: The Great War and the Afro-Asian Assault on the Civilizing Mission Ideology." *Journal of World History* 15, no. 1 (March 2004): 31–63.
Aderinto, Saheed. *When Sex Threatened the State: Illicit Sexuality, Nationalism, and Politics in Colonial Nigeria, 1900–1958.* Urbana: University of Illinois Press, 2015.
Ageron, Charles-Robert. "Les troubles du nord-constantinois en mai 1945: Une tentative insurrectionnelle?" *Vingtième siècle: Revue d'histoire*, no. 4 (October 1984): 23–38.
Akpo-Vaché, Catherine. *L'AOF et la Seconde Guerre mondiale: La vie politique (septembre 1939–octobre 1945).* Paris: Karthala, 1996.
Albord, Maurice. *L'armée française et les états du Levant, 1936–1946.* Paris: CNRS Éditions, 2000.
Aldrich, Robert. *Colonialism and Homosexuality.* New York: Routledge, 2002.
———. "Colonial Past, Post-colonial Present: History Wars French Style." *History Australia* 3, no. 1 (June 2006): 14.1–14.10.
———. "Homosexuality in the French Colonies." *Journal of Homosexuality* 41, no. 3/4 (2002): 201–18.
Allen, Philip M. *Madagascar: Conflicts of Authority in the Great Island.* Boulder, CO: Westview, 1995.
Allman, Jean. "Rounding up Spinsters: Gender Chaos and Unmarried Women in Colonial Asante." *Journal of African History* 37, no. 2 (July 1996): 195–214.

Bibliography

Allman, Jean, and Victoria B. Tashjian. *"I Will Not Eat Stone": A Women's History of Colonial Asante*. Portsmouth, NH: Heinemann, 2000.

Alpern, Stanley B. *Amazons of Black Sparta: The Women Warriors of Dahomey*. New York: New York University Press, 1998.

Amrane, Djamila. "Les combattantes de la guerre d'Algérie." *Matériaux pour l'histoire de notre temps*, no. 26 (January–March 1992): 58–62.

Aouad Badoual, Rita. "'Esclavage' et situation des 'noirs' au Maroc dans la première moitié du XXe siècle." In *Les relations transsahariennes à l'époque contemporaine: Un espace en constante mutation*, edited by Laurence Marfaing and Steffen Wippel, 337–60. Paris: Karthala, 2004.

Appadurai, Arjun. "The Past as a Scarce Resource." *Man*, n.s., 16, no. 2 (June 1981): 201–19.

Arnaud, Georges, and Jacques Vergès. *Pour Djamila Bouhired*. Paris: Minuit, 1957.

Arnaud, Louis. "Étude anthropologique de la Garde Noire des sultans du Maroc." *Bulletin de l'Institut d'Hygiène du Maroc* 10 (1940): 35–36.

Ba, Amadou. *Les "Sénégalais" à Madagascar: Militaires ouest-africains dans la conquête et la colonisation de la Grande-Île (1895–1960)*. Paris: Harmattan, 2012.

Bâ, Amadou Hampaté. *The Fortunes of Wangrin*. Translated by Aina Pavolini Taylor. Bloomington: Indiana University Press, 1999.

Balesi, Charles John. *From Adversaries to Comrades-in-Arms: West Africans in the French Military, 1885–1918*. Waltham, MA: Crossroads, 1979.

Ballantyne, Tony, and Antoinette Burton, eds. *Moving Subjects: Gender, Mobility, and Intimacy in an Age of Global Empire*. Urbana: University of Illinois Press, 2009.

Baratier, Albert. *Au Congo: Souvenirs de la mission Marchand*. Paris: Arthème Fayard, 1914.

Bari, Nadine, and Laby Camara. *L'enfant de Seno*. Paris: Harmattan, 2011.

Bat, Jean-Pierre, and Nicolas Courtin, eds. *Maintenir l'ordre colonial: Afrique et Madagascar, XIXe–XXe siècles*. Rennes, France: Presses Universitaires de Rennes, 2012.

Bay, Edna G. *Wives of the Leopard: Gender, Politics, and Culture in the Kingdom of Dahomey*. Charlottesville: University of Virginia Press, 1998.

Beauvoir, Simone de, and Gisèle Halimi. *Djamila Boupacha*. Paris: Gallimard, 1962.

Benot, Yves. *Massacres coloniaux, 1944–1950: La IVe République et la mise au pas des colonies françaises*. Paris: La Découverte, 2001.

Berenson, Edward. *Heroes of Empire: Five Charismatic Men and the Conquest of Africa*. Berkeley: University of California Press, 2011.

Berry, Sara. *No Condition Is Permanent: The Social Dynamics of Agrarian Change in Sub-Saharan Africa*. Madison: University of Wisconsin Press, 1993.

Berthemet, Tanguy. "Pensions militaires: Français et africains enfin à égalité." *Le Figaro*, 12 July 2010. Accessed 28 October 2018. https://www.lefigaro.fr/international/2010/07/12/01003-20100712ARTFIG00628-pensions-militaires-francais-et-africains-enfin-a-egalite.php.

Betts, Raymond F. *Assimilation and Association in French Colonial Theory, 1890–1914*. New York: Columbia University Press, 1961.

Bibliography

Bodin, Michel. *La France et ses soldats: Indochine, 1945–1954.* Paris: Harmattan, 1996.

———. *Les africains dans la guerre d'Indochine, 1947–1954.* Paris: Harmattan, 2000.

Boittin, Jennifer Anne, Christina Firpo, and Emily Musil Church. "Hierarchies of Race and Gender in the French Colonial Empire, 1914–1946." *Historical Reflections / Réflexions historiques* 37 (2011): 60–90.

Bonnetain, Raymonde. *Une française au Soudan: Sur la route de Tombouctou, du Sénégal au Niger.* Paris: Librairies-Imprimeries Réunies, 1894.

Bouchareb, Rachid, dir. *Hors-la-loi.* Paris: Tessalit Productions, 2010.

———. *Indigènes.* Paris: Tessalit Productions, 2007.

Bouche, Denise. *Les villages de liberté en Afrique noire française, 1887–1910.* Paris: Mouton, 1968.

Boutonne, Jean. "L'expérience de colonisation militaire à Madagascar au temps de Gallieni." *Omaly sy anio: Hier et aujourd'hui* 12 (1980): 7–70.

Bouvier, Pierre. *La longue marche des tirailleurs sénégalais: De la Grande Guerre aux indépendances.* Paris: Belin, 2018.

Branche, Raphaëlle. "Des viols pendant la guerre d'Algérie." *Vingtième siècle: Revue d'histoire,* no. 75 (July–September 2002): 123–32.

Brooks, George E. *Eurafricans in Western Africa: Commerce, Social Status, Gender and Religious Observance from the Sixteenth to the Eighteenth Century.* Athens: Ohio University Press, 2003.

Brownmiller, Susan. *Against Our Will.* New York: Bantam Books, 1976.

Brubaker, Rogers. *Citizenship and Nationhood in France and Germany.* Cambridge, MA: Harvard University Press, 1992.

Brunschwig, Henri. *Brazza explorateur: L'Ogooué, 1875–1879.* Paris: Mouton, 1966.

———. *Noirs et blancs dans l'Afrique noire française, ou, comment le colonisé devient colonisateur (1870–1914).* Paris: Flammarion, 1983.

Buettner, Elizabeth. *Empire Families: Britons and Late Imperial India.* Oxford: Oxford University Press, 2004.

Buggenhagen, Beth. *Muslim Families in Global Senegal: Money Takes Care of Shame.* Bloomington: Indiana University Press, 2012.

Bunting, Annie. "'Forced Marriage' in Conflict Situations: Researching and Prosecuting Old Harms and New Crimes." *Canadian Journal of Human Rights* 1, no. 1 (Spring 2012): 165–85.

Bunting, Annie, Benjamin N. Lawrance, and Richard L. Roberts, eds. *Marriage by Force? Contestation over Consent and Coercion in Africa.* Athens: Ohio University Press, 2016.

Burke, Edmund, III. *The Ethnographic State: France and the Invention of Moroccan Islam.* Oakland: University of California Press, 2014.

Burnet, Jennie E. *Genocide Lives in Us: Women, Memory, and Silence in Rwanda.* Madison: University of Wisconsin Press, 2012.

Burrill, Emily S. *States of Marriage: Gender, Justice, and Rights in Colonial Mali.* Athens: Ohio University Press, 2015.

Burton, Antoinette. *Dwelling in the Archive: Women Writing House, Home, and History in Late Colonial India.* Oxford: Oxford University Press, 2003.

Bibliography

Bush, Barbara. "Gender and Empire: The Twentieth Century." In *Gender and Empire*, edited by Phillipa Levine, 77–111. Oxford: Oxford University Press, 2004.

Byfield, Judith. "Women, Marriage, Divorce and the Emerging Colonial State in Abeokuta (Nigeria) 1892–1904." *Canadian Journal of African Studies* 30, no. 1 (1996): 32–51.

Byfield, Judith A., Cynthia A. Brown, Timothy Parsons, and Ahmad Alawad Sikainga, eds. *Africa and World War II*. Cambridge: Cambridge University Press, 2015.

Byrne, Jeffrey James. *Mecca of Revolution: Algeria, Decolonization, and the Third World Order*. New York: Oxford University Press, 2016.

Camara, Mohamed Saliou. *Political History of Guinea since World War Two*. New York: Peter Lang, 2014.

Camiscioli, Elisa. *Reproducing the French Race: Immigration, Intimacy, and Embodiment in the Early Twentieth Century*. Durham, NC: Duke University Press, 2009.

Cammaert, Jessica. *Undesirable Practices: Women, Children, and the Politics of the Body in Northern Ghana, 1930–1972*. Lincoln: University of Nebraska Press, 2016.

Campbell, Gwyn. *An Economic History of Imperial Madagascar, 1750–1895: The Rise and Fall of an Island Empire*. New York: Cambridge University Press, 2005.

Campt, Tina. *Other Germans: Black Germans and the Politics of Race, Gender, and Memory in the Third Reich*. Ann Arbor: University of Michigan Press, 2004.

Capuano, Christophe. *Vichy et la famille: Réalités et faux-semblants d'une politique publique*. Rennes, France: Presses Universitaires de Rennes, 2009.

Cardoza, Thomas. *Intrepid Women: Cantinières and Vivandières of the French Army*. Bloomington: Indiana University Press, 2010.

Chafer, Tony. *The End of Empire in French West Africa: France's Successful Decolonization?* Oxford: Berg, 2002.

Chakrabarty, Dipesh. "Postcoloniality and the Artifice of History: Who Speaks for 'Indian' Pasts?" *Representations*, no. 37 (Winter 1992): 1–26.

Chanock, Martin. *Law, Custom, and Social Order: The Colonial Experience in Malawi and Zambia*. Cambridge: Cambridge University Press, 1985.

Chavannes, Charles de. *Avec Brazza: Souvenirs de la mission de l'ouest-africain (mars 1883– janvier 1886)*. Paris: Plon, 1935.

Cherki, Alice. *Frantz Fanon: A Portrait*. Translated by Nadia Benabid. Ithaca, NY: Cornell University Press, 2006.

Childers, Kristen Stromberg. *Fathers, Families, and the State in France, 1914–1945*. Ithaca, NY: Cornell University Press, 2003.

Christelow, Allan. "The Muslim Judge and Municipal Politics in Colonial Algeria and Senegal." *Comparative Studies in Society and History* 24, no. 1 (January 1982): 3–24.

Clancy-Smith, Julia, and Frances Gouda, eds. *Domesticating the Empire: Race, Gender, and Family Life in French and Dutch Colonialism*. Charlottesville: University of Virginia Press, 1998.

Clark, Andrew F. "Freedom Villages in the Upper Senegal Valley, 1887–1910: A Reassessment." *Slavery and Abolition* 16, no. 3 (December 1995): 311–30.

———. *From Frontier to Backwater: Economy and Society in the Upper Senegal Valley (West Africa), 1850–1920*. Lanham, MD: University Press of America, 1999.

Bibliography

Clark, Gracia. *Onions Are My Husband: Survival and Accumulation by West African Market Women.* Chicago: University of Chicago Press, 1994.

Clarke, Kamari Maxine. *Fictions of Justice: The International Criminal Court and the Challenge of Legal Pluralism in Sub-Saharan Africa.* Cambridge: Cambridge University Press, 2009.

Clayton, Anthony. *France, Soldiers, and Africa.* London: Brassey's Defence Publishers, 1988.

Clayton, Anthony, and David Killingray. *Khaki and Blue: Military and Police in British Colonial Africa.* Athens: Ohio University Press, 1989.

Cleaveland, Timothy. "Reproducing Culture and Society: Women and the Politics of Gender, Age, and Social Rank in Walāta." *Canadian Journal of African Studies* 34, no. 2 (2000): 189–217.

Clough, Patricia Ticineto, ed. *The Affective Turn: Theorizing the Social.* Durham, NC: Duke University Press, 2007.

Coe, Cati. *The Scattered Family: Parenting, African Migrants, and Global Inequality.* Chicago: University of Chicago Press, 2013.

Cohen, William B. *The French Encounter with Africans: White Response to Blacks, 1530–1880.* Bloomington: Indiana University Press, 2000.

Cole, Jennifer. "Narratives and Moral Projects: Generational Memories of the Malagasy 1947 Rebellion." *Ethos* 31, no. 1 (March 2003): 95–126.

Conklin, Alice L. "Colonialism and Human Rights, a Contradiction in Terms? The Case of France and West Africa, 1895–1914." *American Historical Review* 103, no. 2 (April 1998): 419–42.

———. *In the Museum of Man: Race, Anthropology, and Empire in France, 1850–1860.* Ithaca, NY: Cornell University Press, 2013.

———. *A Mission to Civilize: The Republican Idea of Empire in France and West Africa, 1895–1930.* Stanford, CA: Stanford University Press, 1997.

———. "Who Speaks for Africa? The René Maran–Blaise Diagne Trial in 1920s Paris." In *The Color of Liberty: Histories of Race in France*, edited by Sue Peabody and Tyler Stovall, 302–37. Durham, NC: Duke University Press, 2003.

Conklin, Alice L., Sarah Fishman, and Robert Zaretsky. *France and Its Empire since 1870.* New York: Oxford University Press, 2015.

Connelly, Matthew. *A Diplomatic Revolution: Algeria's Fight for Independence and the Origins of the Post–Cold War Era.* Oxford: Oxford University Press, 2002.

Conombo, Joseph Issoufou. *Souvenirs de guerre d'un "tirailleur sénégalais."* Paris: Harmattan, 1989.

Cooper, Barbara M. *Marriage in Maradi: Gender and Culture in a Hausa Society in Niger, 1900–1989.* Oxford: James Currey, 1997.

———. "Women's Worth and Wedding Gift Exchange in Maradi, Niger, 1907–1989." *Journal of African History* 36, no. 1 (1995): 121–40.

Cooper, Frederick. *Citizenship between Empire and Nation: Remaking France and French Africa, 1945–1960.* Princeton, NJ: Princeton University Press, 2014.

———. "Conflict and Connection: Rethinking Colonial African History." *American Historical Review* 99, no. 5 (December 1994): 1516–45.

———. *Decolonization and African Society: The Labor Question in French and British Africa.* Cambridge: Cambridge University Press, 1996.

———. "From Free Labor to Family Allowances: Labor and African Society in Colonial Discourse." *American Ethnologist* 16, no. 4 (November 1989): 745–65.

———. "From Imperial Inclusion to Republican Exclusion? France's Ambiguous Postwar Trajectory." In *Frenchness and the African Diaspora: Identity and Uprising in Contemporary France*, edited by Charles Tshimanga, Didier Gondola, and Peter J. Bloom, 91–119. Bloomington: Indiana University Press, 2009.

Cooper, Nicola. *France in Indochina: Colonial Encounters.* Oxford: Berg, 2001.

Coquery-Vidrovitch, Catherine. *Brazza et la prise de possession du Congo: La mission de l'ouest africain, 1883–1885.* Paris: Mouton, 1969.

———. *Le Congo au temps des grandes compagnies concessionnaires, 1898–1930.* Paris: Mouton, 1972.

———. "Nationalité et citoyenneté en Afrique occidentale française: Originaires et citoyens dans le Sénégal colonial." *Journal of African History* 42, no. 2 (July 2001): 285–305.

Cornet, Charles J. A. *À la conquête du Maroc sud avec la colonne Mangin, 1912–1913.* Paris: Plon-Nourrit, 1914.

Cott, Nancy F. *Public Vows: A History of Marriage and the Nation.* Cambridge, MA: Harvard University Press, 2000.

Coulter, Chris. *Bush Wives and Girl Soldiers: Women's Lives through War and Peace in Sierra Leone.* Ithaca, NY: Cornell University Press, 2009.

Cousturier, Lucie. *Des inconnus chez moi.* Paris: La Sirène, 1920.

Crowder, Michael. *Senegal: A Study in French Assimilation Policy.* London: Methuen, 1967.

———, ed. *West African Resistance: The Military Response to Colonial Occupation.* London: Hutchinson, 1971.

Curran, Andrew S. *The Anatomy of Blackness: Science and Slavery in the Age of Enlightenment.* Baltimore: Johns Hopkins University Press, 2011.

Dalloz, Jacques. *The War in Indo-China, 1945–54.* Translated by Josephine Bacon. Dublin: Gill and Macmillan, 1990.

Davis, Shelby Cullom. *Reservoirs of Men: A History of the Black Troops of French West Africa.* Chambéry, France: Impriméries Réunies, 1934.

Decker, Alicia C. *In Idi Amin's Shadow: Women, Gender, and Militarism in Uganda.* Athens: Ohio University Press, 2014.

———. "What Does a Feminist Curiosity Bring to African Military History? An Analysis and an Intervention." *Journal of African Military History* 1, no. 1 (2017): 93–111.

Delafosse, Maurice. *Haut-Sénégal-Niger (Soudan français).* 3 vols. Paris: E. Larose, 1912.

Delanoë, Nelcya. *Poussières d'empires.* Paris: Presses Universitaires de France, 2002.

Deroo, Éric, and Antoine Champeaux. *La force noire: Gloire et infortunes d'une légende coloniale.* Paris: Tallandier, 2006.

Descostes, François. *Au Soudan (1890–1891): Souvenirs d'un tirailleur sénégalais, d'après sa correspondence intime.* Paris: Picard, 1893.

Diallo, Bakary. *Force-bonté.* Paris: F. Reider, 1926.

Diamond, Hanna. *Women and the Second World War in France, 1939–1948: Choices and Constraints.* London: Pearson, 1999.

Diouf, Mamadou. "The French Colonial Policy of Assimilation and the Civility of the Originaires of the Four Communes (Senegal): A Nineteenth Century Globalization Project." *Development and Change* 29, no. 4 (October 1998): 671–96.

Donadey, Anne. "'Y'a bon Banania': Ethics and Cultural Criticism in the Colonial Context." *French Cultural Studies* 11, no. 31 (2000): 9–29.

Doudou, Aziza. "Fragmentations identitaires des soldats marocains durant la guerre d'Indochine." Paper presented at the annual meeting of the French Colonial History Society, Seattle, Washington, 30 May–2 June, 2019.

Douroux, Philippe. "Aïssata Seck, Marianne Noire." *Libération*, 11 June 2017. Accessed October 29, 2018. https://www.liberation.fr/debats/2017/06/11/aissata-seck-marianne-noire_1576018.

DuParc, Camille. "Les femmes des tirailleurs Sénégalais de 1857 à nos jours." 2 vols. Master's thesis, Université du Havre, 2009.

Dussaulx, Émile. *Journal du Soudan (1894–1898)*. Edited by Sophie Dulucq. Paris: Harmattan, 2000.

Dutton, Paul V. *Origins of the French Welfare State: The Struggle for Social Reform in France, 1914–1947.* Cambridge: Cambridge University Press, 2002.

Echenberg, Myron. *Colonial Conscripts: The Tirailleurs Sénégalais in French West Africa, 1857–1960.* Portsmouth, NH: Heinemann, 1991.

———. "Les migrations militaires en Afrique occidentale française, 1900–1945." *Canadian Journal of African Studies* 14, no. 3 (1980): 429–50.

———. "'Morts pour la France': The African Soldier in France during the Second World War." *Journal of African History* 26, no. 4 (1985): 363–80.

———. "Slaves into Soldiers: Social Origins of the Tirailleurs Senegalais." In *Africans in Bondage: Studies in Slavery and the Slave Trade*, edited by Paul E. Lovejoy, 311–33. Madison: African Studies Program, University of Wisconsin-Madison, 1986.

———. "Tragedy at Thiaroye: The Senegalese Soldiers' Uprising of 1944." In *African Labor History*, edited by Peter C. W. Gutkind, Robin Cohen, and Jean Copans, 109–28. London: Sage, 1978.

Edgerton, Robert B. *Warrior Women: The Amazons of Dahomey and the Nature of War.* Boulder, CO: Westview Press, 2000.

Ellis, Stephen. *The Rising of the Red Shawls: A Revolt in Madagascar 1895–1899.* Cambridge: Cambridge University Press, 1985.

Enloe, Cynthia. *Bananas, Beaches, and Bases: Making Feminist Sense of International Politics.* 2nd ed. Berkeley: University of California Press, 2014.

———. *Ethnic Soldiers: State Security in Divided Societies.* Athens: University of Georgia Press, 1980.

———. *Globalization and Militarism: Feminists Make the Link.* 2nd ed. Lanham, MD: Rowman & Littlefield, 2016.

———. *Maneuvers: The International Politics of Militarizing Women's Lives.* Berkeley: University of California Press, 2000.

Bibliography

———. *The Morning After: Sexual Politics at the End of the Cold War.* Berkeley: University of California Press, 1993.

Ennaji, Mohammed. *Serving the Master: Slavery and Society in Nineteenth-Century Morocco.* Translated by Seth Graebner. London: Macmillan, 1999.

———. *Soldats, domestiques, et concubines: L'esclavage au Maroc au XIXème siècle.* Paris: Balland, 1994.

Epprecht, Marc. *Heterosexual Africa? The History of an Idea from the Age of Exploration to the Age of AIDS.* Athens: Ohio University Press, 2008.

Ezzaini, Aboulqasem Ben Ahmed Al-. *Le Maroc de 1631 à 1812.* Translated by Octave V. Houdas. Amsterdam: Philo Press, 1969.

Fall, Babacar. *Le travail forcé en Afrique occidentale française, 1900–1946.* Paris: Karthala, 1993.

Falola, Toyin, and Christian Jennings, eds. *Sources and Methods in African History: Spoken, Written, Unearthed.* Rochester, NY: University of Rochester Press, 2003.

Fanon, Frantz. *The Wretched of the Earth.* Translated by Constance Farrington. New York: Grove Press, 1968.

Fargettas, Julien. "La révolte des tirailleurs sénégalais de Thiaroye: Entre reconstructions mémorielles et histoire." *Vingtième siècle: Revue d'histoire*, no. 92 (2006): 117–30.

Fehrenbach, Heide. "Black Occupation Children and the Devolution of the Nazi Racial State." In *After the Nazi Racial State: Difference and Democracy in Germany and Europe*, edited by Rita Chin, Heide Fehrenbach, Geoff Eley, and Atina Grossmann, 30–54. Ann Arbor: University of Michigan Press, 2009.

Feierman, Steve. "Colonizers, Scholars, and the Creation of Invisible History." In *Beyond the Cultural Turn: New Directions in the Study of Society and Culture*, edited by Victoria E. Bonnell and Lynn Hunt, 182–216. Berkeley: University of California Press, 1999.

Feraoun, Mouloud. *Journal, 1955–1962: Reflections on the French-Algerian War.* Translated by Mary Ellen Wolf and Claude Fouillade. Lincoln: University of Nebraska Press, 2000.

Ferme, Mariane C. "Deterritorialized Citizenship and the Resonances of the Sierra Leonean State." In *Anthropology in the Margins of the State*, edited by Veena Das and Deborah Poole, 81–116. Santa Fe: School of American Research Press, 2004.

Finch, Michael P. M. *A Progressive Occupation? The Gallieni-Lyautey Method and Colonial Pacification in Tonkin and Madagascar, 1885–1900.* Oxford: Oxford University Press, 2013.

Firpo, Christina Elizabeth. *The Uprooted: Race, Children, and Imperialism in French Indochina, 1890–1980.* Honolulu: University of Hawai'i Press, 2016.

Fletcher, Yaël Simpson. "Unsettling Settlers: Colonial Migrants and Racialised Sexuality in Interwar Marseilles." In *Gender, Sexuality, and Colonial Modernities*, edited by Antoinette Burton, 79–93. New York: Routledge, 1999.

Fogarty, Richard S. *Race and War in France: Colonial Subjects in the French Army, 1914–1918.* Baltimore: Johns Hopkins University Press, 2008.

Foster, Elizabeth A. *Faith in Empire: Religion, Politics, and Colonial Rule in French Senegal, 1880–1940.* Stanford, CA: Stanford University Press, 2013.

Foucault, Michel. *The History of Sexuality: An Introduction.* Translated by Robert Hurley. New York: Vintage, 1990.
———. "Nietzsche, Genealogy, History." In *The Foucault Reader*, edited by Paul Rabinow, 76–100. New York: Pantheon Books, 1984.
Foster, Elizabeth A. *Faith in Empire: Religion, Politics, and Colonial Rule in French Senegal, 1880–1940.* Stanford, CA: Stanford University Press, 2013.
Frey, Henri. *Campagne dans le haut Sénégal et dans le haut Niger (1885–1886).* Paris: Plon, 1888.
Galli, Henri. *La guerre à Madagascar: Histoire anecdotique des expeditions françaises de 1885 à 1895.* Paris: Garnier, 1897.
Gallieni, Joseph-Simon. *Deux campagnes au Soudan français, 1886–1888.* Paris: Hachette, 1891.
———. *Neuf ans à Madagascar.* Paris: Hachette, 1908.
Gavron, Laurence, dir. *Si loin du Vietnam.* Senegal: Mbokki Mbaar Productions, 2016.
Gelvin, James L. *Divided Loyalties: Nationalism and Mass Politics in Syria at the Close of Empire.* Berkeley: University of California Press, 1998.
Germain, Félix, and Silyane Larcher, eds. *Black French Women and the Struggle for Equality, 1848–2016.* Lincoln: University of Nebraska Press, 2018.
Gershovich, Moshe. *French Military Rule in Morocco: Colonialism and Its Consequences.* London: Frank Cass, 2000.
Getz, Trevor R. *Slavery and Reform in West Africa: Toward Emancipation in Nineteenth-Century Senegal and the Gold Coast.* Athens: Ohio University Press, 2004.
Getz, Trevor R., and Liz Clarke, *Abina and the Important Men: A Graphic History.* New York: Oxford University Press, 2012.
Geva, Dorit. *Conscription, Family, and the Modern State: A Comparative Study of France and the United States.* Cambridge: Cambridge University Press, 2013.
Ghosh, Durba. *Sex and the Family in Colonial India: The Making of Empire.* Cambridge: Cambridge University Press, 2006.
Giblin, James. "Passages in a Struggle over the Past: Stories of Maji Maji in Njombe, Tanzania." In *Sources and Methods in African History: Spoken, Written, Unearthed*, edited by Toyin Falola and Christian Jennings, 295–311. Rochester, NY: University of Rochester Press, 2003.
———. "The Victimization of Women in Late Precolonial and Early Colonial Warfare in Tanzania." In *Sexual Violence in Conflict Zones: From the Ancient World to the Era of Human Rights*, edited by Elizabeth D. Heineman, 89–102. Philadelphia: University of Pennsylvania Press, 2011.
Gill, Aisha K., and Sundari Anitha, eds. *Forced Marriage: Introducing a Social Justice and Human Rights Perspective.* New York: Zed Books, 2011.
Ginio, Ruth. "African Soldiers, French Women, and Colonial Fears during and after World War II." In *Africa and World War II*, edited by Byfield et al., 324–38. Cambridge: Cambridge University Press, 2015.
———. "'Cherchez la femme': African Gendarmes, Quarrelsome Women, and French Commanders in French West Africa, 1945–1960." *International Journal of African Historical Studies* 47, no. 1 (2014): 37–53.

———. *The French Army and Its African Soldiers: The Years of Decolonization.* Lincoln: University of Nebraska Press, 2017.

———. *French Colonialism Unmasked: The Vichy Years in French West Africa.* Lincoln: University of Nebraska Press, 2006.

Glasman, Joël. "Penser les intermédiaires coloniaux: Note sur les dossiers de carrière de la police du Togo." *History in Africa* 37 (2010): 51–81.

Goerg, Odile. "Femmes adultères, hommes voleurs? La 'justice indigène' en Guinée." *Cahiers d'études africaines* 47, no. 187/188 (2007): 495–522.

Gomez, Michael A. *Pragmatism in the Age of Jihad: The Precolonial State of Bundu.* Cambridge: Cambridge University Press, 1992.

Goodman, R. David. "Expediency, Ambivalence, and Inaction: The French Protectorate and Domestic Slavery in Morocco, 1912–1956." *Journal of Social History* 47, no. 1 (Fall 2013): 101–31.

Gouraud, Henri Joseph Eugène. *Souvenirs d'un africain.* Vol. 1, *Au Soudan.* Paris: Pierre Tisné, 1939.

Gray, Christopher. *Colonial Rule and Crisis in Equatorial Africa: Southern Gabon, ca. 1850–1940.* Rochester, NY: University of Rochester Press, 2002.

Grosclaude, Étienne. *Un parisien à Madagascar.* Paris: Hachette, 1898.

Guèye, Marc. *Un tirailleur sénégalais dans la guerre d'Indochine, 1953–1955.* Dakar: Presses Universitaires de Dakar, 2007.

Guilleux, Charles. *Journal de route d'un caporal de tirailleurs de la mission saharienne (mission Foureau-Lamy), 1898–1900.* Belfort, France: Schmitt, 1904.

Guiral, Léon. *Le Congo français du Gabon à Brazzaville.* Paris: Plon, 1889.

Gullace, Nicoletta F. *"The Blood of Our Sons": Men, Women, and the Renegotiation of British Citizenship during the Great War.* New York: Palgrave Macmillan, 2002.

Guyer, Jane I., and Samuel M. Eno Belinga. "Wealth in People as Wealth in Knowledge: Accumulation and Composition in Equatorial Africa." *Journal of African History* 36, no. 1 (March 1995): 91–120.

Hacker, Barton C. "Women and Military Institutions in Early Modern Europe: A Reconnaissance." *Signs* 6, no. 4 (Summer 1981): 643–71.

Hale, Dana S. *Races on Display: French Representations of Colonized Peoples, 1886–1940.* Bloomington: Indiana University Press, 2008.

Hall, Bruce S. *A History of Race in Muslim West Africa, 1600–1960.* Cambridge: Cambridge University Press, 2011.

———. "The Question of 'Race' in the Pre-colonial Southern Sahara." *Journal of North African Studies* 10, no. 3/4 (2005): 339–67.

Hamel, Chouki El. *Black Morocco: A History of Slavery, Race, and Islam.* Cambridge: Cambridge University Press, 2013.

———. "Blacks and Slavery in Morocco: The Question of the Haratin at the End of the Seventeenth Century." In *Diasporic Africa: A Reader*, edited by Michael A. Gomez, 177–99. New York: New York University Press, 2006.

———. "'Race,' Slavery, and Islam in Maghrebi Mediterranean Thought: The Question of the *Haratin* in Morocco." *Journal of North African Studies* 7, no. 3 (2002): 29–52.

Bibliography

Hamilton, Carolyn. *Terrific Majesty: The Powers of Shaka Zulu and the Limits of Historical Invention.* Cambridge, MA: Harvard University Press, 1998.

Hannaford, Dinah. *Marriage without Borders: Transnational Spouses in Neoliberal Senegal.* Philadelphia: University of Pennsylvania Press, 2017.

Hardy, Michel Serge. *De la morale au moral des troupes ou l'histoire des B.M.C, 1918–2004.* Panazol, France: Lavauzelle, 2004.

Hay, Margaret Jean, and Marcia Wright, eds. *African Women and the Law: Historical Perspectives.* Boston: Boston University African Studies Center, 1982.

Hoffman, Danny. *The War Machines: Young Men and Violence in Sierra Leone and Liberia.* Durham, NC: Duke University Press, 2011.

Höhn, Maria. *GIs and Fräuleins: the German-American Encounter in 1950s West Germany.* Chapel Hill: University of North Carolina Press, 2002.

"Hollande naturalise 28 anciens tirailleurs sénégalais." *Ouest-France*, 15 April 2017. Accessed 28 October 2018. https://www.ouest-france.fr/culture/histoire/d-anciens-tirailleurs-senegalais-naturalises-francais-4931136.

Huguier, Michel. *De Gaulle, Roosevelt et l'Indochine de 1940 à 1945.* Paris: Harmattan, 2010.

Hunt, Nancy Rose. "The Affective, the Intellectual, and Gender History." *Journal of African History* 55, no. 3 (November 2014): 331–45.

Hunter, Tera W. *Bound in Wedlock: Slave and Free Black Marriage in the Nineteenth Century.* Cambridge, MA: Belknap Press of Harvard University Press, 2017.

Hurl-Eamon, Jennine. *Marriage and the British Army in the Long Eighteenth Century: "The Girl I Left behind Me."* Oxford: Oxford University Press, 2014.

Hynd, Stacey. "'To Be Taken as a Wife Is a Form of Death': The Social, Military and Humanitarian Dynamics of Forced Marriage and Girl Soldiers in African Conflicts, c. 1999–2010." In *Marriage by Force? Contestation over Consent and Coercion in Africa*, edited by Annie Bunting, Benjamin N. Lawrance, and Richard Roberts, 292–312. Athens: Ohio University Press, 2016.

Isaacman, Allen, and Barbara Isaacman. "Resistance and Collaboration in Southern and Central Africa, c. 1850–1920." *International Journal of African Historical Studies* 10, no. 1 (1977): 31–62.

Jean-Baptiste, Rachel. *Conjugal Rights: Marriage, Sexuality, and Urban Life in Colonial Libreville, Gabon.* Athens: Ohio University Press, 2014.

Jeater, Diana. *Marriage, Perversion, and Power: The Construction of Moral Discourse in Southern Rhodesia, 1894–1930.* Oxford: Clarendon, 1993.

Jennings, Eric T. *Free French Africa in World War II: The African Resistance.* Cambridge: Cambridge University Press, 2015.

———. *Vichy in the Tropics: Pétain's National Revolution in Madagascar, Guadeloupe, and Indochina, 1940–1944.* Stanford, CA: Stanford University Press, 2001.

Jennings, Lawrence C. *French Anti-Slavery: The Movement for the Abolition of Slavery in France, 1802–1848.* Cambridge: Cambridge University Press, 2000.

Johnson, G. Wesley, Jr. *The Emergence of Black Politics in Senegal: The Struggle for Power in the Four Communes, 1900–1920.* Stanford, CA: Stanford University Press, 1971.

Bibliography

Jones, Hilary. "From *Mariage à la Mode* to Weddings at Town Hall: Marriage, Colonialism, and Mixed-Race Society in Nineteenth-Century Senegal." *International Journal of African Historical Studies* 38, no. 1 (2005): 27–48.

———. *The Métis of Senegal: Urban Life and Politics in French West Africa*. Bloomington: Indiana University Press, 2013.

———. "Originaire Women and Political Life in Senegal's Four Communes." In *Black French Women and the Struggle for Equality, 1848–2016*, edited by Félix Germain and Silyane Larcher, 3–18. Lincoln: University of Nebraska Press, 2018.

Kaba, Lansiné. "Archers, Musketeers, and Mosquitos: The Moroccan Invasion of the Sudan and the Songhay Resistance (1591–1612)." *Journal of African History* 22 (1981): 457–75.

———. "From Colonialism to Autocracy: Guinea under Sékou Touré, 1957–1984." In *Decolonization and African Independence: The Transfers of Power, 1960–1980*, edited by Prosser Gifford and Wm. Roger Louis, 225–44. New Haven, CT: Yale University Press, 1988.

Kale, Madhavi. *Fragments of Empire: Capital, Slavery, and Indian Indentured Labor Migration in the British Caribbean*. Philadelphia: University of Pennsylvania Press, 1998.

Kanya-Forstner, Alexander S. *The Conquest of Western Sudan: A Study in French Military Imperialism*. London: Cambridge University Press, 1969.

Katz, Jonathan G. "The 1907 Mauchamp Affair and the French Civilizing Mission in Morocco." *Journal of North African Studies* 6, no. 1 (Spring 2001): 143–66.

Keaton, Trica Danielle, T. Denean Sharpley-Whiting, and Tyler Stovall, eds. *Black France / France Noire: The History and Politics of Blackness*. Durham, NC: Duke University Press, 2012.

Kéïta, Sidiki Kobélé. *Des complots contre la Guinée de Sékou Touré (1958–1984)*. Conakry: Les Classiques Guinéens, 2002.

Khiat, Salim. "De la négrophobie en Algérie: Autopsie des mots qui disent le Mal en couleurs." In *Noirs au Maghreb: Enjeux identitaires*, edited by Stéphanie Pouessel, 63–74. Paris: Karthala, 2012.

Khorat, Pierre. *Scènes de la pacification marocaine*. Paris: Perrin, 1914.

Khoury, Philip Shukry. *Syria and the French Mandate: The Politics of Arab Nationalism, 1920–1945*. Princeton, NJ: Princeton University Press, 1987.

Killingray, David. "Gender Issues and African Colonial Armies." In *Guardians of Empire: The Armed Forces of the Colonial Powers c. 1700–1964*, edited by David Killingray and David Omissi, 221–48. Manchester: Manchester University Press, 1999.

Killingray, David, and Richard Rathbone, eds. *Africa and the Second World War*. London: Macmillan, 1986.

Klein, Martin A. "Sexuality and Slavery in the Western Sudan." In *Sex, Power, and Slavery*, edited by Gwyn Campbell and Elizabeth Elbourne, 61–82. Athens: Ohio University Press, 2015.

———. *Slavery and Colonial Rule in French West Africa*. Cambridge: Cambridge University Press, 1998.

Bibliography

Klein, Martin A., and Richard Roberts. "Gender and Emancipation in French West Africa." In *Gender and Slave Emancipation in the Atlantic World*, edited by Pamela Scully and Diana Paton, 162–80. Durham, NC: Duke University Press, 2005.

Klobb, Jean-François Arsène. *Dernier carnet de route: Au Soudan français: Rapport officiel de M. le gouverneur Bergès sur la fin de la mission Klobb*. Paris: Ernest Flammarion, 1905.

Koller, Christian. "Recruitment Policies and Recruitment Experiences in the French Foreign Legion." In *Transnational Soldiers: Foreign Military Enlistment in the Modern Era*, edited by Nir Arielli and Bruce Collins, 87–104. New York: Palgrave Macmillan, 2013.

Kopytoff, Igor, and Suzanne Miers. "African 'Slavery' as an Institution of Marginality." In *Slavery in Africa: Historical and Anthropological Perspectives*, edited by Suzanne Miers and Igor Kopytoff, 3–81. Madison: University of Wisconsin Press, 1977.

Laband, John, ed. *Daily Lives of Civilians in Wartime Africa: From Slavery Days to Rwandan Genocide*. Westport, CT: Greenwood Press, 2006.

Lamothe, Ronald M. *Slaves of Fortune: Sudanese Soldiers and the River War, 1896–1898*. Rochester, NY: James Currey, 2011.

Last, Dick van Galen. *Black Shame: African Soldiers in Europe, 1914–1922*. Translated by Marjolijn de Jager. New York: Bloomsbury Academic, 2015.

Lautour, Gaston. *Journal d'un spahi au Soudan, 1897–1899*. Paris: Perrin, 1909.

Law, Robin. "The 'Amazons' of Dahomey." *Paideuma: Mitteilungen zur Kulturkunde* 39 (1993): 245–60.

Lawler, Nancy Ellen. *Soldiers of Misfortune: Ivoirien Tirailleurs of World War II*. Athens: Ohio University Press, 1992.

Lawrance, Benjamin N., Emily Lynn Osborn, and Richard L. Roberts, eds. *Intermediaries, Interpreters, and Clerks: African Employees in the Making of Colonial Africa*. Madison: University of Wisconsin Press, 2006.

Lee, Christopher J. *Frantz Fanon: Toward a Revolutionary Humanism*. Athens: Ohio University Press, 2015.

———. *Unreasonable Histories: Nativism, Multiracial Lives, and the Genealogical Imagination in British Africa*. Durham, NC: Duke University Press, 2014.

Legassick, Martin. "Firearms, Horses and Samorian Army Organization 1870–1898." *Journal of African History* 7, no. 1 (1966): 95–115.

Lejeune, Léon. *Au Congo: La femme et la famille*. Paris: A. Challamel, 1900.

Le Roy, Alexandre. "Comment-on civilise les races primitives." *Univers*, 15 December 1899.

Lessard, Micheline. *Human Trafficking in Colonial Vietnam*. New York: Routledge, 2015.

Levine, Philippa. *Prostitution, Race, and Politics: Policing Venereal Disease in the British Empire*. New York: Routledge, 2003.

Lindsay, Lisa A. "Domesticity and Difference: Male Breadwinners, Working Women, and Colonial Citizenship in the 1945 Nigerian General Strike." *American Historical Review* 104, no. 3 (June 1999): 783–812.

———. *Working with Gender: Wage Labor and Social Change in Southwestern Nigeria*. Portsmouth, NH: Heinemann, 2003.

Lindsay, Lisa, and Stephan Miescher, eds. *Men and Masculinities in Modern Africa*. Portsmouth: Heinemann, 2003.
Lovejoy, Paul. "Concubinage and the Status of Women Slaves in Early Colonial Northern Nigeria." *Journal of African History* 29, no. 2 (1988): 245–66
Lunn, Joe. "'*Bon Soldats*' and '*Sales Nègres*': Changing French Perceptions of West African Soldiers during the First World War." *French Colonial History* 1 (2002): 1–16.

———. "Kande Kamara Speaks: An Oral History of the West African Experience in France 1914–18." In *Africa and the First World War*, edited by Melvin E. Page and Andy McKinlay, 28–53. London: Macmillan, 1987.

———. "'Les Races Guerrières': Racial Preconceptions in the French Military about West African Soldiers during the First World War." *Journal of Contemporary History* 34, no. 4 (October 1999): 517–36.

———. "Male Identity and Martial Codes of Honor: A Comparison of the War Memoirs of Robert Graves, Ernst Jünger, and Kande Kamara." *Journal of Military History* 69, no. 3 (July 2005): 713–35.

———. *Memoirs of the Maelstrom: A Senegalese Oral History of the First World War*. Portsmouth, NH: Heinemann, 1999.

———. "Remembering the *Tirailleurs Sénégalais* and the Great War: Oral History as a Methodology of Inclusion in French Colonial Studies." *French Colonial History* 10 (2009): 125–49.

Lydon, Ghislaine. "Droit islamique et droits de la femme d'après les registres du Tribunal Musulman de Ndar (Saint-Louis du Sénégal)." *Canadian Journal of African Studies* 41, no. 2 (2007): 289–307.
Lynn, John A., II. *Women, Armies, and Warfare in Early Modern Europe*. Cambridge: Cambridge University Press, 2008.
Lyons, Tanya. *Guns and Guerilla Girls: Women in the Zimbabwean National Liberation Struggle*. Trenton, NJ: Africa World Press, 2004.
Mabon, Armelle. "La tragédie de Thiaroye, symbole du déni d'égalité." *Hommes et Migrations*, no. 1235 (January–February 2002): 86–95.

———. *Prisonniers de guerre "indigènes": Visages oubliés de la France occupée*. Paris: La Découverte, 2010.

Mack, Beverley B. "Women and Slavery in Nineteenth-Century Hausaland." In *The Human Commodity: Perspectives on the Trans-Saharan Slave Trade*, edited by Elizabeth Savage, 89–110. Portland, OR: Frank Cass, 1992.
Mama, Amina, and Margo Okazawa-Rey. "Militarism, Conflict and Women's Activism in the Global Era: Challenges and Prospects for Women in Three West African Contexts." *Feminist Review*, no. 101 (2012): 97–123.
Mamdani, Mahmood. *Citizen and Subject: Contemporary Africa and the Legacy of Late Colonialism*. Princeton, NJ: Princeton University Press, 1996.
Manby, Bronwyn. *Citizenship Law in Africa: A Comparative Study*. 2nd ed. New York: Open Society Foundations, 2010.
Manchuelle, François. "The 'Patriarchal Ideal' of Soninke Labor Migrants: From Slave Owners to Employers of Free Labor." *Canadian Journal of African Studies* 23, no. 1 (1989): 106–25.

Bibliography

———. *Willing Migrants: Soninke Labor Diasporas, 1848–1960*. Athens: Ohio University Press, 1997.
Mangin, Charles. *La force noire*. Paris: Hachette, 1910.
Mann, Gregory. "Immigrants and Arguments in France and West Africa." *Comparative Studies in Society and History* 45, no. 2 (April 2003): 362–85.
———. *Native Sons: West African Veterans and France in the Twentieth Century*. Durham, NC: Duke University Press, 2006.
———. "Old Soldiers, Young Men: Masculinity, Islam, and Military Veterans in Late 1950s Soudan Français (Mali)." In *Men and Masculinities in Modern Africa*, edited by Lisa A. Lindsay and Stephan F. Miescher, 69–86. Portsmouth, NH: Heinemann, 2003.
———. "What's in an Alias? Family Names, Individual Histories, and Historical Method in the Western Sudan." *History in Africa* 29 (2002): 309–20.
———. "What was the *Indigénat*? The 'Empire of Law' in French West Africa." *Journal of African History* 50, no. 3 (2009): 331–53.
Mann, Kristin. *Marrying Well: Marriage, Status and Social Change among the Educated Elite in Colonial Lagos*. Cambridge: Cambridge University Press, 1985.
Mann, Kristin, and Richard Roberts, eds. *Law in Colonial Africa*. Portsmouth, NH: Heinemann, 1991.
Marceau, Hippolyte. *Le tirailleur soudanais*. Paris: Berger-Levrault, 1911.
Marcson, Michael David. "European-African Interaction in the Precolonial Period: Saint Louis, Senegal, 1758–1854." PhD diss., Princeton University, 1976.
Martin, Phyllis M. *Leisure and Society in Colonial Brazzaville*. Cambridge: Cambridge University Press, 1995.
Matsuda, Matt K. *Empire of Love: Histories of France and the Pacific*. Oxford: Oxford University Press, 2005.
Mayer, Holly A. *Belonging to the Army: Camp Followers and Community during the American Revolution*. Columbia: University of South Carolina Press, 1996.
Mbembe, Achille. "African Modes of Self-Writing." Translated by Steven Rendall. *Public Culture* 14, no. 1 (Winter 2002) 239–73.
McDougall, E. Ann. "Discourse and Distortion: Critical Reflections on Studying the Saharan Slave Trade." *Outre-mers: Revue d'histoire* 89, no. 336/337 (2002): 195–227.
———. "A Sense of Self: The Life of Fatma Barka." *Canadian Journal of African Studies* 32, no. 2 (1998): 285–315.
McFadden, Patricia. "Plunder as Statecraft: Militarism and Resistance in Neocolonial Africa." In *Security Disarmed: Critical Perspectives on Gender, Race, and Militarization*, edited by Barbara Sutton, Sandra Morgen, and Julie Novkov, 136–56. New Brunswick, NJ: Rutgers University Press, 2008.
McHale, Shawn. "Understanding the Fanatic Mind? The Việt Minh and Race Hatred in the First Indochina War (1945–1954)." *Journal of Vietnamese Studies* 4, no. 3 (Fall 2009): 98–138.
McMahon, Elizabeth. *Slavery and Emancipation in Islamic East Africa: From Honor to Respectability*. Cambridge: Cambridge University Press, 2013.

Bibliography

Meillassoux, Claude. *The Anthropology of Slavery: The Womb of Iron and Gold*. Chicago: University of Chicago Press, 1991.

Meyers, Allan R. "Class, Ethnicity, and Slavery: The Origins of the Moroccan 'Abid." *International Journal of African Historical Studies* 10, no. 3 (1997): 427–42.

Michel, Marc. *L'Afrique dans l'engrenage de la Grande Guerre, 1914–1918*. Paris: Karthala, 2013.

———. *L'appel à l'Afrique: Contributions et réactions à l'effort de guerre en A.O.F. (1914–1919)*. Paris: Publications de la Sorbonne, 1982.

———. "L'armée colonial en Afrique occidentale française." In *L'Afrique occidentale au temps des Français: Colonisateurs et colonisés (c. 1860–1960)*, edited by Catherine Coquery-Vidrovitch, 57–78. Paris: La Découverte, 1992.

Miescher, Stephan. *Making Men in Ghana*. Bloomington: Indiana University Press, 2005.

Miller, Christopher L. *Blank Darkness: Africanist Discourse in French*. Chicago: University of Chicago Press, 1985.

Mills, Ivy. "Sutura: Gendered Honor, Social Death, and the Politics of Exposure in Senegalese Literature and Popular Culture." PhD diss., University of California, Berkeley, 2011.

Mittelstadt, Jennifer. *The Rise of the Military Welfare State*. Cambridge, MA: Harvard University Press, 2015.

Mirza, Sarah, and Margaret Strobel, eds. *Three Swahili Women: Life Histories from Mombasa, Kenya*. Bloomington: Indiana University Press, 1989.

Monson, Jamie. "*Maisha*: Life History and the History of Livelihood along the TAZARA Railway in Tanzania." In *Sources and Methods in African History: Spoken, Written, Unearthed*, edited by Toyin Falola and Christian Jennings, 312–30. Rochester: University of Rochester Press, 2003.

Monteil, Parfait-Louis. *De Saint-Louis à Tripoli par le Lac Tchad*. Paris: Félix Alcan, 1895.

Mora-Kpai, Idrissou, dir. *Indochine, sur les traces d'une* mère. France: MKJ Films, 2011.

Morgenthau, Ruth Schachter. *Political Parties in French-Speaking West Africa*. Oxford: Clarendon, 1964.

Mourre, Martin. *Thiaroye 1944: Histoire et memoire d'un massacre colonial*. Rennes, France: Presses Universitaires de Rennes, 2017.

Moyd, Michelle. "Making the Household, Making the State: Colonial Military Communities and Labor in German East Africa." *International Labor and Working-Class History*, no. 80 (Fall 2011): 53–76.

———. *Violent Intermediaries: African Soldiers, Conquest, and Everyday Colonialism in German East Africa*. Athens: Ohio University Press, 2014.

Ndiaye, Awa, and Mbaye Gana Kébé. *Un président au service des tirailleurs*. Dakar: Maguilen, 2007.

Nelson, Keith L. "The 'Black Horror on the Rhine': Race as a Factor in Post–World War I Diplomacy." *Journal of Modern History* 42, no. 4 (December 1970): 606–27.

Niane, Anne-Marie. *L'étrangère*. Paris: Hatier International, 2002.

Nora, Pierre. "Between Memory and History: *Les Lieux de Mémoire*." *Representations*, no. 26 (Spring 1989): 7–24.

Bibliography

———. "General Introduction: Between Memory and History." In *Realms of Memory: Rethinking the French Past*, vol. 1, *Conflicts and Divisions*, edited by Pierre Nora, English-language edition edited by Lawrence D. Kritzman, translated by Arthur Goldhammer, 1–20. New York: Columbia University Press, 1996.

Obissier, Louis-Jules-Albin. *Notice sur les tirailleurs sénégalais (race, caractères, moeurs et coutumes)*. Tananarive: Typographie de l'Etat-Major, 1903.

Onana, Charles. *1940–1945: Noirs blancs beurs: Libérateurs de la France*. Paris: Duboiris, 2006.

Osborn, Emily Lynn. *Our New Husbands Are Here: Households, Gender, and Politics in a West African State from the Slave Trade to Colonial Rule*. Athens: Ohio University Press, 2011.

Osborne, Michael A., and Richard F. Fogarty. "Views from the Periphery: Discourses of Race and Place in French Military Medicine." *History and Philosophy of Life Sciences* 25, no. 3 (2003): 363–89.

Osborne, Myles. *Ethnicity and Empire in Kenya: Loyalty and Martial Race among the Kamba, c. 1800 to the Present*. Cambridge: Cambridge University Press, 2014.

Oyěwùmí, Oyěrónkẹ́. *The Invention of Women: Making an African Sense of Western Gender Discourses*. Minneapolis: University of Minnesota Press, 1997.

Parsons, Timothy H. *The African Rank-and-File: Social Implications of Colonial Military Service in the King's African Rifles, 1902–1964*. Portsmouth, NH: Heinemann, 1999.

———. "All *Askaris* Are Family Men: Sex, Domesticity and Discipline in the King's African Rifles, 1902–1964." In *Guardians of Empire: The Armed Forces of the Colonial Powers c. 1700–1964*, edited by David Killingray and David Omissi, 157–78. Manchester: Manchester University Press, 1999.

Pateman, Carole. "Women and Consent." *Political Theory* 8, no. 2 (May 1980): 149–68.

Paton, Diana, and Pamela Scully. "Introduction: Gender and Slave Emancipation in Comparative Perspective." In *Gender and Slave Emancipation in the Atlantic World*, edited by Scully and Paton, 1–34. Durham, NC: Duke University Press, 2005.

Peabody, Sue. *There Are No Slaves in France: The Political Culture of Race and Slavery in the Ancien Régime*. New York: Oxford University Press, 1996.

Pedersen, Jean Elisabeth. *Legislating the French Family: Feminism, Theater, and Republican Politics, 1870–1920*. New Brunswick, NJ: Rutgers University Press, 2003.

Pedersen, Susan. *Family, Dependence, and the Origins of the Welfare State: Britain and France, 1914–1945*. Cambridge: Cambridge University Press, 1993.

Perinbam, B. Marie. *Family Identity and the State in the Bamako Kafu, c. 1800–c. 1900*. Boulder, CO: Westview Press, 1997.

Péroz, Marie Étienne. *Au Soudan français: Souvenirs de guerre et de mission*. Paris: Callman Lévy, 1891.

Perry, Adele. *Colonial Relations: The Douglas-Connolly Family and the Nineteenth-Century Imperial World*. Cambridge: Cambridge University Press, 2015).

Person, Yves. *Samori: Une revolution Dyula*. 3 vols. Dakar: IFAN, 1968–75.

Pesnot, Patrick. *Les dessous de la Françafrique: Les dossiers secret de Monsieur X*. Paris: Nouveau Monde, 2014.

Bibliography

Peterson, Brian J. "History, Memory, and the Legacy of Samori in Southern Mali, c. 1880–1898." *Journal of African History* 49, no. 2 (2008): 261–79.

Peyton, Nellie. "How Spring Rolls Got to Senegal." Roads and Kingdoms, 6 November 2016. Accessed 21 May, 2017. https://roadsandkingdoms.com/2016/spring-rolls-got-senegal.

Vũ Trọng Phụng, *Lục Xì: Prostitution and Venereal Disease in Colonial Hanoi*. Translated by Shaun Kingsley Malarney. Honolulu: University of Hawai'i Press, 2011.

Pierce, Steven. "Farmers and 'Prostitutes': Twentieth-Century Problems of Female Inheritance in Kano Emirate, Nigeria." *Journal of African History* 44, no. 3 (2003): 463–86.

Planche, Jean-Louis. *Sétif 1945: Histoire d'un massacre annoncé*. Paris: Perrin, 2006.

Pollard, Miranda. *Reign of Virtue: Mobilizing Gender in Vichy France*. Chicago: University of Chicago Press, 1998.

Proschan, Frank. "'Syphilis, Opiomania, and Pederasty': Colonial Constructions of Vietnamese (and French) Social Diseases." *Journal of the History of Sexuality* 11, no. 4 (October 2002): 610–36.

Provence, Michael. *The Great Syrian Revolt and the Rise of Arab Nationalism*. Austin: University of Texas Press, 2005.

Quirk, Joel, and Darshan Vigneswaran. "Mobility Makes States." In *Mobility Makes States: Migration and Power in Africa*, edited by Vigneswaran and Quirk, 1–34. Philadelphia: University of Pennsylvania Press, 2015.

Rabut, Elisabeth. *Brazza, commissaire général: Le Congo français 1886–1897*. Paris: Éditions de l'École des Hautes Études en Sciences Sociales, 1989.

Raffin, Anne. *Youth Mobilization in Vichy Indochina and Its Legacies, 1940 to 1970*. Lanham, MD: Lexington Books, 2005.

Randrianja, Solofo. *Société et luttes anticoloniales à Madagascar de 1896 à 1946*. Paris: Karthala, 2001.

Randrianja, Solofo, and Stephen Ellis. *Madagascar: A Short History*. Chicago: University of Chicago Press, 2009.

Ranger, Terence O. "The Invention of Tradition in Colonial Africa." In *The Invention of Tradition*, edited by Eric Hobsbawm and Terence Ranger, 211–62. Cambridge: Cambridge University Press, 1983.

———. *Revolt in Southern Rhodesia, 1896–97: A Study in African Resistance*. London: Heinemann, 1967.

Ray, Carina E. *Crossing the Color Line: Race, Sex, and the Contested Politics of Colonialism in Ghana*. Athens: Ohio University Press, 2015.

Renault, François. *Libération d'esclaves et nouvelle servitude*. Dakar: Nouvelles Éditions Africaines, 1976.

Rice, Laura. "African Conscripts/European Conflicts: Race, Memory, and the Lessons of War." *Cultural Critique* 45 (Spring 2000): 109–49.

Rich, Jeremy. "Where Every Language Is Heard: Atlantic Commerce, West African and Asian Migrants, and Town Society in Libreville, ca. 1860–1914." In *African Urban Spaces in Historical Perspective*, edited by Steven J. Salm and Toyin Falola, 191–212. Rochester, NY: University of Rochester Press, 2005.

Bibliography

Rives, Maurice, and Robert Dietrich. *Héros méconnus, 1914–1918, 1939–1945: Mémorial des combattants d'Afrique noire et de Madagascar.* Paris: Association Française Frères d'Armes, 1990.

Rivet, Daniel. *Lyautey et l'institution du protectorat français au Maroc, 1912–1925.* Vol. 2. Paris: Harmattan, 1988.

Robcis, Camille. *The Law of Kinship: Anthropology, Psychoanalysis, and the Family in France.* Ithaca, NY: Cornell University Press, 2013.

Roberts, Mary Louise. *What Soldiers Do: Sex and the American GI in World War II France.* Chicago: University of Chicago Press, 2013.

Roberts, Richard. "The Case of Faama Mademba Sy and the Ambiguities of Legal Jurisdiction in Early Colonial French Soudan." In *Law in Colonial Africa*, edited by Kristin Mann and Richard Roberts, 185–201. Portsmouth, NH: Heinemann, 1991.

———. "History and Memory: The Power of Statist Narratives." *International Journal of African Historical Studies* 33, no. 3 (2000): 513–22.

———. *Litigants and Households: African Disputes and Colonial Courts in the French Soudan, 1895–1912.* Portsmouth, NH: Heinemann, 2005.

———. "Long Distance Trade and Production: Sinsani in the Nineteenth Century." *Journal of African History* 21, no. 2 (1980): 169–88.

———. *Warriors, Merchants, and Slaves: The State and the Economy in the Middle Niger Valley, 1700–1914.* Stanford, CA: Stanford University Press, 1987.

Robertson, Claire C., and Martin A. Klein. "Women's Importance in African Slave Systems." In *Women and Slavery in Africa*, edited by Robertson and Klein, 3–19. Portsmouth, NH: Heinemann, 1997.

Rodet, Marie. "Continuum of Gendered Violence: The Colonial Invention of Female Desertion as a Customary Criminal Offense, French Soudan, 1900–1949." In *Domestic Violence and the Law in Colonial and Postcolonial Africa*, edited by Emily S. Burrill, Richard L. Roberts, and Elizabeth Thornberry, 74–93. Athens: Ohio University Press, 2010.

———. "'Le délit d'abandon de domicile conjugal' ou l'invasion du pénal colonial dans les jugements des 'tribunaux indigènes' au Soudan français, 1900–1947." *French Colonial History* 10 (2009): 151–69.

———. *Les migrantes ignorées du Haut-Sénégal (1900–1946).* Paris: Karthala, 2009.

———. "Le sous-lieutenant Mansouka (c. 1860–1920): Un parcours d'esclave affranchi entre rébellion et allégeance au temps de la conquête coloniale française en Afrique." In *Résistances et mémoires des esclavages: Espaces arabo-musulmans et transatlantiques*, edited by Olivier Leservoisier and Salah Trabeisi, 75–97. Paris: Karthala, 2014.

———. "Sexualité, mariage, et esclavage au Soudan français à la fin du XIXe siècle." *CLIO: Femmes, Genre, Histoire*, no. 33 (2011): 45–64.

Roos, Julia. "Nationalism, Racism and Propaganda in Early Weimar Germany: Contradictions in the Campaign against the 'Black Horror on the Rhine.'" *German History* 30, no. 1 (2012): 45–74.

Bibliography

Rossi, Benedetta. "Introduction: Rethinking Slavery in West Africa." In *Reconfiguring Slavery: West African Trajectories*, edited by Benedetta Rossi, 1–25. Liverpool: Liverpool University Press, 2009.

Rydstrom, Helle. "The Politics of Colonial Violence: Gendered Atrocities in French Occupied Vietnam." *European Journal of Women's Studies* 22, no. 2 (May 2015): 191–207.

Saada, Emmanuelle. *Empire's Children: Race, Filiation, and Citizenship in the French Colonies*. Chicago: University of Chicago Press, 2012.

Sackur, Karen Amanda. "The Development of Creole Society and Culture in Saint-Louis and Gorée, 1719–1817." PhD diss., School of Oriental and African Studies, University of London, 1999.

Saletes, Jean-Loup. "Les tirailleurs sénégalais dans la Grande Guerre et la codification d'un racisme ordinaire." *Guerres mondiales et conflits contemporains*, no. 244 (December 2011): 129–40.

Sarich, Jody, Michele Olivier, and Kevin Bales. "Forced Marriage, Slavery, and Plural Legal Systems: An African Example." *Human Rights Quarterly* 38, no. 2 (May 2016): 450–76.

Sarzeau, J. [pseud]. *Les Français aux colonies: Sénégal et Soudan français, Dahomey, Madagascar, Tunisie*. Paris: Bloud et Barral, 1897.

Savaron, Calixte. *Mes souvenirs à Madagascar avant et après la conquête (1885–1898)*. Tananarive: G. Pitot, 1932.

Scheck, Raffael, *Hitler's African Victims: The German Army Massacres of Black French Soldiers in 1940*. Cambridge: Cambridge University Press, 2006.

Schmidt, Elizabeth. "Anticolonial Nationalism in French West Africa: What Made Guinea Unique?" *African Studies Review* 52, no. 2 (September 2009): 1–34.

Scott, Joan Wallach. *Gender and the Politics of History*. Rev. ed. New York: Columbia University Press, 1999.

Scully, Pamela. "Gender, History, and Human Rights." In *Gender and Culture at the Limit of Rights*, edited by Dorothy L. Hodgson, 17–31. Philadelphia: University of Pennsylvania Press, 2011.

———. *Liberating the Family? Gender and British Slave Emancipation in the Rural Western Cape, South Africa, 1823–1853*. Portsmouth, NH: Heinemann, 1997.

Searing, James F. "Aristocrats, Slaves, and Peasants: Power and Dependency in the Wolof States, 1700–1850." *International Journal of African Historical Studies* 21, no. 3 (1988): 475–503.

———. *West African Slavery and Atlantic Commerce: The Senegal River Valley, 1700–1860*. Cambridge: Cambridge University Press, 1993.

Sembène, Ousmane, and Thierno Faty Sow, dirs. *Camp de Thiaroye*. New York: New Yorker Films, 1988.

Shadle, Brett L. *"Girl Cases": Marriage Disputes and Colonialism in Gusiiland, Kenya, 1890–1970*. Portsmouth, NH: Heinemann, 2006.

Shereikis, Rebecca. "From Law to Custom: The Shifting Legal Status of Muslim *Originaires* in Kayes and Medine, 1903–13." *Journal of African History* 42, no. 2 (2001): 261–83.

Bibliography

Sjoberg, Laura, and Sandra Via, eds. *Gender, War, and Militarism: Feminist Perspectives*. Santa Barbara, CA: Praeger, 2010.

Smallwood, Stephanie E. *Saltwater Slavery: A Middle Passage from Africa to American Diaspora*. Cambridge, MA: Harvard University Press, 2007.

Smith, Richard L. *Ahmad al-Mansur: Islamic Visionary*. New York: Pearson Longman, 2006.

Spear, Thomas. "Neo-Traditionalism and the Limits of Invention in British Colonial Africa." *Journal of African History* 44, no. 1 (2003): 3–27.

Spears, Edward. *Fulfillment of a Mission: The Spears Mission to Syria and Lebanon, 1941–44*. London: Leo Cooper, 1977.

Stallard, Patricia Y. *Glittering Misery: Dependents of the Indian Fighting Army*. San Rafael, CA: Presidio, 1978.

Stapleton, Timothy. *African Police and Soldiers in Colonial Zimbabwe, 1923–80*. Rochester, NY: University of Rochester Press, 2011.

Stockreiter, Elke E. "Child Marriage and Domestic Violence: Islamic and Colonial Discourses on Gender Relations and Female Status in Zanzibar, 1900–1950s." In *Domestic Violence and the Law in Colonial and Postcolonial Africa*, edited by Emily S. Burrill, Richard L. Roberts, and Elizabeth Thornberry, 138–58. Athens: Ohio University Press, 2010.

Stoler, Ann Laura. *Along the Archival Grain: Epistemic Anxieties and Colonial Common Sense*. Princeton, NJ: Princeton University Press, 2009.

———. *Carnal Knowledge and Imperial Power: Race and the Intimate in Colonial Rule*. Berkeley: University of California Press, 2002.

———. "Making Empire Respectable: The Politics of Race and Sexual Morality in 20th-Century Colonial Cultures." *American Ethnologist* 16, no. 4 (November 1989): 634–60.

———. *Race and the Education of Desire: Foucault's History of Sexuality and the Colonial Order of Things*. Durham, NC: Duke University Press, 1995.

Stoler, Ann Laura, and Frederick Cooper. "Between Metropole and Colony: Rethinking a Research Agenda." In *Tensions of Empire: Colonial Cultures in a Bourgeois World*, edited by Cooper and Stoler, 1–56. Berkeley: University of California Press, 1997.

Stora, Benjamin. *Messali Hadj, 1898–1974*. Paris: Sycomore, 1982.

Stovall, Tyler. "Love, Labor, and Race: Colonial Men and White Women in France during the Great War." In *French Civilization and Its Discontents: Nationalism, Colonialism, Race*, edited by Tyler Stovall and Georges Van Den Abbeele, 297–322. Lanham, MD: Lexington Books, 2003.

Straussberger, John F., III. "The 'Particular Situation' in the Futa Jallon: Ethnicity, Region, and Nation in Twentieth-Century Guinea." PhD diss., Columbia University, 2015.

Streets-Salter, Heather. *Martial Races: The Military, Race, and Masculinity in British Imperial Culture, 1857–1914*. Manchester: Manchester University Press, 2004.

Sunseri, Thaddeus. "Statist Narratives and Maji Maji Ellipses." *International Journal of African Historical Studies* 33, no. 3 (2000): 567–84.

Taraud, Christelle. *La prostitution coloniale: Algérie, Tunisie, Maroc (1830–1962)*. Paris: Payot, 2003.

Thiam, Iba Der. *Le Sénégal dans la guerre 14–18 ou le prix du combat pour l'égalité*. Dakar: Nouvelles Éditions Africaines du Sénégal, 1992.

Thilmans, Guy, and Pierre Rosière. *Les sénégalais et la Grande Guerre: Lettres de tirailleurs et recrutement (1912–1919)*. Dakar: Musée Historique du Sénégal (Gorée), 2012.

Thomas, Lynn M. *Politics of the Womb: Women, Reproduction, and the State in Kenya*. Berkeley: University of California Press, 2003.

Thomas, Lynn M., and Jennifer Cole, "Thinking through Love in Africa." In *Love in Africa*, edited by Cole and Thomas, 1–30. Chicago: University of Chicago Press, 2009.

Thomas, Martin. "From Sétif to Moramanga: Identifying Insurgents and Ascribing Guilt in the French Colonial Post-war." *War in History* 25, no. 2 (2018): 227–53.

Thompson, Elizabeth. *Colonial Citizens: Republican Rights, Paternal Privilege, and Gender in French Syria and Lebanon*. New York: Columbia University Press, 2000.

Thompson, J. Malcolm. "Colonial Policy and the Family Life of Black Troops in French West Africa, 1817–1904." *International Journal of African Historical Studies* 23, no. 3 (1990): 423–53.

———. "In Dubious Service: The Recruitment and Stabilization of West African Maritime Labor by the French Colonial Military, 1659–1900." PhD diss., University of Minnesota, 1989.

Thornberry, Elizabeth. *Colonizing Consent: Rape and Governance in South Africa's Eastern Cape*. Cambridge: Cambridge University Press, 2019.

———. "Sex, Violence, and Family in South Africa's Eastern Cape." In *Domestic Violence and the Law in Colonial and Postcolonial Africa*, edited by Emily S. Burrill, Richard L. Roberts, and Elizabeth Thornberry, 117–37. Athens: Ohio University Press, 2010.

Titley, Brian. *Dark Age: The Political Odyssey of Emperor Bokassa*. Montreal: McGill-Queen's University Press, 1997.

Todd, Lisa M. *Sexual Treason in Germany during the First World War*. Cham, Switzerland: Palgrave Macmillan, 2017.

Tonkin, Elizabeth. *Narrating Our Pasts: The Social Construction of Oral History*. Cambridge: Cambridge University Press, 1992.

Torcy, Louis Joseph Gilles de. *La question des troupes noires en Algérie*. Paris: Augustin Challamel, 1911.

Toy-Cronin, Bridgette A. "What is Forced Marriage? Towards a Definition of Forced Marriage as a Crime against Humanity." *Columbia Journal of Gender and Law* 19, no. 2 (2010): 539–90.

Tracol-Huynh, Isabelle. "Between Stigmatisation and Regulation: Prostitution in Colonial Northern Vietnam." *Culture, Health, and Sexuality* 12, no. S1 (August 2010): S73–S87.

———. "La prostitution au Tonkin colonial, entre races et genres." *Genre, Sexualité, et Société*, no. 2 (Autumn 2009): 1–19.

Trouillot, Michel-Rolphe. *Silencing the Past: Power and the Production of History.* Boston: Beacon Press, 1995.

"Troupes Noires." *L'Afrique française: Bulletin mensuel du Comité de l'Afrique française et du Comité du Maroc* 19, no. 8 (August 1909): 274–78.

Trustram, Myna. *Women of the Regiment: Marriage and the Victorian Army.* Cambridge: Cambridge University Press, 1984.

Turrittin, Jane. "Colonial Midwives and Modernizing Childbirth in French West Africa." In *Women in African Colonial Histories,* edited by Jean Allman, Susan Geiger, and Nakanyike Musisi, 71–92. Bloomington: Indiana University Press, 2002.

Vail, Leroy. *The Creation of Tribalism in Southern Africa.* Berkeley: University of California Press, 1989.

Valensky, Chantal. *Le soldat occulté: Les malgaches de l'armée française, 1884–1920.* Paris: Harmattan, 1995.

Vann, Michael G. "The Good, the Bad, and the Ugly: Variation and Difference in French Racism in Colonial *Indochine.*" In *The Color of Liberty: Histories of Race in France,* edited by Sue Peabody and Tyler Stovall, 187–205. Durham, NC: Duke University Press, 2003.

———. "Sex and the Colonial City: Mapping Masculinity, Whiteness, and Desire in French Occupied Hanoi." *Journal of World History* 28, no 3/4 (December 2017): 395–435

Vansina, Jan. *Oral Tradition as History.* Madison: University of Wisconsin Press, 1985.

Veistroffer, Albert. *Vingt ans dans la brousse africaine: Souvenirs d'un ancien membre de la mission Savorgnan de Brazza dans l'ouest africain (1883–1903).* Lille: Mercure de Flandre, 1931.

Verney, Sébastien. *L'Indochine sous Vichy: Entre révolution nationale, collaboration et identités nationales, 1940–1945.* Paris: Riveneuve, 2012.

Vigné d'Octon, Paul. *La gloire du sabre.* Paris: Flammarion, 1900.

———. *Journal d'un marin: Premiers feuillets: Sur la route d'exil.* Paris: Flammarion, 1897.

Virgili, Fabrice. *Shorn Women: Gender and Punishment in Liberation France.* Translated by John Flower. Oxford: Berg, 2002.

Weil, Patrick. *How to Be French: Nationality in the Making since 1789.* Translated by Catherine Porter. Durham, NC: Duke University Press, 2008.

Westwood, Sarah Davis. "Military Culture in Senegambia and the Origins of the *Tirailleur Sénégalais* Army, 1750–1910." PhD diss., Boston University, 2018.

White, Luise. *The Comforts of Home: Prostitution in Colonial Nairobi.* Chicago: University of Chicago Press, 1990.

White, Luise, Stephan F. Miescher, and David William Cohen, eds. *African Words, African Voices: Critical Practices in Oral History.* Bloomington: Indiana University Press, 2001.

White, Owen. *Children of the French Empire: Miscegenation and Colonial Society in French West Africa, 1895–1960.* Oxford: Clarendon, 2000.

Whitehouse, Bruce. *Migrants and Strangers in an African City: Exile, Dignity, Belonging.* Bloomington: Indiana University Press, 2012.

Wigger, Iris. *The "Black Horror on the Rhine": Intersections of Race, Nation, Gender and Class in 1920s Germany.* London: Palgrave Macmillan, 2017.
Wildenthal, Lora. *German Women for Empire, 1884–1945.* Durham, NC: Duke University Press, 2001.
Wilder, Gary. *The French Imperial Nation-State: Negritude and Colonial Humanism between the Two World Wars.* Chicago: University of Chicago Press, 2005.
Woodfork, Jacqueline. "'It is a Crime to be a Tirailleur in the Army': The Impact of Senegalese Civilian Status in the French Colonial Army during the Second World War." *Journal of Military History* 77, no. 1 (2013): 115–39.
Wright, Marcia. *Strategies of Slaves and Women: Life-Stories from East/Central Africa.* New York: Lilian Barber, 1993.
X, Jacobus. *L'amour aux colonies: Singularités physiologiques et passionelles observées durant trente années de séjour dans les colonies françaises, Cochinchine, Tonkin, Cambodge, Guyane et Martinique, Sénégal et rivières du sud, Nouvelle-Calédonie, Nouvelles-Hébrides et Tahiti.* Paris: Isidore Liseux, 1893.
Zeiger, Susan. *Entangling Alliances: Foreign War Brides and American Soldiers in the Twentieth Century.* New York: New York University Press, 2010.
Zimmerman, Sarah. "Apatridie et décolonisation: Les tirailleurs sénégalais guinéens et la Guinée de Sékou Touré." *Les temps modernes,* no. 693/694 (April–July 2017): 111–45.
———. "Citizenship, Military Service and Managing Exceptionalism: *Originaires* in World War I." In *Empires in World War I: Shifting Frontiers and Imperial Dynamics in a Global Conflict,* edited by Andrew Tait Jarboe and Richard S. Fogarty, 219–48. London: I. B. Tauris, 2014.
———. "*Mesdames Tirailleurs* and Indirect Clients: West African Women and the French Colonial Army, 1908–1918." *International Journal of African Historical Studies* 44, no. 2 (2011): 299–322.
Zuccarelli, François. "Le recrutement de travailleurs sénégalais par l'État indépendant du Congo (1888–1896)." *Revue française d'histoire d'outre-mer* 47, no. 168/169 (1960): 475–81.

Index

Page numbers in *italics* denote illustrations.

Abattoir Village, 135–37
Abid al-Bukhari. *See* Black Guard
Abidjan, 159, 181
administrators. *See* French West Africa: administrators
African American soldiers, 92, 94, 227n41, 251n4
Africa, Equatorial, 2, *65,* 190, 199
Africasian, 171, 251n3
Afro-Malagasy, 153. *See also* household
Afro-Vietnamese, *xii,* 2, 26, 169, 179, 191, 251n3, 263–64; children, 27, 170–71, 188–90, 193, 255, 256n86; relationships, 182. *See also* children; households: Afro-Vietnamese
Agninga, 84
Aguibou, Pierre, 170–71, 187, 193
Aho, Lieutanant Philippe, 164
Ahosí ("Amazons"), 72, 225n15, 233n45
Air Force, Imperial Japanese Army, 176
Al-Atrash, Sultan Pasha, 158
Alawi, 89–90, 91–93, 95, 102–3, 113
Algerçiras, Treaty of, 88
Algeria, *197;* and cordon sanitaire, 103; decolonization, 16, 195–*197*, 200, 202, 204, 206–8; Muslims, 119; tirailleurs' families in, 21; tirailleurs in, 114, 139, 198–99, 211, 238n58, 241–42n15. *See also* French-Algerian War
Allied Forces, 157, 163, 176–77, 196
allocations: and households, 13, 113, 125–29, 131, 135, 138; and long-distance household maintenance, 26, 115; military control over, 76, 79, 133, 136, 140, 142–45, 152, 165, 181; and prosperity, 20; and reciprocal ties, 15; wartime urgent assistance (*secours d'urgence*), 147; and widows, 21. *See also* widows
Amane, Chief Onwango, 83–85
Aminata, Ciraïa, 30, 44–49, 56, 229n67
Amrane, Djamila, 201–2, 257n26
anciens combattants. See veterans
Angoulvant, Lieutenant-Governor Gabriel, 122
Antananarivo, 70–73, 77, 198
anticolonial sentiment, 190, 195–96, 201
anticolonial warfare, 26, 184, 186, 199
Antonetti, Lieutenant-Governor Raphaël, 122, 159–60
Aouangis, 82–83
Arab, 87–89, 100, 102, 148, 186; Arabo-Berber, 89, 90, 93, 101; women and wives, 149, 155, 159. *See also mesdames tirailleurs*
Atlas Mountains, 92, 94, 98, 102, 154
Az-Zayani, Ahmad, 92

Bâ, Abdou Karim, 1–2, 10
Ba, Sacoura, 167
Bâ, Sergeant Mamadou, 130
Baliquet, Marie Louise, 167
Bamako, 45–46, 52, 181
Bamana, 33, 51, 80; Bamanakan, 60; speakers, 96, 115, 151; states, 52
Bambara, Fatamata, 150–51, 153
Banafia, 145
"bar-dancings," 183; and dancehalls, 182–83

Index

Bastien, Paulette, 167–68
Baté, 45–48
Bateke/Tio kingdom, 59
Benhazin, 70
Benin/Nigeria borderlands, 70
beriberi, 97
Bertin, Andrée, 167
Beye, Imbrahima, 177, 191
Beye, Ninh, 176–77, 191, 214
Bieye, Bakary, 191
biological determinism, 91–92, 94
bivouac, 50–52, 72, 77
black (*nègre*), 25, 224n92
Black Guard (abid al-Bukhari), 25, 89–90, 91–93, 95–96, 101, 103–4, 113
blackness (*noir*), 61, 89–90, 235n4, 261n84
"Black Villages" (*villages nègres*), 25, 88, 90–91, 101–4, 108–10, 112, 113, 201
Bobo Dioulasso, 144–45, 246n15
Bodjollé, Emmanuel, 209
Bokassa, Jean-Bédel, 190
Bondy, 212–13
Bouhired, Djamila, 202, 258n28
Boupacha, Djamila, 202, 258n28
Brazzaville, 59, 68–70
bridewealth, 53, 84–86, 131, 146, 239n84, 243n50, 244n63, 247n35; and divorce, 133; and marital legitimacy, 12, 42–43, 109, 125, 144
brothel: *Bordels Militaires de Campagne* (campaign military bordellos, BMCs), 164, 183, 201; military-maintained and/or state-funded, 7, 13, 21, 136, 154, 173, 182–84, 201
Bundu, 1, 10, 28, 35, 51
Bureau des Affaires Africaines (BAA), 189, 200
Burkina Faso, 144, 246n15
Burrill, Emily, 11

Camara, Sergeant Malamine, 66, 68
Cambodia, 62, 187, 205
Cameroon, 64, 86
Cap Tourane, 188, 255n70
Casablanca, 88, *89*, 97–98, *103–4*, 107, 111, 114, 134; Easter weekend deaths, 155–56, 198; red-light district in, 157
caste, 12, 42, 50–51
ceddo, 32–33
Central African Republic, 62, 64, 190, 213
certificates: of birth and marriage, 121, 181, 189; of liberty, 35–36
Chad, 62, 64, *65*
Champollion, 188

Chanock, Martin, 11
Chaouia, 97, *103, 105*, 107
Chat, Vuti, 1–4, 10, 15–16, 23, 213, 251n6
children, 3, 12, 47, 57, 63, 70; abuse of, 200; adoption of, 3, 171, 190, 191, 255fn79; Afro-French, 167–68; Afro-Malagasy, 149–50, 152–53, 233n64; Afro-Syrian, 159–60; Afro-Vietnamese, 2, 26–27, 170–71, 174, 178–79, 186–93, 255n69, 255n79; child marriage, 141, 146, 246n18; child-rearing, 53–54, 76, 104, 108–9; and church- or state-run institutions, 190; and concubinage, 42; and emancipation of parents, 37; guardianship of, 192; and home-front wives, 180; interracial, 18–19, 180, 219n42, 231n6, 239n88, 251n6; legal legitimation of, 128, 143, 148–49, 208; marriage to, 246n18; military benefits to, 10, 14, 25, 79, 106, 128–29, 140, 145, 212–13; in military camps, 49–51, 109, 134, 151; of originaires, 126; out of wedlock, 41, 164, 190, 192; social legitimation of, 41–44, 52; travel by boat, 73, 75; welfare and health of, 76, 97–98, 107, 112. *See also métis*
Christian: converts, 82; marriage ceremonies, 53; names, 192; religious ceremonies, 12; Vietnamese, 192; weddings, 179, 253n28
Cissé, Anttia, 132–33
Cissé, Tiemoko, 166
citizenship, 116, 238n60; and decolonization, 260n63; and the Four Communes, 120–21; French, 2, 118, 123, 128, 210, 212–13; and French females, 165; and 1958 constitutional referendum, 204, 207; status, 25, 117, 169, 171, 209. *See also* Communes, Four
citizen/subject binary, 25, 138, 175, 178, 193, 208, 241n11, 243n43; and Muslims, 241–42n15; *originaires* vs. *indigènes*, 116, 118–19; "quality of citizens," 178, 249–50n75; and women, 242n19
Claude-Bernard, 191
Clozel, Governor-General François Joseph, 121, 125–26
collaboration/resistance dichotomy, 29, 224n2
colonial conquest, French, 6–7, 9–10, 16, 29, 50–51, 56, 58–59, 64–65, 73–74, 78, 138, 214; of Madagascar, 68, 72, 79, 198; of Morocco, 25, 78, 88, 90–91, 100–101, 104, 108, 111, 149, 150, 154; of North Africa, 96; of West and Equatorial Africa, 1, 24, 28, 31–32, 35, 44, 60, *65*, 67, 70, 79, 87, 115

Index

colonial/imperial/French state, 8, 10–18, 121, 193, 207; assistance, 14, 25, 79, 83, 124, 127–28, 138–143, 150–56, 159, 165, 167; expansion of, 28–37, 44, 88–89; obligation, 117–18; power and protection of, 19–20, 35, 43, 137, 158; reliance on, 37, 48, 50, 115, 186, 188. *See also* conjugal relations; French Empire; marriage; West Africa
colonialism, 5–6, 24, 60; anti-, 190, 199; chronologies of, 22, 214; and conjugal relationships, 2, 8–9, 16–18, 48, 81, 83–84, 96, 219n43; and emancipation, 24; end of, 174, 202; French Republican, 15, 28, 94, 186, 198; future of, 60; geographies of, 6; injustices of, 195; legacies of, 15–16, 23, 27, 210–11, 196, 261n84
colonizer/colonized, 26, 29, 62, 171
colonizer/colonized binary, 15–16, 26, 29, 62, 171
Combes, Colonel, 54, 73
Communes, Four, *115*, 119, 129; and Afro-Vietnamese population, 188; and citizenship, 120–21, 171; and military service, 123; and originaires, 118, 122, 124. See also *originaires*
Conakry, *xii*, 21, 181, 188, 205–6, 208–9, 256
concessionary companies (French), 32, 67, 74, 232n20
concubinage, 39, 42, 56, 64, 182; as an accusation, 84, 87; characteristics of, 56; in Congo and Madagascar, 78; forced, 244n63; French meaning of, 182; as marital tradition, 43; as social incorporation, 42
concubines, 1, 4, 42
Conde (African Officer), 200
conduct, disorderly: as racialized and feminized, 110; sexual misconduct, 81, 84, 141
"congaïes," 184. See also *encongayement*
Congo, French, 60, 64, *65*, 67, 70, 73–74, 83, 99, 213, 230n2, 232n20; Congolese women, 19, 81–82; and conjugal unions, 1, 5–6, 24, 57–59, 62, 75–77, 80, 84–85, 87; racial difference in, 61; relationships in, 24, 68, 72, 78–79, 87, 141; sex trafficking in, 86
Congo Free State, 59, 67
Congo River basin, 59, 65
conjugal relations, 1–2, 5–9, 15, 17, 21–22, 74–75, 138, 141, 214; abusive or unsanctioned, 45, 83; and assistance, state, 129, 142–43, 147, 153, 159, 181, 213; and domestic services, 76, 78, 136; forced, 5, 39, 48, 50, 81; French control and concern over, 13, 55, 60–64, 77, 79–84, 86–87, 104, 110, 132, 145, 158, 175; legitimation and contestations of, 3–4, 14, 18, 27, 59, 130, 168–69, 219; legitimation of, 10, 30, 42, 85, 109, 113, 117, 131–33, 166, 189, 208; missionary concern, 82; and monogamy, 182; and morality, 11; strategies, 2, 16, 211; traditions, 12, 23–24, 28–29, 31, 38, 53, 56, 114, 127, 146, 182, 192; in Vietnam, 63, 174. *See also* households: and migration; race: and conjugal relations; slave(ry); women: local
conscription, 33, 93, 122, 140, 173, 203; and coerced labor and *deuxième portion*, 202; evading, 71, 122, 240n3; 1912 Recruitment Decree, 99; of originaires, 122–23; quota-based, 91, 95, 113, 115, 117, 140; of slaves, 92. See also *originaires*
consent and coercion, 8–9, 13, 16, 41, 60, 77; of brides, 147; continuum of, 8, 16; of husbands, 146; and inter-African encounters, 81; of kin to marriage, 41, 43, 84
Côte d'Ivoire, 28, *30*, 66, 115, 121, 124, 140, 144, 146, 153, 159–60
Coulibaly, Mamadou, 109
courts, 140; colonial, 11, 36, 96, 132; customary, 131; Muslim, 118; native, 118–19
Cousturier, Lucie, 162
customs: codifying, 12, 218nn35–36; familial, 153; Islamic, 119; local, 7, 83, 101, 109, 117, 146; marital, 2–5, 12, 16, 26, 29, 40, 81, 142, 148; martial and marital, 1, 10–11, 30; prenuptial, 12; West African, 17, 56, 133

Dadjo, Kléber, 209
Dahomey, 28, 56, 70–72, 74, 80, 87, 167; Dahomeyan soldier, Koto, 144
Dai, Bao (Nguyen Phuc Vinh Thuy), 176, 187
Dakar, 2, 208–9; military spaces in, 134, 137; military vessels in, 76, 155, 173, 188, 209; Paris-Dakar seasonal migration, 212; Vietnamese in, 2, 178, 191–93; wives of tirailleurs in, 116, 135, 207. *See also* households: Afro-Vietnamese; *originaires*
Damascus, 157
dancehalls and "bar-dancings," 182–83
de Brazza, Savorgnan, 59, 65–66, 74, 79–80
debt: to African soldiers, 15, 210; blood debts, 213
Decker, Alicia, 4–5

Index

decolonization, 2, 16, 27, 189, 192–94, 196, 205; and citizenship, 207, 260n63; wars of, 10, 202, 213
De Gaulle, Charles, 147, 204
Delafosse, Maurice, 100, 238n49
demobilization: and Algeria, 199; from France, 139; and Guinea, 196, 206; Japanese, 173; and Madagascar, 152; and repatriation, 162; and Vietnam, 187
desertion, 99, 184
d'Estaing, Valéry Giscard, 208
Diagne, Blaise: Laws, 116, 120–21, 123–24, 127–28, 138, 174; politician, 25, 119, 138; trial of, 243n43
Diagne, Urbain, *xii,* 178, 190
Diallo, Bakary, 105, 114
Diallo, Bilaly, 131
Diallo, Fatou, 155
Diba, Auguste, 170
Diba, Moundo, 171
Dieme, Seargent, 181
Dien Bien Phu, 170–*172,* 178, 186, 192, 194, 198
Dieye, Alioune, 166–67
Dieye, Corporal Assane, 167
Diop, Omar, 179
Diouf, Fatou, 127
divorce, 154–56, 166, 175, 192, 229n57, 244n58; French control over, 46, 131–32; "illegal" vs. legal, 130–31, 133; local authority over, 85, 109–10, 117, 132; and loss of benefits, 145; and remarriage, 41
Djebel Druze Uprising (also known as the Great Syrian revolt), 139, *141,* 158, 245n2
D'Octon, Paul Vigné, 49
Dodd, Colonel Alfred-Amédée, 72
Dolisie, Albert, 81
Drame, Mamadou Lamine, 1, 28, 35; conjugal partners of, 1–4, 16, 23, 31, 39–40, 213
Dravalo, Azana and Ravao, 153

Echenberg, Myron, 23
École de Formation des Officiers Ressortissants des Territoires d'Outre–Mer (EFORTOM), 203
École des Enfants de Troupes, 102–3
economy: colonial, 39, 140; domestic or household, 10, 97; French imperial and military political economy, 10; moral, 13, 56; urban cash, 136; wartime, 135; women's labor and, 39
El Abel, Aminé ben Mohamed, 160, 248n59

elders, 131, 143, 166; autonomy from, 16; and childbirth, 108; and youth sexual relations, 13, 41
El Hamel, Chouki, 93, 102
El moudjahid, 201
El Thomi, Fadona Selim, 159, 248n58
emancipation, 24, 28, 30–33, 34–37, 44, 49, 56, 71, 93, 95, 100, 235n15; of domestic slaves, 32; gendered, 38, 40, 79, 176; lack of enforcement of, 96; and women, 50, 54, 78, 135. *See also* slave(ry)
Empire, French. *See* French Empire
Enloe, Cynthia, 3–4
encongayement, 182
enslavement, 39, 46, 92–93; female, 7, 24, 39, 45, 77–78, 84, 86–87, 151, 213; and kinship groups, 32; and marriage, 37. *See also* conjugal relations: forced
Epprecht, Marc, 100
ethnicity, 50, 61
ethnolinguistic group, 15, 51, 34, 71, 96
Eyadéma, Étienne Gnassingbe, 209

Faidherbe, Louis Léon, 2, 12–13, 23, 32, 35, 60, 118
Fall, Colonel Amadou, 210
Fall, Biran, 67
Family Code, French, 7, 161, 219n40, 245n8
fanompoana, 71
Fanon, Frantz, 200–202, 257n19
Faye, N'gor, 52
femininity, 2, 191
Fez, 88–*89,* 98, 155, 157
Fofana (African officer), 200
force noire. See La force noir
Foreign Legion, 173, 207
Franceville, 86
Free France, 147
Fréjus, 162, 203
French-Algerian War (1954–62), 27, 194–95, 197–99, 200–202
French Community, 204–5, 207–8, 211
French Constitution (1946), 202–3; and nationality law, 165, 250n81
French Empire, *3–4,* 17, 19, 21, 27, 147–48, 195, 204, 214; defending, 211; expansion of, 2, 15, 91. *See also* French West Africa
French Finance Law of 1960, 210–11
French Indochina (contemporary Vietnam, Cambodia, and Laos), 21, 62, 64, *172,* 200–201; military service in, 62–63, 171,

Index

179, 189, 205, 211; sex and race in, 182; tirailleurs' sexuality in, 175–76
French Indochina War (1945–54), 1–2, 16, 195, 202; children and brides, 1–2, 26–27; conclusion of, 186, 191; conjugal life during, 180, 190; and international relocation, 187; legacy of, 193; and originaires, 169, 174, 178; outbreak of, 175; tirailleurs serving in, 170, 173, 177, 193, 198–99
French marine corps, 27, 196, 203–4
French military officers, 20, 54; authority over conjugal disputes, 8; and Guinean soldiers, 20; involvement in conjugal and marital relationships, 10; prohibition of Moroccan slave markets, 96
French National Assembly, 25, 116, 119, 173, 188, 204, 245n8, 261n84
French Union, 175, 178, 199, 202–203
French West Africa, 11, *30*, 99, 127, 142, 148, 167, 181, 195, 211, 254n43; administrators of, 58, 64, 79, 96, 121, 132, 150, 152, 160–62, 164, 166, 225n4; and Afro-Malagasy children, 153; and Afro-Vietnamese families, 170; and childbirth, 108; circulations of Europeans in, 19, 59; citizens and subjects of, 116, 118; decolonization of, 27, 194, 196, 199, 206; French army in, 130, 134; legal practices, in 17; and Moroccan wives in, 154; peripheries of, 26; as political unit, 116–17, 204; repatriation to, 163
Gabon, 62, 64–*65*, 73, 80, 82–83, 86
Gallieni, Lieutenant Colonel Joseph-Simon, 35, 39–40, 55, 69, 74, 78, 149, 215n1; and the Ciraïa Aminata trial, 45–49; promotion to General, 70, 72, 77
Gallieni Tunnel, 150–52
Gaye, Amady Moutar, 179
gender(ed), 4–5, 90, 158; and biological and social reproduction, 37, 52–53; imbalance, 76, 104, 110; and imperialism and hierarchies, 20, 23, 51, 129, 148, 158, 176; and militarism, 4, 29, 38, 52, 216n15; and military conquest, 79, 103–4; order and roles, 3, 14, 78, 88, 90, 105, 148, 161, 174, 214; power and processes, 9, 11, 16, 26, 31, 38–39, 44, 56; relations in Morocco, 101, 111–13; violence, 5–6, 8, 55, 61, 186, 202, 213
Geneva Accords (1954), 187, 189
Germany: and gender and race, 175, 51n4,

251n6, 252n17; occupation, 139, 257n20; prisoners of war, 163
gerontocratic authority, 29, 84, 129, 131, 166, 180
Gold Coast, 124, 227n40, 242n32, 258n42
Gomis, Emile, 177–78
Gomis, Jean, 177–78, 183
Gorée, 35, 118–19, 122
Great Syrian Revolt (also known as the Djebel Druze Uprising), 139, *141*, 158, 245n2
Great War. *See* World War I
Grosclaude, Étienne, 86–87
guerrilla-style warfare, 184, 199
Guèye, Marc, 183
Guilleux, Charles, 55
Guinea and Guinea-Conakry, 27–28, *30*, 42, 45 109, 115, 121, 124, 153, 256n86; and conspiracy, 250n74; decolonization of, 27, 194, 196, 204–6, 209, 260n74; diplomatic relations with France, 208; tirailleurs from, 27, 140, 196, 207, 210
gynecological exams for sex workers, 183; specialists for tirailleur families, 108

Hadj, Messali, 196
Haidara, Fatoum, 155
Haiphong, *172*, 176–77, 187, 191, 199
Haiphong River, 177
Hanoi, 1–2, *172*, 177, 178, 187, 199
harems, 102
heteronormative(ity), 4, 11, 13–14, 29, 39, 44, 75, 104, 143–44, 168, 175, 182–83, 213
Ho Chi Minh (Nguyen That Thanh), 173, 187, 190
Hollande, François, 212–13
homesickness, 99
homestead, 34, 37, 47, 51, 78, 82, 97, 146, 159
homosexuality, 99–100, 238n50
Houdas, Octave, 92
households, 9–10, 20, 58, 75–76, 87, 180, 196, 224n1, 227n40; Afro-French, 161–63, 168; Afro-Malagasy, 153; Afro-Moroccan, 161; Afro-Syrian, 160–61; Afro-Vietnamese, 2, 170, 173–74, 177, 184, 186–87, 189, 191, 193–94; cross-colonial and transnational, 17, 26, 142, 148, 169, 222n68; inter-African, 18–19, 24, 60, 62, 68, 75–77, 79, 81–83, 85–87, *141*, 148; interracial or hyphenated, 25, 101, 161, 167–78, 174, 182; legitimacy, 3–4, 24, 108–9; long-distance, 26; and migration, 50, 221n64; multiwife, 34, 41, 52, 82, 116, 123–25, 166, 193, 208;

Index

households (*cont.*)
  nuclear-family, 13–14, 38; and paternalism, 44; and race, 90, 108–9; resource allocation, 54–56, 106, 126, 128–29, 133, 143, 147, 179, 193; and sources, 19–20, 23, 29, 73. *See also* allocations; pension; polyandry; polygyny
Hova, 77, 79
Hué, Nguyen Thi, and Martine, 190
human trafficking, 81, 86

Indian Ocean, 59, 68–*69*, 73
indigénat, 202
Indochina Amendment, 173
infections: pulmonary, 98; sexually transmitted, 99, 136
inter-African households/relationships, 18–19, 24, 60, 62, 68, 75–77, 79, 81–83, 85–87, 141, 148
intermediaries, 117, 124, 129, 259n47; colonial, 70, 81; critiques of, 16, 240n2; military, 102; rural, 128; and women, 5, 240n3
interwar period, 26, 140, 155, 171, 214; conjugal relations during, 14, 25, 126, 141, 145–46, 148–50, 153–54, 156, 168, 175, 213; tirailleurs in France during, 163; tirailleurs in Syria and Lebanon during, 248; and Vietnam, 174
Islam, 12, 92–93, 119, 126, 191–92
Ismail, Sultan Mawlay, 92–94, 96, 102

Jacobus X, Dr., 100
Jacquinot Decree, 7
Japan, 26, 171, 173, 176–77, 187, 191, 252n21
jihad, jihadist, 1, 92, 199
jus solis and *jus sanguinis*, 120

Kaarta, 33, 46, 52
Kabylia, 199
Kadidie, 160
Kamara, Alpha, 160
Kati, 205, 207
Kayes, 35, 68, 73–74
Kébémer, 167
Keita, Mambé, 98
Kenitra, 88
Khorat, Pierre 111–12; pseudonym for Pierre Ibos, 240n90
kin, 2, 32, 153; distance from, 15, 34, 38, 76, 104, 126, 135, 137, 156; fictive, 13, 171; French officials as extended kin, 43, 50, 53, 83–84; and interracial households, 191; kinship groups, 32, 50, 191; and lineage, 8, 32–33, 41–43, 51–54, 61, 84, 166, 180; and marriage, 10, 14, 41, 43, 84–85, 133, 166; and resource distribution, 37–39, 42, 143, 147, 180–81, 214
Kinajy, 77
Komé, Sira, 207
Konaté, Samba, 150–52
Koné, Aissata, 109
Kone, Demba, Warrant Officer, 144
Kone, Koufiembaye, 144–45
Koné, Sekou, Lieutenant, 164
Konté (soldier), 184
Kourouma, Koly, *xii*, 196, 204–10

labor, 36, 63, 196; coerced or forced, 16, 24, 71, 140, 202; domestic, 2, 17, 31, 36, 39, 50, 61, 77–78, 80, 97, 104, 106, 136, 213; French colonial schemes (*laptots, engagé à temps, rachat*), 18, 31–32, 34, 37, 50; gendered, 104–5; and marriage, 12–13, 42, 47, 116; migrant, 221n61–62; military, 60, 68, 72, 103, 138; slave, 77, 95
La force noir, 91–95, 113, 235n9
Lambaréné, 83–84
Lamine Guèye, 178
Lamine Guèye law, 164, 202, 249n75
Laos, 62–63, 187
Lastourville, 82–83
Law, Framework (Loi Cadre), 195, 203
laws, 7–8, 11, 125, 166, 218n37
League of Nations, 26, 138, 157–58
Lebanon, 26, 138, *141*, 148, 157, 248n56
legal pluralism, 8, 16–17, 46, 114, 116–17, 119, 124–25, 127, 226n35
legal status, 10, 14, 16, 27, 96, 120, 142, 149, 196; and state-allocated benefits, 11, 15, 183, 199–200
Le Roy, Bishop Alexandre, 82
Levant, 2, 138, 157–160, 248n51; Armée du, 157–58, 248n51
Liberia, 66, 242n32
Liberty Villages, 30–32, 35–37, 47, 151
love, 190; difficulty of historicizing, 49, 229n74
Lyautey, Louis-Hubert, 95

Madagascar, 5–6, *69*, 230n2, 231–32, 233n64; colonialism in, 79; 1895 treaty with France, 71; French military incursions

296

Index

into, 1–2, 26, 59, 68, 99; and interracial children, 168; Madagascans/malgaches/Malagasy, 6, 19, 24, 60–61, 73–74, 77–81, 87, 149–50, 153–54, 160, 197–98; relations with Senegalese, 198; tirailleurs in, 12, 24, 56–62, 70–87, 104, 138–39, 141, 148–53, 195, 198, 206; tirailleurs' relationships in, 17, 82, 97, 104

Madeleines (military base), 135, 137
Mahajanga, 70
Maharidaza, 77
Maiga, Sekou, 159, 248n58
maître vs. *mari* (master vs. husband), 46–47
makhzen (imperial government), 102
Makoko, Chief, 59
Malebo Pool, 59
male breadwinner, 13–14, 38–39, 54, 76, 106, 126, 140, 143, 224, 229n47
Mali, 52, 208; Federation, 208–9
Malinké, 51, 115
Mama, Amina, 4
Mamelukes, Egyptian, 92, 94
Manding, 46
Mangassa, Della, 160
Mangin, Lieutenant Colonel Charles, 91–95, 102, 117; and the Recruitment Law, 117
Mann, Gregory, 5
maquis, 163, 201, 257n20
marabout, 53, 230n100
marraines de guerre, 162, 249n63
Marrakech, 88–89, 96, 155–156
Massa, 158
Massu, General Jacques, 199, 257n13
marriage, 17–18; abandonment of, 82–83, 154, 186; and abduction, 44, 46–47, 49, 60, 84, 229n72; à la mode du pays, 12, 43–44; arranged, 41, 102; child and/or levirate, 141, 146, 246n18; Christian ceremonies of, 53; disputes, 243n53 (or possibly p. 244 depending on if formatting changes); and divorce, 46, 110; and extramarital, 9, 63; French regulation of and involvement in, 3, 12–15, 82, 116–17, 133, 189; forced, 9, 13, 45, 87, 213, 219n44, 244n63; "illegal," 130; and infidelity, 82; interracial military marriages, 25–26, 66, 159, 249n74, 250n89, 250n6; as a legibility project, 11–12; legitimate or legal 4, 38–45, 53, 109, 125, 138, 144–49, 165–66, 182, 207–8, 219n39, 219n43 ; minimum age for, 7; and originaires, 124; proof of, 134, 136; by proxy, 146; registers, 85, 128, 143, 187; remarriage, 130, 145; and separation indemnity (*indemnité de separation*), 140, 143–47; and slavery, 29–31, 39–40, 44, 48, 56, 77, 80, 86, 93, 135, 155–56; as a social institution, 8, 10, 37; as a strategy, 7, 42, 79; temporary, 62, 64; "war bride," 14–15, 27. *See also* consent and coercion; heteronormative(ity)

Manas, French commander, 83–84
Mandel Decree, 7, 146
Manding, 46, 53
marabout, 53, 239n100
martial race, 5, 90, 92
Martiniquan soldiers, 176
masculinity, 2–3, 5, 29, 100, 173, 175, 182, 216n11, 258n42
Mashra ar-Ramla camp, 92
matrilineal society, 12, 38–39, 41, 84, 123, 190
Mazillier (Captain), 78–79
Mbembe, Achille, 61
McFadden, Patricia, 5
Meknes, 88, 92, 157
memory, *xii*, 15, 23, 152, 179, 203, 223nn83–84, 223n87
Menalamba uprising (November 1895), 71–72
Merina Kingdom, 59
meritocracy, 50–51
Mery, Amadou, 122
mesdames tirailleurs, 38, 56–57, 62–63, 67–68, 99, 101, 104, 114, 214, 225n7; and childbirth, 54, 108; domestic responsibilities of, 31, 50, 53, 91, 111; as expendable liabilities, 117; French control over, 54–55, 64, 89, 101, 107–108, 110, 113, 148; and historiography, 214; in Madagascar, 72–73, 76, 78; mesdames sénégalais, 72, 77; in Morocco, 25, 88, 90, 100, 105–6, 109, 111–12, 134, 201; and repatriation, 137, 148, 152, 155; tensions between mesdames and local women, 51–55, 111; as wards of the colonial state, 76, 137, 152. *See also* households: and migration

Messaouda, 155–56
métis, 18–19; adoption of, 171, 188, 255n79; and the colonizer/colonized binary, 171. *See also* children: interracial; households
miliciens, 60, 66, 68, 73–74, 79, 85
militarization, 10, 21, 43–44, 258n42; colonial, 6–7, 28–29; of society, 4, 29; and women's lives, 24, 30, 38, 40, 45, 213

Index

militarism, 4–5, 205, 215nn5–7; colonial, 1, 23, 48, 61, 84, 173; and gender, 9–10, 29, 214; globalization of, 6–7, 217n24

military, 3–4, 28–31, 211; active soldiers vs. reservists, 140; bases and camps, 134–35; as a career, 22, 116, 195, 205–6; distinction with civilian, blurred, 6, 60, 69, 217n17; schools (Écoles Militaires de Préparation de l'Afrique, EMPA), 203. *See also* conjugal relations; gender(ed); marriage; *originaires*; recruitment

migration, 18, 20, 240n3; "en famille," 18, 50, 58, 62, 134; expansion of, 60, 154; forced, 93; labor, 17, 221n62; long-distance, 24, 75–76, 87, 134–35; south-south, 18; of tirailleurs' partners, 17, 170. *See also* conjugal relations; households: and migration

Milo River valley, 45, 48

miscegenation, 162, 175, 252n17. *See also* race

Missaré, Karifa, 98

missionaries, 59, 81–83, 87

mixed-race (*métis*), 18, 62, 119, 171, 188, 222nn69–70, 222n72, 231n6, 231n18

Mohammed, Zaira Bint Sidi, 156

morale, of troops, 99, 102–4, 131, 133, 138, 164, 199, 201, 255n79

morality, 11, 112, 142, 159

Moramanga, attack at/uprising, 198

Morocco, 6, *89*; Afro-Moroccan, 154–56, 161; colonial knowledge of, 90; French Protectorate of (1912–25), 95, 154; health issues of troops in, 98; and homosexuality, 100; military/civilian contact, 97, 201; military conquest of, 88–93, 107; postcards from 90, 101, *103*; and race and slavery, 91, 94, 102–4, 149, 201, 235n5, 236nn16–17, 237n31; suppression of anticolonial insurrection in, 195; troop morale in, 99; West African tirailleurs and/or families in, 25, 87, 96, 101, 104, 109–10, 112–114, 138–39, 154, 205; and wives, 106, 148, 157, 175

Moudjahidines, 199

Moyd, Michelle, 5

muleteers, 66, 71

Muslim: Algerians, 119; courts, 118, 241n15; and divorce, 132, 228n57; and enfranchisement in Algeria, 241–42n15; marital practices, 25, 53–54, 124, 127; and sharia, 118; and slaves/slavery, 32, 54, 93; tribunal, 122

name-switching, 122

Napoleon III, 23, 219n40, 245n8

National Liberation Army (ALN), 201

National Liberation Front (*Front de Libération Nationale*, FLN), 198–99

N'Diaye, Aissatou, 130–31

N'Diaye, Ali, 126–27, 243n38

N'Diaye, Karim, 192–93

N'Diaye, Madame, 192–93

N'Diaye, Malick, 122–23

N'Diaye, Makhoni, 126

N'Diaye, Ngor, 155

Niger, *30*

Nigeria, 70–71, 74, 124

Nigerien, 55, 183

Niger River, 35, 60, 70–72, 151, 229n69

North Africa, 2, 25–26, 88, 109, 139, 205, 214; racial hierarchies in, 90, 113; repatriation to or from, 137, 154, 210; vs. sub-Saharan/West African, 25, 95–96, 98–101, 104–8. *See also troupes noires* debates

Ogowe River basin, 65, 84

Olympio, Sylvanus, 209

Okazawa-Rey, Margo, 4

oral history, *xii*, 20, 201

Oranais, 199

originaires: and assimilation, 221n60; and citizenship status, 25, 116, 171, 178; and independence, 193; and interracial households, 174; and military service, 118–24, 138, 169, 175–77, 189; and reintegration, 187, 210; wives of, 125–28. *See also* citizenship

orphan, 1, 10, 54, 80, 171, 188, 255n79, 256n86

Ottoman, 82, 93, 157

Pasteur, 180

patriarchal, 2, 5, 8; African culture, 85, 166; culture of military, 8, 13–14, 55–56, 133, 140, 180; traditions, 38, 129; and Vichy France, 147

patron-client relations, 31, 42, 50, 80, 121

pay scale, 175, 203

pension, 165, 195, 243n43; post-West African independence, 15–17, 21, 193, 196, 206, 208, 210–14; and widows, 2, 143, 152, 160

Pernot, Hugette, 167

Péroz, Marie Étienne, 54

personal status (*statut personnel*), 164; French Republic vs. French Union, 202; and

Index

originaires, 118–20, 124, 127; and polygyny, 143, 165
Pétain, Marshal Phillipe, 147–48
Piegard, Gabrielle Mayrse Josette, 166
polyamorous, 9, 43, 63, 75, 104, 136, 145, 166, 174
polyandry, 110, 130
polygyny, 12, 25, 41, 52, 63, 104, 127, 138, 143, 145, 174, 192; officials and, 9, 124–26, 165–66, 193, 210
Ponty, William, 95, 117–19
porters, 59, 66, 71, 77
Porto Novo, 80
postcards, from Moroccan campaign, 90, 101, *103*
postcolonial, 17, 23, 194; Africa, 5, 212; conflicts, 5; France, 16, 20, 27, 193, 196, 204, 210, 213; militarism, 29
precolonial, 22–23, 33; states, 30–31; symbols of power, 95
premarital, 6, 159; customs, 81; intimate interactions, 41; rites, 12, 43, 116
prenuptial arrangements, 45, 179, 243n50
prenuptial customs, 12, 24, 40, 84, 144, 166
prenuptial rites, 10–11, 41, 43, 56, 81, 83, 109, 140, 142, 191
Poto-Poto, 68
prisoners, 92; and Algerian war, 200; conjugal partners as, 55; of war, 33, 35, 43, 44, 72, 74, 77–78, 93, 147, 163, 211, 253n50
propaganda, 158, 175, 178, 200–201; French booklets and posters, 184–*85*, 234n83, 254n57
prophylactics, 164, 183
prostitution, 9, 84, 87, 136, 173, 218n26
Psychological Bureau, 195, 200–201
PTSD, 199–200, 213

race, 17, 19, 23, 26, 61, 91, 112, 148, 161, 171; and acclimatization, 94; and conjugal relations, 44, 91, 101, 112, 148–50, 161–62, 164–65, 167; and gender, 176; in France, 20, 116, 240–41n6; and interraciality, 62; martial, 5, 92; in Morocco, 122–23; and racial difference, 89, 234n3, 235n4; racial order, 4, 169; and science, 94, 190, 236n19–20; segregation, 90; and skin color, 112, 149
Radama I, King, 59
railway workers, 66, 73, 150, 152
Rainilaiarivony, Prime Minster, 71
Ramata, Hannah, 55
Ranavalona I, Queen, 59
Ranavalona III, Queen, 71
reciprocity, 31, 50, 210

recruitment, 31, 33, 34, 116, 122, 128, 175, 179; agents, 37, 46, 92, 124; civilian, 50, 67; and the Indochina Amendment, 173; 1918 effort, 138; slavery and, 24, 32; substitution, 123; women as central to, 31, 72, 109
Recruitment Decree/Law of 1912, 95, 113, 117
Referendum, September 28, 1958, 204–8
remittances, 180–81
reproduction: social and biological, 10, 31, 41, 61, 166; of the military community, 56, 90, 104
Republic, French: Third, 23, 25, 32, 36, 103, 119; Fifth, 27, 195, 204; Fourth, 26–27, 164, 171, 178, 195, 199, 202, 204; Second, 34, 118
Republicanism, French, 17, 23, 94, 103, 121, 161
reservists, 140, 148; and *deuxième portion*, 202, 258fn31
Rhineland, German, 138–39, 175
Rif War, 139, 154, 245n2
Rives, Colonel Maurice, *xiii*, 176
Rufisque, 118, 135, 187
Roume, Ernest 117

Saar, Binta, 127
Saar, Seïdou, 127
Saigon, 173, 177–78, 183, 188–89, 199
Saint-Louis, *xii*, 1, 35, 58, 67, 73, 75, 122
Saint-Raphael (military base), 162
Sakalava, Kingdom of, 68
Sakho, Sergeant Biram, 133
saligan/saligani, 96
Sall, Macky (president), 212
Saloum, Saida Mint, 155–56
Sambaké, Moussa, 97
Sangha River Basin, 65, 79
Sarkozy, Nicholas, 212
Sau, Nguyen Thi, 177
Savaron, Calixte, 77
Saveurs d'Asie, 193
Seck, Aïssata, 213
Seck, Baye, 167
Second World War. *See* World War II
secularism, 12, 119
Segu, 28, 35, 52, 166
Senegal, *30*, 55, 58, *115*, 119, 192, 212; decolonization of, 192; emancipation decree in, 34–35; Moroccans in, 155; and *nems*, 193; Vietnamese in, 2, 16, 170, 191–92. *See also* Communes, Four; French Empire; French West Africa: administrators of; *originaires*

Index

"sénégalais" (misnomer in Madagascar and French Congo), 60–61, 66–68, 70, 79, 82–86
Senegal River, 1, 16, 35, 52, 70–71, 75, 229n83
Senghor, Lamine, 243n43
Senghor, Léopold Sédar, 188, 209
Sétif, 196–97
settler colonies, 34, 61
17th parallel, 187
severance pay, 177, 186, 208
sex/sexual, 2–3, 7, 10, 18, 24, 55, 101, 171; behavior, of tirailleurs, 3, 11, 13, 138, 161, 164, 174; behavior, of women, 12, 50, 110; French management of African soldiers, 2, 63, 163, 182, 201, 214; interracial, 104, 112; labor, 53, 61; misconduct, 81, 84, 141; nonconsensual, 8, 45, 81; and race, 19, 175–76; trade/trafficking, 81, 86; transactional, 26, 154, 158, 162, 182; transgressive, 82, 156; work/worker, 9, 17, 21, 136, 157, 201. *See also* consent and coercion; heteronormative(ity); prostitution; violence: gendered
sexuality, 2, 4–5, 9, 16, 19, 63, 171, 175–76, 195, 214, 220n46, 237n47; of wives, 130
Sidibé, Bakari, 150–51
Sidibe, Dioucounda, 12–13
Siguiri, 35, 37, 44–47, 49
Sikasso, 54, 234n67
Simone, Marie-Désirée, 178
Sjoberg, Laura, 4
slave(ry), 46, 84, 100, 215n2, 217n25, 225n11, 227n40, 228n58, 229n70; abolition of, 32, 34–35, 81, 118, 226, 276; and abolitionist, 36, 40, 94; ancestry, 12, 25, 50–51, 82, 110, 151, 156; and assimilation, 32; and biological determinism, 93–94; domestic, 3, 32, 78; emancipation, 29, 34–36, 71, 135, 227nn44–45, 235n15; female, 9, 31, 37–38, 52, 54, 61, 70, 87, 132, 137, 213, 227n42; female trafficking, 40, 43, 81 (*see also* human trafficking); former, 32, 72; markets, 95–96; and marriage, 39, 42, 44–45, 47–49, 77, 80, 102; military service and, 24, 30, 33, 91–92, 95; and race, 235n4; Slavery Convention (1926), 7; as social status, 12, 56, 82, 235n5; trade, 58, 88, 90, 92, 96, 111–13, 155
social status, 12, 33, 40–42, 49, 51, 93, 129
SODAICA (state-operated industrial agricultural development agency), 209

sofas (soldiers), 33–35, 45–47, 226n18
soldiers: decommissioned, 67; French, 50, 63, 125, 136, 158, 165, 177, 182, 188, 203; unmarried, 107. *See also originaires; tirailleurs sénégalais*
Soudan, French, 30, 70, 150–51, 155–56, 205, 207, 210; and the referendum, 208
Soudanese soldiers, 55, 63, 208–9
Sous region (Morocco), 102
Southeast Asia, 2, 174, 177, 192; conjugal practices in, 201; French occupation of, 63; gendered constructions of, 5; as "secular," 12; soldiers serving in, 15, 26, 61–62, 170–71, 175, 179–80, 186, 188, 199
Sori, Igoulelé, 144–45
sources, 201; absence of wives and women in, 67, 73, 78, 81, 97, 181; archival, 18–19, 141, 257n22; and gossip/rumor, 22; interviews, 21–22, 201; memoirs, 19
Stanley, Henry Morton, 66
steamships, military, 88, 113, 134
subject/citizen binary, 16, 128, 142, 178, 203. *See also* citizen/subject binary
sutura, 22, 223n82
Sykes-Picot Agreement, 157
Syria, 26, 138, *141*, 148–49, 157–61, 245n2, 248n51

Taî denh, 186
Taouré, Alfa, 80, 234n70
Tall, Amadu Seku, 28, 35
Tall, El Hajj Umar, 52, 151
tax abatements, 14, 26, 116, 129, 140
Thiaroye, 15, 135, 179, 211, 220n54, 253n30
Thiès, *xii*, 135, 178–79
Thompson, Elizabeth, 158
Tiecoura (African Officer), 200
Tiefoura (African Officer), 144
Tiemoko (African Officer), 166, 200
tirailleurs sénégalais. *See* conjugal relations; households; French West Africa; military
Toamasina, 70
Togo, 209
Tonkin, *172–73*, 187, 189
Toulon, 166
Touré, Samory, 28, 35, 45–46, 56, 151
Touré, Sékou, 205–9, 260n74
transoceanic voyages, 76, 113, 173, 190, 193
Traoré, Fanta, 166
Traoré, Moussa, 54
Triande (African Officer), 200

Index

tribal identities, 11, 61, 100
tribunal: colonial, 36; military, 36, 44–49; Muslim, 122, 132; native, 117
troupes noires debates, 88–91, 94, 99, 101, 106, 113, 201, 234n2
Tukulor, 28, 46, 52, 135
Tunisia, 139

Ubangi-Shari River basin, 58, 65
Upper Senegal-Niger, 115, 124
Upper Volta (Haute Volta), 115, 116

Van Hollenhoven, 130–31
Veistroffer, Albert, 80, 86
veterans, 31, 35, 76, 128, 189, 212, 230n80, 261n85; inequalities between, 190, 211, 213; interviews with, *xi*, 20–23, 174, 182, 199, 201, 203; legal status of, 27, 193, 196, 243n43; opportunities for, 36, 149. *See also* pension
Via, Sandra, 4
Vichy regime, 26, 139, 171, 176, 139; defeat of, 158; and Indochina, 177; and National Revolution, 147; "Patrimony, Work, and Family," 177–78
Viet Minh, 184, 186, 189, 254n54
Vietnam, 17, 26, *172*, 176, 191, 193, 214; decolonization of, 186, 192; French presence in, 63, 173, 175; soldiers' experiences in, 26, 61–62, 174, 178, 180, 182, 186. *See also* households: Afro-Vietnamese
vivandières, 110
violence, 4, 28, 50, 79, 82–83, 159, 195; and the French-Algerian War, 199–200; and French colonialism, 70, 159; gendered, 5–8, 21, 24, 55, 60–61, 87, 173, 186, 202, 227n46; and rape and assault, 9, 24, 48, 80, 87, 201–2

Wade, Abdoulaye (president), *xii*, 211, 261n85
war crimes, 8
Wassulu Empire, 28
wealth, 42, 52, 54, 84, 116, 143
welfare, 129; and French state, 14, 25, 138, 213, 246n10; and military, 56, 75, 140, 143, 168, 193; policies, 4. *See also* allocations; pensions
West Africa, 1, 5, *30;* caste and class, 42; early administrators in, 225n4; emancipation in, 24, 40; inheritance traditions, 146; inland conquest of, 1, 28; refugees, 35; warrior-based states in, 33. *See also* households

widows, 20–21, 150–51, 160–61, 176, 191–92, 196, 208; interviews with, *xi–xii*, 22, 174, 186; legal status of, 27, 166; pay, 2, 15–16, 54, 143, 152, 193, 210, 212–14
wives, 57; and abuse, 55, 200; accompaniment of, 75, 109, 134, 154, 175; as civilians, 1–2, 5; and *femme,* 9; and order, 14; terminology, 8–9, 182; as "wives," 1, 144. *See also mesdames tirailleurs;* slave(ry): female
Wolof: ethnic group, 135; kingdoms, 32; language, 21–22
women, 3–4, 12, 14, 16–18, 24, 45, 52, 62, 134, 214; Algerian, 201–2; Arab, 87, 149, 155; as auxiliary combatants, sutlers, and domestic laborers, 6; captured, 3; as civilians, 44, 50, 143; "clandestine," 183; Congolese, 19, 61, 68, 82, 87; control over, 11; as covert militants, 201; and economic production, 39; exploitation of, 61; French, 149, 161–66, 168; living conditions of, 107; local, 81, 83, 86, 97, 109, 111, 141, 148, 156, 170, 198; Malagasy/Madagascan, 19, 61, 73–74, 79, 153; market women, 39, 51; as midwives, 108; Moroccan, 93, 99, 101, 113, 122, 154; pubescent, 41; and race, 25, 90–92; sexual and conjugal habits of, 110; as subjects, 17; subjugation of, 5; Syrian, 158–60; Vietnamese, 2, 26, 171, 173–74, 177, 179, 182–84, 186–88, 191–93; vulnerability of, 6, 43, 77, 151; West African, 29–31, 49, 57, 63–64, 75, 78, 105, 113, 129, 133, 136, 138. *See also* labor; *mesdames tirailleurs;* slave(ry): female; wives
World War I (Great War), 6, 13, 113, 117, 120–22, 126–42, 157, 161, 175, 198, 217n20, 244n63; beginning of, 25, 68, 114, 116, 138; post-, 18, 26, 142, 154, 168, 214; prior to, 132
World War II/ Second, 15, 163, 158, 166, 171, 174–78, 179, 188, 220n53, 257n20; conclusion of, 162, 164, 198, 202, 255n79; outbreak of, 139, 146–47; post-, 26, 157, 163, 168, 194–95, 205, 251n4, 251n6

Yandjo, 84–85
Yenou, Albert, 167–68
youth, 41, 122–23, 188

Zeiger, Susan, 9, 251n6
Ziguinchor, *xii,* 170
Zinder, 55, 130

Printed by Printforce, United Kingdom